SOCIAL SYSTEMS
AND THE EVOLUTION
OF ACTION THEORY

SOCIAL SYSTEMS AND THE EVOLUTION OF ACTION THEORY

Talcott Parsons

THE FREE PRESS
A Division of Macmillan Publishing Co., Inc.
NEW YORK
Collier Macmillan Publishers
LONDON

The Free Press
A Division of Macmillan Publishing Co., Inc.
866 Third Avenue, New York, N.Y. 10022

Collier Macmillan Canada, Ltd.

Library of Congress Catalog Card Number: 76–55100

Printed in the United States of America

printing number
1 2 3 4 5 6 7 8 9 10

Library of Congress Cataloging in Publication Data

Parsons, Talcott
    Social systems and the evolution of action
    theory.

    Includes index.
    1. Sociology--Addresses, essays, lectures.
I. Title.
HM24.P284   301   76-55100
ISBN 0-02-924800-0

Page 134: "Commentary on Talcott Parsons' Review of H. J. Bershady's *Ideology
and Social Knowledge*," by H. J. Bershady. Reprinted with permission from *Sociological Inquiry*, Vol. 44, no. 4 (1974), pp. 279–282.

To
Jan J. Loubser
Rainer C. Baum
Andrew Effrat
and
Victor Meyer Lidz
Editors of
*Explorations in General Theory
in Social Science*
and to the Contributors to those volumes
in appreciation of their
signal contributions
to the development of general
theory in our field

Contents

Preface

To me, as author, it is a particularly welcome venture on the part of The Free Press to resume adding to the series of my collected essays, which they first started publishing in 1949. This will be the first addition to the series since 1969, and 1977 will be the most important year for the whole series, since the present volume is to be followed, within the year, by another, to be entitled *Action and the Human Condition*.

It is well known to those who have followed my rather long career as a contributor to the literature of my field that I have devoted a rather large fraction of my attention to articles and commentaries rather than to book-length works, to say nothing of multivolume treatises. This has of course continued in the last decade.

This practice has had both its advantages and its disadvantages. One of the former seems to be that it is in line with the times; thus, how many living social scientists of the present generation have written treatises, especially with such a title as "Principles of . . ."? In the generation of the turn to the present century, many did. Again, one aspect of this may be that publishing papers rather than treatises is a practice more in accord with that of our neighbors in the natural sciences.

Underlying these considerations seems to be the fact, of which many of us have become increasingly aware, that the intellectual frameworks within which we have been working have been involved in processes of rapid and complex development. Hence, perhaps especially for an author who is concerned with problems of general theory, awareness of the fact, noted by many others, that such attempts are, if they try to transcend the level of the empirical monograph, or that of a highly specialized piece of theoretical analysis, likely to prove distressingly soon to be out of date, an awareness which may help to discourage them. In fact, more than a quarter century ago, in my book the *Social System* (1951), I made an attempt of that sort, only to find that my own thinking and that of persons with whom I was then closely associated had evolved beyond the stage reached in that book, almost before it was published, as was docu-

mented in *Working Papers in the Theory of Action* (1953, with Bales and Shils).

I have devoted considerable attention to the problem of the implications of this situation in the introductory materials I have written for the present volume, particularly the General Introduction, but also in the Introductions to each of the three parts into which the papers are divided.

My concern here with theory, of course, is in no way meant to suggest that, in this most recent phase of my development as a social scientist, there has been a cessation or indeed any diminution in my level of concern with a variety of empirical problems. The period in question saw the publication in 1973 of my book, with Gerald Platt, *The American University,* which was an empirical-theoretical study. Especially in Part III of the present volume, and even more in its sequel, this concern for empirical problems also comes through. Indeed, it is my firm conviction that only theory which is oriented in terms of its relevance to empirical problems deserves to be called scientific theory at all.

It is my confirmed view that the present is, at least in the field of the theory of action, not a time for syntheses which make any sort of pretense to the attainment and exposition of a stable "closed" theoretical system. This view, however, does not suggest to me that we are and have been, in the relevant fields of theoretical culture, living in a state of disorganization or generalized *anomie*. Quite the contrary, I think that we have been living in a situation marked by creative opportunities and attendant intellectual ferment, or what Durkheim called "effervescence," and much significant progress has occurred. It has been and is a time of high creativeness in our thinking in the most recent of the great fields of Western scientific endeavor, namely that dealing with the symbolically meaningful phenomena of human action.

It is in the nature of the modern intellectual enterprise that any one publication should be indebted to many others besides the explicit author. This statement clearly includes the present book but, with one exception, it does not seem feasible to list them here. The exception is Martin U. Martel of Brown University. From the inception of the idea of a new collection I stood in close consultation with Professor Martel, and his judgment has had an important influence on the Table of Contents both of this volume and of its sequel. They are both better books and more representative of my work than would have been the case without his counsel.

Talcott Parsons
January 1977

SOCIAL SYSTEMS
AND THE EVOLUTION
OF ACTION THEORY

General Introduction

THIS IS THE SEVENTH or, according to the way it is counted,[1] the sixth volume in the series of my collected essays issued by The Free Press starting in 1948; a not inconsiderable proportion of them continue to be co-authored with others. Like its predecessors, the present volume includes essays of varying types: Many, like the two articles reprinted from the *International Encyclopedia of the Social Sciences,*[2] were written by request, but a few of those nonetheless show my own initiative, at least with respect to topic. Above all they include topics that range in type from highly empirical to rather abstract theoretical matters.

When this collection was originally planned, it was contemplated that, for the present phase, one volume of collected papers would emerge. Reflection, consultation with others, and new developments, however, resulted in substantial additions to the contents of that single volume. The decision has therefore been reached to publish two volumes.[3]

The present volume of essays and its sequel will be published in the fortieth anniversary year of the first publication of *The Structure of Social Action,*[4] which first brought my name to fairly prominent attention in the social science world. In view of the six (or five) preceding collections of

[1] The question is whether the first collection—Talcott Parsons, *Essays in Sociological Theory Pure and Applied* (New York: Free Press, 1949)—and the second— *Essays in Sociological Theory* (1954)—are to be counted as one or two. The second reprinted about half the contents of the first, omitting the rest, but included as about half of its contents material not previously printed in book form. The other four— Talcott Parsons, *Structure and Process in Modern Society* (New York: The Free Press, 1960), *Social Structure and Personality* (1964), *Sociological Theory and Modern Society* (1967), and *Politics and Social Structure* (1969)—overlap very slightly with each other and do not contain any materials previously published in book form with myself as principal author.

[2] Chapters 7 and 8 in this volume.

[3] The first is scheduled by The Free Press for its spring list for 1977. The sequel is scheduled for the fall of 1977. The division made between the two volumes will be explained later in the present introduction.

[4] Talcott Parsons, *The Structure of Social Action* (New York: McGraw-Hill, 1937). Reprinted by The Free Press, New York, 1949.

1

essays, and of the various other publications bearing my name over the whole period, I have foreseen a problem for the readership of this volume and its successor. Some readers more or less near my own age are likely to have some awareness of the whole range. At the other end of the continuum, however, will be much younger readers, many of whom have relatively little acquaintance with my earlier work or with the trends of development or the intellectual setting of that work.

For this reason, not only in this general introduction but in all of the introductory materials prepared for this volume and its sequel, I have struck an autobiographical note more strongly than before. This takes mainly the form of commenting on the relation of the essay in question, or clusters of them, to earlier publications, their places in sequences, and the like.

Besides the introductory material, this consideration has prompted the selection of Chapter 1 for inclusion in this volume and the position in which it has been placed. It is the most comprehensive intellectual autobiographical statement that I have made in print, and its coverage extends down to 1969. A brief supplementary statement will be included in the general introduction to the volume to follow. For the reader who is interested in the developmental aspects of my work, it should provide a helpful focus of orientation. In this connection I should like particularly to call attention to the importance for me of early interest in the status of economic theory and its relation to sociology, and the relation of that both to the decision to study the modern professions, starting with medical practice, and to the much later concern with the symbolic media of interchange.

If an author's personal self-interpretation is appropriate here, I should like to suggest that my career as theorist has been characterized by a complicated balance between continuity and developmental change. With respect to certain conceptual fundamentals, for example, Dean Gerstein [5] is right that there has been essential continuity over the forty-years period since *The Structure of Social Action*. This continuity has centered above all on the "mining" of the theoretical richness of the works of Émile Durkheim and Max Weber, attempting not only to understand them but to use them constructively for further theoretical development. As I have noted in Chapter 1, the completion of that study was followed almost immediately by intensive study of the writings of Sigmund Freud. Those three have stayed with me as fundamental anchor points ever since.

One major feature of my relation to their work has been that I have made repeated "revisits" to them, some of which are reported in this volume and its successor. My clear experience is that one reading of works

---

[5] Dean Robert Gerstein, "A Note on the Continuity of Parsonian Action Theory," *Sociological Inquiry*, Vol. 45, No. 4, (1975), pp. 11–15.

of such a theoretical caliber perhaps never permits a merely human reader to exhaust the subtle connotations and implications of the work. The revisits have almost always yielded new insights that, on previous readings— often more than one—I had not attained. Surely one explanation of this experience is that, if a reader's own thought has developed between readings, on a revisit he does not approach the work as, in a simple sense, "the same" reader. I hope this account will sensitize the reader to the idea that what may appear superficially to be "contradictory" statements about these and other classic works may often have more to them than simple manifestations of intellectual inconsistency.

One further matter of personal style should perhaps be commented upon. The reader will note that a large proportion of the papers included in the present volume, as well as its predecessors, has been written in response to requests of various sorts, such as by editors of journals, symposia, or encyclopedias. There may be some question regarding the bearing of such origins on the author's intellectual independence: May this not imply an overresponsiveness to the wishes of others rather than presenting "my own" thinking?

By and large, I think not. In most cases topics have, in a broad way, been assigned, though sometimes alternatives have been discussed in advance. Overwhelmingly, however, the *way* in which I dealt with the topic has been left to my own responsibility. There have been very few exceptions to this, and for the most part they have been ironed out by discussion. I regard my experience in this respect as a strong vindication of the solidity of institutionalization of the standards of academic freedom in our society, one of the most important normative complexes of the intellectual world. I, at least, do not at all have the feeling that important patterns of my thought have been "imposed" upon me by the pressures of editorial wishes. I have very generally interpreted editors' requests as opportunities rather than pressures.

By the standards of the time, my early concern with the relations between economic and sociological theory in *The Structure of Social Action* may have seemed to some a very, if not excessively, broad one. Such concern, however, all fell within the range of what would be called the theory of the social system, a conceptual scheme which, however, required, and still does, an immense amount of elaboration and filling out,[6] as well as clarification of its main framework.

Soon after the publication of that work, however, a process of extension of interest beyond the social area, first mainly into the psychological,

---

[6] For a notable recent contribution by another, see Rainer C. Baum, "The System of Solidarities," *Indian Journal of Social Research*, vol. 16, nos. 1 and 2 (1975), and a number of the essays in J. Loubser, R. Baum, A. Effrat, and V. Lidz (eds.), *Explorations in General Theory in Social Science: Essays in Honor of Talcott Parsons* (New York: Free Press, 1976).

began. This was especially stimulated by a study of medical practice and by extensive reading of Freud. It involved many elaborations which, up to that point, were documented especially in the volume of essays *Social Structure and Personality* (1964) but also earlier in *Family, Socialization and Interaction Process* (1955).[7]

Parallel with that, but in emphasis tending to come somewhat later, was an increasing concern with the theoretical analysis of cultural systems and their relations to social systems. This particularly concerned the nature of the differentiation between these two subsystems of action, a matter on which older sociological theory, even including Durkheim and Weber, had by no means been clear.

As Victor Lidz has recently made clear,[8] progress in analysis of the role of the cultural system had lagged behind that in analysis of the social system, having reached a more satisfactory state only in relatively recent years, which is partially documented in the essays included in the present collection and its sequel as well as in Gerald Platt's and my book, *The American University*.[9]

At any rate, a first attempt to generalize these extensions was made in the collaborative volume *Toward a General Theory of Action* (1951, co-edited with Edward Shils)[10] and closely accompanied by a corresponding attempt to achieve a more analytically satisfactory account of the social system in the volume with that title (1951).[11] The former saw the partial emergence of the outline of a general theory of action.

That outline was, however, seriously incomplete, in an important degree because the relation of the level of action to that of the organism, or more generally what we call the biological level, had not been satisfactorily worked out. At the time of *Toward A General Theory* this problem was simply not faced at all, but a system of general action was conceived as involving three subsystems: social, cultural, and personality systems. This was in spite of the fact that I had at that time paid considerable attention to the relevance of biological to social thinking, *e.g.*, of W. B. Cannon's conception of *homeostasis*.[12]

The clarification that has proved to be necessary occurred in two main stages. The first was stimulated by the emergence of the four-function par-

---

[7] Talcott Parsons and Robert F. Bales, in collaboration with J. Olds, M. Zelditch, Jr., and P. Slater, *Family Socialization and Interaction Process* (Glencoe, Ill.: Free Press, 1955).

[8] Victor M. Lidz, "The Functioning of Secular Moral Culture," Ph.D. dissertation, Harvard University, Department of Sociology, 1976, Chapter 3.

[9] Talcott Parsons and Gerald M. Platt, in collaboration with Neil J. Smelser, *The American University* (Cambridge, Mass.: Harvard University Press, 1973).

[10] Talcott Parsons and Edward A. Shils (eds.), *Toward a General Theory of Action* (Cambridge, Mass.: Harvard University Press, 1951).

[11] Talcott Parsons, *The Social System* (New York: Free Press, 1951).

[12] Walter B. Cannon, *The Wisdom of the Body* (New York: W. W. Norton, 1932).

adigm in the 1950s and its suggestion that the organic component, at the individual "phenotypical" level, could well fit in as a fourth primary functional subsystem of the general system of action, defined not as the total organism but as an analytically defined part of it, the "behavioral" organism.

This solution of the problem was provisionally so satisfactory that it persisted for a number of years. Its substantial revision was precipitated by two developments. The first was the reading of a manuscript, published only now in 1976, by Charles and Victor Lidz,[13] which proposed that the adaptive subsystem of the general system of action should not be conceived to overlap with the organic, but to be nonorganic and to comprise primarily the structuring of cognitive functions at the action level, leaning heavily on Piaget's formulations in this area. This suggestion proved, after careful consideration, to be acceptable to me, but its acceptance and the development of its implications have barely begun to see the light of publication.

The other influence came from a developing interest in and sophistication about certain central problems of the nature of biological theory in its relations to the theory of action.[14] This background led to a serious reconsideration of the nature of the organic world and its relation to that of human action. This in turn was stimulated by renewed interest in the problem of evolution, which of course in my case centered on social and cultural evolution, but in a way that made careful relating of these problems to those of organic evolution imperative.

If, within the boundaries of what came to be defined increasingly clearly as the general system of action, the problem of the relation of the social system to the subsystems of personality and culture clamored for answers that were not available in the literature of the most immediately relevant branches of the discipline in question, then a problem parallel to that of the definition of the boundaries of the social system arose on another level.

After all, in the history of modern thought, by the end of the nineteenth century the theoretical interpretation of the organic world, of which man was obviously a part, as well as the only recorded observer, had come to be one of the central cognitive structures of modern civilization. If "social" science, which I prefer to categorize more generally as that of "action," was to find a real place in modern cultural development, it *had to* come to terms with this knowledge of the organic world, especially since Darwin. The story is one of skittish ambivalence, sometimes "overidentification" in attempting to treat human action as simply a "special case"

---

[13] Charles Lidz and Victor Lidz, "The Psychology of Intelligence of Jean Piaget and Its Place in the Theory of Action," in Loubser et al., *Explorations in General Theory*, vol. 1, Chapter 8.

[14] See Gerald Holton (ed.), *The 20th Century Sciences: Studies in the Biography of Ideas* (New York: W. W. Norton, 1972).

of the organic, sometimes avoiding altogether the statement of any significant relation.

It was on this background that I began to take a more serious and systematic interest in the problems of social and cultural evolution.[15] In our field the evolutionary perspective seemed to be an essential complement to the comparative perspective, which had already come to be quite well established.[16] In a way, exploring it meant going back to the sociological influence of my graduate training with Hobhouse and Ginsberg in London, but with important differences, especially growing out of lines of thought developed by Durkheim and Max Weber.

The concern with the theory of sociocultural evolution led logically to deeper concern with the organic side. Here such modern authors as Alfred Emerson,[17] G. G. Simpson,[18] Theodosius Dobzhansky[19] and above all Ernst Mayr[20] proved particularly illuminating. Besides considerations touching the pattern of evolution itself, let me mention two cases of analogy between the organic field and that of human action,[21] in addition to that between genetic and cultural heritage, which I had learned some years previously from Alfred Emerson.[22] The first was that the sociological concept of society, as an abstractly defined basis of collective organization, is directly parallel to the concept of species as it is used by evolutionary biologists, especially Mayr. Of course, there is only one human species, but many societies, so that the organic composition of a society constitutes a *population* rather than a species, in the biological sense.

The second insight has concerned the fact that the famous process of natural selection, which has been so central to evolutionary biology since

[15] An early phase of it took place in a collaborative seminar with Robert Bellah and S. N. Eisenstadt (spring 1963). My contribution was in part summarized in the essay "Evolutionary Universals in Society" (*American Sociological Review*, 29 [June 1964]: 339–357. Reprinted in Talcott Parsons, *Sociological Theory and Modern Society* [New York: Free Press, 1967], Chapter 15, pp. 490–520). Both Bellah and Eisenstadt contributed to the same issue of the *American Sociological Review*. This article of mine was followed by two small books, Talcott Parsons, *Societies: Evolutionary and Comparative Perspectives* (Englewood Cliffs, N.J.: Prentice-Hall, 1966), and *The System of Modern Societies* (Englewood Cliffs, N.J.: Prentice-Hall, 1971).

[16] See Chapters 2 and 3 in this volume.

[17] Alfred E. Emerson, "Homeostasis and the Comparison of Systems," in Roy R. Grinker, Sr. (ed.), *Towards a Unified Theory of Human Behavior: An Introduction to General Systems Theory* (New York: Basic Books, 1956).

[18] G. G. Simpson, *The Major Features of Evolution* (New York: Columbia University Press, 1953).

[19] Theodosius Dobzhansky, *Genetics and the Origin of the Species*, 3d. ed. (New York: Columbia University Press, 1951), and *Mankind Evolving* (New Haven and London: Yale University Press, 1962).

[20] Ernst Mayr, *Populations, Species and Evolution* (Cambridge, Mass.: Harvard University Press, 1970).

[21] Cf. "The Present Status of 'Structural–Functional' Theory in Sociology," Chapter 4 in this voulme.

[22] Emerson, "Homeostasis and Comparison of Systems."

Darwin, is paralleled by the process many sociologists have come to call institutionalization, that is, the process by which items of variation, especially from cultural sources, either come to constitute established parts of later action systems or fail to do so. Especially in the historico-sociological work of Max Weber, there are many illustrations of this process to be found.

Another aspect of this renewed interest in the relations between social and biological theory concerned acquiring some knowledge of the striking developments that have been occurring in microbiology, especially microgenetics. This went back especially to a conference held in Bellagio, Italy, in 1969.[23] Here, among the biologists contributing, particularly important were Gunther Stent (though in absentia) and Curt Stern,[24] but in the background, and subsequently significant to me, J. D. Watson[25] and S. E. Luria.[26] One important realization for me was that there was a special continuity of "organization" in the organic world all the way from species and phylae at the macroevolutionary level to that of the individual cell or microorganism. There seemed here to be certain parallels with the case of human action, whether in terms of the famous but so often misconceived relation between "individuals and society" or in terms of that, within the social category, between macro and micro collectivities, the latter context including the now well-known "small groups."[27]

Partly antedating these influences and converging with them was that of certain perspectives in physiology, emanating above all from the traditions initiated by the French physiologist Claude Bernard[28] and brought to bear in my intellectual environment by the influence of Lawrence J. Henderson[29] and of the book by W. B. Cannon, *The Wisdom of the Body*. In this later phase of my thinking, all three strands of influence from the biological sciences came to focus in a new perspective.

The upshot of this experience has been to heighten the salience of the

[23] The papers presented at this conference have been published in *Daedalus*, journal of the American Academy of Arts and Sciences, Fall 1970. An expanded version has been published in Holton, *20th Century Sciences*.

[24] Gunther S. Stent, "DNA," and Curt Stern, "The Continuity of Genetics," in Holton, *20th Century Sciences*.

[25] See J. D. Watson, *Molecular Biology of the Gene*, 2d. ed. (New York: W. A. Benjamin, 1970).

[26] See S. E. Luria, *Life: The Unfinished Experiment* (New York: Scribner's, 1973).

[27] See Dean Gerstein, "Durkheim, Parsons and the Action Paradigm: I. The Structure of Social Action," forthcoming.

[28] Claude Bernard, *An Introduction to the Study of Experimental Medicine*, Trans. H. C. Greene (New York: Dover, 1957). First published in French in 1865.

[29] Lawrence J. Henderson, *The Fitness of the Environment: An Inquiry into the Biological Significance of the Properties of Matter* (New York: Macmillan, 1913), *The Order of Nature: An Essay* (Cambridge, Mass.: Harvard University Press, 1917), and *Pareto's General Sociology: A Physiologist's Interpretation* (Cambridge, Mass.: Harvard University Press, 1935).

problems of the theoretical relationships between the disciplines working in the organic field and those working in the action field.[30] A long series of problem areas have emerged in which there is presumptive evidence of far closer parallels than had previously been appreciated and of closer articulation. On both sides, but perhaps particularly among social scientists, the predominant attitude in this area has been a skeptical caution, in considerable part in the light of overhasty commitments, a long time ago, to "social Darwinism." The suggestion here made, however, is that there is a high probability that theoretical developments on both sides have reached a stage where such skepticism has become "counterproductive" and that a bolder initiative in this direction can be expected to produce important results in the relatively near future.

The problems posed by the cognitive orientation to the physical world are more peripheral to my interests in composing this introduction, so I shall not take space here for such an extensive comment on them. Here I should like only to state for the record that putting the system of human action in the larger context, which has been a principal theme of this introduction, inherently involves a variety of problems concerning the physical world with which a fuller analysis would be obligated to deal carefully, and its relevance in this broader context should be carefully kept in mind.

There is, however, another open boundary of the action system that demands more immediate attention. This one has been continually held before me especially because I have been a career-long student of problems of the sociology of religion,[31] starting with the work of Malinowski, Durkheim, and Weber in my student days. This concerns what, in *The Structure of Social Action,* I called the "nonempirical" aspect of the world of "reality" in which the human actor must be conceived to be placed. The refusal to "reduce" this to an aspect of the empirical world, as that has been conceived in terms of the philosophy of science, was the most important single reason for repudiating the positivistic tradition as this had figured in the philosophical background of some of the authors and traditions treated in that work. In that repudiation I was particularly strongly influenced by the position of Weber.

"Nonempirical" was clearly and from the beginning admittedly a residual category. Another set of themes in forming the present collection of essays, but especially its sequel, concerns the problems of clarifying the nature and significance for the human condition of this category of "reality." As on previous occasions, the attempt to deal with these themes has not taken shape mainly by first trying to establish an overall philosophical framework, from the application of which the "answers" to the problems

[30] See Chapters 4 and 5 in the present volume.

[31] Talcott Parsons, "The Theoretical Development of the Sociology of Religion," *Essays in Sociological Theory,* rev. ed. (Glencoe, Ill.: Free Press, 1954), pp. 197–211.

of concern could be rigorously deduced, but rather, using the extremely variegated problem structure that has continually emerged from the consideration of theoretical problems in the action area, to state with increasing clarity, and seek directions for the solution of, a variety of these problems. In this respect at least, the author, though an "inveterate theorist," has tended to proceed more inductively than otherwise.

Concern with the clarification of the nature and status of this reference of the analysis of action has steadily grown during the period of gestation of the present collection of essays and of its sequel. The general trend of thought in this connection has been strongly to emphasize the relation of the system of action to a wider setting. Its relation to the organic world, which has been briefly reviewed from the autobiographical point of view above, has constituted one primary aspect of the problem of clarification of the status of action. Another has been the problem of the relation of the action system to the physical world, especially as known to and used by human actors through science and technology. The third context then has been that of the "nonempirical" reference just mentioned.

In this connection in turn, two general unifying themes have come to be especially important. These are the concept of evolutionary development, which is a major theme of the present volume, especially with reference to the conception of "sociocultural" or, more precisely, action evolution seen in its relations to organic evolution. The second theme is the problem of the status, in relation to action, of the conception of cybernetic hierarchy and control in relation to that of conditional factors.[32]

The second volume of this set of essays, to follow the present one shortly, will be primarily organized about these themes, but the present one may be regarded as an important preparation for it.[33] The title will be *Action and the Human Condition*. The first three parts will deal with problems of concern to the analytical student of human action systems, which also involve clear reference to its boundaries and what may lie beyond those boundaries. The first of these problems is the study of health and illness, which, as an old concern of mine, has been the object of a "revisit" in recent years. This obviously is one principal area in which human interests are involved in concern for the organic aspects of the

[32] See Norbert Wiener, *Cybernetics* (New York: Wiley, The Technology Press, 1948).

[33] During the latter part of my incumbency as a Visiting Professor at the University of Pennsylvania (1974–76) these problems, which, following André Malraux, we called those of the "Human Condition," were the subject matter of a small faculty discussion group. I am particularly indebted to its other members, namely Harold Bershady, Willy de Craemer, Renée Fox, Victor Lidz, and, near the end, Charles Bosk, for their major contributions to my own thinking in this area. It will be noted that Malraux's famous novel, which in English translation bore the title, *Man's Fate*, was in the original French *La condition humaine*. See André Malraux, *Man's Fate*, Trans. H. M. Chevalier (New York: Modern Library, 1934). Originally published as *La condition humaine* (Paris: Librairie Gallimard, 1933).

human condition, and the many respects in which man is an "animal," though of a rather special sort, as well as an "actor."

The second problem area is that of higher education. It does not seem to be too much to say that the most important single focus of what is special about modern Western higher education, relative to earlier times and other cultural traditions, has been the phenomenon of modern science that, it will be remembered, first crystallized in a radically new way of looking at the *physical* world and has in a sense spread from there to the organic and the action worlds.

The third focus, then, will be on religion in relation to human action, society, and culture. It is here, above all, that the problems of the status of the "nonempirical" boundary of action come to a head.[34]

The final part of the next volume will directly address the central problems of the relation of the action system to the wider setting of the human condition as a whole. It will be introduced by an essay entitled, "Death in the Western World," written for the *Encyclopedia of Bioethics*.[35] This is my third attempt to deal—the other two in collaboration [36] —with this central problem. Here I wish to emphasize that it is a topic which serves to connect the level of action with that of organic life, which link is given by the fact that in the first instance it is man the living organism that dies—and of course they *all* do. At the same time it also serves to link the action system with the nonempirical problems of "meaning" in the most acute sense.

The main part of the concluding section will, however, consist of a long essay that has grown out of discussions with a group at the University of Pennsylvania in the years 1974–76 [37] more than from any other single source. It is entitled "A Paradigm of the Human Condition" and is to be interpreted strictly in that sense. It is a tentative attempt to work out a larger frame of reference for the setting in which the system of action as such has to be understood.

That such attempts should be made is in my opinion centrally impor-

---

[34] On all this, see Max Weber, "Author's Introduction" to *The Protestant Ethic and the Spirit of Capitalism*, Trans. T. Parsons (New York: Scribner's 1958), pp. 13–31. The book was first published in German in 1904–1905 and the "Author's Introduction" in 1920. See also Benjamin Nelson, "Max Weber's 'Author's Introduction' (1920): A Master Clue to his Main Aims," *Sociological Inquiry*, vol. 44, no. 1 (1974).

[35] Talcott Parsons, "Death in the Western World," *Encyclopedia of Bioethics* (New York: Free Press, forthcoming).

[36] Talcott Parsons and Victor M. Lidz, "Death in American Society," in Edwin Shneidman (ed.), *Essays in Self-Destruction* (New York: Science House, 1967), and Talcott Parsons, Renée C. Fox, and Victor M. Lidz, "The 'Gift of Life' and Its Reciprocation," *Social Research*, vol. 39, no. 3 (October 1972), reprinted in Arien Mack (ed.), *Death in American Experience* (New York: Schocken Books, 1973).

[37] The role of this group will be further explained in the introduction to *Action and the Human Condition*, forthcoming.

tant. I consider the system of action to be the feature of man that is most distinctive to *this* organic species, resting as it does on a complex set of organic conditions. It is in particular the point at which the "humanity" of man, as so-called humanistic studies understand this term, links with the nature of man as "animal," as I put it above.

It seems pertinent to note here that this attempt may be interpreted in the setting of the general theme sounded at the beginning of this General Introduction. The intellectual journey began with a problem of the relation between a subsystem and the larger system of which it was a part, within the category of social system, namely that of the relation of economics and sociology, or economy and society, a quest that reached a certain "closure" with the book *Economy and Society,* in which I collaborated with Neil Smelser.[38]

The journey continued with work on the problem of the larger setting of the analytically defined conception of the social system and of its empirical counterparts. This led, as was sketched above, first to the consideration of a variety of problems about the "individual" who lived in a "society," leading above all into the problem area of the psychology of personality, as well as other problems. It then also led into considerations of the status of what we have called the cultural system in this setting. It is out of these developments that the conception of a "general system of action" has gradually taken shape. The main framework of the theoretical articulation of that system has developed within a "paradigm" in the above sense, that is, a frame of reference within which more empirically meaningful considerations can be systematically formulated and related to each other.

Working on a paradigm for the level of the Human Condition seems to me to have been a logical extension of the strategy of theory development that underlay the steps which preceded it. The central conception has been that of systems of which one of the most important characteristics has been that they are "open" by virtue of the importance for their functioning of "interchanges" with their environments. The dependence of living organisms on their environments for nutrition and respiration is a classic example. Seen in these terms the system of human action both "gets" essential things from, and "gives" them to, systems that are not, analytically or empirically, part of the action system.

These interchanges, however, are by no means random, but, unless the world from the human perspective is to be considered "meaningless," must be considered to be "structured" in terms of some patterns of intelligible order, both within themselves and in relation to action. In principle the same problems arise in this context as arose with respect to the bound-

[38] Talcott Parsons and Neil J. Smelser, *Economy and Society* (New York: Free Press, 1956).

aries of the economy within the society, and then of the society within the general system of action.

There are, of course, in several directions, ultimate limits to the extension of scientific understanding. These limits, however, *cannot* lie only at the boundaries of the action system, since the latter is bounded by both the organic and the physical worlds, which are the fields of study of highly developed sciences—to be sure, like those of action, developed from an "anthropocentric" point of view. My attempt to develop a paradigm of the human condition is premised in the assumption that the scientific method, in this case of theorizing rather than of empirical investigation, can be extended to contributing to the problem of the systematizing of our knowledge of the "setting," as we have called it, beyond the boundaries of the system of action, in the "environment," if we use that concept, in which human action is placed.

I thought it important to make a brief statement of the above considerations in the General Introduction to the present collection of essays for two reasons. The first is to provide readers with information about the framework within which my own thinking has been developing, which may prove helpful in their interpretation of the materials presented in this volume. The second is to alert them to the future—but not distant future—appearance of a further line of thought, which will be extended beyond that embodied in the essays in the present volume. Unlike many programmatic statements, this one is made with the materials necessary for the fulfillment of its promise already in hand.

In conclusion, I shall very briefly outline the materials presented in this volume. Part I is centered on materials that have been significant in my intellectual autobiography. Three principal themes are represented, along with the general outline presented in the first chapter. The first is my reaction to the intellectual experience of my first exposure to modern social science generally, and sociology in particular, in my first year of graduate study at the London School of Economics. The second concerns the emergence into new prominence in my thinking of problems of the relation between biological and sociocultural or action theory, documented in Chapters 3 and 4, but an interest going back to my undergraduate days. This new emergence has above all concerned the growing importance to me of problems of evolution in the field of action. The third theme is a "revisit" to the old problem that figured prominently in the experience of my study in Germany, subsequent to that in London, and centered on Max Weber's treatment of the relation between the "historical" traditions of German socio-cultural thought and the place of theory in the analytically generalizing sciences. In this connection the book of Harold Bershady provided a highly pertinent point of reference.[39] The bearing of these problems on those of evolution is almost self-evident.

---

[39] Harold J. Bershady, *Ideology and Social Knowledge* (New York: Wiley, 1973).

The essays included in Part II are devoted to problems of systematic formulation of generalized theory with primary reference to the social system, though not without consideration, especially in Chapters 7 and 10, of its relation to the general system of action. All four of these essays have, however, concerned themselves more with systematic considerations as distinguished from the patterning of processes of social change.

Part III, on the other hand, more explicitly raises problems of the nature and sources of social change. In it are treated both the problem of how significant evolutionary change can be conceptualized in the social field, and some of the complex problems of the balance among strain, conflict, and integration in the structure of modern societies.

Part I

ACTION AND LIVING SYSTEMS

Introduction

SINCE, AS NOTED in the General Introduction, the present volume of essays is organized, more than was true of its predecessors, in relation to the structure of my intellectual career, it seemed appropriate to assemble in the first part a few items of special relevance to that context. They fall into three subgroups. The first is, as noted, essentially an autobiographical essay written in 1969 which summarizes some of the main features or stages up to that point. The second and third refer to two important stages of this career, but both have the factor in common of much later evaluation of the experience of the first phase of graduate study at the London School of Economics. The next two refer to very recent phases of intellectual interest and development, which have been in the center of the stage in the last few years. Finally, the last item (Chapter 6), the review of Harold Bershady's book, *Ideology and Social Knowledge,*[1] and his response, deals especially with the pervasive problems of the relation between general theory and "history," but with a variety of other issues also.

The first essay was written for a Conference on the Making of Modern Science, organized by Gerald Holton and Stephen Graubard under the auspices of *Daedalus* and held in the summer of 1969 at the Villa Serbelloni in Bellagio, Italy. The report was published in *Daedalus,* Fall 1970, and subsequently in expanded form in the volume *Twentieth Century Sciences* edited by Holton, 1972.[2] I was specifically asked by the editors and organizers in advance to treat the subject autobiographically. The result therefore presents a convenient way of orienting the reader to certain major developmental features of my intellectual career.

I should like to single out a few steps and influences for emphasis here, in the light of my own retrospective estimate of their significance for the general developmental process. Most generally, perhaps, the London School of Economics year may be regarded as constituting one main phase of

---

[1] Harold J. Bershady, *Ideology and Social Knowledge* (New York: Wiley, 1973).

[2] Cf. Gerald Holton (ed.), *The 20th Century Sciences: Studies in the Biography of Ideas* (New York: W. W. Norton, 1972).

preparation for *The Structure of Social Action*,[3] the plan for which did not emerge until some years later. One part of this consisted above all in study of the historical background of the industrial revolution in England and hence, more generally, the antecedents of modern industrial society. The other main part was an enhanced acquaintance with the social theory that was relevant to these problems and in turn with its history. This included the history of economic thought and what may perhaps be called the "utilitarian orthodoxy" of the sociology of Hobhouse and Ginsberg. It also included an introduction to modern social anthropology through Malinowski, which presented a different perspective. The second major phase of preparation for *The Structure of Social Action* was the experience, following the London School of Economics, of study in Germany, at Heidelberg, and intellectually of course, above all acquaintance with the work of Max Weber.

The synthesis documented in *The Structure of Social Action* of course involved further exposure to economic theory, especially Alfred Marshall, to Pareto's economics and sociology, and above all to the work of Durkheim. Subsequently to that, the problem structure shifted to include the study of the professional component in modern societies and, theoretically, above all of the personality theory of Freud. These concerns led into an order of work with the so-called nonrational aspects of the human condition, which was one of the most conspicuous blank spots of the utiltarian tradition.

The next pair of items constitute retrospective reflections on the evaluation of the London School of Economics experience, though not without substantive theoretical references. The first of them (Chapter 2) is a review, written in 1966, of the posthumously published volume of essays of L. T. Hobhouse entitled *Sociology and Philosophy,* edited by his successor and exceedingly loyal follower, Morris Ginsberg.[4] Hobhouse was the first model of "the sociologist" conspicuously presented to me when I became an apprentice aspiring to professional status in that field. I was impressed by him, both personally and intellectually, especially through his writings. I was also impressed by the learning and graciousness as a teacher of Ginsberg. But in the light of my later experiences, centering on Weber in Germany and independently especially on Durkheim, I decided that *for me* as a sociological theorist the latter two models were the primary ones I would follow. In a sense, this review, written forty years after the experience, documents my "declaration of independence" from the utilitarian tradition more generally, from Hobhouse and

[3] Talcott Parsons, *The Structure of Social Action* (New York: McGraw-Hill, 1937). Reprinted by The Free Press, New York, 1949.

[4] L. T. Hobhouse, *Sociology and Philosophy. A Centenary Collection of Essays and Articles*, edited by Morris Ginsberg (London: G. Bell and Sons, 1966).

Ginsberg in particular. The wisdom of this declaration of independence may be left to "historical" judgment.

The second item of this pair (Chapter 3), the essay on Malinowski and the theory of social systems, is another retrospective evaluation, at least in part, of the London School of Economics experience. At the time of my first extended return visit to England after attending the London School of Economics, when I served for a year (1953–54) as a Visiting Professor of Social Theory at the Univerity of Cambridge, Raymond Firth (now Sir Raymond) proposed the publication of a volume of essays in memory of Malinowski, who had been the teacher of most of our generation of social anthropologists and of myself, as a former student of his at the London School of Economics, as well as of the many British anthropologists.

This essay is my contribution to that volume, published in 1957 but written in 1954, when I was in England. It is another version of the repercussions of my critical orientation to the utilitarian tradition, which had in a sense developed "dialectically" after my London year. My critique was above all based on Malinowski's late work *A Scientific Theory of Culture* [5] which I felt was, for a *social* anthropologist, altogether too much "psychologized," especially in the American behavioristic tradition of Clark Hull, [6] to whose work Malinowski became intensively exposed when he moved from London to Yale. As between the two leading British social anthropologists of that generation, I found myself strongly leaning to the side of Radcliffe-Brown,[7] as a theorist of social systems in something like my own sense. Of course the influence of Durkheim, which was so prominent in Radcliffe-Brown, played an essential part. Malinowski's negative appraisal of Durkheim may be seen to have influenced me greatly, an appraisal shared by my other London teacher, Ginsberg.

The third and fourth items document, not a retrospective evaluation of my early intellectual experiences, but a very recent phase of them. The first of the pair (Chapter 4) was written in response to another request, namely that of Lewis Coser, to contribute to a *Festschrift* volume in honor of Robert Merton (incidentally a *student* of mine, which clearly "dates" me). Coser specifically asked me to write on the topic of the "Present Status of Structural–Functional Theory" in sociology. The first part of the article is a review of the topic indicated by the title, in the course of which I stated my objections to the formula "structural–functional" but broadly reviewed what seemed to me to have happened in this field. In

[5] Bronislaw Malinowski, *A Scientific Theory of Culture and Other Essays* (New York: Oxford University Press, 1960). First published in 1944.

[6] Clark Hull, *Principles of Behavior* (New York: Appleton-Century, 1943).

[7] A. R. Radcliffe-Brown, *Structure and Function in Primitive Society* (Glencoe, Ill.: Free Press, 1952).

the second part of the article, however, I "cut loose," as it were, and seized the opportunity to present a substantially fuller version of my views on the relations of social and biological theory than had yet been published. While I thought that Merton's [8] early recognition of this problem, particularly in his judicious review of Cannon's ideas, had been excellent, he had been unduly self-denying in failing to develop further ramifications of the theme, especially those that linked with post-Cannon developments in biological science. The general importance to my thinking of this problem will have become evident to the reader from the General Introduction.

The second item of this pair (Chapter 5) is essentially a programmatic statement on the biology–social science problem, which was very recently written jointly with A. Hunter Dupree and published in the May 1976 issue of the (privately circulated) *Bulletin* of the American Academy of Arts and Sciences. Its initial reference is to the conference at Bellagio in 1969 referred to above. Growing out of that conference, Professor Dupree and I sponsored the two further conferences, jointly of biologists and social scientists, referred to in the *Bulletin* article, neither of which has yet resulted in publication. Since the second of these conferences, however, Professor Dupree has undertaken the major authorship of a book on these problems, under Academy auspices, and to which I have agreed to contribute. Because of Dupree's interest in these problems and his special competence as a leading historian of science, I am especially pleased that this arrangement has crystallized, with its essential implications for the future development of this field of my central intellectual interests.

The last item in Part I (Chapter 6) is of a different character. Since Harold Bershady's book [9] deals mainly with my work, I hesitated to undertake to review it but was persuaded to do so. In retrospect, I think it provided a useful experience and interchange. I had read the book in manuscript, but the responsibility of reviewing it at some length motivated a more careful study of it. It seems to me that Bershady has presented one of the best analyses available in English of the problem of the relations between generalized theoretical conceptualization and the tradition of "historicity," which has figured so prominently in the German background of my work, especially the contributions of Max Weber. In doing so, Bershady greatly illuminated the nature of my own involvement in these problems.

My review was written during the first year of my close association with Professor Bershady at the University of Pennsylvania. This association has broadened and deepened greatly since then, and I think it is fair

---

[8] Robert K. Merton, *Social Structure and Social Theory*, Revised ed. (New York: Free Press, 1957), "Manifest and Latent Functions," Chapter 1, pp. 19–84.

[9] Bershady, *Ideology and Social Knowledge, op. cit.*

to say that, on most of the problems that figured in our interchange, he and I now stand in quite close agreement. It also seemed to me very important to reprint Bershady's rejoinder [10] to my review in this volume so that the reader has easy access to both sides of the interchange.

[10] H. J. Bershady, "Commentary on Talcott Parsons' Review of *Ideology and Social Knowledge*," included in Chapter 6 in this volume.

1 On Building Social System Theory: A Personal History

THE EDITORS have urged contributors to be autobiographical and to write informally. In this vein, I may start by saying that the main subject matter will be the evolution of a contribution to the generalized theoretical analysis of the phenomena of human action, with special concern for its social aspects—that is, the theory of the social system. This has entailed combining elements from a variety of sources, combinations that are not frequently tapped by persons more inclined to disciplinary specialization.

I was perhaps predisposed in this direction by a highly unorthodox education. As an undergraduate at Amherst, influenced by an older brother who had gone into medicine, I had intended to concentrate in biology with a view either to graduate work in that field or to a medical career. But in 1923, my junior year, I was converted to social science under the influence especially of the unorthodox "institutional economist" Walton Hamilton. Then all concentration plans were disorganized by the dismissal, at the end of my junior year, of Alexander Meiklejohn as president of the college. None of the teachers whose courses I had elected was on hand the next fall. I made do with more courses in biology, some in philosophy, including one on Kant's *Critique of Pure Reason,* and some in English literature.

From the beginning I assumed I would pursue graduate study. But although sociology in a broad and vague sense attracted me, the regular American graduate programs, though I knew relatively little about them, did not. When an uncle offered to finance a year of study abroad, I elected to go to the London School of Economics. There the names of L. T. Hobhouse, R. H. Tawney, and Harold Laski particularly attracted me. Only

Reprinted by permission of *Daedalus,* Journal of the American Academy of Arts and Sciences, Boston, Massachusetts. Winter 1974, *Twentieth Century Classics Revisited;* and reprinted by permission of *Daedalus,* Journal of the American Academy of Arts and Sciences, Boston Massachussetts. Fall 1970, *The Making of Modern Science: Biographical Studies.*

after arriving did I discover the man who proved the most important to me intellectually—Bronislaw Malinowski, the social anthropologist.

I was not a degree candidate at London and my plans were unformed, so I was ripe to seize the offer of an exchange fellowship to Germany, for which I was recommended by Otto Manthey-Zorn, with whom I had had a seminar in German philosophy at Amherst and who also had much to do with my appointment, a year later, as instructor in Economics at Amherst. I was assigned to Heidelberg with no personal voice in the matter, but this located me where the influence of Max Weber, who had died five years before, was strongest. It is significant that I do not remember having heard his name either at Amherst or in London.

Weber's work, especially *The Protestant Ethic and the Spirit of Capitalism* (which a few years later I translated into English) [1] immediately made a strong impression on me. On going to Heidelberg, I had had no intention of taking a degree, but I subsequently learned that this could be accomplished with only three semesters' credit, oral examinations, and a dissertation. I decided to write a dissertation under the direction of Edgar Salin (later of Basel, Switzerland) on "The Concept of Capitalism in Recent German Literature." I began with a discussion of Karl Marx, said something about some less central figures such as Lujo Brentano, and then concentrated on Werner Sombart (author of the huge work *Der moderne Kapitalismus*) [2] and Max Weber. This work crystallized two primary foci of my future intellectual interests: first, the nature of capitalism as a socioeconomic system and, second, the work of Weber as a social theorist.

During the year of teaching at Amherst, which allowed time for a good deal of work on my dissertation, it gradually became clear to me that I wanted to go thoroughly into the relations between economic and sociological theory. I became particularly indebted to discussions with Richard Meriam, who had come to Amherst as chairman of the Department of Economics after my graduation. Meriam persuaded me that although economic theory was one of my examination subjects at Heidelberg, I needed to know much more about it, and I decided to make acquiring this knowledge my next setp. Although a German Dr. Phil. was not the equivalent of a good American Ph.D., I decided not to become a candidate for the latter. Meriam recommended that I go to Harvard and arranged an instructorship appointment for me there for the fall of 1927.

Allyn Young, perhaps the most important man for my interests, had just gone to England, but I was fortunate in having contact with Harvard economists F. W. Taussig, T. N. Carver, W. Z. Ripley, and Joseph Schumpeter (who had a visiting appointment, though later he came permanently to Harvard). Edwin F. Gay, the economic historian, was thoroughly famil-

[1] London: Allen and Unwin, 1930.
[2] 3 vols., 2d ed., Leipzig: Duncker and Humblot, 1916.

iar with the German background of my Heidelberg training and sympathetic to my interests.

Meriam was quite right in maintaining that the knowledge of economic
theory I could acquire at Harvard was far superior to that I had learned
at Heidelberg. It gradually became clear to me that economic theory should
be conceived as standing within some sort of theoretical matrix in which
sociological theory also was included. I tried my hand at statements of
this idea in some articles that Taussig kindly published in the *Quarterly
Journal of Economics*,[3] of which he was then editor. Most important, however, was a decision to explore this theme in the work of Alfred Marshall,
who at that time was the dominant influence in "orthodox" or "neoclas-
sical" economic theory, with a view to extracting Marshall's "sociology"
and its articulation with his strictly economic theory. The results, published
in 1931–1932,[4] crystallized the first stage of theoretical orientation that
seemed to me to go beyond the levels attained by my teachers in articulating the theoretical structures of the two disciplines.

Contact with Schumpeter was particularly helpful in laying the groundwork for this development, because, on the problem of the scope of economic theory, he was a strict constructionist in contrast to Marshall's refusal to draw any sharp boundaries. Knowledge of Vilfredo Pareto, gained
both on my own and through contact with L. J. Henderson, was also
especially important because Pareto had been an eminent economic theorist, a good deal in the same tradition as Schumpeter, but at the same time
he had attempted the formulation of a more comprehensive system of
sociological theory which, in his view, included a rather strictly defined
economic theory.[5] Thus both Schumpeter and Pareto served as critical
reference points from which to attempt to distinguish between the economic and the sociological components of Marshall's thought.

From this starting point there gradually evolved the project of including
not only Marshall and Pareto—on whom I had written a mongraph-length
analytical paper shortly after completing the Marshall study [6]—but also
Weber and Durkheim, in a comprehensive study of this group of "recent
European writers." Weber's general ideas on the nature of modern cap-

---

[3] "Sociological Elements in Economic Thought, I," 49 (1935), 414–453; "Sociological Elements in Economic Thought, II," 49 (1935), 645–667.

[4] "Wants and Activities and Marshall," *Quarterly Journal of Economics*, 46
(1931), 101–140; "Economics and Sociology: Marshall in Relation to the Thought of
His Time," *Quarterly Journal of Economics*, 46 (1932), 316, 347.

[5] Pareto gave the French edition of his book the title *Traité de sociologie gén-
érale*. (The Italian was *Trattato* . . .) It has always seemed to me unfortunate that
the English translation, published some years later than my work, bore the title *The
Mind and Society*.

[6] This paper was never published as such, but its main substance, after considerable revision, was published as the three chapters on Pareto in *The Structure of
Social Action* (New York: McGraw-Hill, 1937).

italism, which had been the principal focus of my dissertation, and more specifically his conception of the role of the ethic of ascetic Protestantism, provided sufficient ground for hope that a Marshall-Pareto-Weber "convergence" could be worked out.

Increasingly, it seemed to be desirable to include Durkheim in the picture, but this presented greater difficulties. Of the four, Durkheim had had by far the least to do with economics as a technical discipline. Moreover, I never had a teacher on Durkheim in the same sense that my Heidelberg teachers were such on Weber, Taussig and Schumpeter were on Marshall, and Schumpeter and Tenderson were on Pareto. Furthermore the exposure to Durkheim I had been given, especially by Ginsberg and Malinowski in London, was not only not very helpful, but also positively misleading: much unlearning of what was not true about Durkheim became necessary. The clue, however, was available. It lay in Durkheim's first major work, *De la division du travail social* (1893),[7] which interestingly was seldom mentioned in the English language secondary literature of that period. Careful study of this book showed that its analysis could be indeed be very directly articulated with Weber's analysis of capitalism, and that in turn with Marshall's conception of free enterprise. The theory as such then articulated with the sociological, rather than the strictly economic, components of the work of Pareto and Weber and, more indirectly, Marshall. The key conceptual complex concerned the institutional framework of property and especially contract as distinguished from the "dynamics" of economic activity as such, and as constituting, for its understanding in the theoretical sense, a field for sociological rather than economic investigation.

A First Major Synthesis

The outcome of this complex series of studies was *The Structure of Social Action,* published in 1937 but completed in first draft—though substantially revised afterward—nearly two years before.[8] The book was meant as a study of the writers' ideas about the modern socioeconomic order, capitalism, free enterprise, and so forth, and, at the same time, of the theoretical framework in terms of which these ideas and interpretations had been formulated. In this respect the most immediate interpretive thesis was that the four—and they did not stand alone—had *converged* on what was essentially a single conceptual scheme. In the intellectual milieu of the

[7] George Simpson, trans., New York: Free Press, 1964.

[8] The first part of this book that I actually committed to paper concerned Durkheim's early empirical work and dealt with the Division of Labor and his (subsequently) very famous study of suicide (Chapter VIII).

time this was by no means simple common sense, but as it unfolded it surprised even me a great deal.[9]

To arrive at this conclusion required three resources in particular. One, of course, was careful critical study of the rather large body of relevant texts, as well as secondary literature, though most of the latter was worse than useless. The second was the development of a theoretical scheme that would be adequate to the interpretation of these materials. The third, finally, in a sense lay back of that. It included a kind of philosophy of science orientation about which a few things ought to be said.

All persons aspiring to some degree of sophistication in intellectual fields, since long before the 1920's when these problems became salient to me, had to develop some conception of the nature and condtions of empirical knowledge, and in particular of the nature and role of theory in that knowledge. I was introduced to such problems partly through courses in empirical science, especially biology, and partly through philosophy, including, as I have noted, an intensive course in Kant's *Critique of Pure Reason*.[10] The Heidelberg experience carried me substantially farther, particularly in studies of the issues involved with Weber's *Wissenchaftslehre*. Notable among these were, first, the problems centering around the German historical traditions and hence the status of generalized theoretical conceptualization in the social and cultural disciplines, and, second, those of the status of the interpretation of subjective meanings and motive in the analysis of human action, what the Germans called the problem of *Verstehen*.

Returning to this country I found behaviorism so rampant that anyone

[9] Thus Sorokin, whose *Contemporary Sociological Theories* was the most widely used compendium in the field in the 1930's, treated Pareto, Durkheim, and Weber as belonging to entirely different schools, and did not once mention a relation between any pair of them. Marshall, of course, he did not discuss at all because he was labeled an economist, not a sociologist.

[10] In retrospect it seems to me that this experience was, even apart from the substantive importance of Kant for my problems, especially important training for my later work. It was reinforced by a seminar and oral exam on the same book under Karl Jaspers at Heidelberg in 1926. The importance lay in the fact that I undertook the detailed and repeated study of a great book, the product of a great mind, to a point of reaching a certain level of appreciation of the nature of its contribution, and not being satisfied with the myriad current rather superficial comments about it. This experience stood me in good stead in working with the contributions of my own authors and coming through to what I felt to be a high level of understanding of them in the face of many distorted interpretations current in the secondary literature, some of which were widely accepted.

After the Pugwash Conference of 1967, I. I. Rabi commented to me on the importance of contact with the operation of what he explicitly called "really great minds." He spoke of his own good fortune in his student or early post-student days of being able to work in the laboratories of Pauli and Bohr. I did not have anyone of that caliber among my teachers in the flesh—though possibly Jaspers was—but I had a good many teachers who had that appreciation and I was able to develop it for myself through intensive study of the writings of great minds. The course on Kant was my first introduction to that experience.

who believed in the scientific validity of the interpretation of subjective states of mind was often held to be fatuously naïve. Also rampant was what I called "empiricism," namely the idea that scientific knowledge was a total reflection of the "reality out there," and even selection was alleged to be illegitimate.

Weber had insisted on the inevitability and cognitive validity of selection among available factual information. The importance of analytical abstraction was further strongly emphasized by Henderson in his formula: "A fact is a statement about experience in terms of a conceptual scheme."[11] The culmination of this conception came for me in A. N. Whitehead's work, especially his *Science and the Modern World,* including his illuminating discussion of the "fallacy of misplaced concreteness."[12] Through channels such as these I arrived at a conception which I called "analytical realism," which treated the kind of theory I was interested in as inherently abstract but by no means as "fictitious" in the sense of Hans-Vaihiger.[13] This seemed to me in particular to fit the treatment of the status of economic theory by Schumpeter and Pareto. I also found various of James B. Conant's writings on the nature of science, especially the role of theory, very helpful.

Closely related to this was the conception of "system." Schumpeter and Whitehead were important in forming the background of this concept, but I think it crystallized above all in the influence of Pareto and Henderson. As Henderson was never tired of pointing out, Pareto's model in this respect was the idea of system as used in the theory of mechanics, but he attempted to apply it both to economics and to sociology. Hence Henderson's statement that perhaps Pareto's most important contribution to sociology was his conception of the "social system," a dictum which I myself took so seriously that I used the phrase as the title of a book some years later.

Henderson's own primary model, which he explicated at some length in *Pareto's General Sociology,* was the physico-chemical system.[14] He related this, however, to biological systems. He was a great admirer of Claude Bernard and wrote a foreward to the English translation of the latter's *Experimental Medicine.*[15] The central idea here was that of the "internal environment" and its stability. This connected closely with the idea of

[11] Bernard Barber, ed., *L. J. Henderson on the Social System* (Chicago: University of Chicago Press, 1970).

[12] New York: Macmillan, 1926.

[13] Hans Vaihiger, *The Philosophy of "As if,"* trans. C. K. Ogden (New York: Barnes & Noble, 1952).

[14] L. J. Henderson, *Pareto's General Sociology: A Physiologist's Interpretation* (Cambridge, Mass.: Harvard University Press, 1935).

[15] Claude Bernard, *An Introduction to the Study of Experimental Medicine,* trans. H. C. Green, repub. ed. (New York: Daler, 1957).

W. B. Cannon of homeostatic stablization of physiological processes and also with the residues of my own exposure to biology.[16]

Thus a certain foundation for the transition from the concept of system as used in mechanics and the physico-chemical system as explicated by Henderson to that of the special character of "living systems" was laid in these early years. This was essential to the later phase of my thinking which is usually referred to as "structural-functional" theory and culminated in my book *The Social System*.[17] Further steps were greatly influenced by a continuing Conference on System Theory held from about 1952 to 1957 under the chairmanship of Dr. Roy Grinker in Chicago. Among the several participants whose ideas were important to me, the social insect biologist Alfred Emerson stands out. What he had to say, including some of his writings, strongly reinforced my predilection for the homeostatic point of view of Cannon. He spoke, however, in such a way as strongly to predispose me, and I think others, in favor of the then just emerging conceptions of cybernetic control, not only in living systems but also in many other kinds of systems. This later became a dominant theme in my thinking.

Finally, Emerson put forth what turned out for me to be an especially fruitful conception which did much to seal my conviction of the fundamental continuity between the living systems of the organic world and those of the human sociocultural world.[18] This was the conception of the functional equivalence of the gene and, as he put it, the "symbol." We can perhaps restate these as the genetic constitution of species and organism and the cultural heritage of social systems. In more recent years this perspective has come to be of fundamental theoretical importance to me.

Personal and Professional Concerns

The Structure of Social Action marked a major turning point in my professional career. Its major accomplishments, the demonstration of the convergence among the four authors with which it dealt, was accompanied

---

[16] W. B. Cannon, *The Wisdom of the Body* (New York: Norton, 1932). In the discussion at the Bellagio conference, when this essay was first presented, a question was raised about the seriousness of this exposure to biology. I was greatly pleased when Professor Curt Stern said: "May I make one very short point in regard to Amherst that not everybody might know. At Amherst, biology was taught at a very advanced, even a graduate level, although Amherst did not give doctors' degrees. These were highly distinguished people, and probably their influence was greater than it would have been had Professor Parsons gone to another college with good but less distinguished professors."

[17] New York: Free Press, 1951.

[18] It should be remembered here that social scientists had been forced to expend much ingenuity and energy on fighting off pressures toward illegitimate and premature biological "reductionism."

by a clarification and development of my own thought about the problems of the state of Western society with which the authors were concerned. The state of Western society which might be designated as either capitalism or free enterprise—and on the political side as democracy—was clearly then in some kind of state of crisis. The Russian Revolution and the emergence of the first socialist state as controlled by the Communist party had been crucial to my thinking since undergraduate days. The Fascist movements affected friendships in Germany. Less than two years after the publication of the book the Second World War was to begin, and, finally, came the Great Depression with its ramifications throughout the world.

My personal concern involved a growing family[19]—three children born from 1930 to 1936—and difficulties of status at the professional level. Though the situation was not strictly comparable to what it would be now, it was even then anomalous that I remained at the instructor level for nine years, the first four in the Department of Economics, the last five in the newly constituted Department of Sociology. I had the misfortune of serving under unsympathetic chairmen—in economics the late H. H. Burbank, in sociology P. A. Sorokin. My promotion to an assistant professorship occurred in 1936 and was pushed not by Sorokin but, notably, by E. F. Gay, E. B. Wilson, and Henderson, all of whom were "outside members" of the Department of Sociology. The first draft of *The Structure of Social Action* was in existence by then, and known to all the principals.

Even with the assistant professorship, however, I was by no means certain I wanted to stay at Harvard. In the (to me) critical year of 1937 I received a very good outside offer. Since Gay had retired the previous year and gone to California, I went to Henderson—not Sorokin. In those days before the ad hoc committee system, Henderson took the matter directly to President Conant who, with Sorokin's consent, to be sure, offered to advance me immediately to the then extant "second term" assistant professorship, with a definite promise of permanency as associate professor two years later. On those terms I decided to stay at Harvard.

On the intellectual side I have noted that I had very good relations with Taussig, Schumpeter, and Gay. The above crisis occurred shortly after the completion of an extraordinary relationship with Henderson. I had known him through his Pareto seminar and in other respects before the manuscript of my book was referred to him for critical comment in connection with my appointment status. Instead of the usual limited response, he got in touch with me (stimulated I think mainly by my discussion of Pareto) and started a long series of personal sessions at his house, something like two hours, twice a week for nearly three months. In these

---

[19] I was married in 1927 to Helen B. Walker, whom I had met as a fellow student at the London School of Economics. She has worked at Harvard for many years, most recently in administration of the Russian Research Center.

sessions he went through the manuscript with me paragraph by paragraph, mainly the sections dealing with Pareto and Durkheim; he passed over Marshall rather quickly and did not enter into my treatment of Weber at all.

This was an extraordinary experience, both personally and intellectually. Those who knew him will remember that Henderson was a formidable person, who could be dogmatic, both on political matters, in which he was a pronounced conservative,[20] and on many intellectual matters, as exemplified by his unfairness—as I judged it—to all but one or two sociologists. He had, however, an immense knowledge of science, especially on the level of the philosophy of science and the nature of theory, and if one stood up to him and did not allow oneself to be overridden, he was an exceedingly insightful critic and very helpful with precisely my intellectual problems.[21] I benefited enormously from this special contact, and took

[20] Thus he was extremely hostile to President Roosevelt, whose general policies I personally supported.

[21] Perhaps, in the process of the present essay going to press for inclusion in a 1977 edition of my essays, it may be permissible to add a comment, on my relation to Henderson, from the point of view of some years later. Since Chapter I was written I have, as the volume of essays to follow this will make very clear (but the Introduction to the present one outlines), become more deeply involved than before in the problems of the relation of the human action system both to the organic and to the physical worlds. In trying to understand especially the organic world in its relation to the physical, I have been driven, it is almost true to say, to a "revisit" to Henderson's work. In that connection I have very thoroughly reread his two notable "essay-books" in the philosophy of science, namely *The Fitness of the Environment* and *The Order of Nature* (1912 and 1917, respectively) and have found them extraordinarily stimulating.

It seems to me that, in these two books, Henderson, in a sense which has been only very fragmentarily appreciated since then, laid the groundwork for the main paradigm of evolutionary development with which I have been concerned. It is of course true that he dealt with the transition between the physical and the organic worlds. However, especially in his conception of the "fitness of the environment" from the point of view of defining the conditions under which organic life could emerge, he went much farther than any of his contemporaries in clarifying a central aspect of the evolutionary problem. The essence of Henderson's position in this respect seems to me to be his contention of the *mutuality* of adaptiveness, between organic life and inorganic environment.

The next truly major transition in the evolutionary process has been from the organic to the *action* levels, as we have defined these terms. It would be our contention that the essential principles which Henderson stated for the organic-inorganic boundary apply, with the appropriate modifications, to the organic-action boundary.

In my recognition of indebtedness to Henderson, stated above in the present chapter, this, perhaps most important set of references, was not included. I think this is simply because, even as late as the 1960's I did not understand the problems for the philosophy of science on the relevant level of generality. It is only because such insight has developed farther in the intervening years that I am able to see it now. I think it probable that Henderson's insights were working away in my "scientific unconscious" all these years, but that it took a special set of circumstances to allow them to emerge into the light of explicit intellectual discussion. This experience at least suggests two things. The first is that, from the point of view of the scientist's personality, these things develop by a process other than the rationalists' paradigm would have us suppose. Secondly, they impede the recognition of the contributions

about a year to complete the revisions which the discussions convinced me should be undertaken.[22]

In these early Harvard years, I also had important experiences with age-peers and, in course of time, students. A group of junior faculty members that met fairly reguarly included Edward S. Mason, Seymour Harris, Edward Chamberlin, and for a time Karl Bigelow in economics, Carl J. Friedrich in government, and Crane Brinton in history. With the move to sociology, which brough me closer to psychology and anthropology, I began to get to know Gordon Allport, who had recently returned to Harvard from Dartmouth, and Henry Murray. In anthropology, there were two particularly significant contemporaries. The first was W. Lloyd Warner, brought to Harvard mainly by Elton Mayo, who, under Henderson, directed the Western Electric Study, to make a community study that eventually became the well-known "Yankee City Series." When Warner left Harvard to go to Chicago he was replaced by Clyde Kluckhohn, a young social anthropologist who was quite independent of the Henderson group but associated with them. He became a close friend of Murray, and with Allport, Murray, and Kluckhohn the nucleus of the eventual promoters of the Social Relations experiment was present.

Also by the mid-thirties significant relations with graduate students, a few of whom received teaching appointments, began. The most important single one was with Robert Merton, who was in the first contingent of graduate students in sociology, but after him came Kingsley Davis, John Riley, and—not as a student—Mathilda Riley, Robin Williams, Edward C. Devereux, Logan Wilson, Wilbert Moore, Florence Kluckhohn, and

---

of those to whom honor is due, contributions the importance of which as input of their thinking which brings about the later product. I hereby freely confess that I failed to make fully appropriate acknowledgment of the, to me now, saliently important contribution of Henderson to the development of my theoretical thinking.

[22] A note on the then, as now, prevalence of the belief that the word was "publish or perish" and that the criteria of conformity were to publish as soon as possible and as much as possible. I can testify that the responsible advice which I received from senior faculty members at Harvard did not fit the formula. It was uniformly to take as much time as necessary to do the best job of which I was capable. Of course, it helped immensely that such people as Henderson, Gay, and Wilson knew what I was doing and had seen samples of it. Another senior critic who should also be mentioned in the same vein was the late A. D. Nock.

As in the case of most formidable personalities, there was an underground reaction to Henderson. He wore a reddish beard and was, behind his back, widely known as "Pinkwhiskers." My sessions with him took place in the late afternoon and I generally went directly home and told my wife what Pinkwhiskers had said. I remember worrying that my children would pick up the name and on some occasion say directly to Henderson: "Are you the Pinkwhiskers my daddy talks about?"

It is fortunate that, between the first and final drafts of this paper, there has appeared *L. J. Henderson on the Social System*, edited by Bernard Barber. It contains most of Henderson's sociological writings, with a long and informative introduction by Barber. Barber's introduction tells in considerable detail the story of Henderson's involvement in the social science scene at Harvard and the various people in it with him.

Bernard Barber. An informal discussion group on problems of sociological theory composed largely of these people met in the evenings in my study in Adams House, while I was still an instructor.

Theoretical Interests After *The Structure of Social Action*

Completion of *The Structure of Social Action* constituted a gratifying accomplishment, though at that time I was not aware how large a reputation it would achieve.[23] The theoretical framework which had enabled me to demonstrate the thesis of convergence clearly had the potential of further use and development, but there were several alternatives of what to attempt next with its help. In the Bellagio conference, where this essay was first presented, there was considerable discussion of why I did not identify with economics as a discipline. By the time *The Structure of Social Action* neared completion that decision had already been made on one level by my transfer from economics to the new Department of Sociology. In spite of the friendliness of Taussig, Gay, and Schumpeter, I am quite sure I could not have counted on a future in economics at Harvard. But basically I did not want to do so, and in retrospect the focus of the reasons lay in my permeation with Weber's thinking, then Durkheim's: Freud was yet to come. Though I wanted to keep my contact with economic theory, and in fact have done so in various ways, I saw clearly that I did not want to be primarily an economist, any more than Weber turned out to be.

There was one interesting episode which might, at a relatively late time, have turned me at last farther in the direction of economics. After my formal transfer to sociology, Schumpeter organized a small discussion group with younger people, mostly graduate students, on problems of the nature of rationality. After a few meetings he proposed to me that the group should aim at producing a volume, of which he and I should be at least coeditors, if not coauthors. Though not specifically rejecting the proposal, at least immediately, I remembered having reacted rather coolly, and in fact I let it die. I am not wholly clear about my motives, but I

[23] Perhaps I may be pardoned for noting that, though I felt I was exceedingly fortunate to get the book published in the first place without subsidy and to have it republished in 1949 by The Free Press, it has maintained a steady substantial sale for over thirty years; indeed, just thirty years after the original publication a paperback edition was brought out which has sold well. In this matter I owe a particular debt to Jeremiah Kaplan, who practically "was" The Free Press, for his imagination in bringing out the 1949 reprint and sticking with this and a considerable series of my other publications. Without Kaplan, and his principal adviser Edward Shils, the postwar efflorescence in sociological publication, a wave on which I rode, probably could not have occurred, at least not so soon.

think they had to do with the feeling that I needed a relatively complete formal break with economics.[24]

The Professions and the Two Aspects of the Rationality Problem

The actual choice I made was to undertake a study of some aspect of the professions as social phenomena. This interest grew logically out of the combination of my concern with the nature of modern industrial society and the conceptual framework in which I had approached it. It was empirically nearly obvious that the "learned professions" had come to occupy a salient position in modern society, whereas in the ideological statement of the alternatives, capitalism versus socialism, they did not figure at all. Indeed, what is now habitually called the "private, nonprofit" sector of organization and activity which is occupationally organized, as distinct, for example, from kinship, did not figure ideologically. In retrospect it can be said that both ideological positions stated versions of the "rational pursuit of self-interest"— the capitalist version, grounded in utilitarian thought, the interest of the individual in the satisfaction of his wants, the socialist version, the interest of the collectivity (on lines deriving from Hobbes and Austin) in maximization of satisfaction of the public interest.

Within this field I chose to study some aspects of medical practice. This choice had, I think, good technical grounds, but it also goes back to personal motives. Certainly I could say that my previous renunciation of biological-medical interests played a part: the role of a sociological student of medical practice was an important way of satisfying both motives. The Henderson–Mayo group, however, also had a bearing. Henderson was himself medically trained, though he never practiced, and his early Harvard appointments were in the Medical School. He had combined his medical and sociological interests in a famous paper, "Physician and Patient as a Social System," [25] which stated an approach highly congenial to me; hence it was natural that I should consult both Henderson and Mayo— but also W. B. Cannon—about my plan of work. All three strongly reinforced my own feeling of the probable fruitfulness of such a study. I pro-

---

[24] I have barely noted above that in my undergraduate days a comparable basic decision was made, namely to go into social rather than biological science. My switch to social science—a qualified economics initially—was associated with my father, who, during my development, was a college teacher and administrator. When I was a student in college my father was president of Marietta College in Ohio. He had begun his career as a Congregational minister and was very much involved with the then important "social gospel" movement, which, it is now clear, had much to do with the origins of sociology in this country.

[25] Reprinted in Barber, ed., *Henderson on the Social System*.

posed, in addition to canvassing the literature, to approach it through the methods of participant observation and interview. The semi-public character of medical practice in the modern hospital made a good deal of the former possible, such as—equipped with a white coat and the (albeit non-medical) legitimate title of doctor—making ward rounds, observing operations, going on the home visit service of the Tufts medical center and the like. (Perhaps, with current concern over ethical aspects of research, this mild deception of patients would now be regarded as unethical.) The other source of data was a series of interviews with a rather large number of physicians, chosen to represent different types of practice.

One other aspect of the situation involved in this choice turned out to be of primary significance. This was a time in which ideas about psychosomatic relations were beginning to take hold among the intellectual elite of medicine—typified perhaps by internists at the Massachusetts General Hospital, where I spent a good deal of time. In the background was psychoanalysis and the fact that the professor of psychiatry at Massachusetts General Hospital, Stanley Cobb, had recently been the principal founder of the Psychoanalytic Institute in Boston. The Henderson–Mayo group had also been very much concerned with this and related movements of thought—they were devotees of Pierre Janet, but also of Jean Piaget.

For me the decisive event was a talk with Elton Mayo about my interests in medical practice, in which he asked point blank how well I knew the work of Freud. My reply had to be, only very fragmentarily. He then earnestly advised me to read Freud seriously and comprehensively. This was fortunately a time when I had a good deal of free time, thanks to an assistant professor's term leave, and I followed his advice. It was too late to build the implications of Freud's ideas into *The Structure of Social Action,* but this proved to be one of the few crucial intellectual experiences of my life. This, of course, prepared the way for formal psychoanalytic training—at the level permitted—about a decade later.

I used the economic paradigm of the "rational pursuit of self-interest" as the major point of reference, but in this case negatively, to throw light on the *differences* between the classical economic model of market orientation and the professional case with which I was concerned. Major differences were not far to seek. In the individual practitioner they were, first, fee-for-service relation to patients' situations—the so-called "sliding scale" or higher charges for well-to-do patients and lower or remission of charges for less well-to-do patients. And, second, the objection to "shopping around"—namely patients testing out various physicians with respect to their judgment of the value of the proferred medical service, financially and otherwise. In later years I was to modify substantially this close assimilation—with the differences—of the professional relation to the ideal type commercial one.

The most important theoretical implications concerned the problem of

the nature of rationality, the very question with which I had been involved, not only in my own work, but also in my work with Schumpeter. What opened up was a distinction, not only between economic and noneconomic aspects of rationality, but also, within the latter category, between two different modes or directions of considering the rationality problem. The first concerned a very old problem, even for me, namely the relation between rational (mainly scientific) knowledge and action in the sense of "application." Medicine, especially at the time I was studying it, was a kind of prototype of the possibilities of generating potentially useful knowledge and applying it to the solution of critical human problems. What was called "scientific medicine" then enjoyed a sort of heyday, and its significance was strongly impressed upon me by my brother, who had been trained at Johns Hopkins. There were, of course, very definite connections between this aspect of medicine and the more general setting of the rationality problem in *The Structure of Social Action,* notably in Pareto's concept of "logical action."

The concern with psychosomatic problems, and eventually those of mental illness, noted above, raised a different set of questions. These concerned the significance of the scientific modes of rational investigation and analysis for the understanding, and in some eventual sense control, of the non- and irrational factors in the determination of human action, in the first instance individual, but clearly also social. Concern with these issues permeated the thought of all of my authors except Marshall, but intensive contact with Freud rounded out the pattern and gave new dimensions to it, notably concerning the relevance of nonrational factors and mechanisms in the more intimate microsocial processes of interaction. I suspect that concern with this complex of problems had a good deal to do with my coolness toward Schumpeter's overture, flattering as that was for a young and still insecure scholar.

In this type of interest I was clearly influenced by my growing association with such colleagues as Clyde Kluckhohn and Henry Murray; Gordon Allport, by contrast, was a psychologist of pronouncedly rationalistic bent. At any rate, *both* facets of the "rationality complex" happened to be combined in my study of medical practice and both stood in sharp contrast to my earlier concentration on the economic-political aspects of rationality. In the background stood concern for the status of religion in any general analysis of social action—a concern which I had come by honestly as a result of my family background and which was brought into focus by Weber's analysis of the Protestant Ethic and his more general studies on the comparative sociology of religion.

As I see it now, these three (or, including religion, four) foci of the "rationality problem" have been nearly dominant in the structuring of my theoretical interests since this crossroads situation of the late 1930's. The first main swing was away from the economic-political complex toward

the socio-psychological, that is, the problem of nonrationality seen more from the perspective of Freud than that of Weber or Pareto, different as these two were from each other. In the course of this move I was fully conscious of the importance of "cognitive rationality" in particular as constituting the cultural basis of the scientific component of medicine. Intensive concern with this, however, was to await my coming around to concern with the anchorage of the professions in the system of higher education and research, a concern that has become central to me in recent years. In a certain sense it is a case of the "return of the repressed."

In the context of the social-emotional aspect of medical practice, I came to analyze some of the phenomena which were then commonly called the "art of medicine" (as contrasted with the "science") in terms of Freud's conception of the relation between analyst and analysand, notably the phenomenon of transference, which I regard as one of Freud's great discoveries. Freud clearly had not invented the physician–patient relationship, which in Western tradition goes back at least to Hippocrates (vide Henderson), but he had accepted it as his primary social framework for psychoanalytic practice and immensely deepened the basis of its understanding. It became clear that the psychoanalytic relation presented the extreme, and, hence, in a kind of limiting sense paradigmatic, example of this relationship, and that the vast and vague range of psychosomatic relationships fitted into this. There was, of course, a basic link between the two primary aspects of the rationality problem of interest here, namely via the aspiration of psychoanalysis to scientific status, which in my opinion in spite of much controversy has been broadly validated and is perhaps in the context of application best symbolized for the process of therapy by Freud's aphorism "where Id was, there shall Ego be."

It was mainly by this path that I came to think of illness as in some sense a form of social "deviance" and of therapy as belonging in a very broad band of types of "social control"—a view for which I have paid dearly in the accusation of being an agent of Establishment interest in maintenance of the status quo. There is, nevertheless, a certain element of truth in this position, truth which I think to be basically independent of the particular form of social order. The important theoretical point is the shift from considering the application of medical science as a biophysical technology only, to considering it as a field of social interaction as well. Put in more technical terms which were crystallized later, the traditional view of medical practice conceived it as a relation between cultural systems (scientific knowledge) and organisms, with social agents only implementing the obvious implications of knowledge, whereas the other perspective involved treating medical relationships, at least in part, as cases of the subtle interplay between unconscious motives at the personality level and particularities of the structure of social systems. There are further sociological correlates of the difference which involve a duality of levels—in the

medical case between physician as competent agent of social control and patient as recipient of these important services—which cannot be gone into in detail here. This turns out, however, to be a major focus of social structure which does not have a place either in the predominantly economic or the political models (capitalism and socialism).

From Medical Practice to the Theory of Socialization

In a period of my career so much under the influence of Freud, it was perhaps natural to shift interest from the analysis of the social situation of psychoanalysis, and more generally of medical practice, to that of the origins of the problems which analyst and analysand confronted. These clearly were problems in the first instance in the personalities of analysands—the bases of "countertransference" were analyzed somewhat later—and for the sociologist led to the consideration of conditions of child development in the family as a social system. Freud himself had increasingly laid stress on "object relations" but could scarcely be said to have developed an adequate sociology of the family. In this connection a major conception on which there had been impressive convergence came to play a central role. In my reading of Freud, I gradually realized the importance of what I and others came to call the phenomeon of "internalization" (Freud's own term was "introjection")—both of sociocultural norms and of the personalities of the others with whom an individual has been interacting, above all a "socializing agent" (the latter case sometimes being called "identification").

This idea first emerged clearly in Freud's thought in the conception of the superego, though one may say it was present from an early stage, especially in the conception of transference (for example, the treatment of the analyst as if he were the analysand's father). Freud came to consider moral standards, particularly as implemented by the father, integral parts of the child's personality, through some phases of the learning process. Gradually the scope of this aspect of Freud's theory of "object relations" widened in the course of his later work to include not only the superego but also the ego and even the id.[26] At about the same time, it became clear to me that a very similar conception, developed from a quite different point of view, was essential to Durkheim, especially in his conception of social control through moral authority. The idea was also at least implicit in Weber's treatment of the role of religious values in determining behavior, and appeared with great clarity in the work of a group of

---

[26] See my paper, "Social Structure and the Development of Personality: Freud's Contribution to the Integration of Psychology and Sociology," in *Social Structure and Personality* (New York: Free Press, 1964).

American social psychologists, notably G. H. Mead and W. I. Thomas. The conception of the internalization, in successive series, of sets of cultural norms and concrete social objects has become a major axis of the whole theory of socialization, figuring in new forms even in the most recent treatments of the problems of higher education.

Internalization is a feature of the structure of the personality as a system. I have called the parallel phenomenon for social systems institutionalization, especially the shaping of social relationships by components of normative culture, which come to constitute direct structural parts of the social system of reference. Perhaps the preeminent theorist of this line of analysis was Weber, especially in his comparative sociology of religion, but Durkheim made contributions of similar importance. Both these conceptions, furthermore, could make sense only if the primary subsystems of a general system of action were conceived to be *interpenetrating* as well as interdependent. Thus, certain components of the cultural system came to be *at the same time* components of certain social and personality systems. This very central conception, in turn, depended heavily on the conception of the abstractness of the subsystems under consideration. Thus a social system—for example, a "society"—is not a concrete entity, but a way of establishing certain relations among components of "action" that are distinctive relative to the manifold of concrete reality.

Concern with this set of problems of the nonrational was certainly reinforced by the circumstances of the times. Discussions of the problem of German character, in connection with which Erik Erikson first became a salient figure to me, were important at this time.[27] So were personal matters, including my medical brother's premature death (1940) and the aging and eventual deaths of my parents (1943 and 1944).

This set of circumstances seems to me to provide the principal explanation of a major failure of my career: not to carry through my intention to publish a major monographic study of medical practice. I had, I think, gained immensely from the venture, but had been diverted into more general concerns with the subtler aspects of social control and the genesis of the problems in socialization processes outside the professional context.[28] In any case, I did stall on completion of this enterprise and, in addition to a good many discussions of aspects of the problems in various papers, settled

[27] See my paper, "The Problem of Controlled Institutional Change," reprinted in *Essays in Sociological Theory*, rev. ed. (New York: Free Press, 1954).

[28] Possibly one precipitating factor in this diversion was the death, in 1938, of my father-in-law, Dr. W. D. Walker of Andover, Massachusetts, at the age of sixty. Dr. Walker was a particularly fine type of general practitioner of medicine and had been exceedingly helpful to me in the working out of the fieldwork phase of my medical study and in general discussions of the medical scene. At the same time, he was sufficiently old-fashioned not to "take much stock" in my more esoteric psychological interests.

for a longish chapter, "The Case of Modern Medical Practice," in *The Social System*.

Starting, perhaps, in the later 1940's there was a shift back from concern with psychological and microsociological problems to the more macro-sociological, including the economic, but also perhaps a renewed sense of participation in the European scene, which was inaugurated by teaching at the Salzburg Seminar in the summer of 1948. In a sense this process culminated in a revisit to the problems of the relation between economic and sociological theory which began during my year as a visiting professor at Cambridge, England (1953–1954).

In 1946, however, I entered into formal psychoanalytic training as a "Class C" candidate at the Boston Psychoanalytic Institute. The more general intellectual grounds for my interest are perhaps clear from the above discussion, though I also had some personal reasons for seeking psycho-therapeutic help. I count myself exceedingly fortunate in having had as my training analyst Dr. Grete Bibring, who had been a member of the original Freud circle in Vienna until forced into exile by the Nazi takeover of Austria. Of course, without a medical degree I could not have aspired to practice psychoanalysis, and according to the rules in force at that time I was not permitted to take control cases; indeed, I was admitted to the clinical seminars only as a special concession. However, I never had any intention of practicing.

In addition to deepening my understanding of psychoanalytic theory and the phenomena with which it dealt, this experience had the effect of contributing to my "weaning" from an overconcern with the psychoanalytic level of dealing with human problems and was hence a kind of corrective to the effect of the original reading of Freud and the early phases of my study of medical practice. Both an efflorescence of concern with more abstract and analytical problems of theory and empirical concern with less psychological areas—for example, economic and political again, and later educational—began to grow in relative strength.

I was not one of the many Harvard faculty members who was called to war service away from Cambridge. I did, however, do some teaching in the School for Overseas Administration, of which my friend Carl Fried-rich was director, which administered Area and Language programs and programs for Civil Affairs officers. I taught in the fields of European and East Asian societies. During the latter part of the war period I served as a consultant to the Enemy Branch of the Foreign Economic Administration, dealing with the postwar treatment of Germany. I wrote several mem-oranda in opposition to the so-called Morgenthau Plan.

In 1944, in response in part to a very good offer from outside Harvard, I was appointed chairman of the Department of Sociology, with something of an understanding that important reorganization would take place soon.

Allport, Kluckhohn, Murray and I had had important discussions on the possibility of reorganization. In 1945 there were two openings for permanent appointments in sociology. One of them went to George C. Homans, who had been in the department before leaving to serve in the Navy. The other went to Samuel A. Stouffer, who was just winding up his eminent service as director of research in the Information and Education Branch of the War Department. These events, late in 1945, made possible the faculty's action in establishing the Department of Social Relations, which opened in the fall of 1946. Stouffer became director of the Laboratory of Social Relations, an associated research organization, and I became chairman of the department, which included, besides sociology, social anthropology and social and clinical psychology. I continued as chairman for ten years until 1956. The role of Paul H. Buck, dean of the Faculty of Arts and Sciences and provost, was of outstanding importance in the establishment and development of the Department of Social Relations.

During this period I also became more active in professional affairs outside Harvard. I had served in 1942 as president of the Eastern Sociological Society, but as it was a war year the post did not entail much activity. I was elected president of the American Sociological Association for 1949 and this, of course, proved to be a much bigger job. The association was then undergoing a major organizational crisis occasioned mainly by growth in membership and activities. During my term a new office was set up, the first paid executive officer was appointed, and the association's constitution was substantially revised. After an interval of a few years I again became active in the affairs of the association, serving as chairman of the Committee on the Profession, then as secretary for five years, and finally for two years as the first editor of *The American Sociologist,* a house organ of the association dealing with matters of concern to the profession rather than "contributions to knowledge." In the 1950's I was also active in the American Association of University Professors, serving on the special committee on loyalty–security cases and for one term each on the Council and the Committee on Academic Freedom and Tenure.

Theoretical Development, 1937–1951

For my role as teacher, especially at the graduate level, the early years of the Department of Social Relations came to be a true golden age. Opening just a year after the end of the war, the department attracted, aided by the G.I. bill, an unusually able sample of the backlog of young people whose training had been interrupted by the war. Among those who had already been at Harvard were Bernard Barber, Albert Cohen, Marion Levy, Henry Riecken, and Francis Sutton, with Robert Bales staying

through the war. New arrivals included David Schneider, Harold Garfinkel, David Aberle, and Gardner Lindsey. A little later came James Olds, Morris Zelditch, Joseph Berger, Renée Fox, Clifford Geertz, François Bourricaud (from France on a Rockefeller Fellowship), Robert Bellah, Neil Smelser, Jackson Toby, Naspar Naegele, Theodore Mills, Joseph Elder, Ezra Vogel, William Mitchell (in the Department of Government), Odd Ramsoy (from Norway), and Bengt Rundblatt (from Sweden).

In the late 1950's and early 1960's came a third wave of especially important graduate students, including Winston White, Leon Mayhew, Jan Loubser, Edward Laumann, Charles Ackerman, Enno Schwanenberg, Victor Lidz, Andrew Effrat, Rainer Baum, Mark Gould, John Akula, and, in a special collaborative relationship after completion of his formal studies, Gerald Platt. Close association with advanced students of such caliber has been one of the most rewarding features of my academic career. Such young minds cannot fail, it seems to me, to have a most stimulating effect on their teachers. My own experience has strongly reinforced my belief in the importance of *combining* the teaching and the research functions in the same organizations and roles.

A few of these direct collaborative relationships—with such people as Robert Bales, James Olds, Neil Smelser, Winston White, Victor Lidz, and Gerald Platt—resulted in collaborative publications. Other important relationships have been with David Schneider, Clifford Geertz, Leon Mayhew, and (though not as a formal student) my daughter, the late Anne Parsons.

In spite of the shifts noted above, there seems to be a certain unity in the period of intellectual interests and theoretical development running from completion of *The Structure of Social Action* to the two major books published in 1951, *Toward a General Theory of Action,* a collaborative work coedited with Edward Shils,[29] and my own *The Social System.* The most important thread of continuity lies, I think, in what came to be called the "pattern-variable" scheme.

This scheme originated as an attempt to formulate a theoretical approach to the interpretation of the professions. Clearly nothing in the capitalism–socialism dichotomy would do, so I turned to a famous distinction crystallized for German sociology by Toennies and used by Weber: that between *Gemeinschaft* and *Gesellschaft* as types of social organization.[30] The problem of self-interest was the initial point of reference, in a sense which posed an alternative far short of the total public interest in the socialistic sense. The professional orientation was, as I initially put it, "disinterested" (later "collectivity-oriented"), in the sense in which the physician

---

[29] Talcott Parsons and Edward Shils, eds., *Toward a General Theory of Action* (Cambridge, Mass.: Harvard University Press, 1951).

[30] Ferdinand Toennies, *Community and Society* [*Gemeinschaft und Gesellschaft*], trans. and ed. Charles P. Loomis (New York: Harper & Row, 1963).

professes to be above all concerned with the welfare of the patient. This criterion put the professions in the *Gemeinschaft* category.

The scientific component of medicine, the universalistic character of the knowledge applied to problems of illness, fitted with an extensive complex of features of modern society which Toennies and his numerous followers would have to classify as *Gesellschaft*. The obvious inference was that the Toennies dichotomy should not be treated only as variation in terms of a single variable, but also as a resultant of a plurality of independent variables. If these were indeed independent, there should be not just two fundamental types of social relationship, but a substantially larger family of such types. My suggestion was that the professional type belonged in this family but neither as *Gemeinschaft* nor as *Gesellschaft*. Important as the problem of self-interest was, it seems to me now that even more so was that of how to bring the universalism especially characteristic of cognitive rationality, and the problem of the status of nonrational emotion or affect, into the *same* analytical scheme. Quite early a dichotomous variable which I called "affectivity—affective neutrality" was formulated and incorporated in the same system which also included "Universalism—particularism."

The pattern-variable scheme underwent over the years rather complex vicissitudes which need not be detailed here. The project that produced the volume, *Toward a General Theory of Action,* however, produced a first genuine synthesis. It was initiated as a kind of theoretical stocktaking of what underlay the social relations experiment, and for this project Edward Shils and the psychologist E. C. Tolman were brought to Harvard on a visiting basis. Shils and I developed a particularly close collaboration from which came our joint monograph, *Values, Motives and Systems of Action,* which is, in a sense, the theoretical core of *Toward a General Theory of Action.* In it we developed the pattern-variable scheme as a theoretical framework not only, as I had initially assumed, for the theoretical analysis of social systems, but also for analysis of action in general, and, especially within our purview at the time, of personalities and of cultural systems. As such it was no longer a catalogue of dichotomous distinctions, but became very definitely a "system," which however, contained seeds of much further complication than we were aware of at the time.

This generalization and systematization seemed to constitute a real theoretical breakthrough which emboldened me to attempt a general statement on my own responsibility of the nature of a social system, including most definitely the macrosocial levels. The outcome, my book *The Social System,* apart from its codification of received sociological wisdom, rested above all on two features which might be considered original. The first of these was the clarification of the relations between social systems, on the one hand, and psychological—or personality—and cultural systems, on the other. The second was the consciously systematic use of the pattern-

variable scheme as the main theoretical framework for the analysis of the social system.

Economics and Sociology Reconsidered

The two 1951 books were in some ways a culmination, but even more important they were a foundation for a major new phase. Shils's and my contribution was organized about the pattern-variable scheme, which our collaborative work generalized from the social system level to that of action generally. Robert Bales [31] and I meanwhile had had many discussions of the relations of this scheme to his scheme for the analysis of small-group interaction. These discussions became so important that we invited Shils to work with us for the summer of 1952, and the three of us produced the *Working Papers in the Theory of Action* (1953).[32]

The crucial outcome, in light of subsequent development, was the emergence of what we now call the "four-function paradigm." Its genesis lay in a convergence between the system comprising the four elementary pattern variables and a classification that Bales had set forth in his *Interaction Process Analysis*.[33] We concluded that systems of action generally could be exhaustively analyzed in terms of processes and structures referable to the solution—simultaneously or in sequence—of the four functional problems that we called "adaptation," "system (not unit) goal-attainment," "integration," and "pattern-maintenance and latent tension-management." Though there were many defects in our formulations at that time, this basic classification has remained with me for the more than fifteen years since it first emerged and has constituted a primary reference point of all my theoretical work.[34]

A consequence, closely related to Bales's work on small groups, was an extension of the analysis to the socialization process, harking back to my study of medical practice. This extension eventuated in the book *Family, Socialization, and Interaction Process*,[35] written in collaboration with Bales, James Olds, and others. Its main theme was that the nuclear family, emergent in modern industrial societies, could be treated as a small group and differentiated according to the four-function paradigm,

[31] Bales had been one of the few graduate students in residence during the lean war years. As a junior faculty member he began his notable program of the experimental study of small human groups.

[32] New York: Free Press, 1953.

[33] Cambridge, Mass.: Addison-Wesley, 1950.

[34] This scheme was explicated in Chapter III of *Working Papers in the Theory of Action*. Shorthand for it became the "A,G,I,L" scheme.

[35] Talcott Parsons, Robert Freed Bales, James Olds, Morris Zelditch, and Philip Slater, *Family, Socialization, and Interaction Process* (New York: Free Press, 1955).

on the axes of generation and sex, in ways closely analogous to the pattern of differentiation of many of the small experimental groups with which Bales and his associates had been working. This was also, perhaps, the point at which I began to be intensely interested in the phenomenon of differentiation in living systems more generally. This interest was linked to my previous biological concerns and stressed the importance of "binary fission."[36]

This line of theorizing, a continuation of the concern with problems of nonrationality discussed above, was soon overshadowed by another which led me back to the old problem of the relations of economic and sociological theory. For the academic year 1953–1954 I was invited to serve as visiting professor of social theory at the University of Cambridge. While there I was invited to give the Marshall Lectures, sponsored by the Cambridge Department of Economics in memory of Alfred Marshall. The subject assigned to me was, specifically, the relation between economic and sociological theory.

For some years I had not been intensively concerned with problems of the status of economic theory. And, on accepting the assignment, I was not sure I could go much beyond the level attained in *The Structure of Social Action*. But the theoretical development in the interim, notably the four-function paradigm, turned out to have laid a basis for a quite new phase of analysis.

In preparation I studied thoroughly, for the first time, Keynes's *General Theory of Employment, Interest, and Money* and carefully reread large parts of Marshall's *Principles of Ecnomics*.[37] It suddenly struck me that Marshall's extension of the basic classification of the factors of production and the shares of income from land, labor, and capital could, with the addition of Marshall's fourth factor, which he called "organization," to the three classical categories, be regarded as a classification respectively of inputs and outputs of the economy as a social system, analyzed in terms of the four-function paradigm.

This insight proved to be the starting point of a fundamental reconsideration of the problem, which was only partially carried out by the time of the delivery of the three lectures in November 1953. By unusual good luck, however, Neil Smelser, whom I had known as an undergraduate at Harvard, was then in the second year of his Rhodes scholarship at Oxford, studying economics. I sent him the manuscript of my lectures, and he responded with such detailed and pertinent comments that we arranged a series of discussions during the academic year in England. Then, the fol-

[36] This interest was, as noted above, strongly stimulated by participation in the continuing conference on theories of systems, organized by Drs. Roy Grinker and John Spiegel. I was particularly influenced, in that conference, by the contributions of the Chicago biologist Alfred Emerson. See Appendix to *Family, Socialization, and Interaction Process*.

[37] New York: Harcourt, Brace, & World, 1936 (Keynes); 8th ed., London: Macmillan & Co., Ltd., 1925 (Marshall).

lowing fall, we were both back at Harvard and completed the collaboration which produced the book *Economy and Society*.[38]

We did, I think, succeed in working out a new and more generalized analysis of the relations of economic and sociological theory. This analysis extended to the relation of the economy, conceived as a subsystem of a society, to the society as a whole. This theoretical restructuring, in addition, proved to be generalizable to a reconsideration of the other primary functional subsystems of societies. Hense it has opened up a whole new view of the structure and functioning of total social systems, of which a society is one particularly important type.

The key connection was that what economic theorists called the economy should be regarded as one of four primary functional subsystems of the society, with a primarily *adaptive* function—that is, as agent of the generation of generalized resources. Three of the factors of production and shares of income then should be regarded as, respectively, inputs from and outputs to each of the other three primary subsystems. The fourth pair—land and rent—should be treated as a special case, as it long had been in the theoretical tradition of economics. The key is the famous doctrine that the supply of land, unlike that of the other factors is not a function of its price. This property fitted the logical requirements of the pattern-maintenance function, which we had been treating as the stabilized reference base of an action system. In the process we considerably revised the traditional economic conception of land to include not only natural resources but also any economically significant resources that were unconditionally committed to the function of production in the economic sense, which included commitments at the value level to production. In our aspect, then, economic rationality became a category of value, not of psychological motivation.

Given that our assignments of sources of input and destinations of output among the other three subsystems were correct and that we were able to work out comparably correct classifications and categorizations for the inputs and outputs of the other three primary subsystems, it has eventually proved possible to work out a complete "interchange paradigm" for the social system as a whole.[39] This has taken several years and has required a long series of conferences between Smelser and myself as well as with others.

This line of thought both introduced a new complication and opened up a new set of opportunities. The primary reference model of interchange for us became the Keynesian focus on the interchange between households and firms: the former are placed in the pattern-maintenance system, which

[38] New York: Free Press, 1956.

[39] The interchange paradigm appears as an appendix to my article "On the Concept of Political Power," *Proceedings of the American Philosophical Society*, 107 (June 1963), reprinted in *Sociological Theory and Modern Society* (New York: Free Press, 1967).

made good sociological sense, the latter in the economy. Two, not four, categories, however, were involved: what economists have called "real" inputs and outputs and the monetary categories of wages and consumers' spending. This naturally raised questions on the status of money as a medium of exchange and on its other functions—for example, as measure and store of economic value.

Monetary theory has, of course, become increasingly central in the discipline of economics, but economists and others have tended to treat money as a unique phenomenon. If the idea of a generalized interchange paradigm for the social system as a whole made sense, however, it would seem to follow that money should be one member of a family of comparable generalized media; indeed there should be four of them for the social system.

It was not too difficult to work out some of the necessary aspects of the sociology of money for it to be treated in this way; but the other media presented greater difficulties. The first success came with the attempt to treat power in the political sense as such a medium, different from but comparable to money.[40] This entailed a far more substantial reordering of conceptualizations used by political theorists than those used by economists working in the monetary context. It necessitated introducing the conception of the "polity" as defined in abstract analytical terms parallel to that of the economy—hence not as government—and concerned with collective goal-attainment to the exclusion of integration as its primary societal function. Above all, the conception of power as a symbolic medium—which is parallel to the property of money as having value in exchange but not in use—was almost totally missing in political thought, where "intrinsic effectiveness" in the Hobbesian tradition has clearly been paramount as a reference point. Nevertheless, I think a coherent paradigm of power as such a medium has been worked out (see note 38). Once this step was taken, it was much easier to extend the analysis to include two other media: "influence" and "value-commitments," these terms being used in a specifically technical sense.[41]

Media of Interchange and Social Process

By this path the stimulus of the Marshall Lectures eventually opened up an approach to not only the structural, but also the processual analysis of social systems that promises to bring treatment of their noneconomic

[40] *Ibid.*

[41] This analysis is in two of my articles: "On the Concept of Influence," *Public Opinion Quarterly* (Spring 1963) and "On the Concept of Value-Commitments," *Sociological Inquiry*, 38 (Spring 1968), both reprinted in *Politics and Social Structure* (New York: Free Press, 1969).

aspects to a level of theoretical sophistication more nearly comparable to that attained for the economy and that includes the dynamics of inter-relation between these other subsystems and the economy. For example, the conceptions of inflation and deflation, as these have been used by eco-nomists, now seem to be generalizable to the other three societal media and their interrelations not only with money but also with one another. One example of the many difficulties in working this out may be cited. The monetary dynamics referred to is clearly incompatible with the idea that money is a "zero-sum" phenomenon. Credit expansion and contraction are, of course, central features of monetary inflation and deflation. Political theorists, however, have been predominantly of the opinion that power should be treated in zero-sum terms. Hence, to make money and power comparable in this vital respect, it has been necessary to investigate the basis of this contention and to show that it was untenable for my purposes.

The conception of action systems and their relation to subsystems, which had crystallized in the four-function and the interchange paradigms, strongly suggested the desirability and importance of extending the analysis. In one direction this has been pursued in considerable detail—namely, to the "general action" level, as we have called it. A first stage was central to the two 1951 books and may be regarded as a development from the two facets of the problem of rationality that emerged in my study of medical practice. This stage treated the social system as being flanked, as it were, by the psychological or personality system on the one hand, and the cultural system on the other, and interdependent with and inter-penetrating with both. The logic of the four-function paradigm gradually made it clear how the "behavioral organism"—not the total concrete organism—could and should be fitted in. This extension was facilitated by the revival and expansion of biological interests, particularly through con-tact with Alfred Emerson and by close association with James Olds, who had gone from social psychology into the field of brain research. The functional locations of the four subsystems of action are clear and stable. They are, namely, in the adaptive position, behavioral organism; in that of goal-attainment, personality; in the integrative position, the social sys-tem; and in that of pattern-maintenance, the cultural system.

This perspective has been prominent now for some years, and attempts at a first-order breakdown of the systems other than the social have been made (for example, the paper on psychological theory for the Koch sym-posium and, on the cultural system, the Introduction to Part 4 of *Theories of Society*).[42] Only recently, and so far only very tentatively, has it proved

---

[42] See the Introduction to Part IV of Talcott Parsons, Edward Shils, Kasper D. Naegele, and Jesse R. Pitts, eds., *Theories of Society* (New York: Free Press, 1961) and my essay, "An Approach to Psychological Theory in Terms of the Theory of Action," in Sigmund Koch, ed., *Psychology: A Science*, III (New York: McGraw-Hill, 1959).

possible to work out a general interchange paradigm for the general-action level.[43] An interesting convergent outcome has emerged. The categories of generalized media that have tentatively been settled on can be identified with those introduced as the "four wishes and the definition of the situation" by the social psychologist W. I. Thomas more than a generation ago. They are, respectively: the adaptive medium, parallel to money at the social system level; intelligence, which can include, in its positive form, Thomas' "wish for new experience" and, in its negative aspect, his "wish for security"; the goal-attainment medium, performance capacity, rewarded by Thomas' "recognition"; the integrative medium, affect— roughly in the psychoanalytic sense—rewarded by Thomas' "response"; and, finally, as the medium of pattern-maintenance process, the "definition of the situation," which, as in the other pattern-maintenance phenomena, should be and is treated by Thomas as a special case.[44]

"Structural Functional Theory?"

The concept of system, in the action field as in others, has been central to my thinking from a very early stage. With it is associated an extensive complex of empirical–theoretical problems that have entered prominently into the critical discussions of this type of theory. These concern such conceptions as equilibrium and its relations to conditions of stability and possibilities and processes of change; the status of the concept function itself; problems of "consensus vs. conflict" as characteristics of social systems; and the relation between what may be called "maintenance processes" in systems and processes of structural change, extending all the way to the conception of evolution or its opposite.

Perhaps, if I may repeat a little, my first introduction to the equilibrium problem was in the form of the Henderson-Pareto version, reinforced as it applied to the economy by Schumpeter. This form used the concept system in the sense of mechanics, with the physico-chemical system as the model. It emphasized the conditions of stability, though Henderson was careful to point out that Pareto's conception of equilibrium was by no means necessarily static. Quite early, however, I came to be influenced by the more physiological conception of equilibrium, especially as formulated by Cannon around the concept of homeostasis.

This physiological conception articulated more directly with the functional perspective then prevalent in the thinking of social anthropologists,

---

[43] See the Appendix to "Some Problems of General Theory in Sociology," in John C. McKinney and Edward Tiryakian, eds., *Theoretical Sociology: Perspectives and Developments* (New York: Appleton-Century-Crofts, 1970), reprinted herein as Chapter 10.

[44] W. I. Thomas, *The Unadjusted Girl* (Boston: Little, Brown, 1923).

especially A. R. Radcliffe-Brown and his followers. Malinowski, though also known as a functionalist, was off on a different theoretical tack.[45] Radcliffe-Brown was much influenced by Durkheim and came into my orbit by that route. For a considerable time, Merton and I came to be known as the leaders of a structural-functional school among American sociologists.

Developments since the emergence of the four-function paradigm and the analysis of generalized media, in particular, have made the designation "structural–functional" increasingly less appropriate. First, it gradually became clear that structure and function were not correlative concepts on the same level—as, for example, universalism and particularism are in the pattern-variable formulation. It became evident that function was a more general concept defining certain exigencies of a system maintaining an independent existence within an environment while the cognate of structure, as a general aspect of such a system, was process. Concern both with the maintenance of boundaries and other aspects of the functioning of an action system increasingly focused attention on problems of control. Money could thus be regarded as a mechanism through the circulation of which economic activities are controlled, in a manner analogous to that in which the circulation of hormones in the blood controls certain physiological processes. Such ideas articulated, in turn, with the strong emphasis in modern biological thinking that living systems are open systems, engaged in continuing interchange with their environments.

Clarification of the problem of control, however, was immensely promoted by the emergence, at a most strategic time for me, of a new development in general science—namely, cybernetics in its close relation to information theory. It could now be plausibly argued that the basic form of control in action systems was of the cybernetic type and not primarily, as had been generally argued, the analogy of the coercive–compulsive aspects of the processes in which political power is involved. Furthermore, it could be argued that functions in systems of action were not necessarily "born free and equal," but had, along with the structures and processes implementing functional needs of the system, differential hierarchical relations on the axis of control.

Here developments of the cybernetic aspects of biological theory, especially the "new genetics," proved to be extremely suggestive for action theory. Particularly important was Emerson's idea that the "system of cultural symbolic meaning" played a role analogous (in the proper biological sense of analogy) to that played by genes in biological heredity. There was a notable theoretical fit between this conception and the role that had been assigned, in the theory of action, to the pattern-maintenance

---

[45] See my article, "Malinowski and the Theory of Social Systems," in Raymond Firth, ed., *Man and Culture* (London: Routledge and Kegan Paul, 1957), reprinted herein as Chapter 3.

function and the structures and processes involved with it generally and to cultural systems particularly.

This perspective offered a way out of the endless circles of argument about the relative predominance of classes of factors in the determination of social processes and developments. For example: Was, in the last analysis, Marxian economic determinism more correct than cultural determinism? In general, such a question is meaningless, being of the same order as the old biological argument over heredity versus environment. The alternative, of course, is that action process involves combinations of factors that have different functions for the systems in which they are combined, and that one major aspect of these functions is control in the cybernetic sense.

The cybernetic perspective also helped to open new possibilities for dealing with the vexing problems of stability and change in action systems. In this connection, it was possible to articulate new perspectives with my previous interest in the socialization of personality and similar themes. Insistence on a radical theoretical distinction between the processes by which a system-pattern is maintained—including for societies the socialization of new members—and those by which its major structure is itself altered seemed to be vindicated, as broadly analogous to the basic biological distinction between physiological processes by which the state of the individual organism is maintained or changed, and evolutionary processes involving change in the genetic constitution of the species.

Social Change and Evolution

The latter problem context has emerged into a strongly revived interest in the theory of social and cultural evolution and its continuities with organic evolution. This interest was particularly stimulated in a 1963 seminar in problems of social evolution given jointly with S. N. Eisenstadt and and Robert Bellah. It has been followed up in various writings.[46] This line of interest, of course, constitutes a continuation of my concern with Weber's comparative and historical perspective, particularly in its relation to the interpretation of the nature and problems of modern society. It is also linked to more detailed problems in a series of studies of higher education on which I have recently been engaged.

A considerable part in the theoretical analysis of processes of structural change in social systems has recently been played by a paradigm

---

[46] "Evolutionary Universals in Society," *American Sociological Review*, 29 (June 4, 1964), reprinted in *Sociological Theory and Modern Society; "Christianity,"* in David Sills, ed., *International Encyclopedia of the Social Sciences* (New York: Macmillan and Free Press, 1968); *Societies: Evolutionary and Comparative Perspectives* (Englewood Cliffs, N.J.: Prentice-Hall, 1966); *The System of Modern Societies* (Englewood Cliffs, N.J.: Prentice-Hall, 1971).

that is another derivative of the general four-function paradigm. This has been labeled a paradigm of a stage in progressive structural change in a system of action, especially a social system.[47] The point of departure for this is the conception of differentiation, a process which seems on good grounds to come to focus on the binary case—that is, the division of a previous structural unit into two functionally and hence qualitatively different units. The paradigmatic case for the social system is the differentiation of the peasant type of household into a residential household and a productive agency from which income for support of the former can be derived.

For very long—for example, in the work of Herbert Spencer—differentiation has been understood to be complemented, on functional grounds, by new integrative structures or mechanisms. Partly for this reason, the newly differentiated system is also involved in new adaptive problems, very much in line with the general biological concept of adaption as crystallized in the Darwinian tradition, but with a new emphasis on active as distinguished from passive adaption. Finally, however, there are components of such a system that are relatively insulated from these overt processes of structural change. These components belong organically in the genetic category; action-wise, in that of pattern-maintenance. Hence a four-fold paradigm becomes appropriate at this level also. We have spoken of differentiation as focusing on the goal-attainment function, integration in the obvious place, but with a special emphasis on what we call "inclusion," upgrading of adaptive capacity as the focal adaptive category and "value-generalization" as the mode of change required to complete such a phase for the system, if it is to have the prospect of future viability.

This paradigm has played a prominent part in the spelling out of the interest in societal evolution mentioned above. The work on social evolution has been documented in a number of articles and in two small volumes written for the Prentice-Hall Foundations of Sociology series (Alex Inkeles, editor): *Societies Evolutionary and Comparative Perspectives* (1966) and *The System of Modern Societies* (1971).[48] The basis of this interest goes back to my dissertation on the nature of capitalism as a social system, which could now be more broadly redefined as an interest in the nature and main trends of modern society. This time, however, it has been approached in a broad evolutionary perspective, very much in the spirit of Max Weber, but with certain important differences from his views.

Comparative perspective has, of course, been very much in my mind, but at the same time I have been frankly concerned with the conditions and processes of modern Western development. With this in mind, and against the background of a survey of primitive and intermediate societies, I have been especially concerned with the way in which Christianity (in the con-

[47] See *Economy and Society*, Chapter 5.
[48] See note 46, above.

text of Judaism and the culture and society of classical antiquity) set the stage for modern development. In this connection, a double set of considerations seemed to be particularly important. One was the idea that in two special cases small-scale societies—namely, ancient Israel and Greece— were able to make special cultural contributions because they became differentiated from their environments *as total societies,* on a basis which, however, did not permit them to survive for long as independent entities. Their cultures could, though, be differentiated from their societal bases and exert a profound influence on subsequent civilizations. I have called these "seed-bed" societies. In a broad sense the contributions of Israel and Greece to the modern world—especially, though not exclusively, via Christianity—are well known, but perhaps the sociology of the process is not so familiar.

The second ruling conception was that of the Christian church as a partially separated subsystem of the whole society of late Mediterranean antiquity, politically unified under Rome, which, with its strategic cybernetic position could eventually have a decisive influence on the whole process of modern development. It can be seen that the seed-bed society and the differentiated religious collectivity could be understood to serve similar functions for the long future—functions that in certain senses are parallel to the functions of investment for the process of economic development. I have tried to put forward this view for Christianity in two articles on its general development and significance.[49] Of course this line of analysis is, in certain respects, an extension and revision of Weber's famous interpretation of the significance of the ethic of ascetic Protestantism.

In this connection I have conceived, as so many others have, of Israel and Greece as contributing principal foundation components of what may be called the "constitutive" culture of modern civilization. These components were synthesized and changed in essential respects in Christianity. Beyond this rather commonplace position I have been concerned with elucidating the social processes by which the connection has taken place over time and with linking these interpretations with emerging interpretations of the essential elements of the modern system.

The Nature of Modern Societies

Weber's view of capitalism, like Marx's clearly rested on capitalism's relation to the industrial revolution. This view was consonant, on the

---

[49] See "Christianity," in Sills, ed., *International Encyclopedia,* and "Christianity and Modern Industrial Society," in Edward Tiryakian, ed., *Sociological Theory, Values, and Sociocultural Change: Essays in Honor of Pitirim A. Sorokin* (New York: Free Press, 1963).

whole, with the assumption that this basic change in economic organization—in close relation to technology, of course—was the most essential feature of the new society. Marx and Weber were in agreement on this main point, though they differed profoundly in their accounts of the factors involved in its genesis and in their analysis of the internal dynamics of the industrial structure.

In their different ways, both were also passionately interested in the political developments that first came to a head in the French Revolution and had immense and complex repercussions thereafter. But Marx, in his focus on class struggle, and Weber, in his focus on the process of bureaucratization, tended to relegate the democratic revolution to a place secondary to the industrial. Increasingly, it has seemed to me that the two should be placed in positions of coordinate importance. From the broad point of view of my paradigm, no matter how highly interdependent they were, one should be interpreted as being of primarily economic and the other of political significance in the analytical senses. In this sense, they can be seen as independent in focus but resting on a common base.[50]

From my interest in the professions, I came gradually to the conclusion that what may be called the educational revolution is of an order of significance for modern society at least commensurate with that of the other two. The educational revolution, of course, began substantially later, toward the middle of the nineteenth century. But with the proliferation of mass higher education in the last generation, this revolution has reached a kind of culmination. As a result, the occupational structure has altered profoundly—having its primary focus in the professions themselves, as specially articulated in and with the system of higher education, rather than in "line" bureaucracy.

The conception of the three revolutions—industrial, democratic, and educational—fits with the paradigm of progressive change because all three involved major processes of differentiation relative to the previous state of modern society. Moreover, all were major agencies of upgrading through the immense increase of generalized and mobile resources. All three have also clearly posed major problems of integration for the societies in which they have appeared and have necessitated major shifts of what we call value-generalization.

In accord with the logic of the four-function paradigm, it has seemed to be meaningful to seek a more fully constitutive base in some sense back of these three major transformative processes, a sense which might well include the temporal dimension. In this context, I have increasingly come to consider the possibility that the principal beginning of the modern phase

---

[50] There are complexities of "crossover" involved. Thus bureaucracy in economic production is a harnessing of *analytically* political components in an economic interest, and the constituency aspect of political democracy is a comparable harnessing of integrative components in the interest of government.

of societal development lay *before* the emergence of the three revolutions—in a cultural and societal milieu that could be conceived to lay foundations common to all three. Once this possibility—as distinguished from the more common tendency to date modernity from either the industrial or the democratic revolution (or both)—was open, it seemed entirely clear that the primary locus lay in what I have called the northwest corner of the seventeenth-century European system: England, France, and Holland. In an important sense, of course, England and Holland were more closely related because both were predominantly Protestant powers with a strong economic emphasis, at that time mainly commercial. It should not be forgotten, however, that France narrowly escaped a Protestant victory and that Calvinism left a lasting influence there.

Not only was ascetic Protestantism especially strong in this whole area, but so was the aftermath of the Renaissance. The two coalesced, in a sense, in the great English and Dutch development of science in that century. The same century saw in England the first culmination in the development of common law and the establishment of the first important parliamentary regime. The France of Louis XIV, on the other hand, developed the most powerful centralized state yet seen, which served as the primary foil to the democratic revolution. The latter questioned, not the conception of the state as such—Rousseau emphasized this concept maximally—but the structure of authority by which it was controlled. Thus in terms of cultural base (especially religion and science), of legal order, and of political organization, these three countries established in the seventeenth century several of the major components of modernity. Nor should it be forgotten that these countries were at that time in the forefront of the institutionalization of the concept of nationality, which served as a basis for some of the conflict among them. The Dutch emancipation from Spanish rule was, of course, a major reference point.

There is an important sense in which all three revolutions presupposed this common base. The first was a kind of extension of economic differentiation and upgrading from the commercial level to the industrial—that is, the mobilization of the deeper-lying factors of production for economic upgrading. The second, intimately involved with nationalism, was a mobilization of deeper-lying factors of political effectiveness, notably the active support of the citizenry, who were no longer subjects of the monarch. The third constituted a mobilization of cultural resources in the societal interest, through the immensely complicated process of internalizing commitment to the major cultural patterns and the implementation of the attendant commitments.

In this connection, a major problem of interpretation of the trend of the modern system arose. The problem may perhaps be stated in terms of the contrast with a view which, with all their differences, may be said to be common to Marx and Weber. In a certain sense, they were agreed that

the core problems of the modern system lay in power relationships. Marx located the core of this relationship in the dichotomous structure of the industrial firm, with its owner-manager versus worker structure, and then generalized this to the all-society basis of class. Weber, more realistically in the light of developments, located it in the conception of a much more differentiated firm as a bureaucratic system *not* bifurcated on a power basis, but in a diffuse and general sense controlling the actions of its participants.

The principal point of reference for a different view in my case has been the work of Durkheim, notably his conception of organic solidarity. The simplest ways to formulate the difference seem to be, first, in terms of the contrast between a predominantly associational and a hierarchical bureaucratic pattern of social structure and, second, between a more monolithic and a more pluralistic type of structure. The relation of associational structure to the problem of concentration versus dispersion of power is relatively obvious and has, of course, been very much involved in the democratic revolution. In discussiong this context, the tendency has been to concentrate on the organization of government as such, and above all on central government. But in many modern societies, perhaps especially the United States, there has been a vast proliferation of voluntary associations of many different sorts. For my own purposes, a particularly important case of associationalism has been the professions, precisely because of their increasingly strategic significance to the occupational structure. They provide a central focus for the differences of opinion between capitalists and socialists and among the theorists who have concerned themselves with the impact of the industrial revolution. The professions clearly do not tend toward a bureaucratic type of organization, but so far as they are involved in collective decision-making, claim considerable autonomy relative to agencies not belonging to the profession in question and act mainly as associational groups. Since the professional role is typically that of a full-time job, I have—following, indeed, Weber's and other usage—been calling this pattern "collegial." Not the least important case is the academic profession, which has over several centuries preserved a predominantly collegial pattern of organization, even though it has had to articulate with more bureaucratic ones especially in the realm of academic administration.

The problem of pluralism is somewhat more subtle. Over a wide range, differentiation of a social structure does not lead to the allocation of the personnel of the previous structure exclusively to one or the other of the resulting ones. Thus when the older peasant type of household became differentiated, the adult males continued to be members of residential households, but *also* became members of employing organizations—that is, factories and offices. The same principle applies frequently to collectivities that are units in more extensive social systems; thus various disciplinary associations are, in their corporate capacity, members of such a

body as the American Council of Learned Societies. Indeed, departments as well as individuals are members of a university faculty.

Since I have attributed such importance to the process of differentiation in societal development generally, but especially in its modern phase, the phenomenon of pluralization with its distinctive features, conditions, and consequences becomes of substantive importance. In his concept of organic solidarity, Durkheim made a centrally important beginning in the conceptual analysis of this range of phenomena, a beginning on which I have increasingly been attempting to build.[51] It has become more and more evident that the phenomena in this range are of critical significance to modern society, not only in the economic sphere, but also in the articulation of occupation with kinship, ethnicity, relgous structures, and various aspects of the category of community. At the same time, for a combination of reasons of ideology and intellectual history, the focus of attention and the development of conceptual tools appropriate to this area have seriously lagged behind. The tendency to focus on the two great figures of Marx and Weber and to employ either a class analysis or a bureaucratic one is indicative of this intellectual situation.

In terms of my own intellectual experience, one particularly important point of reference could be exploited in this direction. Durkheim's approach to the analysis of the modern economy in *Division of Labor* emphasized its *institutional* regulation in the relatively informal senses, but on formal levels it stressed law more than governmental administration. The central focus was on the institution of contract and secondarily on that of property. In terms of later theory, this view directly linked the economy, as the adaptive subsystem of a society, with the integrative system that I have recently begun calling the "societal community." This linkage with Durkheim and its various subsequent ramifications lead to an emphasis on differentiatedness and pluralization of structure in direct contrast to the hierarchial emphasis on power relations that is common to both Marx and Weber.

In developmental terms, it became clear that, with the exception of the organization of the French state, the fundamental structural contributions of seventeenth-century society were of the associational-pluralistic character, notably ascetic Protestantism, common law, and parliamentarism as well as science and the rapid development of a market economy. In its capitalistic form, the industrial revolution certainly moved society farther in that direction, as did the democratic revolution. From this perspective it became clear, perhaps especially under the influence of Tocqueville, that the modern society emerging in North America was beginning

[51] See my essay, "Durkheim's Contribution to the Integration of Social Systems," in Kurt Wolff, ed., *Emile Durkheim, 1858–1917: A Collection of Essays with Translations and a Biography* (Columbus: Ohio State University Press, 1960), reprinted in *Sociological Theory and Modern Society*.

to play a role in the total modern system of the twentieth century somewhat parallel to that of the European northwest corner in the seventeenth. This society owed its primary distinctive features to an associational-pluralistic emphasis and not to the sharpness and rigidity of its class discriminations nor to its especially high level of bureaucratization. In addition to decentralized governmental democracy, examples would be its federalism and separation of powers, the religious constitution of separation of church and state, denominational pluralism, and the capacity to absorb, in the sense of integration by inclusion, large immigrant religious and ethnic groups, though this absorption is far from being complete.

Spelling out the ramifications of these structural trends—assuming that they indeed exist—is a complex empirical–theoretical task, but it has increasingly become my main concern in recent years. One scholar, even when he enjoys collaboration and can connect with the work done by many others, can at best work through such complex problems only in partial and fragmentary fashion.

A substantial part of the hierachy–power preoccupation of so much generalized social thought of the last century or so I attribute to ideological factors. Thus, classically, the socialist reaction to the capitalist conception of an economy governed by the rational pursuit of unit self-interest substituted rigidly centralized control by government in the public interest. In the dilemma stated by these alternatives, attention was diverted from the actual extent to which the new industrial economy was *neither* purely rationally individualistic in the sense of the utilitarian economists nor collectivistic in the socialistic sense. As Durkheim made clear, it was governed, in considerable part, by other factors. Among such factors is a normative structure, legitimized in terms of values grounded in cultural bases, notably at religious levels. In the other direction lies the affective grounding of solidarity, precisely in Durkheim's sense, in the motivational attachments of individuals to roles, to the collectivities in which they participate, and to their fellow members.

Solidarity and the Societal Community

Parallel to the rigid capitalistic–socialistic dichotomy between individual self-interest and public interest, there is a more recent dichotomy between alienation of the individual and various subcollectivities from collective solidarities, on the one hand, and expectations and demands for total absorption of the individual or relevant subcollectivity in some macroscopically conceived community, on the other. Here also a third alternative, not simply an intermediate state, is almost certainly more important

than the recent and current ideological assertions would have us believe. Such alternatives presumably fit in the broad associational–pluralistic range.

Adequate theoretical resources to define these alternatives, to diagnose and further analyze the existent phenomena where they appear as well as the features of many existent structures which block them, are probably in relative terms more inadequate than were the theoretical resources for analyzing pluralistic normative components in Durkheim's time. Above all, it is necessary to establish adequate theoretical links between the psychology of the individual, the functioning of social systems in many different respects, and the grounding of the normative factors in the cultural system. One problem is to avoid simple dichotomization of the *Gemeinschaft–Gesellschaft* type, which is so strikingly parallel to that of socialism–capitalism. There is a distressing tendency among today's intellectuals to posit return to a relatively primitive level of *Gemeinschaft* as the only remedy for what are so widely held to be the malaises and the moral evils of contemporary society.[52]

The approach to this complex problem area that has been most congenial to me has been a continuation of the analysis of the process of socialization of the individual, with special reference to the interrelations between the motivational dynamics involved and the structural setting of the process seen in terms of both the social and the cultural systems. Psychoanalytic psychology at the strict personality level has provided a solid theoretical base for getting a purchase on this problem area. For understandable reasons, however, it has tended to concentrate its attention on the earlier phases of the process—especially in its classical form, the Oedipal. Even here it has needed appreciable correction and modification in the light of sociological analysis of family and kinship systems.

Psychoanalytic theory, however, has with a few exceptions (for example, Erikson on adolescence) [53] notably neglected the progressive stages of the socialization process through the various stages of formal education. It has often been content with therapy and with the ambiguous dictum that character structure has been fully laid down by the end of the first— or more usually the sixth—year of life and that what comes after that can safely be relegated to pathology or its absence.

In earlier phases of my thinking there were some beginnings of successful analysis in this area (as in the early paper on "Age and Sex" as categories of social structure,[54] later in the *Family, Socialization, and Inter-*

[52] See Robert A. Nisbet, *The Sociological Tradition* (New York: Basic Books, 1966).

[53] Erik Erikson, "Youth: Fidelity and Diversity," *Dædalus* (Winter 1962), pp. 5–27.

[54] "Age and Sex in the Social Structure of the United States," *American Sociological Review*, 7 (October 1942), 604–616, reprinted in *Essays in Sociological Theory*.

action Process, and including perhaps the social paradigm of the conditions of psychotherapy advanced in *The Social System* and elsewhere). It has, however, not proved possible to achieve a level of analytical generality in this area comparable to that obtainable in the main areas of the political, economic, legal, and even religious structures of societies.

Important progress in this direction was made by returning after some years to a consideration of problems of kinship and the incest taboo, with special focus on the significance for the associational type of society of the taboo among siblings. This consideration led in turn to an interest in the significance of "symbolic" kinship patterns in Western institutional history, especially religious orders labeled as "brotherhoods and sisterhoods." Indeed, religious celibacy could readily be conceived to constitute a case of the "investment" pattern similar to the seed-bed societies and early Christianity.[55] My views in these areas have been immensely clarified by the work of my old student and friend David Schneider on American kinship.[56]

I had previously also been engaged in a study of the relations of secondary education to social mobility, in collaboration with Florence Kluckhohn and the late Samuel Stouffer. An extension of the thought of this study backward to the elementary-school level produced important clarification of some structural reference points.[57] My empirical interests had also, as noted, extended forward on this continuum to studies of the social structure and dynamics of higher education, especially in terms of its intimate involvement with the professions.

Substantial further theoretical progress has proved to be contingent on the development of another generalized analytical paradigm—the classification of generalized media of interchange and the spelling out of categories of interchange among the four primary functional subsystems at the level of the general system of action, involving cultural, social, psychological, and behaviorally organic systems. As outlined above, these categories converged with the scheme of W. I. Thomas.

It had long been evident that "affect"—in something like the psychoanalytic sense, which should be clearly distinguished from erotic pleasure—should be treated as a generalized medium operating at the general action level. The problem was where it should be placed; the prominence of its psychological associations made its anchorage in the personality system

[55] See "Kinship and the Associated Aspects of Social Structure," in Francis L. K. Hsu, ed., *Kinship and Culture* (Chicago: Aldine Press, 1971).

[56] David M. Schneider. *American Kinship: A Cultural Approach* (Englewood Cliffs, N.J.: Prentice-Hall, 1968).

[57] See my articles, "The School Class as a Social System: Some of Its Functions in American Society," *Harvard Educational Review*, 29 (1959), 297–318, reprinted in *Social Structure and Personality*, and, with Gerald M. Platt, "Higher Education, Changing Socialization, and Contemporary Student Dissent," in Matilda Riley, ed., *Aging in Society*, Volume Three: *A Sociology of Age Stratification* (New York: Russell Sage Foundation, 1972).

especially plausible. The breakthrough came in exploring the possibility and finally making the decision to place it primarily in the social system and, of course, the latter's interchanges with the other primary systems.[58] This decision treats affect as the direct parallel, at the general action level, of influence in the social system—namely, as the primarily intergrative medium. Furthermore, its status as a generalized medium makes it possible to outline a series of steps in its differentiation similar to the historic steps in the evolution of monetary exchange from barter to advanced credit systems—with the marketability of the fundamental factors of production (labor, in particular) developing at an especially crucial stage (essentially that of the industrial revolution).

The solidarity of a social system may then be thought of as a state of solvency of its "affective economy," conditioned both on the flow of instrumentally significant contributions from its members and on their motivational states of gratification, which can be thought of as the positive of which alienation is the negative. In simple social systems, these factors can be conceived to be ascribed; this is true both of primitive societies and of the socializing agencies in which, in a more differentiated society, the child is placed in the earlier stages of his socialization.

How highly differentiated his personality system must become in order to achieve high levels of gratification by full participation depends, of course, on the structure of the social and cultural milieu in which he acts. What we have called pluralization of the structure of the society is thus a major aspect of the much discussed complexity of modern life. Seen in this context, it can be suggested that the development of mass higher education, such a conspicuous and to some extent disturbing phenomenon of our time, may be regarded as a response to the societal need for personalities in sufficient numbers capable of coping with this complexity both in terms of many forms of instrumental competence and of personality integration at affective levels. The new modes of inclusion of individuals and subgroups in social solidarities constitute the primary focus of this set of problems of the stability and other aspects of integration of modern societies.

It is tempting to draw parallels with the states of disturbance that followed the high development of both the industrial and the democratic revolutions. In the former case, two can be distinguished: labor disturbance and that of the business cycle. Smelser has shown convincingly that a new kind of labor disturbance appeared among classes of workers who had not been injured, as had for example the hand-loom weavers, by the transition.

[58] Professor Renée Fox, in a commentary on the original draft of this essay, suggested that the decision to place "affect" primarily in the social system was effectively made much earlier, namely in formulating the pattern-variable, "affectivity vs. affective neutrality." The decision, new or old, has been hotly contested by two of my ablest young collaborators, Victor Lidz and Mark Gould.

These disturbances underlay the development of trade unionism and of the socialist movement, so far as they involved labor movement.[59] Depressions, on the other hand, raised questions of the stability of the new system at over-all systemic levels. It is also notable that attempts to deal with both categories of primarily economic disturbance were couched mainly in terms of self-interest—wages, hours, and conditions of work and the expectations of profit on the part of firms. At the same time there was a tendency, most evident in the socialist aspect and in Marxian theory, to combine these economic considerations with those of political power.

The equivalents for the democratic revolution may be said to be, on the one hand, the struggles over power and authority internal to particular political units (for example, the waves of revolution in Europe of 1789 and its aftermath, 1830, 1848, and indeed 1917–1918) and, on the other hand, the systemic waves of disturbance concerning disequilibrium in the relations among national units. The equivalent of depression here is surely war or, short of it, severely strained international relations, with a tendency for these disturbances to become increasingly generalized. Here the place of the individual self-interest of workers and entrepreneurs has clearly been taken by the collective self-interest of the Powers in their respective positions of power. At the same time, the focus on power has been modified by a highly significant integrative reference, the most prominent manifestation of which has been nationalism. Just as power struggles over economic interests have often become economically irrational, struggles over national prestige have often become politically irrational. Thus a *Realpolitiker* like Bismark could be more rational than a nationalistic political romanticist like Napoleon III.

I suggest that what I have called the educational revolution may be interpreted as the most salient manifestation of a new phase in the development of modern society where integrative problems rather than economic or, in the analytical sense, political problems are paramount. Student disturbances would then be paralled to labor and authority disturbances because students constitute the category of persons exposed to the most massive problem of adjustment to structurally changed conditions. The focus of their problem is, on the one hand, not realistically in power, but in the mode of their inclusion in the course of the educational process itself— a new phase of the socialization process—and in the more general societal world after completion of formal education.

From this point of view, the radicalism of the New Left is parallel to the socialism of the labor movements and to the Jacobinism of the radical democrats. The more systemic disturbance, then, is the propagation of

[59] See Neil Smelser, *Social Change in the Industrial Revolution* (Chicago: University of Chicago Press, 1959) and *Essays in Sociological Explanation* (Englewood Cliffs, N.J.: Prentice-Hall, 1968).

waves of alienation and related forms of malaise, especially among the
more sensitive components of modern populations, notably the intellectuals. This concerns the stability of fulfillment of expectations of improved
social solidarity in the first instance, and hence the evidences of lack of
such solidarity—such as poverty, racial discrimination, crime, and war—
are seen to be particularly distressing. Although it may be argued that the
recent manifestations center on the integrative problem, this series of disturbances resembles the earlier ones in that there is prominent invocation
of the next higher level of concern or control—in this case, that of values.
This is very evident in the special prominence, especially in the more radical circles, of moral concerns.[60]

Thus, over a period of more than thirty years, an empirical interest in
the problem of capitalism came to a special focus on the nature and significance of the professions. A continuing interest evolved in the broadest
categorization of the nature of modern society, but was no longer put in
terms either of capitalism, as such, or of the capitalist–socialist dilemma.
Indeed, I am sympathetic to talk of the post-industrial society, but wonder
whether it should not also be called in some sense the "post-democratic"
society, a suggestion to which there would probably be considerable resistance. (I would not suggest by this term that democracy no longer counted,
any more than that "post-industrial" implies that industry is obsolete.) By
the same token, special attention should be paid to the system of higher
education—and within it the academic profession as the structural core of
the system of higher education. For the medical and academic professions
I have attempted a close approximation to a standard empirical study,
more so than in other aspects of my work. But in both cases I have
wanted to understand the professional groups in question in the context
of the wider system of which they have come to constitute particularly
important parts.[61]

Higher Education as Focus

It is perhaps evident that these concerns with the main trends of development of modern society would naturally bring into sharp focus problems
of the nature and current status of the system of higher education in modern, especially American, society. In evolutionary terms, as the culmination
of the educational revolution, it had an especially salient place; special

---

[60] See Talcott Parsons and Gerald Platt, "The American Academic Profession: A
Pilot Study," multilith (Cambridge, Mass., 1968) and my "Some Problems of General
Theory in Sociology."

[61] Preliminary findings are reported in Parsons and Platt, "The American Academic Profession."

study devoted to it seemed to be far from trivial. Second, this field was particularly important in view of my long-standing interest in the modern professions, since it became increasingly clear that university-level formal training was one of the hallmarks of the professions. Training for the most prestigious of the so-called "applied" professions had developed graduate-level professional schools, which in turn became increasingly closely drawn into the universities.

The main guardian and developer of the great tradition of knowledge had become the central academic profession, mainly that institutionalized in faculties of arts and sciences. This profession of "learning itself" could be felt to be the "keystone of the professional arch" and it was to this group that I turned my primary attention. At the same time, the study of higher education offered an opportunity to continue and develop further my long-standing interest in the processes of socialization, carrying this into much later phases of the process than had occupied the primary attention of most psychoanalytically oriented students.

This interest crystallized before the Berkeley outbreak, in a project to study academic professionals in the United States, first on a pilot basis with samples from the faculties of 8 institutions and then, starting in 1967, a nation-wide sample from 116 institutions all offering four-year liberal arts programs, with or without graduate schools. This study has been generously supported by the National Science Foundation, and the main direction of research has been carried out by my collaborator Dr. Gerald Platt. As of this writing it is nearing completion.

A more autobiographical note may be added here. It is perhaps understandable that a social scientist like myself, who had become so much absorbed in matters of general theoretical concern, should be under a certain amount of tension in relation to the strong American emphasis on the importance of solid *empirical* research. Response to this pressure was surely one factor in my decision to study medical practice. This study was conceived mainly in the anthropological tradition of participant observation and interview.

With the end of the war and the entrance of Stouffer on the Harvard sociological scene survey research had achieved a position of salience in the social science world. Soon after that he and I decided to collaborate and, associating Florence Kluckhohn with us, undertook a study of social mobility among high school boys, which centered about a graduate seminar that the three of us jointly conducted. This project assembled a substantial body of data, mainly from questionnaires administered in a sample of public high schools in the metropolitan Boston area.

A crisis supervened with the premature death of Stouffer in 1960—in the same summer in which Clyde Kluckhohn died, even more prematurely. Florence Kluckhohn and I had plans to bring out a volume and indeed the body of statistical material for which Stouffer had been primarily respon-

sible had been carefully reworked with that in mind by the late Stuart Cleveland, but the vicissitudes of assembling the other desired contributions defeated the project.

There is, hence, a certain psychological continuity in my attempting a second round at involvement with survey research. Indeed, the use of this method had been decided upon before Platt joined the enterprise, and his training in these methods constituted one of his principal qualifications. I have considerable hope that this time it will come off, though my personal contribution will have been that of senior faculty sponsor, theoretical contributor, and critic, rather than operative survey researcher, which had been the job of Platt and the staff working with him. Especially since coming to know Stouffer well I have had a high intellectual respect for empirical social research, and very much hope that still closer alliances between these techniques and the kind of theory I have been concerned with can be worked out.

Another rather obvious continuity between the two ventures in survey research lies in the fact that they both dealt with phases of the sociology of education and both in some sense in relation to the socialization process. The mobility project was especially concerned with linking socialization, in a focus on formal education, with the occupational structure which has been so crucial to modern society since the industrial revolution. In a sense our study of higher education and the academic profession has led into a new sphere where the relations of education to the cultural tradition, coming to focus in the problem of the status of the intellectual disciplines, has taken a kind of precedence over the problems of the allocation of manpower with the occupational system, important as these are.

This is perhaps an appropriate place to take note of another context of significance for the development of my thinking, namely the American Academy of Arts and Sciences. I was elected a Fellow of the Academy in 1945 when, for a variety of reasons, including the war then just ending, it was not very active. I had attended a few "stated meetings" of the Academy, but I think a more active interest was first enlisted through *Daedalus*, my first independent contribution to which was participation in a symposium on youth in 1961. I also became a member of the Research Funds Committee of the Academy and of the Committee on the Social Science Monograph prize.

I became progressively more involved in such *Daedalus* enterprises as those dealing with the New Europe, with science and culture, and with the color problem [62]—and the Poverty Seminar that followed them, independent of *Daedalus*.[63] I also became for a time chairman of the Academy's

[62] *Daedalus* issues on "A New Europe?" (Winter 1964), "Science and Culture" (Winter 1965), "The Negro American" (Fall 1965 and Winter 1966), "Color and Race" (Spring 1967).

[63] Daniel P. Moynihan, ed., *On Understanding Poverty* (New York: Basic Books, 1969); James L. Sundquest, ed., *On Fighting Poverty* (New York: Basic Books, 1969).

Committee on Research Funds and a member of the Commission on the Future of the Academy. Finally, in 1967, I was elected president of the Academy, the first social scientist to serve in this capacity.

It was particularly congenial to me that interests of various groups within the Academy, especially through *Daedalus,* turned in the direction of the study of higher education. This has been evident in a number of ways: the Danforth Project on the governance of universities, the study of the ethical problems of experimentation with human subjects, the discussion of international problems of higher education in industrial societies, the recent studies of the status of the humanities, and the volume in which the present essay is published.[64] I have participated in the Academy's Assembly on University Goals and Governance, initiated in September 1969, as a central staff member, assigned to producing a set of generalized analyses of the nature of the current system of higher education, its place in modern society, and its possibilities of change. I have hence been in the interesting position of functioning in my Academy role mostly as a generalist student of higher education, but—in the role of research supervisor of the faculty study—I am also attempting to pin down some rather specific empirical generalizations about what academic people are really like and what makes them tick.

Participation in the work of the Academy has been particularly rewarding to me in a double sense. As an explicitly interdisciplinary organization, with active participation of members ranging across the whole spectrum of the intellectual disciplines and beyond, it has seemed to me one of the few best antidotes, organizationally speaking, to the alleged and in part actually existent trend to overspecialization in our culture, particularly its academic sector. Hence, for a scholar committed to the importance of highly generalized orientations, active participation in what has been going on in the Academy in the last decade or so has seemed to present an unusual personal opportunity for the kind of interdisciplinary action which is difficult in the local university setting. This has included exposure to stimuli which I would not otherwise have had to take account of—such as the presentations of the biologists in the volume—and an opportunity to act more positively in relation to the cognitive interests and sentiments of people involved in the immense range of different disciplines and intellectual interests represented in the Academy and various of its activities.[65]

From the more objective point of view of understanding the system of higher education and related phenomena, the Academy has increasingly come to represent a potential of generalization in the cultural field, in relation to the social organization of research, teaching, and application, which

---

[64] *Daedalus* issues on "The Embattled University" (Winter 1970), "Ethical Aspects of Experimentation with Human Subjects" (Spring 1969), and "Theory in Humanistic Studies" (Spring 1970).

[65] A broad survey of some of these interests and activities can be gleaned from the annually published *Records* of the Academy. My first two annual reports as president are in the 1968 and 1969 volumes.

is not totally unique but still probably preeminent. The very fact that such an organization can, for the time being at least, flourish in an age of allegedly rampant specialization seems to be some sort of index of the deeper concerns which are, often silently, guiding our main cultural development.

Cognitive Style and Summary of Themes

More than one commentator on the first draft of this essay has raised the question of the relation between a kind of "intellectual opportunism" and a pattern of consistency and continuity in the developments which I have outlined in the preceding pages. An attempted formulation seems more appropriate near the end of this account than near the beginning.

It is quite clear that neither in the occupational sense nor in the sense of intellectual context has mine been a meticulously planned career. The furor over the dismissal of Meiklejohn at Amherst was not foreseen when I went there, nor was the shift from biomedical to social science interests planned. Within a limited range the year at London was, but the German venture, including being assigned to Heidelberg, very definitely was not. Similarly, though going farther with economic theory was planned, involvement in sociology at Harvard clearly was not, nor was the life-long career anchorage at Harvard. Just as, when I went to Heidelberg, I had never heard of Weber, when I decided to come to Harvard I had never heard of Gay or Henderson. I was early predisposed to treat Pareto as rather indifferent and was conditioned to consider Durkheim unsound. I also had no special attraction to or knowledge of Freud until well into my thirties, and I had no special interest in the professions until nearly the same period.

There is a relation between the serendipitous element in these various career decisions at both the occupational status and the intellectual commitment level and another pattern that has continued down to the present. This is the pattern of responding to intellectual stimuli: challenges to organize association meetings and attend conferences, or, most important, to write articles on a wide variety of topics. Two early examples were a request to set up, at a meeting of the American Sociological Association (1941), a session on Age and Sex as coordinates of the role-structure of societies. It is out of this that the most widely reprinted paper I ever wrote, "Age and Sex in the Social Structure of the United States," came. The second was a request from the editor of the *American Anthropologist,* Ralph Linton, to attempt a synthesis of anthropological method in the analysis of kinship with sociological perspective on American society. The result was the paper "The Kinship System of the Contemporary United States" (1943), which also received rather wide attention.

It is perhaps largely in response to this kind of thing that two related

images of my role in American social science have emerged. One is that—largely, I presume, by contrast with "solid" empirical research contributors—I have been held to be primarily a talented and "stimulating" essayist, writing on a variety of topics but without any genuine continuity or solidity of any kind—one might suggest an "esoterically academic" kind of journalist. The second is the attribution to me of a kind of schizophrenic dual professional personality—on the one hand this kind of journalism, on the other hand a wholly unrealistic abstract kind of formalized theorizing, with the strong implication if not assertion that the two personalities had nothing substantive to do with each other.

Professor Renée Fox has especially stimulated me (in a detailed personal communication) to reconsider the problem of continuity of development, especially at theoretical levels. I hope that my conviction that there has in fact, for over forty years, been a basic continuity has come through in the course of the preceding exposition.

In attempting to understand the nature of the psychosocial process by which this continuity has developed, I have found one parallel to be particularly suggestive. In two recent academic years I collaborated with Professor Lon L. Fuller of the Harvard Law School in a seminar under the highly permissive title Law and Sociology. In the course of it I have learned a good deal about law, and not least about the common-law tradition. From the point of view of Continental European systematists of law—an especially prominent example being Hans Kelsen—the state of common law is clearly intellectually scandalous. It allegedly consists of nothing but an aggregate of particular cases and seems almost completely devoid of principles.

Fuller more than any other person,[66] has helped me to see that, far from the "case system" being inherently antithetical to "systematization," under the proper conditions it can be a positive vehicle of systematization. The essential point is that, since in common-law terms, with a few qualifications, courts must adjudicate *any* case put before them in a procedurally acceptable form, they have the problem, not only of rendering decisions, but also of justifying them. An appellate judicial system ensures that dubious justifications are likely to be challenged on appeal and by an intellectually critical profession, for example, in law review articles. Justification in this sense involves subsuming the particular decision, not only under specific precedents, but also under more general legal principles.

There are those in my immediate relational nexus, most notably my colleague George Homans,[67] who hold that the only legitimate use of the

---

[66] Lon L. Fuller, *The Anatomy of the Law* (New York: Praeger, 1968).

[67] George C. Homans, *Social Behavior: Its Elementary Forms* (New York: Harcourt, Brace & World, 1961); *The Nature of Social Science* (New York: Harcourt, Brace & World, a Harbinger Book, 1967); "Contemporary Theory in Sociology," in Robert E. L. Faris, ed., *Handbook for Modern Sociology* (Chicago: Rand McNally, 1964).

term "theory" is to designate a logical deductive system, with explicitly and formally stated axiomatic premises and, combined with appropriate minor premises, a set of deductions from them which fit empirically verifiable statements of fact. From Homans' point of view, all I have produced is a conceptual scheme which is not theory at all. A semantic issue is surely involved here but I, along with many others, have never confined the use of the term "theory" to this narrow type. I do regard it as a legitimate goal for a course of development of theory, but to say that anything short of it is not theory at all is another matter.

However that may be, two things may be said about the development outlined in this essay. First, what is at present available in my more abstract writings is not a mature system of theory in Homans' sense. Second, the process by which it, such as it is, has been arrived at has most emphatically not been one of having sat down and formulated the basic axiomatic principles and then deduced their logical implications and checked these against the known facts.

It has, on the contrary, been a process much more like that of many developments within the common law. The work of which *The Structure of Social Action* was the outcome certainly established a theoretical orientation—in my sense of theoretical—which was not a congeries of random opinions within the areas of relevance. From this conceptual scheme, if you will, as a reference base the process has been one of exploring a rather wide variety of highways and byways of empirical–theoretical problems, not, however, in wholly random succession. In this process, along with my serendipitous encounters with intellectually significant persons and influences, I have indeed reacted to quite a number of externally presented stimuli of the sort that I have characterized, especially requests to write on topics suggested by others.

In a sufficient proportion of such cases, I hope I have reacted somewhat in the manner of a competent common-law appellate judge: namely, that I have considered the submitted topics and problems in relation to a theoretical scheme, which—though its premises were not defined with complete precision and henceforth assumed as fully given in a logically complete sense—has had considerable clarity, consistency, and continuity. In a sufficient proportion of cases, it seems to me that this kind of procedure has yielded empirical insight and rounding out, extension, and revision and generalization of the theoretical scheme. At certain points this has meant intensive concern with formally defined theoretical problems, but at other points primary concern with much more empirical issues. In any case this is essentially what I have meant by the phrase "building social system theory" as used in the title of this essay.[68]

[68] Another important focus of this process lies in the teaching role. This is analagous to the common-law courts in that the teacher, especially at the advanced undergraduate and graduate level, is obligated, within rather wide limits of definition of

If the above considerations throw some light on the process by which some serious continuity has been maintained, I may now say a few words, in a summary fashion, about the themes which, in retrospect, seem to me to have been most important in the continuous theoretical development and the patterns of their succession.

Though a number of primary themes were involved in the theoretical patterning of *The Structure of Social Action,* notably that of the nature of the historic conceptions of economic self-interest and of economic rationality, one came to be particularly salient and has continued to be so with many variants ever since. This was what I have called the "problem of order," with reference to the human condition generally and the social system in particular. The classic early modern formulation lay in Hobbes's concept of the "state of nature" and the problem why human societies, with all their troubles, had not by and large become states of the "war of all against all." (Even with the many wars of history, the combatting units have been social systems, not isolated individuals.) [69]

My assumption throughout has been congruent with that of Hobbes in the sense that even such order as human societies have enjoyed should be treated as problematical, not assumed as obviously "in the nature of things"; in this regard perhaps I have inherited some element of Christian pessimism. Hobbes's personal solution, the "social contract" to set up an absolute sovereign who would coercively enforce order, was by the 1930's obviously unsatisfactory. But the problem remained. One of my most

---

his sphere of competence, to try to deal with questions raised by his students—in class, perhaps especially during seminar discussions; in term papers, honors papers, or other theses; and in personal conferences. Within limits the students, not the teacher, formulate the problems. If he deals with the students with competence and integrity, he must continually refer them to the generalized theoretical structure of the relevant bodies of knowledge. I have long thought that the enormous stimulus of these interchanges, both to good theoretical thinking and to incentive to be empirically informed and sound, constitutes one of the main reasons why too great a separation of the functions of research and teaching is unlikely to be healthy for the academic enterprise.

Certainly, in my own case, interaction with a succession of generations of intellectually able and curious students has constituted a major stimulus to the development of my theoretical thinking and acquisitions of empirical knowledge. The exceptional graduate students named earlier in this essay have played an especially important role in this respect—in a gratifying proportion of cases extending well beyond their student days.

[69] It may be of interest to note that I took a Kantian approach to the problem of order. Very broadly, with respect to the epistemology of empirical knowledge, Hume asked "*is* valid knowledge of the external world possible?" and came out with, by and large, a negative answer. Kant, on the other hand, posed the question in a more complex way. He first asserted that "we in fact *have* valid knowledge of the external world" then proceeded to ask "*how* is it possible?", that is, under what assumptions? Similarly some social theorists have wondered whether social order was possible at all, and often denied its possibility. I, on the other hand, have always assumed that social order in fact *existed*, however imperfectly, and proceeded to ask under what conditions this fact of its existence could be explained.

important reasons for linking Weber and Durkheim and, by teasing out essentially latent conceptions, Pareto, was the growing insight that they had in common the recognition of the intellectual seriousness of the problem and the conviction that, in one way or another, normative factors in human action, which were analytically independent both of economic interests in the usual sense and of interests in political power, were of decisive importance.[70] Durkheim's insight about the normative components in the structure and regulation of systems of contractual relations was a truly clinching contribution to my own conceptualization; Durkheim made specific reference to Hobbes in this connection. I very much stand by the view that order in this sense is genuinely problematical, and that the nature of its precariousness and the conditions on which such order as has existed and may exist is not adequately presented in any of the views of human society which are popularly current, regardless of political coloring. There is a fundamental distinction between an intellectually competent analysis and understanding of this kind of problem and a popularly appealing ideological definition of it. They are not always at sharp variance with each other, but very generally so.

The "problem of order" is quite clearly a central focus in problem-formulation—in the German formulation *Problematik*—of the relations among, and the balances of factors involved in, states of stability, of tendencies to disorganization and dissolution of systems, and trends of change.[71]

The connection between the theme of order and that of convergence must be evident from the above and from earlier discussions. Insight into the problem of the theoretical significance of accounting for order and its further potentials, as well as its failures, could be considered to be a theoretical achievement. My thesis that an otherwise diverse group of theorists had converged on a common "direction of solution" of this problem, which was not obvious to the academic common sense of the time, could, on the other hand, be held to constitute a "finding."

The nature of this convergence has been sketched here and is spelled out at great length in various of my writings. It concerned the component of normative control as distinguished above all from coercive enforcement in ways which linked both with homeostatic conceptions in psychology and cybernetic conceptions over a much wider range.

As noted by Clifford Geertz in discussion of this essay, the theme of

---

[70] That the same was true of Marshall, in the sense that he assumed it but did not let it obtrude too much into his technical economics, goes almost without saying. One may say that if there ever was a late Victorian, "evangelical" Englishman, Marshall was one.

[71] I have been widely accused by critics of being a last-ditch defender of order at any price, the ultimate price usually being interpreted to be fascism. Fortunately the more perceptive of the critics have seen order as a problem, not as an imperative.

convergence did not stop with the cases intensively examined in *The Structure of Social Action,* but has continued to be a major theme of my whole intellectual career. The conviction of some kind of convergence between socioeconomic and biological thinking played an early part. Perhaps above all my concern with Freud made salient both the problem of convergence between social system theory and personality theory, and, gradually, the extent to which this was actually present. Of course such convergence often had to be teased out from what at face value were incompatible positions. The analytical distinction between personality and organism has been indistinct in most psychological thinking—indeed many psychologists today would totally deny its relevance—but, especially because of association with James Olds in the early phases of his work on the brain and with Karl Pribram, it seemed to me to be a case of convergent patterns within a framework of analytical distinctness. Similar considerations have operated in the field of the relation between social and cultural systems, for which I was primed above all by Weber, but also by my many associations with cultural anthropologists. In a sense, perhaps the most extensive convergence of all has seemed to occur under the umbrella of the cybernetic conception, with its many associations and ramifications.

The "problem of rationality" has constituted another very major thematic complex. Phrasing it as "the problem" I hope makes clear that I have not been a naïve rationalist, either in the sense of holding that virtually all human action *is* essentially rational, or that the intrusion of non- or even irrational elements should be condemned. The position, rather, is that to attempt to analyze the role and nature of rational components in relation to those which should not be designated as such has constituted a major focus of theoretical concerns.

It seems clear that my initial focus on problems of economic and, secondarily, political rationality—for example, in the capitalism–socialism debate—was a legitimate but limited focus. To a considerable extent I have built the above account around the relation between this focus and the two others, which in a sense are located—in the spectrum of cognitive concerns with human action—on each side of this middle one. *The Structure of Social Action,* reinforced by Freud and related influences, opened up both. For example, Pareto's conception of "logical action," strictly bound by the canons of scientific validity, opened a door into the scientific basis of the professions, of the functions of higher education, and, more generally, of "cognitive rationality" as a value pattern—as well as opening another door into the elucidation of the "psychological" nonrational.

As I have tried to make clear, for a number of years I was rather more concerned with the other alternative to economical–political rationality, namely that which linked the social system with personality in a way that proved to have highly complex relations, on the one hand to the organic complex and on the other hand to the cultural. Thus in the former con-

text the problem of the significance of the erotic complex was salient, in the latter the problem of the role of internalized values was uppermost, starting with Freud's conception of the super-ego.

The "problem of rationality" in this context has two, or possibly three, facets. One is the question of the roles, in the determination of action, of rational and nonrational forces—for example, for Freud the ego and the "reality principle" and the id in relation to the "instinctual needs" governed by the "pleasure principle." It should be clear to the reader that my views in this area have been much less antirational than those of many other students of the problems, but I hope not naïvely rationalistic either.

The second, very vital, context concerns the accessibility of non- and sometimes irrational forces to rational understanding, that is, in cognitive terms. The intellectual movements into which I came were deeply involved in this situation. This included Freud most conspicuously, but very clearly all of my major authors, with the partial exception of Marshall. Perhaps Freud's most heroic endeavor was to set out a program for the "rational understanding of the unconscious," an entity which was, by his definition, in its very nature nonrational. This is indeed a far cry from either the rational understanding of the "rational pursuit of self-interest," or, indeed, the rational understanding of the pursuit of rationally cognitive knowledge.

The third facet, if there is one, is the link between these two. The classical aphorism is Freud's "where Id was, there shall Ego be." We might even go back to August Compte and his slogan, *savoir, c'est pouvoir*. In what senses and within what limits does rational understanding of the nonrational—which clearly includes the physical world—open the doors to control? In the most general sense of course the answer is that it does open such doors. But this remains one of the most seriously controversial areas of the rationality complex, various aspects of which have been very central to me.

The rational component of psychotherapy shares with economic and political rationality its instrumental character. But two problems beyond this arise. The more obvious one concerns the sources of legitimacy and justification of the ends or goals in the interest of which such instrumental rationality is brought to bear. The utilitarians, and still for the most part, economists, treated consumption "wants" as given, that is, as not constituting the locus of intellectual problems for their purposes. Similarly for Freud and psychiatry mental health was an aspect of general health, and its attainment or restoration almost by definition desirable. But in both contexts, and a variety of others, it is reasonable to raise the question, paraphrasing a famous book title: "Rationality for what?" (Robert Lynd, *Knowledge for What?*)

A seductively simple solution is to say that the goals of instrumentally rational action are *basically* nonrational. But as so often, this is too simple. Weber made a major contribution to further sophistication here with his

concept of "value rationality" (*Wertrationalität*), which he conceived as constituting one of the primary types of action. The essential implication, which cannot be grounded here,[72] is that the "universe of values" is not devoid of rational organization and that decisions of "commitment to" values, including their more or less direct implementation, have a rational component which is independent of instrumentality.

It has turned out that the relevance of this position, which was only most explicit in Weber, has operated in two directions, not one, in a sense somewhat analogous to the "fork in the path" encountered when following out the theoretical problems implicit in the conception of economic rationality. The more obvious of these concerns religion. In a variety of ways, problems of religion have been prominent for me almost from the beginning. It was Weber's Protestant Ethic essay which set off a major development for me, and the *common* concern of Weber, Pareto, Durkheim, and later Freud with the intellectual problems posed by religion as a human phenomenon became a major reference point in the earlier phases of my career. In the circumstances this had to involve the problem of the relation between rational and nonrational components of religion.[73]

This concern with religion—in the role not of a *dis*- but more of an *un*believer, in the terminology of a recent Vatican conference—has been a major orientation point in my intellectual career. It was already a major aspect of my early rejection of "positivism," but at the same time has been a focus of a continuing attempt to understand the balance of the roles of rational and nonrational components in human action. Clearly, however, such a focus of intellectual concern leads one beyond the more purely cognitive problems of religion into those of moral commitment, affective engagement, and practical action.

The other ramification of the concept of "value-rationality" is in some ways more surprising. This concerns the status of the value-component in defining the relation of cognitive structures not to the clearly nonrational characteristics of the phenomena "cognized," such as the Unconscious or the "grounds of meaning" at the religious level, but to cognitive structures themselves. This has come to a head in recent years on the conception of "cognitive rationality" precisely as a *value*-pattern, not simply as a maxim of expedient "want satisfaction." The generalization of this conception was foreshadowed in the interpretation which Smelser and I put forward of the economic category of land as including a *value*-commitment to economic rationality.

The relevance of this perspective to many recent concerns, both of my

---

[72] See my article, "The Sociology of Knowledge and the History of Ideas," in Philip Wiener, ed., *Dictionary of the History of Ideas* (New York: Scribner's, 1974).

[73] Fairly early in my Harvard teaching career I introduced a course in the Sociology of Religion which continued for at least two decades, in the later years in collaboration with Robert Bellah.

own as a theorist and of society, is almost patent. It is clearly very central to the complex of higher education and its relation to the intellectual disciplines. Since the role of empirical cognitive knowledge was so central to the original formulation of the rationality problem, this concern with the value aspect of empirical cognition, both in the grounds of the cognitive validity of the knowledge mobilized in the instrumental aspects of rational action and in the cognitive problems of the justification of commitment of instrumental potentialities among goals, in a sense bring consideration of the problem of rationality full circle in that the considerations involved in the grounding of value-choices, including their more or less religious bases, are seen to be of the same order as those involved in the grounding of the validity of empirical knowledge.[74]

Perhaps I may conclude with a few words about my conception of the significance to me of the most important intellectual role models: clearly, Weber, Durkheim, and Freud, none of whom, it is important to note, I ever knew personally, though they all lived into the period of my attainment of some kind of personal awareness or perhaps of "identity," to use Erikson's term. In terms of substantive influence in the shaping of problems and of the many elements of empirical and conceptual structure which has been central to my thinking, it is quite clear that all three have been crucial. Others have of course been exceedingly important, first perhaps Pareto and Marshall, in that order, but again Schumpeter, Henderson, Cannon, Taussig, Piaget, and many others.

One factor in this attribution of significance is of course, the intellectual location of relevance. Equally or more towering figures in more remote fields have naturally not had the same significance in my development, even though they may have been very important on the periphery. This would have been true of Cannon, of the biological background figures like Darwin, of Whitehead, of Piaget, of Norbert Wiener, and various others. The other factor is, from such a locational perspective, the stature of these figures relative to those of directly comparable relevance.[75]

---

[74] If, without being accused of being a "racist," I may venture to quote an old Negro spiritual, I think the phrase "there's no hiding place down there" sums up the situation admirably. By "down there" in the present context I mean the positivistic view of the total cultural self-sufficiency of science, which has been alleged to have no "deeper" connections with any components or problems of human orientation outside itself.

[75] I am reminded here of a geographical case which I have personally experienced a number of times. Seen from the valley of Chamonix, the Mont Blanc massif is clearly the most important mountain mass in that region of the Alps. If, however, one moves from Chamonix and its neighborhood, not only to Geneva, but beyond to the slopes of the Jura, the preeminence of the massif becomes overwhelmingly salient —providing weather permits visual perception. It is in an analogous sense that I think my three major figures constitute the highest "peaks" of the "range" of intellectual achievement in the field most relevant to me and in the time. This is by no means to deny the importance of the rest of the range.

The sense in which the ideas of Weber, Durkheim, and Freud have permeated my own thinking should be clear from the above account. There remains the question of the senses in which they have been role models mainly in terms of what I have called "cognitive style." Here there emerges an important distinction between Weber and the other two. Substantively, Weber has been at least as important to me as any of the three. Stylewise, however, he was very different from the other two. He was much more, in Erikson's format, a Luther type, who, with all his immense preparation, underwent a single major transformative crisis—in Weber's case involving serious mental illness—from which he emerged as a new Weber, who, with truly dazzling "virtuosity" (a term he was fond of) produced within two or three years the great methodological essays (*Wissenschaftslehre*) and the Protestant Ethic as the opening step in a major reinterpretation of the nature of modern society seen in the broadest comparative–evolutionary perspective. It seems to me significant that, in many of his subsequent writings, Weber particularly stressed the centrality of the "charismatic breakthrough" as the most important process of religious, and more generally of sociocultural, innovation and change. In suggesting that this is not the only way—connecting with the idea of the role of genius—I do not in the least mean to derogate the importance of what I regard as Weber's superlative intellectual achievement.

The cognitive style of Durkheim and Freud was quite different. I do not for a moment think that either was less intellectually ambitious than was Weber. Their method, however, was to settle on and thereby become committed to attempting a radical solution of certain definable problems in their respective spheres. For Durkheim it was a special version of the "problem of order" in the sense in which this has been outlined above. For Freud, it was the problem of rational understanding of the nonrational, with special references to the role of what he came to conceive as the "unconscious."

Clearly, in both cases, the process by which these intellectual commitments were entered into was motivationally highly complex—for example, in Freud's case his liberation by the death of his father. But in neither case was the maturing of his commitment a highly dramatic event, though for each it resulted in a truly seminal book, namely, Durkheim's *Division of Labor* and Freud's *Interpretation of Dreams*.

It is not quite fair, but still broadly accurate, to say that, from his great breakthrough on, Weber's contribution consisted far more in a truly monumental spelling out and empirical validation of the basic insights of the critical reorientation. In the other two cases, it was a process of step-by-step development of theoretical thinking from the original problem-formulation base. In this sense there is a Weberian theory which dates from his new orientation following his recovery from his psychological disturb-

ance—that is, about 1904–1905. In a comparable sense there is no Durk-heimian or Freudian theory, but there is the documentation of an impressive process of theoretical development.

I see no reason to suggest that either of these alternative cognitive styles on the part of intellectual innovators is in any general sense superior to the other; both are critically important, but each is effective in different times and situations. Speaking personally, however, Durkheim and Freud have been my paramount role models as theoretical analysts of human action. Perhaps this has some bearing on the question of the balance between continuity and opportunism in my own intellectual history.

2. Review of L. T. Hobhouse, *Sociology and Philosophy: A Centenary Collection of Essays and Articles**

THE PUBLICATION OF THIS COLLECTION forms a very appropriate recognition of the centenary of Hobhouse's birth. It serves not only to remind us of the important contributions he made to sociology and philosophy in his long series of books, but brings together a number of his articles which have not been widely read because of their original channels of publication. Most of the articles the present reviewer had not read before.

Perhaps as Professor Ginsberg says in his Introduction, the time has not yet come for a full appraisal of Hobhouse's contributions in either of the two fields indicated in the volume's title. However, the time that has lapsed and the intellectual developments that have emerged since the completion of his work, certainly make it possible to approach such a judgment much more closely than before.

I hope that it is permissible for me to approach this material in a somewhat more personal vein than is customary in review articles. The circumstances are somewhat unusual in that the very beginning of my career in sociology—apart from very fragmentary introductions as an American undergraduate—consisted in a year of study (1924–1925) at the London School of Economics when Hobhouse and, of course, Ginsberg were the dominant influences in sociology. Following that year, I went to Heidelberg, Germany, where I came strongly under the influence of the recently deceased Max Weber. Back in the United States, I undertook a thorough study of the theoretical work of Emile Durkheim, and came to an interpretation and evaluation very different from that taught me at LSE by

From *Sociological Inquiry,* Toronto, Canada, Vol. 43, No. 1 (Spring 1973), pp. 85–87. Reprinted by permission.

* Edited by Morris Ginsberg. London, G. Bell and Sons, Ltd., 1966. *Ed.'s Note*: This review was not published at the time it was written in 1966. Being in the realm of "eternal ideas," we feel it useful to make available to our readers even at this date.

Ginsberg (and Malinowski). The problem I wish to set forth in this review, then, is the justification, if any, of turning away from Hobhouse as the primary model and source of ideas for my own work in sociological theory and of turning to the two Continental theorists—one of whom was, so far as I remember, never mentioned during my London year, and the other of whom was treated with a good deal of disparagement, in the words of Professor Ginsberg's Introduction to the present volume, as the proponent of "a mystical view of society as a new entity qualitatively distinct from the members composing it, which always operating in a powerful and distinctive manner, but whose mode of operation remains wrapped in total obscurity" (p. xiv). Although the main works of Weber and Durkheim were available at the time, the intellectual climate of LSE clearly did not favor their creating a strong impression on a young research student.

Hobhouse's work certainly contained many elements which were highly congenial and, as the reading of the present volume makes clear, have remained so. A major one for me is the dominant concern with the problems of social evolution. Here Hobhouse was clearly the most important thinker in the English language world after Herbert Spencer, and his trend of thought has been handsomely vindicated after the period of "cultural relativism" we have been through—he shares this honor, however, with the broadly contemporary, and to me much more incisive, Weber, and Durkheim was by no means so oblivious to these problems as Professor Ginsberg suggests (cf. p. xv and, for a different interpretation, Robert N. Bellah, "Durkheim and History" *A.S.R.* 1959).

Certainly he was one of the very few most important pioneers in the comparative study of social institutions, a field of course most intimately connected with that of evolution. The Hobhouse, Wheeler and Ginsberg monograph remains a classic, and *Morals in Evolution* a landmark. Of course, also his strong concern for problems of social justice in modern society, and the broad direction his thinking in these areas took, is very sound.

The primary difficulty for me lies at the level of analytical theory and can perhaps best be stated in terms of intellectual history. As I should put it, Hobhouse was essentially a social utilitarian and as such the most eminent successor of John Stuart Mill. He benefitted from a whole series of developments since Mill wrote. Notable of course was the major development of biological science, but to a considerable extent also of psychology, though Hobhouse was notably unresonant to the most important movement in psychology in his time which was close to sociology, namely psychoanalysis. He can hardly have been said to have been much influenced by the more technical developments in economic theory since Mill, notably the concept of an economic system as formulated by Marshall and several Continental writers. Thus, though he shared Mill's and Hobhouse's British type of "empiricism," Marshall, in such matters as his treatment of the

relations of "wants and activities," gave a much sharper formulation to the problems of the scope of economics than Hobhouse did, who spoke of it as dealing with the "industrial and commercial organization of society as a thing apart . . .," i.e., a rather concretely conceived entity.

Hobhouse pushed the theme of the *social* aspect of utilitarianism above all through his conception of mind as a "harmonizing" agency. Underlying it is the utilitarian assumption that somehow "wants" are unproblematical, combining as they do biologically given "needs" and a learned component which tends to be treated as an individually variant matter of "taste." It is very revealing that the component of social systems which many of us have treated as a common set of norms and values is formulated by Hobhouse as a category of "purpose" which is his central category of mind.

What seems to be missing is the analytically independent category of *cultural system.* The more immediate source of this lies in the contributions of Idealistic thought. Hobhouse, in his critique of idealism, seems in a sense to have thrown out the baby with the bath water and eliminated all of this element except the lowest order component, namely collective goal-attainment. Weber, on the other hand, who was perhaps just as severe a critic of idealism in social theory, was able to lay the foundations of a very extensive analysis of the cultural components of concrete social action systems which involved basic religious orientations, systems of economic and social ethics, systems of law and others, all of course interdependent with each other and with noncultural components. Cultural systems thus understood are not simply the modes of "harmonization" of the motives and interests of individuals. They are not aspects of "mind" if by that is meant the personality of the individual, though Hobhouse in his concept of mind did not make the basic distinction between personality and the cultural "content" of knowledge, norms and beliefs as they function in the individual. Correspondingly Hobhouse gives no clear conception of what we call the institutionalization of cultural elements in social systems, nor of their internalization in personalities.

Similar difficulties appear at the social level. Curiously, in the light of current usage, Hobhouse defines a "society" as *any* concrete set of socially related, equally concrete individual persons. He does not closely approach the conception of a social system as an *analytically* defined subsystem of action in which the components deriving from interaction as such are abstracted analytically. To him the unit of a society in his sense is the concrete individual; the basic concept of role is not developed theoretically, though it is in some sense implicit.

Durkheim is, in my opinion, the most important single theoretical father of the concept of social system. He was not discussing a "mystical entity," the operation of which remains totally mysterious, but was formulating, in the course of many difficulties, a usable analytical scheme. In-

deed, only when such a scheme, involving both cultural and psychological as well as social systems, has been worked out can an acceptable social psychology be established.

These problems seem to me to relate in turn to two other very central ones. One of them is the conception of sociology as the synthesis of all our knowledge of human behavior in so far as it is in any sense "social." The most obvious difficulty of this conception lies in defining the position of economics. In spite of Professor Ginsberg's quotation from Durkheim as agreeing with Hobhouse (Introduction, p. viii), I think Durkheim's tendency was very much more in the direction of an analytical definition, dealing above all with the focal problems of the basis of solidarity including the ways in which solidarity is impaired and broken as well as promoted. Though of course economic "factors" are always concretely involved, this is not a focus which analytically includes economics. It has certain affiliations with Hobhouse's harmony, but is far more specific theoretically.

The second problem concerns Hobhouse's view that social philosophy should be conceived as a branch of sociology. This of course runs counter to the main tradition that sociology should be an empirical science and thereby differentiated from all branches of philosophy. The treatment of culturally grounded values and norms as components of social systems, which have a fundamental bearing on their states of solidarity, is a very different view from Hobhouse's that the normative grounding of judgments of value should be a part of the task of sociology. This conception that there is in the last analysis no basic difference between empirical science and philosophy is one of the "positivistic" implications of a utilitarian position which is to me one of the best evidences that Hobhouse was, indeed, basically a utilitarian.

Allowing, then, for the fact that in a brief review only the barest bones of a justification for it can be given, I would sum up my own judgment somewhat as follows. Hobhouse was, I think it fair to say, the most advanced and sophisticated of the utilitarians. He carried the possibilities of contribution to sociology, in general terms and in many specific fields, about as far as can be done within that framework. Further major advance required a major theoretical break with the utilitarian frame of reference, along lines which I tried to formulate in my *Structure of Social Action* some thirty years ago, and, along with many others, have tried to develop farther since then.

This path of theoretical innovation above all has meant willingness to work with much more abstract theoretical schemes than had been common in social science, using, with suitable modifications, the model of economic theory as the closest available. It meant defining social systems analytically as one category of system in the human action field which was differentiated from, but also interdependent and interpenetrating with, independently conceived cultural systems and psychological systems of per-

sonality. It meant, further, building, on the foundation of this greatly elaborated frame of reference, a much more elaborate body of theoretical analyses and interpretations than any utilitarian theorist had attempted.

To me, this is to say, exposure first to the work of Hobhouse, then to that of Weber and Durkheim, presented a fundamental choice to a person ambitious to make a contribution to theory in sociology. It is my firm conviction after so many years that choosing the latter path in preference to following Hobhouse was a sound choice. Great as Hobhouse's contributions were, following his lead could not be nearly so fruitful as has been, for many of us, building more fully on the work of his two great Continental contemporaries.

3. Malinowski and the Theory of Social Systems

THE PHASE of Malinowski's work to be discussed in this paper is his relation to the development of the theory of social systems, a principal common interest of sociology and social anthropology. It seems to me that the most adequate way to approach the problem is to recognize that there are two relatively distinct levels on which such theorizing may be attempted. The first is the level closest to the ethnographic facts, the immediate conceptual framework in terms of which observed activities are described and interpreted. The second is the level of general theory where such facts serve illustrative and demonstrative purposes, since the main concern of the theorist is to discern general lines and patterns of order in his subject matter.

The first level of theorizing is so close to the treatment of concrete anthropological subject matters that in Malinowski's case it has been rather fully discussed in the other contributions to this volume. It is directly involved in his concrete discussions of kinship, of gardening, of chieftainship, of magic, of funeral ceremonies and a variety of other topics. I therefore take it that my task is to discuss Malinowski's theory in the second sense.

I would, however, like to say a few words about the former since it is so typical of the man and so important to his place in the history of social science. Indeed, at one remove as it were, it can be said of Malinowski as he himself said [1] of Frazer that his anthropological work as a whole is of far higher quality than his explicit general theory. Indeed the latter is, in my opinion, far from being the strongest part of his work. His "clinical" theory is in general of a higher order of excellence.

From *Man and Culture,* edited by Raymond Firth (London: Routledge & Kegan Paul Ltd.; Humanities Press, Inc., New Jersey. Reprinted by permission.

[1] Bronislaw Malinowski, *A Scientific Theory of Culture (and Other Essays),* with a Preface by Huntington Cairns (Chapel Hill, N.C.: University of North Carolina Press, 1944).

82

Perhaps the most distinguishing characteristic of Malinowski's "clinical" theory is his intense interest in human motivation, and the very high level of insight which he displayed in describing and interpreting it. He was at his best in his analytical descriptions (if I may use such an expression) of his Trobrianders in their regular lives, at work in their gardens or on their canoes, participating in a funeral ceremony, on the occasion when the chief's son was forced to leave the village, and in many other similar cases. And he was at his best as a theorist when he tried to give humanly understandable meaning to behavior which the reader would otherwise find bizarre and unfathomable.

Indeed, if anything like a general agreement about Malinowski's place in the history of social anthropology were to be sought among the professionals of that field, it would probably center more than anything in the high quality of his field observation and his contribution to the development of field techniques and the training of a whole generation of students as field workers. It should, however, be clear that anything like this level of field work could not be attained without at least implicit theory, and on this level Malinowski was undoubtedly a theorist of considerable stature.

What were the main lines of his theoretical thinking on this level? They were, I think, characterized by a strong effort to remain close to the relatively direct interpretation of the motives of the individual, to carry a psychological emphasis in this sense. But at the same time it was a "psychologism" strongly tempered by keen awareness of the social and cultural context in which the individual lived. How far this empirical tempering of a psychological tendency was worked out on the level of more general and formal theory will have to be discussed later.

The main lines of Malinowski's interpretation of motivation were, I think, laid down in the duality of the conceptual scheme he formulated in *Magic, Science and Religion.*[2] The gist of his position may be said to have been that, in interpreting the "mind of primitive man" it was not legitimate to accept either the rationalism of Tylor and Spencer, or the irrationalism of Lévy-Bruhl. Within certain spheres the "savage," as Malinowski liked to call him, was as matter-of-fact and rational as any modern European, he possessed considerable empirical knowledge of the world he lived in and applied it in an entirely rational way to meet his needs. But at the same time his serious belief in the efficacy of ritual, in the necessity of performing magical rites in certain contexts, and in the rightness of religious rituals, including the myths behind them, was a cardinal

[2] "Magic, Science and Religion," in *Science, Religion and Reality*, J. A. Needham (ed.) (London: 1925), pp. 20–84. Reprinted in 1948. It is perhaps pertinent to note that my first acquaintance with Malinowski's work was a course of lectures (London School of Economics, Michaelmas term, 1924) based on the manuscript of this justly famous essay (then as yet unpublished) given under the title, "The Psychology of Primitive Peoples."

tenet for Malinowski. One had to accept the reality and importance of *both* aspects of primitive behavior.

There is a sense then in which Malinowski's central problem was to make both types of behavior humanly understandable to the modern European through a theory of function of some sort. Above all an adequate theory had to account for the fact that both types of behavior characterized the same people under different circumstances. It would not do, to characterize "primitive man" as in essence the one *or* the other. This seems to be one primary focus for the genesis of the concept of functionalism as Malinowski used it.

A second focus derives from his objections to "trait" theory as this had been used by other schools of anthropology, and among his own contemporaries, particularly by the "diffusionists." There seem to have been two main bases of his objection to trait theory. One was the assertion of the independence of traits which then allegedly could be arbitrarily shuffled and reshuffled in the course of historical processes. This violated what Malinowski felt to be a cardinal principle, that of the interconnectedness of all the elements of a contemporary culture.[3]

The second principal of his attack in this connection was the doctrine of "survivals," the view that many traits present in a contemporary culture could be interpreted as having originated in connection with a function in some situation of the past, and then have survived into the present without reference to their connection with other traits or their functions.[4]

The primary starting points of Malinowski's theorizing, then, may be said to be, first the making of any given mode of behavior humanly understandable in terms of the motivation of individuals, second the inclusion within this requirement both of rational, "scientifically" validated, behavior and of "irrational," ritual, magical, or religious, behavior on the part of the same persons, third the recognition of the interconnectedness of the different items which constituted a "culture" to form some kind of system, and fourth the reference of the particular item to some kind of function in the current contemporary operation of this culture, as a basis of its understandability.

All of these starting points are in themselves fully acceptable to the contemporary, theoretically interested, social scientist. It can furthermore be conceded that they are justified in critical terms, in the sense that one or more of these requirements was violated by an important part of the litera-

---

[3] A typical statement is "I am deeply convinced that there is a fundamental misunderstanding in any attempt at isolation of separate traits" (Malinowski, *A Scientific Theory of Culture*, p. 34).

[4] His concept with the relation of theory to field-work is illustrated by the following quotation: "The real harm done by this concept (survivals) was to retard effective field-work. Instead of searching for the present-day function of any cultural fact, the observer was merely satisfied in reaching a rigid, self-contained entity" (Malinowski, *A Scientific Theory of Culture*, p. 31).

ture available to Malinowski especially in the early stages of his career. But the question which interests us is what he did on the basis of this platform. In what direction did he go, and how far? Did he reach a point which is satisfactory for the theoretical needs of our generation?

It is now necessary to set up a frame of reference within which some analysis of the problem can be carried out, and on which Malinowski's views can be projected. The development of thought which covered Malinowski's career span, and periods before and since, has involved a process of differentiation as between the types of system within which the factors which can be said to play a part in the determination of human behavior can conveniently be analyzed. In one sense perhaps one of the greatest accomplishments of anthropology before and during Malinowski's time was to establish a clear distinction between man as a biological organism and man as the creator, bearer, and transmitter of culture. The importance of this distinction can be considered to be common ground between the functional school and its trait or diffusionist or other predecessors. Perhaps it can be said that Malinowski's greatest theoretical effort was devoted to re-establishing the connection which this process of differentiation had made precarious and in many respects unclear.

In the sense of full establishment in the field of professional common sense, the next stage of differentiation can hardly be said even yet to have been completed, but there are many signs that this is the main trend of theoretical development in the area. What I refer to is the further differentiation of the cultural system, which has been considered to be independent of man as organism, into two categories, first of culture in the narrower sense, and second, social systems, as analytically distinct references for theoretical analysis. Concomitantly the older conception of "the individual" as primarily a biological organism has tended to become differentiated into the organism in the physiological sense, and the *personality* as the system of behavior emanating from that organism.

It has been noted that, wherever this type of theoretical differentiation occurs, there arises a new problem of integration. When, as in the older anthropological sense, the organism came to be differentiated from culture, the problem arose of what is the relation between them, since living human beings are obviously both organisms and culture-bearers at the same time. Similarly, when the more refined differentiation of theoretical analysis to which we have referred occurs, again the problem arises of how social system, residual culture, organism and personality are related to each other, and how they all together fit into a larger entity, the scientific analysis of the human being, as individual and as related to others in the species and its various subcategories.

It seems to me that the theory of human behavior has now reached a stage where it is not possible to deal adequately with most concrete problem areas within it without carefully discriminating these four system types

or levels from each other, namely the organism, (1) as physiological system and (2) as behaving system or personality, (3) the systems constituted by the interaction of a plurality of behaving organisms, i.e. social systems, and finally (4) the systems of cultural pattern which are generated in concrete social interaction, but which survive the lifetime of particular living organisms and can be transmitted or diffused from one social system to another.

I would like to suggest that Malinowski thought primarily in terms of the first level of differentiation of system references, between that of the organism and of the "culture" in the less differentiated sense of the term, and within this dual frame of reference his main concern was to establish an integration between them by working out a theory of motivation which was adequate to the facts of cultural behavior, as he knew it from the literature, but above all from his own field work experience. There is much in his work which foreshadows a later technical theory of social systems, but he did not even take full advantage of what was available in the literature at the time,[5] and his most valuable personal contribution to it are on the "clinical" level already referred to rather than in his attempts at more generalized formulation.

Given these principal preoccupations, it seems probable that Malinowski, in the role of general theorist, was a somewhat unfortunate victim of the stage of development of theoretical thinking at the time of his most active professional life. It seems probable, that is to say, that this attempt of a synthesis between cultural and psychological considerations was, given the theoretical materials he had to work with, or choose from in the literature, premature. Neither a satisfactory psychology for his purposes nor a satisfactory theory of social systems could be developed without a further process of theoretical differentiation which discriminated four and not merely two system levels and which established the requisite relationships between them. Though he did not achieve the high synthesis to which he aimed, Malinowski's experience may be considered to have constituted a notable attempt and to be very instructive for our own generation with respect to the difficulties in which he became involved as well as to the positive accomplishments.

The justification for treating Malinowski as operating mainly on the less differentiated of the two levels of theoretical discrimination we have discussed, is to be found on the one hand in his concept of culture and the way he relates it to that of institutions, and on the other hand in his concept of needs. I shall discuss each of them in turn.

The feature of Malinowski's use of the concept of culture which is most striking is its encyclopedic inclusiveness. "It obviously [sic!] is the integral whole consisting of implements and consumers' goods, of con-

---

[5] See p. 98.

stitutional charters for the various social groupings, of human ideas and crafts, beliefs and customs. Whether we consider a very simple or primitive culture or an extremely complex and developed one, we are confronted by a vast apparatus, partly material, partly human, and partly spiritual by which man is able to cope with the concrete specific problems that face him."[6]

In the first place it seems clear that, in accord with much anthropological usage, particularly perhaps in the United States, Malinowski's definition includes what otherwise are three quite disparate categories, namely, "material culture," i.e. in his definition implements and consumers' goods, which are artefacts, i.e. physical objects, the products of human activities, or instrumental to the satisfaction of human wants; second, concrete categories of human activity, particularly under the term "custom"; and third, constitutional charters for the various social groupings and beliefs, the last being what in a narrow sense we might call specifically cultural objects. Social organization is not singled out even as a specific category within culture but is most obviously included under the term customs, and less directly under the charters for social groupings.

Essentially it can be said that Malinowski follows anthropological tradition in treating culture as everything pertaining to human life and action which cannot be treated as a property of the human organism as a physiological system, in the somatic sense, or the genetic, i.e. as a direct manifestation of biological inherited patterns of behavior. Culture is that aspect of behavior which is learned by the individual, and which hence may to a greater or less extent be "held in common by pluralities of individuals, and transmitted to other individuals, together with the physical objects associated with such learned patterns and activities.

The essential point is that Malinowski makes no attempt, in discussing culture as such, to draw any theoretical lines of distinction within this encyclopedic category. The only line which is at all clear cut, though it is not strongly emphasized, is between material objects which function as implements and consumers' goods, on the one hand, and those aspects of culture like customs, beliefs and, social groupings which are properties of behaving human beings or pluralities of them.[7]

To be sure Malinowski does not treat culture as simply undifferentiated. The essential point I am making is that he does not, in his differentiation of it, directly or indirectly pay primary attention to the kinds of line of analysis which would be involved in a discrimination of the three

[6] Malinowski, *A Scientific Theory of Culture*, p. 36.

[7] Though he explicitly includes material objects on the one hand, and beliefs and values on the other, there seems to be a sense in which Malinowski *tends* to identify culture and society or social systems. Thus we find him, perhaps inadvertently, speaking of the "members of a culture" (Malinowski, *A Scientific Theory of Culture*, p. 89). A human being can be a member of a social group, but certainly not of a category of consumers' goods or of a belief or value.

types of systems discussed above which do not belong to the organism in a physiological sense. He introduces two cross-cutting classifications which are both employed in connection with his concept of *institution,* one a classification of the elements or components which go to make up an institution, the other of the different types of institutions themselves. Let us therefore turn to this concept.

Malinowski treats institutions as "the concrete isolates of organized behavior." Since such behavior always involves a plurality of persons, an institution in Malinowski's sense is thus a social system, not a society but a "partial" social system which is in some sense a subsystem of a society.[8]

An institution in this sense is, though functionally differentiated from others, a segmentary cross-section of culture in that it involves *all* the components which Malinowski has included in his definition of culture. Thus he enumerates charter, norms, material apparatus, activities, and in addition function.[9] To be sure he did not say directly that personnel and function were part of culture, but all the other elements of an institution are, by his formal definition, and it is quite clear from [his] discussion that every type of component of culture is involved in every institution.

The distinctive features of Malinowski's conception of institutions within this framework are the concepts of charter and of function. Function will be taken up presently, but it is noteworthy that Malinowski, in his conception of the charter of an institution, was well in line with developing sociological theory in that he treated as the central feature of the charter "the system of values for the pursuit of which human beings organize, or enter organizations already existing."[10] Closely related to this is his clear conception of the normative control of behavior—on a certain level—and hence of the relations between norms and activities as, in his terminology, components of culture. In these respects, and in spite of the late influence on his thinking of the Yale school of behaviorism, Malinowski escaped the confusions which have been associated with many behavior-

---

[8] It may be noted, purely as a terminological matter, that Malinowski used the concept *institution* as referring to a concrete social system or, as he often said, a group. This is one of two alternatives both of which are deeply rooted in social science tradition, the other being to refer to an element of "pattern" in the structure of social relationships. By Malinowski's conception obviously property and contract cannot be institutions. For British anthropology it is interesting to note that Radcliffe-Brown followed the other alternative (cf. for example, A. R. Radcliffe-Brown, *Structure and Function in Primitive Society* [Glencoe, Ill.: Free Press, 1952], pp. 10–11), a usage he shared with Durkheim who may very well have been the source of it. I also have chosen to use the pattern rather than the group reference. Neither can be said to be canonically "correct," but since there are considerable ranges over which they are irreducibly contradictory (e.g., property in much usage is certainly an institution but cannot in any way be made out to be a group) it is important to be clear which usage is meant.

[9] Malinowski, *A Scientific Theory of Culture,* p. 53.

[10] *Ibid.,* p. 52.

istically inclined attempts at psychological interpretations of social behavior. There is no indication in his writings that he was worried about the
legitimacy of using verbal accounts of motives and sentiments or any suggestion that these should be treated as simple epiphenomena of some
underlying physiological process. However inadequately he analyzed it, the
independent significance of the cultural level of behavior-structuring was
deeply taken for granted by Malinowski.

What now of the concept of function? In the first place it clearly fits
into the scheme of culture as so far discussed. It is the primary basis of
the differentiation of institutions within the same "culture" from each other.
Institutions differ in that they are "organized about" different functions.
But functions for what? The sense of the term Malinowski has in mind is
clearly that current in the biological science referring to essential conditions
of the continuing life and "normality" of an organism or an aggregate of
organisms such as a species.

There are in Malinowski's writings a good many rather loose references
to function where apparently are included individual human beings as organisms, groups of such human beings, institutions as such groups organized
in a specific culture, and the culture itself. The two poles of Malinowski's
analysis, however, between which the analysis is couched are clearly the
individual biological organism, qualified mainly by the reproductive function on behalf of the species, and the culture, which is only equivocally
and indefinitely related to any particular social system.

A key problem in this context is that of the classification of institutions.
Malinowski attempted this on several occasions and in different ways. One
such attempt which he spoke of as "a fairly common sense statement," [11]
does not lean very strongly toward the biological pole, since only two out of
seven main categories suggested have clear biological primacy, namely reproduction (a case of species, not individual primacy) and what is called
"physiological" referring above all to age and sex as points of reference
for social differentiation. The other five categories, territorial, voluntary
associations, occupational and professional, rank and status, and a final
"comprehensive integration" in which both political and cultural references
are involved, are by no means obviously biological in reference. Indeed
even the first two mentioned are biological only in the sense that relatedness through biological criteria constitutes a point of reference for ascriptive categorization of and assignment to social statuses.

This is a classification which any sociologist might take as a promising
beginning for the analysis of social structure as such. Malinowski, however, showed surprisingly little interest in exploring such possibilities at
all. In what was unquestionably meant to be his major theoretical work,
after setting forth this classification he immediately went off on another

[11] *Ibid.*, pp. 63–65.

tack and never returned to it. The tack in question was the development of a theory of needs, the main focal point of which is clearly a theory of the biological needs of the individual organism. He was quite clear about his own conviction that the primary reference of the concept of function was to such a theory of needs. Thus: "It is clear, I think, that any theory of culture has to start from the organic needs of man, and if it succeeds in relating (to them) the more complex, indirect, but perhaps fully imperative needs of the type which we call spiritual or economic or social, it will supply us with a set of general laws such as we need in sound scientific theory." [12]

Within the polarity defined by the human organism and the culture, then, Malinowski ascribed casual priority to the organism, and his basic theoretical attempt was to *derive* the main characteristics of the culture, and hence of social systems, from a theory of the causally precultural needs of the organism. This orientation is again made quite explicit in his many statements that, however important, however differentiated, culture is always *instrumental* to the satisfaction of organic needs in the sense in which he is using that term. Indeed what he did was to assimilate the concept of culture to that of environment in the specifically biological sense of that term. He referred to culture, thus, as a "secondary milieu" in which the organism exists.[13]

Before attempting to follow the logic of Malinowski's theorizing farther let us make explicit a fundamental theoretical problem at this point. The primary focus of biological theory as it has influenced the behavioral sciences has been on the physiological as distinct from the behavioral interchanges between organism and environment. The typical object of primary environmental significance has not been another behaving organism but for example a source of food. Though with respect to reproduction and defense particularly, relations to other organisms are important to biology, the drawing of a sharp distinction between objects with which there is and is not a process of *interaction* on a behavioral level, has not been a prominent feature of biologically influenced theory in the social sciences. Indeed, where the focus has been on behavior as such, as in the theory of learning in experimental psychology, the typical experimental situation has not included other organisms, but rather the maze is set up by the experimenter to operate entirely independently of any behavior except that of the experimental animal.

But it is this very process of interaction between two or more behaving organisms which is the point of departure for a theory of social systems. Here the behavior of one must acquire meaning as sign, cue or symbol for the other and vice versa. But in his assimilation of the culture to the concept of environment in a biological sense, Malinowski gives no intimation

---

[12] *Ibid.*, pp. 72–73.
[13] *Ibid.*, p. 68.

that he is giving special importance to this distinction; on the contrary it is clear that he conceived organic needs as altogether independent of any phenomena of interaction; it is only as instrumental means to their satisfaction that interactive features of the situation acquire significance. To be sure he speaks of symbolic behavior from time to time, but apparently does not connect the problem with this context.

Thus we have seen that on two levels Malinowski missed an opportunity to take a path which would have led directly into a theory of social systems. First he did not follow up his "fairly common sense" classification of institutions as elements of social structure, and secondly in relation to the idea that culture is an environment of behavior, he did not bring out the significance of the phenomena of social interaction, but left them merged in the general biological concept of environment.

What he did was to attempt first to work out a theory of "basic needs" which gave specific content to what he called "human nature," i.e. "the biological determinism which imposes on every civilization and on all individuals in it the carrying out of such bodily functions as breathing, sleep, rest, nutrition, excretion, and reproduction. We can define the concept of basic needs as the environmental and biological conditions which must be fulfilled for the survival of the individual and the group." [14]

His basic problem, then, was how to get from the system of biologically basic needs of the organism to the facts of culturally organized behavior. As has already been noted he utilized one very general formula, namely that culture is always of instrumental significance in the satisfaction of biological needs. This formula represents in a sense the dividing line between the path Malinowski took and other paths of theoretical development, since in principle it categorically denied the independent casual significance of *learned* goals and values. There is a sense in which what Malinowski put into culture and institutions with his concept of the charter as the system of values for the pursuit of which human beings organize, he took away again with his conception of the causal priority of basic needs and the conception that culture must always be instrumental to the satisfaction of such needs. It is perhaps correct to say that on the clinical level Malinowski operated mainly with the conception of charter; here values were very real and were not treated simply as instrumentalities. But when he attempted to be a general theorist he tended to shift his ground to the detriment of the sociological quality of his thinking.

What, however, of his own explicit attempt to build the bridge? His first major step was to set up a classification of basic needs which could be directly related to a classification of "cultural responses" which could then in turn be brought into relation to institutions. The familiar table [15]

---

[14] *Ibid.*, p. 75.

[15] *Ibid.*, p. 91, and *Man and Culture*, Raymond Firth (ed.) (London: Routledge and Kegan Paul, 1957), p. 35.

includes among the seven basic needs reproduction, movement and growth; and as the corresponding cultural responses, kinship, activity, and training.

In the first place it would seem that the catalogue of basic needs is somewhat skewed from one which would be acceptable to biological theory. But this is not a very serious departure. The one item which is perhaps most dubious in his list is the need for movement which surely most biologists would refer to some other functional context, probably breaking it down into relevance to several such as safety, food-getting and the like.

But more serious is the arbitrariness involved in the way Malinowski attempts to relate this classification of needs to the classification of cultural response. Let us take three examples. The relation of kinship to reproduction is obvious. But particularly in nonliterate societies kinship units perform a wide range of functions which certainly include all seven of Malinowski's categories both of basic needs and of cultural responses. It is a very general fact of course that only in organized kinship relationships is human reproduction ordinarily legitimated but this fact does not justify treating kinship as a whole as primarily a cultural response to the biological need of reproduction.

Secondly let us note the category of "training" as a cultural response. Most surely this cannot be said to be a response simply to the need of the organism to grow in the strict biological sense. The only basis for such a view would seem to be that biological maturation provides necessary conditions for the effectiveness of various sorts and stages of training. If culture is learned, there clearly must be some kind of ordered sequence in the learning process which is concomitant with and in part dependent on the process of growth of the organism.

Finally, third, perhaps the most tenuous connection of all is that between activities as a cultural response and the alleged basic need for movement. The basic difficulty here is the extreme generality of the categories, both of cultural response and of need. *All* social behavior is in some sense activity. Presumably activity devoted to satisfaction of the other six needs would not be included in this category; hence it becomes a residual category of all activity which is not devoted to some other function than satisfying the need for movement. To be sure Malinowski suggests that particularly play and recreation should be placed in this category, presumably because they otherwise appear functionless. But this is an example of the familiar logic of the *ad hoc* hypothesis. There exists a category of empirical phenomena which are otherwise unexplained. Then what one does is to invent a "need" or some other "force" of which they can be treated as a manifestation.

Clearly Malinowski's classification of cultural responses, however, even granting that they stand in a satisfactory relation to a satisfactory classification of basic needs, does not get him very far toward bridging the gap between the concept of needs and even his own classification of institutions discussed above. He must have recourse to some further theoretical devices

in order to get within shouting distance of his goal. The principal device he adopts is the insertion of a second category of needs between his basic needs and the institutional integrates of collective behavior. These are what he calls "derived needs" and are clearly the outcome of applying the concept of "secondary drive" as utilized in Hullian learning theory to his problems.

Three main questions arise about this shift from emphasis on basic biological needs to that on derived needs and their relation to cultural imperatives. The first concerns the implications of the shift for Malinowski's thesis on the primacy of basic needs in functional theory. The second concerns the actual classification of derived needs at which he arrived and its implications, whereas the third concerns his analysis of the motivational mechanisms by which the connections are established. The three questions, particularly the first and third, are of course interdependent.

There seems to be no doubt that, in this part of his discussion, Malinowski talked about the relative independence of culture and institutions from biological needs in a way that stands in striking contrast to his many pronouncements about the functional primacy of basic needs. He thus speaks of culture as "imposing a new type of specific determinism on human behavior." [16] And again "Man does not, by biological determinism, need to hunt with spears or bow and arrow; use poison darts; nor defend himself by stockades, by shelters, or by armour. But the moment that such devices have been adopted, in order to enhance human adaptability to the environment they also become necessary conditions of survival." And yet again "A permanent deterioration in material equipment, in social solidarity, in the training of the individual and the development of his abilities, would lead in the long run not merely to disorganization of culture, but also to starvation, large-scale disease, the deterioration of personnel efficiency; hence also, obviously, to depopulation." [17]

On one level the bridge he attempts to build is through the concept of adaptation and hence of the instrumentality of culture. Once cultural instrumentalities have been adopted then man becomes dependent on them in such a way that biological survival itself, and of course the satisfaction of the basic needs, becomes dependent on them. In this connection the source of difficulty lies in such phrases as the one quoted, that man does not, by biological determinism, need to hunt with spears, etc. Then there is the problem, why, if biological determinism is paramount, does he do so? In a broad way Malinowski's answer seems to be that he does so because he has found that he can *better* gratify his basic needs through cultural instrumentalities than without them. This raises certain questions in the theory of personality to which it will be necessary to return presently.

However this may be, there has, when Malinowski talks in this vein,

16 Malinowski, *A Scientific Theory of Culture*, p. 119.
17 *Ibid.*, pp. 121, 122.

been at least a relative abandonment of what may be called the "passive" conception of the role of the cultural environment of action. Now, if man is even to survive he not only has this cultural environment available to take advantage of if he wishes, but he must do so in order to survive. Above all, perhaps, he must learn the content of his culture and he must conform to its norms and rules. To this extent at least the cultural level has acquired theoretically independent signficance. The cultural element of the environment is *man-made,* and is perpetuated and sustained by human action. It is not something which is simply there, independent of human life, to which man must adapt because he is unable to change or control it.

From this type of consideration there emerges in Malinowski's work a classification of cultural imperatives and responses which is of the greatest theoretical interest to the sociologist. It is worth while to quote his tabular presentation in full: [18]

Imperatives	*Responses*
1. The cultural apparatus of implements and consumers' goods must be produced, used, maintained and replaced by new production.	1. Economics
2. Human behavior, as regards its technical, customary, legal, or moral prescription must be codified, regulated in action and sanction.	2. Social Control
3. The human material by which every institution is maintained must be renewed, formed, drilled, and provided with full knowledge of tribal tradition.	3. Education
4. Authority within each institution must be defined, equipped with powers, and endowed with means of forceful execution of its orders.	4. Political organization

This, it can be said, is an authentic, if sketchy, classification of the functional imperatives of *social systems.* With respect to it, the formless encyclopedic character of Malinowski's more general discussions of culture evaporates and relatively clear relationships between "material culture" at least in its economically relevant aspects, norms, values and social organization come to the fore.

This is the more notable to me personally because this classification

[18] *Ibid.,* p. 125.

corresponds very directly to one which I and various people associated with me have been using in our recent theoretical work. With some modifications, but retaining in essentials the four basic categories, and particularly the number four, it can be treated as the master classification of functional imperatives of any social system, or indeed of any system of action.[19]

I should maintain, then, that Malinowski's late classification of the functional imperatives of culture, or as I should prefer to say of a social system, could well have constituted a basic starting point for a general theoretical analysis of social systems in their own right, not just as derivatives of basic biological needs. Unfortunately, however, this notable contribution stands as a virtually isolated fragment. Not only is it not developed or used in any technical theoretical sense, but Malinowski did not even attempt to relate it to the classification of institutions which he had presented earlier in the same volume.

Part of the explanation of this fact undoubtedly is to be found in the fact that this was one of the very last things Malinowski wrote; had he lived longer, it might have been developed. But at the same time, the further sequence of the *Scientific Theory* would seem to indicate that there was another aspect of the matter. For he immediately returns to his overpowering theoretical interest, namely how he can relate these derived needs to a theory of motivation of the behavior of the individual. Theoretically at every crucial point he seems to have done this, to have abandoned the structural analysis of culture and of social systems in favor of a certain level of psychological interest. This brings us to the third of the three questions we raised in connection with the theory of derived needs, namely his analysis of the motivational mechanism involved.

What he finally adopted, and is developed in the last part of the *Scientific Theory,* is, as I suggested, a modified version of Hullian learning theory. The essential point is that he adopted the concept of learned or acquired drive so that one could for example on this basis speak of a need to conform with rules or norms of the culture.

But even here it is notable how narrowly he circumscribes his analysis. First an acquired drive, which he refers to as "drive (2)" is stated always to be instrumental in significance relative to a basic need which he refers

<hr />

[19] I shall not attempt to elaborate this statement here. The classification in substantially the form now being used was first put forward by R. F. Bales (Cf. R. F. Bales, *Interaction Process Analysis: A Method for the Study of Small Groups* [Cambridge, Mass.: Harvard University Press, 1950], Chapter II). It turned out that the "pattern variable" scheme with which Shils and I had been working (Cf. T. Parsons and E. A. Shils [eds.], *Toward a General Theory of Action* [Cambridge, Mass.: Harvard University Press], 1951; and T. Parsons, *The Social System* [Glencoe, Ill.: Free Press, 1951]) also involved this classification and could be derived from it. In its current form the fourfold scheme was first stated in T. Parsons, R. F. Bales, and E. A. Shils, *Working Papers in the Theory of Action* (Glencoe, Ill.: Free Press, 1953), Chapters III and V.

to as "drive (1)." Second he roundly asserts that, presumably in every case the satisfaction of an acquired drive, of a derived need is also and in its meaning to the individual essentially a satisfaction of a particular and specific basic need in the original sense. As he says "after the instrumental phase has been adequately accomplished, the immediate drive of nutritive or sexual appetite, of removal of pain or noxious bodily conditions leads directly to the physiological performance, whether this be positive or negative, the satisfaction of pleasure or the removal of pain." [20]

This is a very tenuous bridge indeed and almost undoes what Malinowski has been saying about the independent significance of culture and social organization. Furthermore even on the basis of learning psychology alone, Malinowski takes up only the one idea of instrumental learning and altogether ignores the possible significance of contiguity learning and classical conditioning. Even more serious, he seems to be guilty of a basic confusion, namely between the necessary conditions for a process of learning to take place, and the motivational structure of psychological process after the learning has occurred. There is no reason to doubt that the motivation of all secondary drives or derived needs goes back in the genetic history of the individual to the satisfaction of primary drives. But that in the mature individual the "ultimate" motive for any specific act of learned behavior must be the continuing satisfaction of a specific primary drive is certainly not an established psychological doctrine.

Above all, perhaps the most serious source of the difficulty of Malinowski's position lies in his failure to consider the problems of the *organization* of human personality as a motivational system. He clearly leaves it as a bundle of biologically inherited basic needs about each of which there then develops a cluster of learned instrumental patterns of behavior. But the motivation of the instrumental patterns *remains,* in the last analysis, the basic need. Insofar as the personality can be conceived to operate as a system its fundamental organization must be referred to the cluster of discrete basic needs. There is no central organization of learned motivation.

Perhaps this aspect of the matter can be summed up by saying that Malinowski failed to establish a theoretically adequate link between the observed facts of cultural behavior and the psychological sources of motivation to such behavior. He reduced the connection to an instrumental one, leaving the structure of the motivational system essentially untouched as a system of given, i.e. biologically inherited, basic needs which are independent of, and prior to culture itself. Essentially Malinowski's social psychology turns out to be a modification of the instinct theory of McDougall.

Above all it is perhaps significant that Malinowski by-passed the opportunity to utilize the conception of internalization of culture patterns, which was very much in the air in the later years of his career. The dif-

---

[20] Malinowski, *A Scientific Theory of Culture,* p. 138.

ference between Malinowski's position and that of the "culture and personality" school, however, which utilized this conception on one level (e.g. Kardiner or Margaret Mead) lies essentially in the relative weights that they gave to the organic and the cultural reference points in the scheme we have seen that Malinowski worked with. The culture and personality school took the fullest possible advantage of the conception of the plasticity of human nature, and tended to push it to the point where the personality was only a kind of mirror image of the culture, wholly formed by it. Malinowski on the other hand reduced the learned elements of personality functioning to instrumental status and essentially left the biologically given structure of "instincts" untouched as the prime mover.

It seems to me that the dilemma between these two positions is a false dilemma. The only way to escape it, however, is to develop a more differentiated conceptual scheme that either Malinowski or the "culture and personality" school have given us. The essence of the necessary differentiatedness is that the conception of a social system must be differentiated from the encyclopedic conception of culture which both groups on the whole share, leaving a more restricted conception of "cultural tradition." Secondly the personality as a behavioral system must be clearly differentiated from the organism as a phsyiological system.

If these theoretical differentiations are fully carried out it becomes possible to raise in a fully technical sense the questions of the structure of social systems and of personalities and their relation to each other. Malinowski was quite right that cultural man is subject to certain imperatives which are independent of the exigencies imposed by the physiological needs of the organism. Furthermore, it is legitimate to interpret these imperatives as above all those of the social systems in which he is involved.

All this is correct. But Malinowski grossly underestimated the theoretical import of these facts. The systems could not be made to fit together at all if their connection were restricted to the levels with which he deals. A much more radical step is necessary, to the doctrine that the *primary structure of human personality as a system* is not organized about the physological needs of the organism, but about the social structure of the society and its various subsystems. To a point the position taken by the personality and culture school is, seen in this light, correct. But it is not the "culture" in the most general sense, but the circumstantially detailed role structure of the social system which is the focus of personality structure and its development. This starts, in virtually all societies, with the family, not as an agency for securing biological reproduction, but as an agency of the *socialization* of the child, and goes on by a series of successive stages of development which institute a process of differentiation of a simple structure and further organization and integration of the differentiated parts. Only by conceiving a process of personality development in an ordered system of social interaction situations can we conceive the development of complexes

of motivation by which human beings could conceivably meet the exigencies imposed on them by the imperatives of their culture and society. Instrumental patterns for meeting physiological needs have their place in such a motivational system, but the departure from this simple paradigm which must be accounted for is far more profound than Malinowski realized.[21]

At the conclusion of this review of Malinowski's theoretical treatment of social systems, the verdict must be that on the level of general theory his contribution left much to be desired, both in the most general respects and with respect to his field of special interest, the motivation of social behavior. On the other hand his performance on what I have called the "clinical" levels of theorizing about social behavior is far more satisfactory.

At certain points suggestions of a general analysis of the social system and its structure did emerge in Malinowski's work, notably in his classification of institutions and in his account of the functional imperatives of cultural life. But he never disentangled the concept of the social system as such in any clear way from his encyclopedic concept of culture, which would have been a necessary prerequisite of further theoretical development. But above all he entirely failed to carry out any technical development from these starting points. It seems clear that his heart was not in it, that whenever he had established what he felt to be a useful reference point his theoretical interest immediately turnd in a psychological direction.

In this connection it may again be noted that he failed to make significant contact with the eminent theorists of social systems whose work was available to him; there is so far as I am aware no reference either to Max Weber or to Pareto anywhere in his work, and his references to Durkheim are either on too particularized points to be of great interest to general theory, or were negatively critical with respect to certain general aspects such as the alleged "group mind" aspect of his thought. He apparently entirely failed to appreciate the profound contributions Durkheim made to the analysis of social systems.[22]

Malinowski's special field of interest, the motivation of social behavior, is one of the greatest importance to sociology and anthropology as well as to psychology. But here again in terms of general theory his work cannot be judged to have been highly successful. Essentially it was characterized

---

[21] For an attempt to develop this point of view of the relation between social structure and personality development, see T. Parsons and R. F. Bales, *Family, Socialization and Interaction Process* (Glencoe, Ill.: Free Press, 1955). For a critical review of psychological theories in this context and others related to the motivation of social behavior, see T. Parsons, "Psychology and Sociology," in *Toward a Science of Social Man*, J. L. Gillin (ed.) (New York: 1954), pp. 67–101.

[22] The purpose of this essay is not to make a comparison between Malinowski and Radcliffe-Brown, but the contrast in this respect is striking. Throughout his work Radcliffe-Brown has been extremely clear about the concept of social system—and Durkheim's use of it—and has consistently made it the main focus of his theoretical work. On a comparably general level this cannot be said of Malinowski.

by premature resort to psychology. His failure to carry through sustained structural analyses of social systems meant that he did not develop, or take over from others, an analysis of the structural setting which would have enabled him to state the problems of the nature of social motivation and its genesis in the individual more fruitfully than he did, or to get more deeply into the theory of personalities in its relation to social systems.

Again in this context Malinowski seems to have been rather peculiarly insensitive to the sources available in the literature of the time which might have been of help to him. He was one of the early social scientists to become interested in Freud's work. But having, to an important degree prematurely and without full understanding, decided that Freud's theory was culture-bound and could not explain Trobriand facts, he dropped it and never made serious use of it in his own theoretical structure. Moreover, there was a school of social psychology in the United States centering on the names of G. H. Mead and W. I. Thomas, which might have been very useful to him, but so far as one can judge from his writings, had no influence on him. What he did take up was one version of behavioristic learning theory in perhaps its least directly fruitful form for these purposes.

In sum, I am afraid that my verdict must be that so far as the *general* theory of social systems is concerned, including as a vitally important branch, the motivation of social behavior, there is with one exception no point at which Malinowski has more to teach us than one or several of his contemporaries or predecessors. The one exception to which I refer is the classification of the functional imperatives of "culture" and the responses to which they relate. It is tragic that, having set this forth, he entirely failed to follow it up.

The harshness of this verdict [23] is mitigated above all by two circumstances. The first of these concerns the eminence of Malinowski's contribution to anthropology and more broadly to social science in other directions, as a field-worker, a teacher,[24] and a "clinical" theorist. It is only as a general theorist of social systems that I think we must conclude that Malinowski was not definitely first-rate.

The second circumstance concerns the state of the subject in his time. By contrast with the older evolutionary and trait theories he unquestionably was, in his general theoretical orientations, on a fruitful track and exercised a healthy influence. This influence, I think it is clear, considerably increased sensitivity to the need for good general theory, and for recognition of examples of it when it was available.

[23] This verdict seems to be shared on the whole, though from a somewhat different point of view, by the only other attempt at a rather general appraisal of this aspect of Malinowski's work I have found, namely by Gluckman (M. Gluckman, "Malinowski's Sociological Theories," *The Rhodes-Livingston Papers*, No. 16 Oxford: 1949).

[24] In this respect I have a heavy personal debt to Malinowski which I fully recognize and do not wish anything said in this essay to invalidate.

4. The Present Status of "Structural-Functional" Theory in Sociology

SINCE ROBERT MERTON and the present author are generally labeled what might be called the "arch-functionalists" in contemporary sociology— among whom Marion Levy [1] would also often be included—it seems appropriate that in a volume honoring Merton on the occasion of his sixty-fifth birthday his old teacher and fellow functionalist should say something on the topic indicated by the title of this paper. After an interval of some years, I have reread Merton's seminal essay "Manifest and Latent Functions" [2] and tried to fit his thought and my own together. In that essay and in other writings,[3] he clearly made a major contribution to the understanding and clarification of the theoretical methodology of what he, I think quite appropriately, called "functional analysis"—what it was about, what its assumptions were, what some of its potentialities were, and the like.

I well remember at a meeting of the International Sociological Association, held in Washington, D.C., in 1961, Merton very cogently made the point of objecting to the phrase "structural-functionalism." He particularly did not like having it labeled an "ism" and suggested that the simple descriptive phrase "functional analysis" was more appropriate. I heartily concur in this judgment.

The hyphenated label "structural-functionalism" has seemed to me to

---

[1] Marion J. Levy, Jr., *The Structure of Society* (Princeton, N.J.: Princeton University Press, 1952) and *Modernization and the Structure of Societies,* 2 vols. (Princeton, N.J.: Princeton University Press, 1966).

[2] Robert K. Merton, "Manifest and Latent Functions," in his *Social Theory and Social Structure,* rev. ed. (New York: Free Press, 1957), pp. 19–84.

[3] See Merton, *Social Theory and Social Structure.*

be decreasingly appropriate. I might, therefore, begin with a statement of my grounds for this feeling. They consist essentially in the view that the two concepts "structure" and "function" are not parallel. Both are entirely indispensable in sociology and any other theoretical enterprise that deals with living systems, but it is important to understand the relation in which they stand to each other. I will not, as Piaget [4] does, extend my consideration beyond the category of so-called living systems, which is common to the biological and the social sciences and indeed, in certain respects, the humanities as intellectual disciplines. [5]

System seems to me to be an indispensable master concept, the meaning of which is directly concerned with its relation to the concept "environment." The crucial point is that the state of affairs internal to a living system is always different from the state of affairs in its environment and is in general more stable. Merton, [6] following Walter B. Cannon, [7] has given an exposition of the nature of this system–environment relation with exemplary clarity in the paper on "Manifest and Latent Functions." The idea, in turn, was derived from the great French physiologist Claude Bernard, [8] but particularly developed by Cannon. The difference between system and environment has two especially important implications. One is the existence and importance of boundaries between the two. Thus, the individual living organism is bounded by something like a "skin" inside of which a different state prevails from that outside it; for example, in the so-called warm-blooded organisms the internal temperature is different from the environmental temperature and is maintained at a nearly constant level in the face of major variations in environmental temperature. There are many other examples of this, such as the level of sugar in the blood. Cannon [9] discusses both these cases at considerable length.

The second basic property of living systems is that in some sense they are self-regulating. The maintenance of relative stability, including stability of certain processes of change like the growth of an organism, in the face of substantially greater environmental variability, means that, again as Merton puts it, there must be "mechanisms" that adjust the state of the system relative to changes in its environment. Thus, a fall in environmental temperature, again for a warm-blooded organism, necessitates either some

---

[4] Jean Piaget, *Structuralism*, trans. and ed. Chaninah Maschler (New York: Basic Books, 1970).

[5] See Talcott Parsons, "Theory in the Humanities and Sociology," *Daedalus* 99, no. 2 (Spring 1970): 495–523.

[6] Merton, "Manifest and Latent Functions," op cit.

[7] Walter B. Cannon, *Bodily Changes in Pain, Hunger, Fear and Rage* (New York: Appleton, 1929) and *The Wisdom of the Body* (New York: Norton, 1932).

[8] Claude Bernard, *An Introduction to the Study of Experimental Medicine*, trans. Henry Copley Greene (New York: Dover, 1957; first published in French, 1865).

[9] Cannon, *Bodily Changes in Pain, Hunger, Fear and Rage*, op cit.

mechanism that has the effect of checking the rate of heat loss or some mechanism that has the effect of increasing the rate of heat production, or some combination of the two. It is in this kind of setting that the relevant meaning of the concept "function" for present purposes is to be understood.

It is taken as a matter of empirical fact, verified by observation, that certain kinds of living systems maintain certain kinds of constancies and boundaries relative to the environments in which they live. Given the empirical state of affairs then, the question inevitably arises, "How is it maintained?" Or we might put it slightly differently in the phrase used by the eminent biologist Ernst Mayr,[10] in his paper "Teleological and Teleonomic," that in the study of living systems, three basic questions, not two, must always be asked. The first is, "What are the characteristics of the living system?" The second, "How do these characteristics develop and are they maintained?" And the third, as Mayr puts it, "Why?" "Why?" in Mayr's sense is a functional question. Thus, why do human beings outdoors on a very cold day jump up and down? Cannon's answer, with which Mayr would clearly agree, is that they are counteracting the loss of body heat in a cold environment by muscular activity, which is a way in which heat is produced in the body.

It is, of course, important in this connection that the functions of bodily or other events may be in Merton's sense latent rather than manifest. If we take the case not of jumping up and down but of shivering, which Cannon discusses, most of us are unaware that shivering is another form of muscular activity which increases the rate of heat production and is thereof functionally related to the problem of maintenance of constant body temperature. It is a mechanism in this context.

The examples I have been giving are drawn from biology, but the same principles are equally relevant to social systems or personality systems. Thus, fund raising activities, initiated by officers of a university administration, may be said to have the function of maintaining or enhancing the financial support on which the operation of the university as a social organization is dependent. Correspondingly, let us suggest that a living human person driving a motor vehicle will consult maps and road signs in order to make the directional decisions that will insure arriving at his planned destination. The function of observing the maps and or the road signs, therefore, is to facilitate the regulation of the person's behavior in the interest of attainment of a postulated personal goal, that is, arrival in "good time" at a projected destination. Seen in this context, the concept "structure" does not stand at the same level as that of function,

[10] Ernest Mayr, "Teleological and Teleonomic: A New Analysis," in Marx Wartovsky, ed., *Method and Metaphysics: Methodological and Historical Essays in the Natural and Social Sciences*, Proceedings of the Boston Colloquium for the Philosophy of Science, 1969–72 (Leiden, Holland: Brill, 1974), vol. 6, pp. 78–104.

but at a lower analytical level. It is a cognate with the concept "process," not function.[11]

We do not wish to hypostatize structure. It is any set of relations among parts of a living system which on empirical grounds can be assumed or shown to be stable over a time period and under a set of conditions relevant to a particular cognitive enterprise. Broadly speaking, the anatomical structure of an organism can be safely assumed to be constant over considerable periods of, we might say, maturity or adulthood. If, however, the concern is with the growth from fertilized ovum to mature organism, its structure is continually changing. Similarly, various kinds of disease lead to changes in the structure of the organism. If our concern is with social systems or personalities, the relevant considerations are entirely parallel.

Process, then, is the correlative concept designating the respects in which the state of a system or the relevant part or parts of it changes within the time span relevant and significant for the particular cognitive purpose in mind. A physiologist studying the process of digestion does not assume that the input of food substances from the environment will remain constant over a period of, let us say, several hours. In the stomach and intestines, food materials undergo a complicated set of changes, a major part eventually being absorbed into the bloodstream, other parts being rejected and eventually evacuated through defecation. Correspondingly, in a social organization, there are continual changes taking place: members of university faculties change their status by promotion, by its failure to materialize, by breaking their contracts, by retirement, or by resignation. Similarily, every academic year new cohorts of students are admitted and become members of the organization and old ones leave by graduation or some other process. Clearly, they are all processes, not structures, but they usually occur within a relatively stable and constant structure.

Thus, to make it as clear as possible, the concept "function," unlike that of structure and of process, is not a rubric in terms of which an immediately empirical description of a set of features of a living system can be stated. It is, rather, a concept that stands at a higher level of theoretical generality and is more analytical than either structure or process. Its reference is to the formulation of sets of conditions governing the states of living systems as "going concerns" in relation to their environments. These conditions concern the stability and/or instability, the survival and/or probable extinction, and not least, the temporal duration of such systems. In the organic field, crucial distinctions must be made between different system references, for example, the individual organism and the species, and we

---

[11] Sometimes, the levels are consolidated or fused by reference not to functions but to function*ing*. From this point of view, the verb form may be considered to be a synonym for process.

will argue that parallel distinctions must be made for the analysis of human systems of action, including social systems.

The concept "function," then, is the rubric under which the larger theoretical problems involving the general character of a class of living systems, and its relation to one or more environments, can be effectively stated and their solution approached. It concerns, above all, the *consequences* of the existence and nature of certain empirical describable structures and processes in such systems. Included, of course, are considerations relevant to the conditions under which the structures and processes of reference can arise, or the probabilities that they will in fact develop, or persist.

All this seems very simple and straightforward. Perhaps the only serious issue concerns the question, following Ernst Mayr,[12] of "Why?" Certain types of "reductionists" and "positivists" allege that such questions do not need to be asked, whether they be about organisms, species, social systems, or human personalities. The next question, however, is in certain respects more difficult. Our use so far of the term "system" has referred to classes of objects "out there," in the sense that they are not to be identified with the seeker of knowledge about them. The seeker of knowledge or the investigator must, however, if he is to know something about these objects, form the equivalent of what E. C. Tolman has called "cognitive maps." [13] He must, that is to say, describe, conceptualize, and analyze the "data" available concerning the objects in which he is interested. But the cognitive products coming out of this process must not be identified with the objects themselves. They are entities of quite a different order.

The crucial point we must emphasize is that, although there is presumptively some kind of correspondence between the cognitive structures produced by investigators and the objects the nature of which they are investigating, literally *never* is the cognitive account of the object a complete and concrete reproduction of everything that can be known or "felt" about such an object. It is always and in the nature of the case in some sense abstract, in that it formulates and calls to attention certain structures and processes pertaining to the object but omits consideration of many others or plays them down. This point has become standard in the methodology of science, in my own experience, having been particularly clearly elucidated by Max Weber [14] and by A. N. Whitehead.[15] The illusion that

---

[12] Mayr, "Teleological and Teleonomic," op. cit.

[13] Edward C. Tolman, "A Psychological Model," in Talcott Parsons and Edward A. Shils, eds., *Towards a General Theory of Action* (Cambridge, Mass.: Harvard University Press, 1951), part 3, pp. 279–361.

[14] Edward A. Shils and Henry A. Finch, eds. and trans., *Max Weber on the Methodology of the Social Sciences* (Glencoe, Ill.: Free Press, 1949).

[15] Alfred N. Whitehead, *Science and the Modern World* (New York: Macmillan, 1925).

a "conceptual scheme" reproduces the full reality of the concrete object is what Whitehead so illuminatingly analyzed as the "fallacy of misplaced concreteness." [16] When, therefore, we refer to living systems—whether it be a human organism, a human personality, a social system, or what not—the cognitive structure in which we attempt to describe and analyze it is *always* in some degree and in some senses abstract. I wish to emphasize the word "always." It therefore becomes extremely important for investigators to be as clearly aware as they possibly can of the nature and extent of the abstraction they are undertaking and the consequences of these cognitive processes for the solution of a very wide variety of problems involving the classes of objects with which they are concerned.

I may use an example of special concern to that category of investigators labeled "sociologists." From a common sense point of view, what we sociologists call a "society" is usually conceived to be a completely concrete entity, comparable, let us say to a stone or a dog. For technical theoretical purposes, however, it is strictly impossible for any investigator to deal with an entity he calls "American society" in its full concreteness. He can fill vast encyclopedic volumes with statements about it, but he will never come anywhere near exhausting what can validly be said to be true of it.

Does this mean that the cognitive enterprise is inherently self-defeating or impossible? Of course not. But the investigator must quite self-consciously select the "aspects" or features or properties of what he calls a society with which he can deal feasibly in a cognitively meaningful way. This imperative goes to the point that his very concept of the society itself becomes an abstraction in a sense parallel to that in which in the theory of the solar system in classical mechanics the earth is a truly heroic abstraction. Its units are said to have only the properties of mass, location in space, and velocity and direction of motion. There is no mention in the theory of the solar system of the flora and fauna, societies and cultures on the planet Earth, or even of its geological features. Newtonian mechanics was not for this reason simply wrong or incompetent. Indeed, Einstein's versions are, from this point of view, even less concrete than Newton's. It is, indeed, one of the most difficult features of the role of scientific investigator to become and stay critically aware of the nature and extent and directions of abstraction with which he is working. One of the commonest sources of difficulty in intellectual discourse is that parties to such discourse "talk past each other" because they do not assume the same patterns of abstraction.

Coping with the implications of the above consideration has been a perennial source of difficulty in all sophisticated fields of cognitive endeavor, not least the social sciences. Presumably, it is inherently impossible to exhaust the possiblities of awareness of the relations between what is

---

[16] *Ibid.*

being selected for specific consideration and what is being left out. Nevertheless, in the course of the evolution of knowledge, certain extremely important steps have been taken along this line.

The most important of these steps which I have in mind is the gradual realization that what we call a "social system" in sociological terminology, including a society, is only *one* analytically distinguishable sector or subset of the much larger complex we call "human action." It has gradually become theoretically imperative to make clear, first, a distinction between social and cultural systems. Beyond that, it has become evident that it is not legitimate—theoretically speaking, that is—to identify either a cultural or a social system with the psychological or personality system of an individual or class of them, any more than it is legitimate to identify a particular living organism with a species. Finally, it has also become clear that what is usually called "the personality system" is by no means the only major theoretical reference for consideration of the "individual." I have tended to deal with a fourth primary subsystem of what I would call the general system of action under the heading of the "behavioral organism." [17]

These considerations have very major implications for what sociologists ought to mean by societies or other categories of social system. The conceptual formulation of such systems, not only in the logical but also in the empirical-referential sense, abstracts from other considerations which bear on cultural, personality, and behavioral problem areas, but it implies that these analytically distinguishable systems function as environments to each other around the clock and across the board. It is a very difficult conception to grasp, for example, that the personality systems of individual "members" of a society should be treated as constituting an environment for purposes of analyzing the functioning of the society. Common sense will always tell us that since the personalities of its members are internal to the society they do not constitute an environment to it or vice versa. The society is alleged to be "composed" of individuals.

[17] I have, however, recently come to be convinced through a paper written by Victor and Charles Lidz that this particular designation of the fourth primary subsystem of "action" is not correct and should be replaced by what the Lidzes call the "behavioral system," which centers on what we sometimes call "cognitive functions." See Victor Lidz and Charles Lidz, "The Psychology of Intelligence of Jean Piaget and Its Place in the Theory of Action," in J. Loubser, R. Baum, A. Effrat, and V. Lidz, eds., *Explorations in General Theory in the Social Sciences* (New York: Free Press, 1976). The essential thesis of the paper is that what I, in a number of publications, most recently *The American University* (Cambridge, Mass.: Harvard University Press, 1973), have been calling the "behavioral organism," as one of four primary subsystems of action, should not be treated as part of the action system but as part of its environment. They propose substituting for it what they call the "behavioral" system, the nature of which they outline in a very ingenious analysis, which takes its departure from Piaget's well-known studies of intelligent human cognitive patterns and capacities, adapting Piaget's discussion to the framework of the general theory of action. I have been in general terms willing to accept this highly original theoretical innovation; indeed, this is the first occasion on which I have done so in print.

To my knowledge, Durkheim was the first social scientist to have a profound insight into this tremendous complexity of the analytical task of the social sciences when he spoke of the social environment from the point of view of the acting individual as being factually given to him.[18] His two basic concepts of "social facts" and the *milieu social* incorporate this insight. Once the purport of Durkheim's insight is understood, the action-system parallel to the physiological distinction between the external and the internal environment, stressed so strongly by Claude Bernard and by Cannon, becomes striking indeed.[19]

In Durkheim's work this view was first clearly suggested in his *Rules of Sociological Method* (1895), but its significance was difficult to "tease out" because of Durkheim's own confusing tendency to treat "society" as a concrete entity.[20] It comes out much more clearly in Durkheim's late work, *The Elementary Forms of the Religious Life,* essentially because by that time Durkheim had explicitly theorized at the level of the "general system of action," as I and several colleagues have called it. By discriminating subsystems, this made it possible to treat the "individual" as acting in relation to a "social environment" external to himself but still part of the system of action. This provides a new clarification of Durkheim's early conception of "social facts" as concerning, from the point of view of the individual actor, properties of a given set of objects in the external world.

All of this has an exceedingly important bearing on problems of the nature and status of functional analysis. The most important single proposition is that attempts at functional analysis will become intolerably confusing if there is not the best possible clarification of "system references." This obviously has to be a problem concerning data about the objects of investigation "out there." At the same time, however, it must concern the theoretically defined cognitive system with which the investigator is working.[21]

---

[18] Emile Durkheim, *The Elementary Forms of the Religious Life*, trans. J. W. Swain (London: George Allen & Unwin, 1915; first published in French, 1912), and *The Rules of Sociological Method*, trans. S. A. Solovay and J. H. Mueller (New York: Free Press, 1964; first published in French, 1895).

[19] See Talcott Parsons, "Durkheim on Religion Revisited: Another Look at *The Elementary Forms of the Religious Life*," in C. Y. Glock and P. E. Hammond, eds., *The Scientific Study of Religion: Beyond the Classics?* (New York: Harper & Row, 1973), pp. 156–80.

[20] Cf. Robert N. Bellah, ed., "Introduction," to *Émile Durkheim on Morality and Society* (Chicago: University of Chicago Press, 1973).

[21] In the classical literature of the "functional point of view," this point is very sharply illustrated by the difference between the theoretical positions of the two most prominent so-called functionalists in the last generation of British social anthropology, namely, Radcliffe-Brown (see A. R. Radcliffe-Brown, *Taboo* [New York: Cambridge University Press, 1939] and *Structure and Function in Primitive Society* [New York: Free Press, 1952]) and Malinowski (see Bronislaw Malinowski, *Magic, Science and Religion* [Glencoe, Ill.: Free Press, 1948] and *A Scientific Theory of Culture and*

We therefore cannot emphasize too strongly the importance of being clear about exactly what system is the frame of reference for raising and trying to answer functional questions. The problem is the more complicated and urgent because it has become so evident that the field of human action cannot be dealt with in terms of one system reference, such as "society," but must involve multiple system references: perhaps the problem of keeping these system references straight has been the most prolific single source of difficulty and confusion in theoretical analysis in this field.

Essentially, all of the above is in very close agreement with Merton's position, although it lacks his very careful and illuminating analysis of the many confusions which have appeared in sociological writings over functional analysis. I have differed from him mainly in my strong stress on the importance and centrality of the concept "system," on the inevitability of abstraction, and on the necessity for the self-conscious use of plural or multiple system references.

I also agree with him strongly on two further points, which I would like to mention now. The first is that the status of functional analysis is entirely independent of any ideological implications in the usual sense. In particular, it has nothing to do with political conservatism or a defense of the status quo. It has nothing essentially to do with judgments about the specific balances between elements of integration in social systems and elements of conflict and/or disorganization. The concept "dysfunction" is, of course, just as legitimate and important as that of function in the positive sense and is entirely central. We are, I think, entirely agreed in our repudiation of the Dahrendorf idea of "two theories," a consensus theory and a conflict theory.[22] This consideration again emphasizes continuity with biology. Biology does not have two basic theoretical schemes, a theory of healthy organisms and one of pathological phenomena in organisms, but health and pathological states are understandable in basically the same general theoretical terms. This proposition, of course, implies that "theory" in the present sense does not refer to empirical generalizations about certain classes of concrete phenomena but to an abstractly analytical "conceptual scheme."

Other Essays [Chapel Hill: University of North Carolina Press, 1944]). Radcliffe-Brown, taking his cues especially from Durkheim, adhered quite consistently to the consideration of social systems, notably societies, as his systems of reference. Malinowski, on the other hand, very conspicuously refused to do this and quite explicitly included the personality of the individual in his definition of systems of reference. It is not surprising that the two eminent anthropologists arrived at such very different empirical generalizations about societies, or more correctly we should say human action systems, in their respective work. See Talcott Parsons, "Malinowski and the Theory of Social Systems," in Raymond Firth, ed., Man and Culture (London: Routledge & Kegan Paul, 1957), reprinted herein as Chapter 3.

[22] Ralf Dahrendorf, Class and Class Conflict in Industrial Society (Palo Alto, Calif.: Stanford University Press, 1959), chap. 5, pp. 157–65.

A related polemical orientation is the claim frequently put forward that "functionalists" are incapable of accounting for social change: that is, their type of theory has a built-in "static" bias. This also is entirely untrue. If we have any claim to competence as social scientists, we must be fully aware that there are problems both of stability and of change, as there are problems of positive integration and malintegration.[23] The student's orientation to these problems is not a matter of the type of general theory he subscribes to but of his more empirical interests and his empirical judgments.

There is, however, one complicating consideration in this general area which needs to be made explicit. This derives from the very deep-seated human propensity to put forward what is perhaps best called "utopian" ideas—a propensity very strongly expressed in many ideologies. By utopian I mean specifically assertions about the desirability or feasibility of social states of affairs, statements which do not take adequate and competent account of the conditions necessary if the state of affairs discussed is in actual fact to be brought into being and/or maintained. Functional analysis, however, like any other solid and competent scientific procedure, must make a special point of pushing the analysis of conditions as far as it can. Since in response to utopian ideas it often says, yes, that might be nice, but for such and such specific reasons we think it cannot be accomplished, the sociologist of the functional persuasion, as well as others, is likely to be felt to be intolerably conservative because he seems to be placing obstacles in the way of the realization of what is clearly considered to be desirable. The problem of planned or advocated social change is scientifically, of course, a very complicated one. The errors in such a field are by no means only those pointing in a utopian direction—belief in the possibility of the impossible—but frequently errors in the other direction—failure to see the possibilities of change. In this, as in so many other contexts, the only remedy is command of information, careful analysis, and balanced judgment. None of us, however, can expect perfection in such a complex combination, and both types of errors are certain to recur again and again.

Functional Analysis in the Biological and the Psychosocial Disciplines

Merton makes very competent and effective use of the theoretical models of Walter B. Cannon as they were developed for physiological study. At the same time, however, he states a negative polemical attitude

[23] See Francesca Cancian, "Functional Analysis of Change," *American Sociological Review* 25, no. 6 (December 1960): 818–27.

toward the use of biological "analogies" by social scientists, citing the unfruitfulness of the use of many of them made by an earlier generation of sociologists such as Herbert Spencer, René Worms, and others.[24] I quite agree with his strictures on that set of uses. But I would like to raise certain further questions. First, it is interesting that in the biological sciences, as is also true of law, the term "analogy" does not have the pejorative connotations which have been so prominent in connection with its social science uses. For biologists, an analogy exists between two or more anatomical structures or physiological processes that are similar in function but differ from each other in mechanism. A classical example is the analogy between organs and processes of vision in the insects on the one hand, the vertebrates on the other.[25]

The existence of fruitful analogies between the phenomena of organic life and those of human personalities, societies, and cultures rests essentially on the common features and continuities of different types of living systems. To take one example, both sociologists and anthropologists went through a stage of violent objection to the use of evolutionary ideas with reference to human societies. Very often these objections have been based on misunderstanding of the biological theory of evolution and on its misapplication to human social phenomena. I, however, would subscribe firmly to the view that social science cannot be complete without the careful study of dimensions that can properly be called "evolutionary."

Let us cite, however, certain other examples. The first of these is the analogy between the concept "society," as used by at least some sociologists, and the concept "species," as used by some biologists of high standing. I think particularly of Ernst Mayr in his notable book *Populations, Species, and Evolution*.[26] Mayr defines a species in a very careful statement as having three primary foci or aspects. First, it is a reproduction community; for the most part, only members of the same species interbreed with each other. Put in these terms, it is a bounded system with respect to the reproductive function. Second, it is a territorial community; it has a habitat, or a niche, that in most cases is shared with other species, but the distribution of organisms of the same species is never random in territorial location. In this respect also it is a bounded system. Third, it is a genetic community that share a common genetic pool which is distinctive relative to the gene pools of all other species.

A human society, of course, is not a species. All human biologists,

[24] Herbert Spencer, *Essays*, 3 vols. (London: Longmans, 1858–76), and *A System of Synthetic Philosophy* (London: Appleton, 1862–96), vols. 9–10, *Principles of Sociology*; René Worms, *Organisme et Société* (Paris: Giard & Brière, 1896).

[25] George Wald, "Molecular Basis of Visual Excitation," *Science* 162, no. 3850 (October 11, 1968): 230–39.

[26] Ernst Mayr, *Populations, Species, and Evolution* (Cambridge, Mass.: Harvard University Press, 1970), esp. chap. 1.

to my knowledge, are agreed that there is only one human species. The analogy of the reproductive community is at the level of what biologists, including Mayr, call a "population," which is a subunit of a species; a society organizes a population, which is a subsector of the human species. It also does so with a territorial reference sometimes characterized by the phrase "politically organized." Finally, a society is also characterized by a common culture, although the sharing of this need not be absolutely uniform among its whole population, any more than every member of an organic species has the same genetic composition. Clearly, in all these respects the mechanisms by which a society functions as a bounded system differ from those by which organic species do, but the functions are clearly comparable.[27]

Another important analogy between the two classes of living systems lies in the applicability to both of the fundamental concepts *adaptation* and *integration*. Adaptation was, of course, one of the few key concepts of Darwin's theory of evolution [28] and is universally central to the conceptual armory of the biological sciences. It, of course, concerns the relations of a living system to its external environment, whether that system be an individual organism or a species.

Integration concerns the relations internal to the system of parts with each other. It is intimately related to the conception of the internal environment mentioned above. The integration of a system is in one primary aspect the adaptation of its parts to the internal environment. In our field, I, together with Neil Smelser, have conceived of the function of economic production as primarily an adaptive mechanism of the society in relation to several of its environments.[29] It will be remembered that we mean here not only the physical environment but also the personalities of individuals. Durkheim was probably the most seminal theorist in the field of studying the integration of social systems, notably in his conception of organic solidarity. As I have noted, this was also intimately connected with the sociological analogue of the biologists' conception of the internal environment.

Another way in which I differ from Merton is that, to my knowledge, he has never seriously attempted to achieve theoretical closure of the set of primary functions of a social system. I have attempted to do so in the four-function paradigm I have been using extensively for nearly twenty years. This paradigm developed out of the so-called pattern-variable

[27] For a sociological conception of a society, see Talcott Parsons, *Societies: Evolutionary and Comparative Perspectives* (Englewood Cliffs, N.J.: Prentice-Hall, 1966), chap. 2, and *The System of Modern Societies* (Englewood Cliffs, N.J.: Prentice-Hall, 1971), chap. 2.

[28] Charles Darwin, *The Origin of Species by Means of Natural Selection*, ed. J. W. Burrow (Harmondworth, Eng.: Penguin Books; first published, 1859).

[29] Talcott Parsons and Neil Smelser, *Economy and Society* (New York: Free Press, 1956).

scheme by emphasis on one specific set of relations among the four central pattern-variable pairs.[30]

I think it is now possible to say with confidence that this set as a whole is part of a highly generalized analogy between organic and sociocultural living systems. Unless the use of the terms "adaptation" and "integration" in the scheme is simply arbitrary labeling, those two concepts are central to it and are clearly of functional significance; that is to say, they designate aspects or phenomena of living systems that are of functional significance to the systems.

Besides adaptation and integration, a third consideration has to do with the concept goal attainment, or purposiveness, as it has so frequently been called. This has been extremely controversial among comparative psychologists for a long time, but I think we can say that the balance has now tipped in the direction of consensus about the fundamental importance of purposiveness in the behavior of living organisms. This goes across the line between psychology and biological science and is, for example, strongly endorsed by Mayr [31] in the paper referred to above, as it was by Tolman.[32] Of course, in the lower phylae of the evolutionary scale, goal directedness is relatively rudimentary, but when we come to virtually all of the higher species it is very central indeed. The concept is sometimes confused with that of adaptation bcause it has to do with relations between organism and external environment, but they should be analytically distinguished.

Finally, there is the concept that my associates and I have long called *pattern maintenance*. On the biological side, the analogy has been immediately strengthened by some of the most important advances of biological science in the last generation, especially those connected with molecular genetics.[33] I was first made aware of it by a statement made by an eminent biologist, Alfred Emerson,[34] at an interdisciplinary conference in which I participated. Emerson explicity used the terminology in the tech-

[30] Talcott Parsons, Robert F. Bales, and Edward A. Shils, *Working Papers in the Theory of Action* (New York: Free Press, 1953), esp. chaps. 2 and 4, and Talcott Parsons, "Some Problems of General Theory in Sociology," in John C. McKinney and Edward A. Tiryakian, eds., *Theoretical Sociology: Perspectives and Developments* (New York: Appleton-Century-Crofts, 1970).

[31] Mayr, "Teleological and Teleonomic," op cit.

[32] Edward C. Tolman, *Purposive Behavior in Animals and Men* (New York: Appleton-Century, 1932).

[33] See Curt Stern, "The Continuity of Genetics," and Gunther S. Stent, "DNA," in Gerald Holton, ed., *The Twentieth-Century Sciences: Studies in the Biography of Ideas* (New York: Norton, 1972).

[34] Alfred E. Emerson, "Homeostasis and the Comparison of Systems," in Roy R. Grinker, Sr., ed., *Towards a Unified Theory of Human Behavior: An Introduction to General Systems Theory* (New York: Basic Books, 1956). See also Talcott Parsons and Robert F. Bales, *Family, Socialization, and Interaction Process* (New York: Free Press, 1955), Appendix A.

nical biological sense, and his formula was that in the human action fields the *symbol* is analogous to the gene in the organic field. I think a better way of phrasing it would be to say that in the action sciences the patterns of culture are analogous to the genetic heritage of a species. This way of looking at it means drawing a careful distinction between the cultural and the social systems, which is parallel to that drawn by biologists between germ plasm on the one hand, somatoplasm on the other—or genotype and phenotype.

That there is an analogy from the functional point of view of control of the development of individual organisms or social units has been enormously strengthened by the dramatic development of the science of linguistics, again in about the last generation. Symbolic communication through speech utterances is, in the linguistic case, made possible through the operation of what some linguistic scientists call a "linguistic code" or Chomsky calls "deep structures." [35] Such codes are not themselves meaningful utterances at all but rather the symbolic frame of reference within which meaningful utterances can be formulated. The famous biochemical molecule DNA is looked at by microgeneticists from very much the same point of view as embodying the genetic code and a more detailed "program," which regulates the processes of synthesis of the biochemical components of the living cell, notably the proteins.[36]

The understanding of phenomena of this sort, extending all the way from the microbiology level through the theory of evolution and species formation to language and human society and culture has been enormously furthered by another development in general science, the relevance of which extends even beyond the sciences dealing with living systems. I refer to cybernetics and information theory. What is common between the genetic code and the gene pool on the one hand, linguistic codes and other aspects of human culture on the other, is that they can function as cybernetic mechanisms which, in certain fundamental respects, control life processes. This perspective has dealt what will probably turn out to be a death blow to the older ideas of biological "mechanism" and to various kinds of biopsychological reductionism which have been so prevalent in the history of the social disciplines. If we can successfully adapt sociological and other action science data to cybernetic models—and vice versa—we have the possibility of greatly enhanced analytical power in our fields, and an enormous range of codification between these and the other relevant fields.

There is a further point about cybernetics which bears very directly on functional analysis. This is the fact that functionally specialized or differentiated sectors of living systems stand in some kind of an order of cybernetically hierarchical control relative to each other. This is quite a

[35] Noam Chomsky, *Syntactic Structures* (The Hague: Mouton, 1957).
[36] Cf. Stent, "DNA."

fundamental principle of ordering of such systems and, as such, is an enormous aid to the solution of a wide variety of theoretical problems.

There is one further analogy in the present series which in my opinion helps enormously to clarify a very difficult and controversial sociological problem area. This is the problem of understanding the processes by which what we call "institutionalization" takes place. The commonest reference is to the incorporation of normative elements of cultural origin into the structure of a social system. Certain patterns of legal ordering can serve as a convenient example. The problem, however, comes up whenever new elements that have not previously been incorporated into social structure in fact become so.

The organic analogy is with nothing less than the famous principle of natural selection. The mere fact of the presence of certain genes in the gene pool of a species is not a sufficient determinant of their role in the generation of phenotypical organisms. For this to occur, there must be integration of the genetically given patterning with a series of exigencies defined by the nature of the species' life in its environment. In the course of meeting such exigencies, some genetically given patterns arising as variations or mutations, or from new combinations, will be built into the actual structure of the species and its members, whereas others will be eliminated by the processes of natural selection. Similarly, in social subject matters some cultural values or norms arising in processes of social change do in fact become constitutive of concrete social structures, whereas others fail to do so. The problem of institutionalization is the problem of understanding the exigencies and mechanisms by which these differential outcomes occur. For codification of the analogy, it is a crucially important fact that the theory of natural selection has made very substantial advances [37] since Darwin's first epoch-making formulation of it.[38] Had this not occurred, I do not think a sociologist would have perceived that there was potentially a very fruitful analogy present in this area.[39]

Finally, there is one still further theoretical development in the action theory area which seems to me to be an integral part of functional analysis and to hold very great promise for the furtherance of the dynamic analysis of process in systems of action, not least social systems. There are certain elements of analogy here also to comparable phenomena in the organic

[37] Mayr, *Populations, Species, and Evolution.*

[38] Darwin, *The Origin of Species.*

[39] Since submitting the manuscript of the present article, further investigation in the biological literature has convinced me that the analogy between institutionalization and natural selection can be extended also to the microbiological level. In this case the problem concerns the processes by which the patterns of DNA are, as the microbiologists themselves say, "transcribed" and "translated" through the mediation of RNA and the enzymes into the synthesis of proteins, which are the principal operative agents of the functioning of the cell. For further reference see Stent, "DNA," op. cit., and S. E. Luria, *Life: The Unfinished Experiment* (New York: Charles Scribner's Sons, 1973).

world, but the analogies are not so highly developed or well known as in some of the other cases. I refer to the role in action processes of what I and some of my associates have come to call "generalized symbolic media of interchange." The prototypical case is money, which has come to play such a very important role in highly developed and differentiated economic systems.[40] Indeed, some go so far as to say that the core of economic theory is to be found in the understanding of monetary phenomena. Money, however, is a paradigmatic case of a phenomeon that is high in information but very low in energy. This point was already understood by the classical economists as expressed in their formula that money has value in exchange but no value in use. It is essentially a phenomenon of symbolic communication. Money is anchored, institutionally speaking, in the property system; hence, its special relation to economic relations.

It has been widely assumed that money was an entirely unique phenomenon in social systems, but there has developed increasingly cogent reason to question this. In fact, we have identified three other generalized media that operate at the social system level, becoming visible, of course, only when the system's level of differentiation has advanced sufficiently far. These are, specifically, political power, influence, and value commitments. To fit them into the paradigm of generalized symbolic media, since their common sense meanings are not adequately specific or consistently clarified, they have to be redefined in technical senses. An attempt to do this has been made in three of my essays over a period of years.[41] More recently, it has proved possible to develop a comparable set of generalized media that are conceived to operate at the level of the general system of action, not the social system. We have defined these as intelligence, performance-capacity, affect, and definition of the situation—a list owing a great deal in different ways to W. I. Thomas, to Freud, and to Piaget.[42]

I will not take space in the present brief essay to attempt to explicate them, especially the latter set which operates at the general level of action. One publication [43] has made a beginning, but a full statement is yet to be made. However, they have been very much further developed in one re-

[40] Cf. J. M. Keynes, *General Theory of Employment, Interest and Money* (New York: Harcourt Brace Jovanovich, 1936).

[41] Talcott Parsons, "On the Concept of Political Power," "On the Concept of Influence," and "On the Concept of Value-Commitments," in *Politics and Social Structure* (New York: Free Press, 1969), chaps. 13, 14, and 16.

[42] William I. Thomas, *The Unadjusted Girl* (Boston: Little, Brown, 1931); Sigmund Freud, *The Interpretation of Dreams*, vols. 4 and 5 of the *Standard Edition of the Complete Psychological Works of Sigmund Freud*, trans. James Strachey (London: Hogarth Press and Institute of Psycho-Analysis, 1953), esp. chap. 7 (first published, 1900); and Jean Piaget and Bärbel Inhelder, *The Growth of Logical Thinking from Childhood to Adolescence* (New York: Basic Books, 1958).

[43] Parsons, "Some Problems of General Theory in Sociology." Also Talcott Parsons and Gerald M. Platt, *The American University* (Cambridge, Mass.: Harvard University Press, 1973). See Chapter 10 of this volume.

cently published book (*The American University*, with Gerald M. Platt, 1973) and a second one in preparation, the title of which has not been finally settled upon yet but which will focus on the integrative problems of social systems.

When I said above that the media of interchange are integrally part of the functional context, one of the things I wished to convey was that their clarification and use as analytical tools would not have been thinkable had it not been possible to see them in a functional perspective. They operate essentially as mechanisms that regulate the flow of interactional transactions among the different unit components of social and other action systems. Again, as I noted, they fit very definitely into the cybernetic frame of reference because they are uniformly, predominantly mechanisms for the exchange of information, not of energy, and have functions of control, for example, of the allocation and combination of factors and outputs.

There are, presumably, many analogues at organic levels. One of the most prominent sets of them, significant for physiological process, is the hormones, knowledge of which was relatively new in Cannon's day and of which he made a great deal, for example, in presenting a rather detailed analysis of the nature and functions of insulin in the regulation of levels of blood sugar.[44] In recent years, the microbiologists have been paying intensified attention to another set—namely, the enzymes—which play an essential role in the synthesis of proteins.[45] Finally, there have been immense advances in the recent period in understanding the functioning of the central nervous systems of the higher animals, including, of course, man, and it would seem that neural process is essentially a communication process within the central nervous system and between it and other parts of the organism. With improved relations between the two sets of disciplines and further development within each set, a much fuller picture of these extremely important phenomena should gradually take shape.

Conclusion

In recent years there has been considerable talk about the decline of concern with "structural-functional" theory, or, as I prefer to call it, "functional analysis," in favor of other types of conceptualization and theoretical generalization. It is my considered opinion that, to paraphrase Mark Twain's famous remark about the rumors of his own death, these rumors are "slightly exaggerated." I think Kingsley Davis, in his Presidential Address to the American Sociological Association, was nearer the

44 W. B. Cannon, *Wisdom of the Body*, op cit.
45 Cf. Stent, "DNA."

mark when he took the view that there was less talk about functional analysis because essentially all serious theory in the field had become functional and took this for granted.[46] Of course, there will be considerable difference of opinion on the point and there are, indeed, exceptions, particularly where what I would think of as theoretical considerations are subordinated to political movements and goal seeking and where generalization, insofar as it figures, tends to become mainly empirical generalization, as in many strictly quantitative studies.

I think the kind of developments I have sketched in this paper indicate a very lively intellectual ferment in this field, and it should not be forgotten that a quite substantial number of people are self-consciously working wihin a somewhat similar framework or others that bear sufficiently close relation to it so that it would be arbitrary to allocate them to radically different "schools." Not least important to note is the fact that I think the great development of economic theory on the one side, and of linguistics on the other, should definitely be judged to belong to the category of functional analysis.

I have in the present paper strongly stressed how the kinds of developments with which I have been concerned in the social field relate to those in the biological sciences and, to a lesser degree, in linguistics. One could say comparable things about a good deal of psychology, political science, and social anthropology. Within all this, however, the relation to the biological sciences seems particularly impressive because they cover such a wide range of the problems of living systems and some of them occur at such a high level of theoretical development and generality. Given more space, I could have included others, but I think the ones reviewed will suffice.

I think we can look forward to at least a strong possibility, if not a probability, that in coming years there will be a good many advances beyond analogy in anything like the usual sense to very fruitful interaction between the various disciplines involved, especially insofar as suggestions emanating from one of them turn out to be usable to develop theory in one or more others. I, for one, find the present reality and prospects very exciting and do not have in the least the feeling of being identified with a moribund theoretical perspective. Let us salute Robert Merton for his highly creative role in developing the foundations of this challenging intellectual situation.

---

[46] Kingsley Davis, "The Myth of Functional Analysis as a Special Method in Sociology and Anthropology," *American Sociological Review* 24, no. 6 (December 1959): 757–72. Presidential Address read at the annual meeting of the American Sociological Association, Chicago, Ill., September 1959.

5. The Relations between Biological and Socio-Cultural Theory

THE RELATIONSHIP between biological and social theory has been a subject of considerable intellectual concern ever since the publication of Darwin's *Origin of Species* and the rise of disciplines concerned with human social and cultural phenomena in the late nineteenth century. Our mutual interest in these matters goes back to a conference held at Bellagio, Italy, in 1969 which resulted in the publication of a *Daedalus* issue on "The Making of Modern Sciences" (published in hard cover as *The Twentieth-Century Sciences,* edited by Gerald Holton, 1972). The belief that certain of the questions raised or implied at the conference deserved further consideration led to the organization of two planning meetings held at the House of the Academy in 1972 and 1973. Subsequent informal discussions indicate that the promise of a fruitful interplay of ideas between biological and social theory continues to grow.

Underlying this mounting intellectual interest is the conviction that, over a broad front, a notable convergence has taken place on the two sides of this particular intellectual "fence" which merits substantial further exploration. An important keynote was sounded by the late Lawrence J. Henderson in his book, *The Fitness of the Environment,* written more than a half-century ago (Beacon Press, 1959; first published by Macmillan Co., 1913). Henderson presented a very general treatment of the nature of living systems on the assumption that they were set off by boundaries from their environment. The human skin is such a boundary. In Henderson's own phrasing, these systems presupposed first, complexity, by which he meant the potential for high degrees of differentiation among the components which came to constitute such systems. The second property, regulation, was defined along lines worked out by the French physiologist

---

From *Bulletin of the American Academy of Arts and Sciences,* Vol. XXIX, No. 8 (May, 1976) (In collaboration with A. Hunter Dupree). Reprinted by permission.

Claude Bernard, by Henderson himself, and by his contemporary, Walter B. Cannon. An example of regulation, stressed by Cannon, was the maintenance of a constant body temperature by mammals. Henderson termed the third characteristic, metabolism, that is, the combination of components introduced into the organism from its environment, the processing of these inputs, like food and oxygen within the organism, and the output to the environment of various products of these processes, including especially the energizing of behavior. The work Henderson did later in his life on the sociological thought of Vilfredo Pareto was an important stimulus to the extension of this analysis of the nature of living systems to the socio-cultural level.

The directions of the search for theoretical relationships may be made somewhat clearer by brief mention of the major topic which emerged at the Academy's two planning meetings and in subsequent discussions. One of the most important is the idea that through the appearance of language and related symbolic systems, a duality of determinants in the life process has developed at the human socio-cultural level. This duality bears a strong theoretical resemblance to the one very fully established in biological science between, on the one hand, the genetic constitution of species and their constituent individual organisms, and on the other, what biologists call the phenotypical level of organization. It is the phenotype which directly interacts with the detailed features of the non-living environment and with other species. Some twenty years ago, the biologist, Alfred Emerson, promulgated a short-hand formula of the equivalence of gene and symbol to designate this relationship. Preliminary exploration seems to indicate that this is a fruitful analogy, in the nonpejorative sense of the term "analogy" which has been prevalent in the biological sciences.

Of course, the role of genetic heritage in the organic world is comprehensible, in terms of modern biological theory, only because of its relation to the complementary conceptual complex which falls under the heading of natural selection. With certain qualifications, the genetic factors are, in the organic evolutionary process, the primary sources of evolutionary innovation. However, variations at this level do not have uniform prospects of contributing to evolutionary consolidation in subsequent generations of the species and other organic aggregates which are under consideration. The complex of processes which are responsible for a kind of winnowing process among the effects of genetic variations has come to be called natural selection. Evidence from the recently developed field of microgenetics and microbiology at the level of the particular cell suggests that closely analogous processes take place here.

It has come to be the conviction of the group discussing this topic that similar selective and consolidating processes are at work in socio-cultural systems at the human symbolic level and that there are many formal similarities between these two sets of processes, which may be summed up

under the concept "institutionalization." There are many resemblances between these processes of success or failure in institutionalization and those of natural selection as the latter have come to be conceived in biological theory.

Perhaps the broadest basis for the promise of comparability between the organic and the socio-cultural types of living systems lies in an intellectual movement which has gained increasing prominence in the middle third of the twentieth century—cybernetics, a concept associated with Norbert Wiener. However, cybernetics had extremely important antecedents in physiology in Henderson's day, notably in the work of Claude Bernard, extended by Henderson himself, and, as noted, by Cannon. It is safe to say that this kind of thinking became an increasingly prominent aspect of the theoretical discussions in both the field of evolutionary theory and of microbiology in the generation past.

The central theme of this line of thought is the relation between the genetic and the selective components of the determinants of both organic maintenance and evolutionary change. The cybernetic formula concerns the possibility that, under appropriate conditions, systems high in information but low in energy can control systems high in energy but low in information. There seems to be general agreement in biological circles that the genetic factors in the biological process are predominantly centered on informational content and that such energy factors as the organic energy released by metabolic processes of oxidation can be and are, in fact, controlled by these informational factors. Indeed, it is very striking to social scientists that biologists have gone as far as they have in adopting linguistic terminology to characterize their own preoccupations. For example, DNA is said to carry information which is "transcribed" onto RNA which, in turn, is "translated" through the action of enzymes into the synthesis of proteins at the cellular level. Further, the three successive genes in DNA, called a "codon," have been designated by microbiologists as "subject," "verb," and "predicate." (Gunther S. Stent, "DNA", in Gerald Holton, ed., The Twentieth-Century Sciences, pp. 198–226).

The development of linguistics has been one of the most important elements of the more general intellectual revolution to which we refer, and is, in our opinion, closely linked to developments in social and cultural theory in the social sciences. Indeed, we consider linguistics to constitute a very important intellectual bridge between the biological and the socio-cultural sciences.

Underlying this whole conception is the fact that, whatever may be the case with regard to the nonliving cosmos, living systems require some kind of relatively constant "code" or "program" and another set of symbols which implement the genetically given patterns at the phenotypical levels in organisms. In the same way in the socio-cultural field,

patterns of culture and biological organisms interact through the process of institutionalization.

Admittedly, we are faced with a highly complex field that is far from being codified at this juncture in intellecutal history. Taking this project seriously involves the hope, indeed, we may go a step further to say the faith, that serious theoretical work on the borderlines between biological and socio-cultural systems may make an important contribution to their eventual synthesis, understandable in terms of a wider conceptual framework acceptable both to biologists and social scientists.

6. Review of Harold J. Bershady, *Ideology and Social Knowledge**

Since this book is predominantly devoted to the analysis and evaluation of my own theoretical work, there is a certain delicacy in my undertaking to review it. From certain points of view, I would have preferred to see it competently reviewed by someone not so intimately involved, but the editor has been relatively insistent that I undertake it, and I have consented to do so.

First, I think that the title is not altogether appropriate. The book has rather little to do with the theory of ideology except insofar as the author stressed that many of the critics of my work have imputed ideological positions to me and have themselves been actuated by ideological considerations. The main concern of the book, however, is with the structure of theory in a sense which is not usually classed as ideology.[1]

The book is an important contribution and surely both one of the most competent and most sympathetic analyses of my own work. Professor Bershady quite correctly points out that the theoretical position has not remained unchanged over a rather long career of publication. But in spite of important differences between the stress on the means–ends schema in *The Structure of Social Action,* the more "structural–functional" position of a somewhat later period and the still different position of perhaps the last fifteen years, Bershady notes a certain constancy of fundamental theoretical aims throughout. I think he is correct in this judgment. This is the more acceptable to me in that Bershady does not make this stress the ground of an attack alleging me to be a rigidly fixed person unable to change views in the light of developing evidence.

From *Sociological Inquiry,* Toronto, Canada, Vol. 44, no. 3 (Fall 1974), pp. 215–221. Reprinted by permission.

* Oxford, England: Basil Blackwell, 1973.

[1] For example, see R. K. Merton in his essay, "A Paradigm for the Sociology of Knowledge," who rather strongly stresses this distinction. The essay is reprinted in his recent volume, edited by N. W. Storer, *The Sociology of Science* (Chicago: University of Chicago Press, 1973).

It is, of course, quite correct to use the terminology of a relatively famous discussion with Robert Merton. From the time when the outline of my first book, *The Structure of Social Action,* took shape, I have been deeply concerned with the position and possibilities of what I have called "general theory," [2] specifically in contrast to Merton's stress on "theories of the middle range." [3]

I have also consistently believed in and stressed the essential role in general theory of universalistically defined concepts and abstract analytical generalizations. Bershady quite consciously interprets this in terms of an attempt to avoid the kinds of relativism which have played so prominent a place in the tradition of German historicism and related movements of thought. From the very beginning of my acquaintance with his work, I was very greatly impressed by Weber's concern with these problems and by his insistence that the historicist position was not scientifically acceptable.[4]

This background in relation to Weber's position raises what to me is an interesting question about Bershady's book. This concerns the rather scant attention he pays to the importance in my own development of the critical and comparative analysis of the theoretical work of a group of predecessors. Indeed, it was only through the analysis of the work of Alfred Marshall, Pareto, Durkheim, and Weber, that I was able to arrive at an autonomous theoretical position of my own. Without the autonomy of an independent position, furthermore, it seems to me that it would not have been possible to clarify the extremely important convergence which I maintain was to be found in the work of this group. Further critical analysis of others' work, notably perhaps Freud's, has also been extremely important to me.

Related to this is another rather curious omission, or at any rate, playing down—as it seems to me—on Bershady's part. This has to do with his lack of at all intensive concern with what came to be the most important substantive problem of the early phases of my theoretical work, namely, the problem of the relations between economic theory and what at the time I thought of as sociological theory. This concern provided the sole rationale for including a study of the work of Alfred Marshall and an

---

[2] T. Parsons, "The Present Position and Prospects of Systematic Theory in Sociology" and "The Prospects of Sociological Theory," in *Essays in Sociological Theory,* revised edition (N.Y.: The Free Press, 1954).

[3] R. K. Merton, *Social Theory and Social Structure,* revised and enlarged edition (N.Y.: The Free Press, 1957).

[4] This issue has arisen again quite recently in what might be called a certain controversy with Reinhard Bendix. See my review (*Contemporary Sociology,* 1972, 1: 200–203) of the book by Reinhard Bendix and Guenther Roth, *Scholarship and Partisanship: Essays on Max Weber* (Berkeley, Calif.: University of California Press, 1971). In that book Bendix took what seemed to me the rather extreme position that Weber should not be classed as concerned with general theory in any deep sense, but rather that he used theoretical conceptualization as a kind of useful tool in furthering his historical studies. This is to say that Bendix tends to put Weber's role as a historian far ahead of his role as a theorist.

exceedingly important part of the rationale for the amount of attention I gave to that of Pareto, and it surely was not absent from the impact of Max Weber's work, and indeed of Durkheim's.

It was a revisit to this set of theoretical problems, stimulated by the invitation to give the Marshall Lectures at the University of Cambridge in 1953–1954, which further led to or played a very important part in the initiation of what I would now consider to be the last main phase which might even be called the "post-structural-functional" phase. The primary innovations of that phase, theoretically speaking, started with the reorganization of the pattern variable scheme to produce what I and others have been calling the "four-function schema." The four-function schema then has underlain increasing concern with what I have been calling the general level of action as distinct from the social system alone and has been essential to the development of the analysis of generalized symbolic media of interchange. The analysis of the general action level has so far been carried furthest in the book in which I collaborated with Gerald Platt, *The American University*.[5] Of course it is important that this was not available to Bershady for his own book since it was not published until the Fall of 1973.

Perhaps this is the most appropriate point to come to a recurring theme of Bershady's discussion. This is the theme of the importance for my work of a philosophy of science model of what he calls the "covering law" conception of scientific theory—a term which I understand through personal conversation with him he has adopted primarily from Hempel.[6] The conception is that scientific theory should eventuate in the formulation of laws in what I think could be called in terms of his historic models, above all, the Newtonian sense. On the whole Bershady tends to impute to me this ambition for "sociology" and I think he has a good deal of justification for this imputation.

In my own case, this certainly goes back to the prestige of the analytical model of the "logico-deductive" system which derived laws from a kind of Aristotelian logic of major and minor premises verified by specific empirical data. I was certainly encouraged in this view of scientific theory by L. J. Henderson and by Pareto as seen in the light of Henderson's interpretations.[7]

One particularly important modification of this tradition, however, which Bershady does not stress, played a decisive role in my early theo-

[5] T. Parsons and G. M. Platt, in collaboration with J. Smelser, *The American University* (Cambridge, Mass.: Harvard University Press, 1973).

[6] C. G. Hempel, *Aspects of Scientific Exploration* (N.Y.: The Free Press, 1965).

[7] L. J. Henderson, *Pareto's General Sociology: A Physiologist's Interpretation* (Cambridge, Mass.: Harvard University Press, 1935). See also, B. Barber (ed.), *L. J. Henderson on the Social System* (Chicago, Ill.: Heritage of Sociology Series, University of Chicago Press, 1970).

retical development. This was Whitehead's conception of the importance of what he called "the fallacy of misplaced concreteness." [8] Whitehead applied this concept above all to interpretation of what had changed in physical science between the era of Newton and that of his own lifetime which was the era of relativity and eventually quantum physics. His position was that the Newtonian view was not in any simpleminded sense "wrong," but had tended, especially among its philosophical interpreters, to generalize the relevance of a rather particularized conceptual scheme to a broader range and set of levels of phenomena than were justified.

For me, this perspective was particularly important in connection with the problem of the relations between economic and what at that time I interpreted to be sociological theory. Economic theory, which had undergone a somewhat comparable process of generalization of applicability to that of the Newtonian theory of the solar system, had in certain quarters been claimed to be the key to the understanding of human social interaction in general.[9] It was this tendency of thinking which was my most important polemical foil in searching out the sociological premises of people who, like Marshall implicitly, and like Pareto and Weber explicitly, had challenged the all sufficiency of economic theory. I think that I was fully aware even in this period that the broader sociological theory I attempted, borrowing very heavily from preceding authors, to formulate, did not fully meet the criteria of developing a new, if one will in the present subject matter, "post-economic" theory of social interaction. The task of doing so should define highly important concerns of the social theorist.

I think a certain turn occurred when I diverted my attention somewhat from preoccupation with the economic–sociological problem and began to consider the theory of the social system in what to this day has stuck with me as a label, a "structural–functional" sense. One of the decisive intellectual influences governing that turn was that of the popular book of the physiologist W. B. Cannon, *The Wisdom of the Body*. This seemed to me also to have a certain fit with a number of other intellectual traditions which were in a position to avoid the basic dilemma, consciousness of which Bershady quite correctly imputes to me, between the Scylla of historical relativism and the Charybdis of what my late colleague Samuel Stouffer picturesquely called "dust-bowl empiricism."

If I was unduly partial to the covering law model, that is, that of a logico-deductive system of which the great historical example has been that of Newton, for a good many years, I was early sensitized to one prob-

---

[8] A. N. Whitehead, *Science and the Modern World* (N.Y.: Macmillan, 1925).

[9] By no means only by Marxians, but in an even subtler way by utilitarian-oriented economists such as Lionel Robbins and Milton Friedman. See especially Robbin's *An Essay on the Nature and Significance of Economic Science*, and my review article in the *Quarterly Journal of Economics*, 4: 511–545.

lem about it, namely, the problem of level of abstraction. This came to me, above all, as noted earlier, through the work of Whitehead in his notable book, *Science and the Modern World,* and particularly his notion of the "fallacy of misplaced concreteness."

In the course of a good many years, however, it gradually became clear to me that there was a certain sense in which Whitehead had not gone far enough. His formulation served my purposes admirably with relation to the problem of the relations of economic and sociological theory at the level at which I apprehended it in that phase, notably, leaning on L. J. Henderson, Schumpeter, and Pareto. Gradually, however, the implications of a more "functional" approach began to elaborate and develop. This, finally, as a result of certain developments starting from the pattern variable scheme, eventuated in the four-function paradigm which has ever since its appearance in the later 1950's been a central point of reference for my more general theoretical thinking. One major development which came out of this was a rather drastic. revision of the concept of social system and in particular society, making any social system including societies a member of one of four primary categories of functional subsystems of the general system of action.

The beginnings of this development were clearly present in *Toward A General Theory of Action* and *The Social System,* but they flowered in the years after that, as Bershady clearly points out, especially with the addition of a fourth primary system which for a number of years I identified as the "behavioral organism," in addition to social system, cultural system, and personality system.[10]

In certain respects these developments represent the culmination of a long process of modification of the more general point of view toward theory. Some of its groundwork was laid in the very early days, but, again, as I have noted, the particularly important influence was that of W. B. Cannon in *The Wisdom of the Body,* which became available to me and made a major impression in the period immediately following the completion of *The Structure of Social Action.* On recently rereading Robert Merton's famous essay on "Manifest and Latent Functions," [11] I have been struck by the fact that Merton also was immensely impressed by this book. At any rate, it was largely responsible, along with certain influences emanating from Durkheim and from the British type of social anthropology,

---

[10] I have accepted a revision of this scheme occasioned by a notable paper by Victor and Charles Lidz, who have proposed that the behavioral organism should be replaced by what they call the "behavioral system," the main content of which they base on the work in cognitive psychology of Jean Piaget. See Victor Lidz and Charles Lidz, "The Psychology of Intelligence of Jean Piaget and Its Place in the Theory of Action," in J. Loubser, R. Baum, A. Effrat and V. Lidz (eds.), *Explorations in General Theory in Social Science* (N.Y.: Free Press, 1976).

[11] R. K. Merton, "Manifest and Latent Functions," in *Social Theory and Social Structure,* revised edition, N.Y.: Free Press, 1957.

for my moving from a point of view which, as Bershady quite correctly notes, centered on the means–ends schema to a functional type of analysis of systems. This is the primary basis of labeling my work as "structural-functionalism." I am very grateful to Bershady that he does not take the permanent appropriateness of this label with the same seriousness that many commentators on my work have done.

In the sense meant by most of the commentators, especially those who take a negatively critical stance, I am no longer a "structural-functionalist," but one person with whom I recently discussed the problem said, "Protesting against that label is totally useless—you're stuck with it.' " Even if this is true in the jungle of certain kinds of communication, I would still like to be on record as protesting that it is no longer totally appropriate.[12]

This turned out not to be a permanently stable phase of theoretical orientation, but to lead over into a phase in which three developments have been particularly salient. As I just suggested, the foundation of these developments lay in the four function paradigm.[13]

The first primary fruit of the four function paradigm stage was a major revision in the conception which had been put forward in *The Structure of Social Action* of the theoretical relations between economic and "sociological" theory. This was documented in *Economy and Society* in which I collaborated with Neil J. Smelser and which was based on the Marshall Lectures. Again, one of my milder strictures against Bershady's book is that he does not emphasize the continuing importance of this problem.

When, however, in the previous paragraph I put the word sociological in quotation marks, I had in mind the revision of the place of the concept of social system in the general system of action to which I referred a brief time ago. Before the development of the four–function paradigm and related considerations, I had been willing to follow Pareto and most other theorists in considering "society" to be a nearly concrete entity which did not need to be treated in terms of a very special kind of procedure of analytical abstraction, a procedure the main pattern of which I derived from Whitehead's views.[14]

Bershady does introduce, toward the end of the book, a rather brief discussion of what some of us have been calling, to use an awkward

---

[12] I have commented on the status of this concept in my contribution to the Festschrift in honor of Robert Merton, edited by Lewis Coser, and reprinted as Chapter 4 in this volume.

[13] The primary rationale of that paradigm was more fully stated in print in my essay, "Some Problems of General Theory in Sociology," included in the volume edited by J. C. McKinney and E. A. Tiryakian, *Theoretical Sociology* (N.Y.: Appleton-Century-Crofts, 1970).

[14] T. Parsons, "Pareto's Approach to the Construction of A Theory of the Social System," in the Proceedings of the *Convegno Internazionale su Vilfredo Pareto*, sponsored by the Accademia Nazionale dei Lincei, Rome, 1975.

phrase, the "generalized symbolic media of interchange." The prominence of this theme in my own work was a direct outgrowth of the reorientation with respect to the problem of the status of the relations between economic and "sociological" theory which was documented in *Economy and Society*. The analysis of that book, one might say, was just on the verge of exploiting the idea of media. This entailed a sociological reanalysis of money, as, in a sense, the prototypical medium, but more important than that, a program of generalization from the case of money to that of other media, first at the social system level, and considerably later at that of the general system of action. It seems to me that Bershady's discussion of this endeavor is one of the less satisfactory parts of his book—an impression somewhat confirmed by personal conversations with him since the publication of his book.

Quite seriously, I do not consider that the theoretical foundations of the conception of generalized media are really shaky. I have felt on very firm ground in an interpretation of money as an institutionalized phenomenon resting very heavily on the authority of the classical economists and of Keynes.[15] I think it has been possible from a sociological point of view to introduce certain extensions of the complex with which they were concerened, notably with respect to relevance of the institutions of property and contract in terms derived particularly from Durkheim's work. The fundamentals of their analysis, centering about the conceptions of money as a medium of exchange which has value in exchange but not in use, and the extensions of that to consider money as a "measure of value" and a "store of value" remain completely unshaken. The major problem has been whether the same principles, with the appropriate alterations of reference to content, could be generalized beyond the case of money to that of other media.

In this connection the first case, and I think it is legitimate to regard it as a test case, was that of political power. The result of work on that is documented in my paper "On the Concept of Political Power." [16] Whereas dealing with money from the special sociological point of view of its status as a medium could rest on very solid reference points in the views of the most eminent economic theorists, unfortunately the same is not true with respect to the concept of power conceived as another such medium. When I was working on that, I made, with the help of a very able research assistant (now Professor Leon H. Mayhew, University of California at Davis), a careful study of discussions of the nature of power among the most eminent political theorists, from Hobbes on. The result

[15] J. M. Keynes, *General Theory of Employment, interest and Money* (London: Macmillan, 1936).

[16] T. Parsons, "On the Concept of Political Power," *Proceedings of the American Philosophical Society* (Vol. 107, no. 3, June 1963); reprinted in T. Parsons, *Sociological Theory and Modern Society* (N.Y.: The Free Press, 1967), and in *Politics and Social Structure* (N.Y.: The Free Press, 1969).

was to make clear that recent consensus among political theorists has been in reconfirming the Hobbesian conception (which incidentally was taken over by Max Weber) that essentially power is the capacity to prevail in getting what one wants in a system of human relations, independent of the resistance against this which is offered by interaction partners. This conception is not at all sufficiently specific from my point of view. It treats, for example, both money and influence as "forms of power."

Having ascertained this and in the search for a more adequately specific conception, several things emerged. One was the importance of the collective reference. I have recently defined power as the capacity to formulate collectively acceptable or legitimated decisions which in turn are binding on the collectivity and, of course, the same reasoning applies to the actions involved in the implementation of such decisions. The factor of coercion merging at the extreme into the use of force is referable at a more general theoretical level to that of the bindingness of decisions. It can scarcely occur, for example, that a decision is announced as binding by government authority and that, at the same time, failure to comply with the implications of the decision be treated indifferently by the responsible collective implementors.

Another centrally important theoretical problem with respect to power was that of whether power can correctly be considered to be a "zero sum" phenomenon. There has been impressive authority on the side of so considering it. This, however, would introduce a quite fundamental difference from money where the phenomenon of increase of the monetary supply through credit creation is clearly fundamental and fully recognized by economists. On balance, the evidence seems to be clear that an analogous feature of power systems also exists, that power can in fact be created by certain processes of leadership which are analogous to the banking operations involved in the creation of credit in the monetary field.

Radical as this way of looking at political power is, it seems to me to have stood the test of a good deal of critical analysis, and to be institutionally grounded in the institutional complexes of leadership and, above all, of authority in a way that is directly parallel to the institutional grounding of money in the complexes of property and contract.

However that may be, I and my colleagues have at the social system level extended the conception of generalized media to include two further examples beside money and political power, namely, what we have called *influence,* which like power, has to be redefined in our own technical sense and should not be understood in the senses current in general usage. We think of influence as a medium above all concerned with the function of integration at the social system level. In addition to that, we have put forward the conception of *value-commitments* which we think of as anchored in the pattern-maintenance subsystem of societies. I will not take space to elaborate these somewhat difficult conceptual complexes further on the

present occasion, but will refer the reader to two articles in *Politics and Social Structure*.[17]

In certain respects, closely connected with the theme of the place in action systems of generalized media of interchange is that of the theoretical analysis of social change, culminating eventually in the conception of what might most precisely be referred to as "action evolution," but which is usually called socio-cultural evolution. I would like to present my thinking in this area on two levels. The first and simpler level Bershady somehow does not mention at all. This concerns a paradigm which I have called that of a single phase of a process of "progressive" action evolution. By progressive is not meant a reference to total social progress, but in the first instance a process of change, the outcome of which is a substantial increase in the adaptive capacity of the system of reference in relation to its environments. The four categories we have used in this connection are differentiation, adaptive upgrading, inclusion, and value-generalization.[18] The version of the paradigm stated in the Vallier volume is a revision of its original statement in an article in *Rural Sociology* [19] which has been rather widely quoted. The later and more complete version should, however, be used for critical reference.

On the whole, this schema seems to have held up rather well in a certain series of empirical tests in a variety of historical–sociological problem areas. One such area, for example, is the religious development of Western Christendom from the stage of medieval Catholic unity to the stage of modern denominational pluralism and ecumenicism.[20] Another major example is to be found in the complicated relations between cultural and social system reference levels which have been concerned with the "educational revolution." [21]

There is an extremely important connection between the analysis of the media and the paradigm of phases of progressive change. This is the theme that the media constitute mechanisms whereby an action system is able to achieve a new level of "value-added" combination. This implies, on the one hand, a freedom of action for its individual component member-units, but on the other hand, new mechanisms of control which make the functioning of such freedoms feasible at increasingly generalized levels.

[17] T. Parsons, "On the Concept of Influence" and "On the Concept of Value-Commitments," in *Politics and Social Structure, op. cit.*, Ch. 15 and 16.

[18] The fullest theoretical exposition of this schema is to be found in Parsons, "Comparative Studies and Evolutionary Change," in I. Vallier (ed.), *Comparative Methods in Sociology* (Berkeley, Calif.: University of California Press, 1971), PP. 97–139.

[19] T. Parsons, "Some Considerations on the Theory of Social Change," *Rural Sociology* (Vol. 26, no. 3, September 1961).

[20] See, T. Parsons, *The System of Modern Societies* (Englewood Cliffs, N.J.: Prentice-Hall, 1971).

[21] See Parsons and Platt, *The American University, op. cit.*

I have developed these themes of the subtle relations between freedom and control in the three articles referred to above on the social system media other than money.

The building of these considerations into a more generalized theory of action evolution involves very considerable further theoretical complications. We think that in this connection the analogy or parallel of the biological theory of evolution is particularly crucial. There is one point in particular which has not been widely recognized by social scientists. This is that, in biological evolutionary theory, certainly ever since Darwin, there has been universally assumed to be a bifactoral set of determinants. One of these has concerned the genetic heritage of species and other intergenerational biological systems. The other has concerned the complex relations between this genetic heritage and the complex of environmental factors to which members of such species have been exposed.[22] In catchwords one may put it that one primary focus of the problems of biological evolution has concerned genetic composition, the other has concerned natural selection as the primary focus of interchange between phenotypical units of biological species and populations and their respective environments.

We think that the analogy holds up extremely well in the socio-cultural field. We would conceive what in a very broad and hence confessedly vague sense have often been called the "patterns of culture" to constitute the analogue of the gene pool,[23] to use a phrase common among contemporary biologists, for socio-cultural systems. We do not, however, consider that the potentialities of a genetic component of this size and complexity for embodiment in actual concrete living organisms is any simple function of the constitution of the genetic complex itself. Quite the contrary, we conceive that there is a complex process of interaction at the biological level between genetic and environmental conditions, and at the socio-cultural, between cultural components and what have in German tradition been called the "real factors" of the determination of social structures and processes.[24] Clearly it is only in limiting cases that one-to-one correspondences of the neat sort which are always central points of reference for argument appear. Most of the interrelationships turn out to be distressingly complex when they are carefully analyzed.

However that may be, I do not think that Bershady's verdict is completely just when he suggests that the approach in my own work to evolu-

---

[22] Cf. E. Mayr, *Populations, Species and Evolution* (Cambridge, Mass.: Harvard University Press, 1970).

[23] See A. Emerson, "Homeostasis and the Comparisons of Systems," in R. R. Grinker, Sr. (ed.), *Towards a Unified Theory of Human Behavior*, N.Y.: Basic Books, 1956.

[24] The reference is to the ubiquitous discussions in the German literature of 50 years and more ago of the relations of and presumptive priorities among *Idealfaktoren* and *Realfaktoren*.

tionary theory is "confused." It surely leaves innumerable problems, either altogether or to important degrees unresolved, but I do not myself have the feeling that there is a basic set of theoretical–philosophical ambiguities which vitiates the whole procedure. On the contrary, I think a lot of this work is proceeding on a rather firm foundation, but I have not yet had opportunity to follow up with adequate clarity, precision, and detail many of the intermediating mechanism problems.

This brings me back to a slightly more commonsense set of considerations which have figured prominently in the literature, namely, the question of the achievements of this type of theorizing in facilitating the solution of problems "in the middle range" to use Merton's formulation. The middle range, like the middle class in social stratification theory, is not easy to define in terms of its boundaries. I have already called attention to Bershady's relative neglect of the problem complexes in my own personal intellectual history centering on the one hand on the problems of the relation of economic and sociological theory, and on the other of concern with the modern professions as a sociologically significant phenomenon.

It may well be that the fact that I have not followed a simple and consistent program of research in middle range matters has contributed to the impression of lack of conclusive results in this area. I would like, however, in addition to the above two problem areas, to cite that of the complex of deviance, social control, and therapy. It does seem to me that though final closure was not reached in that area, a contribution of appreciable significance was made and I for one would not wish to derogate the extent to which this contribution was made possible by clarification of problems at the more general theoretical level.

In the complex previously referred to, it seems to me in particular that the work having to do with family and kinship structure and its relation to the socialization process had a considerable significance as contribution to theories of the middle range. More specifically, a paper I once wrote on the interpretation of the incest taboo [25] seems to me to have been a considerable contribution. The latest field in which perhaps comparable contributions have been achieved is that of the analysis of education, in particular higher education. We have observed earlier that *The American University* was not available to Bershady in the work on his own book. There were, however, a number of preliminary essays in this area and even treatments of such subjects as the school class as a social system and Dreeben's notable small book, *On What Is Learned in School*.[26] Here again it seems to me difficult to maintain a position that there is a drastic

[25] T. Parsons, "The Incest Taboo in Relation to Social Structure and the Socialization of the Child," *British Journal of Sociology*, 1954, 5: 101–117.

[26] T. Parsons, "The School Class as a Social System," *Harvard Educational Review* (Fall 1969); reprinted in Parsons, *Social Structure and Personality* (N.Y.: The Free Press, 1964); R. Dreeben, *On What Is Learned in School* (Reading, Mass.: Addison-Wesley, 1968).

hiatus between the level of general theory and that of middle range contribution. Having, however, called attention to these cases, I think I will leave it at that.

In conclusion let me come back to the general problem of the status of categorization in general theory, which is Bershady's main preoccupation throughout the book. In his concluding statements he raises the question of the possible helpfulness of a new, in the more German sense, "methodological" doctrine of the importance of what he calls "practical reasoning." Unfortunately, I do not know the sources in the philosophy of science on which he relies, namely, Anscombe and Von Wright, and have not been able to take the time to familiarize myself with them in the course of writing this review. I had the impression that they relax some of the to my mind unnecessarily rigorous criteria of validity of authors like Hempel, perhaps Nagel, and I think legitimately Homans.[27] I would have to reserve judgment, however, about the adequacy of an alternative set of proposals for this most general categorial level of theory until I had a command of this material.

I have noted above that on various occasions and with various degrees of intensity I have "played with" the applicability and relevance to our subject matter of basically the Newtonian model of a theoretical system. On the whole, however, I think that gradually with the passage of years of time and experience I have become increasingly skeptical of this. There have been, I have become aware, developments in the physical sciences which have questioned the adequacy of this model. I have also been increasingly impressed by the biological model and the extent to which very impressive results at the level of empirical generalization have proved to be attainable with the use of a concept of living systems which certainly does not meet the Newtonian requirements specifically with reference to the formulation of "laws." One major difference between the biological and the classical mechanics orientation clearly seems to be with reference to the logical character of variables which are given a prominent place. I cannot help but contrast the intimacy in the Newtonian synthesis between the differential and integral calculus and the theory of celestial mechanics, with the pattern of conceptualization which has developed in the more sophisticated versions of modern biology, particularly micro-biology, where one might say that the underlying Mendelian paradigm of shuffling and re-shuffling of qualitatively distinct units through what in Mendelian literature is called the principle of segregation, continues to play an exceedingly important part.[28]

---

[27] Hempel, *op. cit.*; E. Nagel, *The Structure of Science* (N.Y.: Harcourt, Brace and World, 1961); George C. Homans, *Social Behavior: Its Elementary Forms* (N.Y.: Harcourt, 1961), and "Contemporary Theory in Sociology," in R. E. L. Faris (ed.), *Handbook of Modern Sociology* (Chicago: Rand McNally, 1964).

[28] See C. Stern, "The Continuity of Genetics," in G. Holton (ed.), *The Twentieth-Century Sciences: Studies in the Biography of Ideas* (N.Y.: Norton, 1972).

My own present view is that the theoretical logic of social science theory should be closer to the Mendelian than to the Newtonian model.[29] This would seem to hold with the important exception of mathematical economics.

Finally, if in Bershady's formula of a "pragmatic orientation" is included a theoretical stance which does not insist upon the level of conceptual rigor which has been achieved in classical mechanics and is highly advocated by certain philosophers of science heavily influenced by the discipline of logic, it does not seem to me that this is necessarily a basic obstacle to the progress of the disciplines in which this "less than perfect" logical rigor operates at the theoretical levels. My own personal view of the development of theory in the fields of social system theory and system of action theory in approximately the last half century is that very substantial progress has been made, though many of our critics take the view that our failure to conform to the above mentioned extremely rigorous criteria vitiates *any* claim to theoretical progress whatever. I think Bershady has made an important contribution to the clarification of the issues underlying the judgment of the state of an important branch of knowledge.

Commentary on Talcott Parsons' Review of H. J. Bershady's *Ideology and Social Knowledge*

by H. J. Bershady

I am most gratified that Professor Parsons has responded so generously to my book, not least because he has raised searching questions concerning the categorial bases of action theory and of social knowledge in general. I should like to pursue these questions briefly here as their subject is the main preoccupation of my effort in *Ideology and Social Knowledge*.

Why indeed "ideology" in the title? Because in either of the two senses in which the term is commonly used—to refer to a particular economic, political or class interest cloaked in doctrine, or to refer to a master set of categories undergirding all the thoughtways of an epoch—a relativistic consequence for thought, sometimes pernicious in its implications, is frequently drawn. The major views on this topic formulated over the past 150 years are laid out in chapters 1 and 2 of my book and need not be dwelt on here. I think it is among the great merits of Parsons' work that he has faced the relativistic issues unflinchingly, with a full awareness of their complexities, and has gone a long way towards resolving them. But the rational solution of such issues will give us no guarantee they will not

[29] T. Parsons, "On Building Social System Theory: A Personal History," *Daedalus, Journal of the American Academy of Arts and Sciences* (Vol. 99, No. 4, Fall 1970); reprinted in G. Holton (ed.), *The Twentieth-Century Sciences, op. cit.*

reappear in their destructive forms in the future, if for no other reason than that they have been raised repeatedly throughout the entire history of Western philosophy, from Protagoras to Mannheim, have been as repeatedly vanquished, and have arisen again.

Whatever may be made of the recurrence of skeptical, relativistic ideas—and surely this is a subject deserving of social, historical study—it is important to note that, in his efforts to undo the throttling forms of relativism, Parsons joins the great line of rationalist thinkers who have made major contributions to the Western intellectual tradition. He thus holds with other rationalist thinkers, as I do, to the general assumption that human beings are, in the very first instance, minded or thinking beings. What this means is that his own efforts to explain human social life may be seen as consisting of theories, or systematic thoughts, on beings who themselves think and are thoughtful.

I put the matter in this slightly exotic way to underscore the following propositions. First, that action theory has as its core concern the analysis of *meaningful* human behavior. And second, that thought on thoughtful beings—beings whose actions are meaningful—is of an order logically higher and more complex than thought on non-thoughtful beings, such as theories whose reference is to high energy particles. To clarify the second proposition somewhat, consider that when we analyze the meaning of physical theories the reference of our analysis is to the theories themselves, to the definitions of their terms, the structure of their explanations, the categories of their logical framework, but not to the references *of* the theories which have to do with an exclusively physical subject matter. The place occupied by social knowledge in this perspective, then, is *structurally* analogous to the place of epistemology in the analysis of the physical sciences. However, social knowledge is *not* epistemology: no such equation is here being proposed. Indeed, the epistemological analysis of social knowledge has yet to be developed. But it has already proceeded far enough to make us wary of the simple identity so often struck between the logics of the explanatory enterprises of all the sciences. Epistemological analysis is itself not a form of deductive or inductive nomological explanation, but nevertheless provides us with a kind of explanation or knowledge of knowledge. And if social knowledge is structurally analogous to epistemology, we may raise the question whether the logic of explanation and the categorial structure of social knowledge are also distinctive in kind from the physical sciences. I will take up a few implications of this argument in a moment.

Although relatively novel [30] and briefly stated, the preceding argument

[30] A recent statement of similar import is by Herminio Martins, "Time and Theory in Sociology," in John Rex (editor) *Approaches to Sociology*, London: Routledge, 1973. A much earlier statement is by Felix Kaufmann, *Methodology of the Social Sciences*, N.Y.: Oxford, 1940.

is, I think, coherent and not logically difficult to grasp. But there are difficulties in comprehending even the terms of the argument. And these difficulties are rooted largely in the fact that a vastly different and opposed set of assumptions on social life and social knowledge is held by the great majority of scholars who are concerned with such matters. For convenience this opposed set of assumptions may be placed under the general heading of positive thought. The writings of Hempel, Nagel and Braithwaite on the logic of explanation are canonical within this rubic, and I will assume they are so well known as to require no exposition.

One of the implications of the antipositivist argument sketched above is that social knowledge, which has as its primary cognitive aim the analysis of meaningful social action, is an essentially reflexive endeavor. In fact, Parsons has said as much of his own work by referring often to the "inherently subjective" aspect of the theory of action—a stance for which he has been condemned frequently by radicals and positivists alike, the former because of an utter, perhaps even a deliberate, lack of comprehension of his meaning, the latter because the word "subjective" in scientific inquiry is a taboo term which violates the most sacred premises of the positivist metaphysic. For to be reflexive means literally to turn the mind back upon itself. In any reflexion, therefore, under any philosophical or political auspices, there must be something to which the mind turns, something already realized but not well understood, a former rather than a future state of the mind, whether of one's own or that of another, for the future cannot be *re*-flected: it is empty of meaningful action. Parsons has made this point repeatedly and incisively from his first major work on: ". . . the normative elements (of social action) can be conceived of as 'existing' only in the mind of the actor. They can become accessible to an observer in any other form only through their realization. . . ." [31] The reflexive stance thus directs one to gaze upon an aspect of the mind that *has* appeared, to interrogate and further explicate that appearance, and to render it increasingly intelligible. It is in this respect that epistemological analysis is also an essentially reflexive endeavor, pointed to prior cognition, and thus "inherently subjective."

Another implication, then, of the anti-positivist argument is that the explanatory effort of action theory is not, and cannot be, geared to prediction in the sense entailed by the nomological model of explanation. Does this mean action theory is no more than a kind of immensely elaborate hermeneutic? Or if not predictive can action theory then be—to use the common analytical term—"retrodictive"? There is no doubt that a large portion of the theory of action is interpretive in nature, aimed at clarifying and systematically ordering the nuances of a vastly complex

[31] *Cf. The Structure of Social Action,* Glencoe: The Free Press, 1949, 2nd edition, p. 733.

range of cultural meanings. Although positivist inspired critics have often dismissed the interpretive components of action theory as being "mere classifications," therefore, presumably, not explanations and perhaps not much of anything at all, I would insist upon the cognitive importance and the legitimate explanatory character of classifications. Classifications give us answers to questions of the "what is it?" sort. But think what it would mean for our discourse if for every new definition of a thing we had to invoke a new kind of differentiating principle. Our cognitions of things would then consist of a hodge-podge of disparate elements, and discourse on many things would be clogged by the sheer plenitude of our definitions, and perhaps cease altogether.[32] It is a homily but nonetheless true that when we can define a great many things by the use of a few principles we can achieve a gain in the coherency of our cognitions. To have provided such definitional answers in so large a measure and with such great economy as action theory has done has resulted in a kind of semantic explanation of culture itself. Very much remains to be done in further sharpening this explanation. But now we can speak with increased intelligibility and definiteness of many of the ingredients of any culture we now have an understanding of various of the modalities of culture, and thus we now possess a clearer idea of the general meaning of culture. However, the explanatory ambit of action theory does not come to rest on the interpretive explication of meaning alone, although this sort of effort should and will doubtless continue. There is the matter of the sort of propositions entertained by action theory, of retrodictions, and to this I now turn.

I have been at some pains in my book to bring out and assess certain of the features of Parsons' theoretical efforts. Action theory has great intrinsic interest. But as the concern of the book was to clarify philosophical and epistemological themes that pertain to a theory of social knowledge, the manner of action theory often took some precedence over its substance—although too sharp a distinction should not be drawn. I found a logical characteristic common to each of Parsons' formulations. Whether he has proceeded from a voluntarist, functionalist, evolutionist or cybernetic framework, each of the logical or conditional relationships he has proposed is cast in the form of a putative necessity. To speak in more common logical parlance, action theory in each of its phases is formulated as a set of nomic relationships between various of the components of action. The ubiquity of this kind of proposition in action theory is so marked and so distinctive, and so sets action theory off from many other endeavors at social knowledge, that the question arises of unearthing the rationale of its employment. Surely such pervasive usage is not unwitting. I have called the form of the reasoning of such propositions "a priori,"

---

[32] For a striking presentation of this view, see Jorge Luis Borges, "Funes the Memorious," in *Labyrinths*, N.Y.: New Directions, 1962, pp. 59–66.

and have interpreted their use as a strategy devised by Parsons to solve simultaneously a variety of philosophical and scientific problems. But if there is truly a strategy being deployed here it is obviously crucial to understand the objectives the strategy is intended to achieve—or the very idea of a strategy becomes nonsensical.

This is not the place to review a large part of the argument of my book or the evidence mustered in its support. But I may mention one of the objectives being pursued by this presumed strategy to which I have tried to call attention. A kind of explanation is being sought which nomic propositions will allow us to make when they are properly qualified. By employing propositions of nomic connection in our theories, that is, we can deduce occurrences which have taken place in the past. Whether our deductions are materially correct is of course another matter. But we cannot by employing propositions of nomic connection deduce occurrences that will take place "in the future." We can deduce the lack of such occurrences in the future, for nomic propositions answer questions of the "how is it possible?" sort. But I strongly doubt the deduction of such a lack falls within the meaning of a prediction. Nomic propositions allow us to construct retrodictive but not predictive explanations. The reason commonly given in the logical literature is that as nomic propositions state necessary relationships they are law*like* statements. Nomological propositions, on the other hand, state universal relationships from which both predictions and retrodictions may be constructed. They are law*ful* statements.

What is gained, then, and what is lost by composing a theory consisting solely of statements of necessary connection? I will leave aside discussing a very considerable logical gain examined in detail in my book, namely, the destruction of skepticism implied by various doctrines of the relativism and ideology of knowledge. But notice that if one holds to something very like the nomological model of explanation, then explanation by means of nomic propositions will be considered "second best"—as in fact Parsons has dubbed the explanatory formulations of the functionalist phase of his work.[33] A philosophical victory has been gained, let us say, but not yet an allegedly full scientific victory. Nevertheless, certain relations of the components of action are preserved for possible future reformulation. I think this very brief account recapitulates in miniature much of the logical view held by Parsons up to the mid 1950s. Much but not all. For action theory, remember, is inherently subjective and was first articulated under the rubric of voluntarism. Although it has developed under new rubrics, the voluntary and subjective components of action theory have never been relinquished. There has been a tension from the outset between the statement of the explanatory goal, a "nomological explanation" of action, and the actual formulations of the categories and the substance of

---

[33] Talcott Parsons, *The Social System*, Glencoe: The Free Press, 1951, p. ix.

the theory. For a lawful explanation of action would seem to impose a "determinism" upon beings who are held to be free in their essence. At this point precisely an ambiguity has arisen concerning the explanatory form of action theory. I have in my concluding chapter referred to the ambiguity as a kind of conceptual confusion between the categories and the professed explanatory goals of the entire theoretical effort. But it is as though the fashioner of action theory, by being reluctant to proceed to the goals he had staked out, by developing only "second best" explanations, has prevented the loss of certain of the components fundamental to social action. I would consider this to be an incomparable gain. But was there truly a reluctance? And if so, did the reluctance become one of the grounds of a strategy? Parsons has said little on the question of explanation for the past twenty years. The evidence up to now has thus been too fragmentary to permit of a judgement, and I was content mainly to lay out a range of plausible interpretations. But with Parsons' statement in his review of my book we can presently see that there may have been some reluctance even at an early stage. He has grown increasingly skeptical, he says, of the pertinence of the nomological model of explanation to action theory. Is it too much to surmise there was a shred of doubt from the very beginning? So that perhaps not clearly understood as such at first, a strategy was put together and advanced against an uncertainty: to provide an explanation of the creative human actions of the past which would leave inviolate the most basic assumptions of the concept of action and yet not foreclose the option of lawful explanations if they could be devised. Thus it may have been. And what is the upshot?

I think it is highly significant that in his review Parsons has now explicitly rejected the explanatory model he had accepted in *The Structure of Social Action*. His statement is not to be taken lightly. Nor should it be mis-taken. It is an assessment of the *relevance* of the nomological model to the explanatory purposes of action theory. The grounds for his judgement are in fact more experimental than formal as he speaks on the basis of decades of profound theoretical involvement. It is true that precedents were to be found earlier in biological theory for challenging the claim to explanatory hegemony of the covering-law model. However, this would have meant a challenge not only to much received logical opinion, but to opinion which carried with it the weight of a cultural force. For the nomological or covering-law model was fashioned from an analysis of the Newtonian mechanics—"the science," as it was called for centuries, held up as an exemplar for all the sciences to emulate. With a few notable exceptions, logicians and philosophers of science have paid scant attention to the kinds of explanations actually to be found in the social sciences and biology. Thus epistemological analyses of these disciplines which are truly congenial to their subject matters have been undertaken largely by the practitioners of these disciplines themselves. There has been no loss of

logical acuity thereby, but understandably there has been less concentration of effort.

Parsons suggests that the explanatory form of action theory more closely resembles the Mendelian model that is found in biological theory. Following the terminology of von Wright I have called this kind of explanation as it pertains to Parsons's efforts "quasi teleological." [34] "Quasi teleological" and "teleonomic" are approximately equivalent expressions, although the latter term is more consistent with the language of this essay. Do teleonomic explanations capture fully what Parsons is after? There is no doubt that a large part of the theory of action is cast in the form of sets of teleonomic propositions. Teleonomic propositions express relationships which are necessary and metaphorically "purposive." In the theory of natural selection, for example, the perpetulation of a genotype is explained as a necessary relationship between genetic and environmental characteristics.[35] To speak figuratively, one could characterize the selective process as having taken place for "the purpose of" adapting a genotypical individual to an environment. Consider as another instance the explanation of certain processes in the human body—say, respiration—as being necessary for, or as being for "the purpose of," the maintenance of a homeostatic state of the body. In each of these instances the supposed purpose in the explanation is in fact mechanical.[36] We can grant that there are many aspects of social action which are equally mechanical. But the concept of social action includes much more. There are voluntary and active components to social action in which human purposes are not construed metaphorically but are taken as ontologically "real." Teleonomic explanations alone do not seem to capture these active, intentional characteristics of social action. It is for this reason that, again following the fertile leads provided by von Wright, I have tentatively suggested the practical argument as an explanatory model pertinent to action theory.

I do not think it is possible at present to judge decisively whether the practical argument is fully adequate to the explanatory objectives of action theory. For action theory seeks to interrelate enormously complicated and disparate elements among which may be found teleonomic, teleological and even nomological relationships. Not each of these relationships has been fathomed, nor is the particular order of these relationships to one another clear. Current work on the theory of social evolution and the generalized symbolic media of interchange may—I think it will—produce a fuller and more organized body of social theory which will be amenable to careful logical analysis. I suspect the results of such analysis will be

[34] Georg von Wright, *Explanation and Understanding*, London: Routledge, 1971.

[35] *Cf.* Ernst Mayr, *Populations, Species, and Evolution*, Cambridge: Harvard Press, 1970, p. 108.

[36] *Cf.* S. E. Lusia, *Life—The Unfinished Experiment*, N.Y.: Scribner's, 1973, p. 80.

surprising, that if the Newtonian and Mendelian theories have given rise to powerful but different explanatory structures, the Parsonian theory will be seen to give rise to an equally powerful but unprecedented explanation of social action. To rid ourselves of prevailing logical prejudices and to open up new possibilities was part of the purpose of my book.

Part II

FUNCTIONAL ANALYSIS
OF SOCIETIES:
RECONSIDERATIONS
AND EXTENSIONS

Introduction

PART II CONSISTS of four rather long and substantial essays, each of which was addressed to a set of theoretical problems within the province of the theory of action. They fall rather naturally into two pairs. The first pair (Chapters 7 and 8) includes two theoretical papers written for the new *International Encyclopedia of the Social Sciences,* which was published in 1968. These essays both clearly belong in the heartland of my theoretical interests over a long period. Of the two, I have placed the article on "Social Interaction" first for two reasons. The first is that it includes an historical survey of the genesis of the problem since the time of Descartes. The second is that the subject of social interaction is in a fundamental sense logically prior to that of social system.

The "Social Interaction" article may be considered to be a mature statement about this theoretically central problem area. First, I may note that there was no "collusion," either positive or negative, with my good friend G. E. Swanson. At the time I wrote it, I did not know that he was at work on the next article under the title "Symbolic Interaction." [1] Comparsion of the two may, in the light of more recent discussions, throw some light on the state of integration versus separation into "schools" in contemporary sociology. [2]

Another theoretical theme may be mentioned here. At the beginning of the article I related the paradigm of the subject-object relation in Cartesian epistemology to that of the actor-situation relation in the theory of action, and I tried to outline some of the intellecual history bearing on

---

[1] Guy E. Swanson, "Symbolic Interaction," *International Encyclopedia of the Social Sciences,* David L. Sills (ed.) (New York: The Macmillan Company and The Free Press, 1968), Vol. 7. The articles by T. Parsons and G. E. Swanson are among 6 articles on Interaction in *The International Encyclopedia of the Social Sciences.* The others are: Kenneth Burke, "Dramatism"; Peter M. Blau, "Social Exchange"; William C. Schutz, "Interaction and Personality"; and Robert F. Bales, "Interaction Process Analysis."

[2] See Jonathan Turner, "Parsons as a Symbolic Interactionist," *Sociological Inquiry,* Vol. 44, No. 4 (1974), and Talcott Parsons, "Comments" on Turner's article in *Sociological Inquiry,* Vol. 45, No. 1 (1975), pp. 62–65.

this relationship. Perhaps here I need add only that the significance of this background theme has not diminished for me in the intervening decade but has grown in relative importance. Though I have just characterized this article as a "mature statement," I hope this will not be interpreted to mean that I think nothing more needs to be said or thought in this area. On the contrary, I think the field has been opened up more than it has reached "closure."

In a parallel sense, I think it is justified to speak of the "Social Systems" article as a mature statement. It clearly is a far more mature one than that contained in the book entitled *The Social System* [3] of about fifteen years earlier, which is still frequently referred to as comprising "Parsons' theory." To signalize the difference, perhaps two points may be noted. First, there is an even stronger emphasis than before on the necessary abstractness of what is treated as a system in scientific theory, a development from the earlier influence on me of Whitehead [4] and Henderson [5] and of Max Weber.[6] Second, far more explicitly than before, the concept of social system was even then placed in the context of the general system of action.

As in the case of social interaction, however, the situation here was not "closed" in 1968. I should like again just to note two points. The first is that the account of the structure of the general system of action which was presented in the first part of this article has subsequently undergone a major modification. This came through the article of Charles and Victor Lidz [7] which, as noted in the General Introduction, has recently been published, and which radically challenges the status of what had been called the "behavioral organism" in the paradigm of the general system of action. The action system was redefined as not to include the organism at all, and in its place was put a "behavioral system" with primarily cognitive-adaptive functions in action. I have personally accepted this far-reaching suggestion. Readers seriously interested in this question should read Lidz and Lidz in the work, *Explorations in General Theory in Social Science,* edited by Loubser, Baum, Effrat, and V. Lidz.[8]

[3] Talcott Parsons, *The Social System* (New York: Free Press, 1951).

[4] Cf. Alfred N. Whitehead, *Science and the Modern World* (New York: Macmillan, 1925).

[5] Cf. Lawrence Joseph Henderson, *The Order of Nature: An Essay* (Cambridge, Mass.: Harvard University Press, 1917).

[6] Max Weber, *The Methodology of the Social Sciences,* transl. by Edward A. Shils and Henry A. Finch (Glencoe, Ill.: Free Press, 1949). The essays contained in this book were originally published in German in 1904, 1905, and 1917.

[7] Charles Lidz and Victor Lidz, "The Psychology of Intelligence of Jean Piaget and Its Place in the Theory of Action," in J. Loubser, R. Baum, A. Effrat, and V. Lidz (eds.), *Explorations in General Theory in Social Science, Essays in Honor of Talcott Parsons* (New York: Free Press, 1976).

[8] *Ibid.*

The second main point is to note that, since the writing of this article, the integration of the theory of action with that of living systems more generally, and of course primarily their organic aspects, has proceeded much farther. The point of specific relevance here is that, as I did not realize before, the concept of society in the usage of this article is formally directly parallel to that of species, as used in modern evolutionary biology.[9] If this parallel, or in the nonpejorative sense "analogy," holds up, as I think it will, it should prove to be a major contribution to the theoretical generalization of our knowledge in this extremely broad field.

It may be noted that the definition of the concept society, as a particularly important type of social system, has been a serious source of difficulty for sociologists. Most have tended to assume what may be called the "Spencerian" conception of an "organized" aggregate of concrete "individuals."[10] The reasons why this view simply "won't do," if there is to be an intellectually sophisticated theory of social systems, may be illustrated by two cases important in my recent personal experience.

The first concerns Pareto. In 1973 I was invited to a conference in Rome commemorating the fiftieth anniversary of Pareto's death and was asked to give a paper on Pareto's concept of the social system, which Henderson[11] had earlier celebrated as Pareto's most important theoretical contribution to sociology. On "revisiting" Pareto's relevant writings, it became perfectly clear to me that there were major difficulties in Pareto's attempt to deal with the "society" as a concrete entity, as he attempted to do, and then to treat it as a special type of social system.[12] At the time of writing *The Structure of Social Action*[13] I had only dimly appreciated these difficulties, especially that even Pareto had not given adequate attention to the necessary problems of abstraction. For example, had there not been this difficulty, Pareto would not have exposed himself to the allegation that he was an "instinct" theorist in the traditional sense.[14]

The second example is that of Durkheim. In a recent article criticizing my interpretation of Durkheim, especially in *The Structure of Social Action*

[9] See Ernst Mayr, *Populations, Species and Evolution* (Cambridge, Mass.: Harvard University Press, 1970).

[10] Cf. Herbert Spencer, *The Study of Sociology* (Ann Arbor: University of Michigan Press, 1961). First published in 1873.

[11] Lawrence Joseph Henderson, *Pareto's General Sociology: A Physiologist's Interpretation* (Cambridge, Mass.: Harvard University Press, 1935).

[12] See Talcott Parsons, "Pareto's Approach to the Construction of a Theory of the Social System." Paper presented at the International Conference on Vilfredo Pareto in Rome, October 25-27, 1973, published by the Accademia Nazionale dei Lincei, Rome, 1975.

[13] Talcott Parsons, *The Structure of Social Action* (New York: McGraw-Hill, 1937). Reprinted by The Free Press, New York, 1949.

[14] Cf. George C. Homans and Charles P. Curtis, Jr., *An Introduction to Pareto, His Sociology* (New York: Alfred A. Knopf, 1935); and Pitirim A. Sorokin, *Contemporary Sociological Theories* (New York: Harper & Brothers, 1928).

but also since, Whitney Pope [15] put forward the view that it was nearly obvious on grounds close to common sense what Durkheim had meant by the term "society." In my criticism of Pope,[16] I countered with extensive quotations from the Introduction to Robert Bellah's notable volume of selections from Durkheim's work.[17] Bellah there began his discussion of Durkheim by commenting at length on the extreme complexity of the concept of society in Durkheim's work. Indeed, it has seemed to me that, if we are to make sense of what Durkheim meant, especially in his earlier works, in speaking of "society as a reality *sui generis*,"[18] we must interpret him to mean not what I have meant by "society" in the present article on social systems, but something very much like the general system of action.[19] As Pareto said, "let us not dispute about words." This admonition does not, however, dispose of the definitional problem. A discipline with a claim to conceptual rigor cannot have it all ways, that the key concept for defining its subject matter is an analytically defined aspect of a given reality, is the concrete totality of that reality, and is to be deliberately left undefined.

The third paper (Chapter 9) in Part II is also on a major theoretical topic but is one of the most recent of my major theoretical papers. It was written at the request of the then President of the American Sociological Association, Peter Blau, to be read at one of the plenary sessions of the Association meeting in Montreal in 1974 and was published in the volume, edited by Blau, entitled *Approaches to the Study of Social Structure*.

It follows well on the social systems paper, because the latter contains a brief summary discussion of what I have been calling the "generalized symbolic media of interchange" which operate at the social system level. In response to Professor Blau's invitation to present a paper bearing on the central theme of the 1974 meeting, namely "social structure," in the light of my considerable concern with analyzing these media over several years,[20] I decided to try to present a more generalized account of the nature and significance of the media which operated in the social system.

[15] Whitney Pope, "Classic on Classic: Parsons' Interpretation of Durkheim," *American Sociological Review*, Vol. 38 (August, 1973), pp. 399–415.

[16] Talcott Parsons, "Commentary on 'Classic on Classic: Parsons' Interpretation of Durkheim' by Whitney Pope," *American Sociological Review*, Vol. 40 (February 1975), pp. 106–110.

[17] Robert N. Bellah, "Introduction" to Emile Durkheim, *On Morality and Society*, edited by R. N. Bellah (Chicago: University of Chicago Press, 1973).

[18] Cf. Emile Durkheim, *The Rules of Sociological Method*, 8th ed., edited by G. Catlin, translated by S. A. Solovay and J. H. Mueller (New York: Free Press, 1964). Originally published in French in 1895.

[19] Talcott Parsons, "Durkheim on Religion Revisited: Another Look at the *Elementary Forms of the Religious Life*," in Charles Y. Glock and Phillip E. Hammond (eds.), *Beyond the Classics? Essays in the Scientific Study of Religion* (New York: Harper and Row, 1973).

[20] Cf. Talcott Parsons, "On the Concept of Political Power," "On the Concept of Influence," and "On the Concept of Value-Commitments," Chapters 14, 15, and 16 in *Politics and Social Structure* (New York: Free Press, 1969).

This is a problem area of quite special significance to my recent theoretical work more generally. The discerning reader will note the connection with my special early concern with the relations between economic and sociological theory. It was shortly after publication of a major revision of my views on that topic, stated in the small collaborative volume with Neil Smelser, *Economy and Society*,[21] that I began to realize the significance of the place of money and monetary theory, not mainly within the discipline of economics, but as a theoretical model for other branches of the theory of social systems. Perhaps the combination of the publication in Blau's volume and various themes in the present collection of my essays and its sequel will help to enhance the professional attention accorded to this theoretical theme, not only among sociologists but related professional groups.[22]

The main reason why the article from the Blau volume was placed third in Part II is that the one which follows it (Chapter 10) was, though written earlier, the first attempt, a very crude one as it now appears, to extend the conception of generalized symbolic media from the social system level to that of the general system of action. Though crude, it has seemed worth while to reprint this attempt here, since it illustrates for the reader interested in such matters some of the difficulties and vicissitudes of theory construction in new fields, considered as a process of action and not of logical deduction. A torough revision of the scheme of media for the general system of action will be published in my forthcoming book, *The Action of Social Structure*.[23]

The tentatively proposed schema of media of general action takes up the second main part of the "Problems of General Theory . . ." paper. The first part is concerned with the problem of the underlying rationale of the four-functional paradigm, particularly in the light of enhanced concern by that time with more technical problems arising at the level of the general system of action. It is important to note that this paper was writ-

[21] Talcott Parsons and Neil J. Smelser, *Economy and Society* (New York: Free Press, 1956).

[22] My most important partner in this intellectual adventure has been Victor Lidz (Charles Lidz and Victor Lidz, "The Psychology of Intelligence of Jean Piaget and Its Place in the General Theory of Action," and "Introduction" to Part II in J. Loubser, R. Baum, A. Effrat, and V. Lidz [eds.], *op. cit.*). The collaboration began when Lidz was still a graduate student at Harvard, and worked as my research assistant. He then went to a teaching appointment at the University of Chicago, and it chanced that this overlapped with my being at Chicago on a visiting appointment. We took advantage of this by offering, at Chicago, a joint seminar on "The Generalized Symbolic Media . . ." After that, by another fortunate coincidence, we were both together at the University of Pennsylvania, he on a regular teaching appointment, I as a Visiting Professor, and we again took advantage of this opportunity, two academic years running, to offer a joint seminar on the same topic. I clearly owe a very great intellectual debt to him for his contribution in these connections, which it is by now impossible to separate from my own thinking.

[23] To be sure, the latter part of the Blau article does include a brief account of this tentative attempt.

ten before Chapter 4 in Part I, namely the one on the status of "structural-functional" theory. It was written after a conference, in which I participated, held at Duke University in 1969.[24]

This order of writing is important because the "Duke" article, if I may call it that, had a different theme from the "Merton" article. In the former, it was the problem of why we should fasten on *four* categories of function, and of course which four, rather than some other number and list, or even possibly a completely "open" list, ending with "etc.," which had been the common practice in sociology almost ever since functions were discussed at all.[25] By the time of writing the "Duke" article, I had become much more self-conscious about the problem of the relation of the functional categories relevant to the theory of action to those used in biology. Hence, I made a serious and, though partial, I think not altogether unsuccessful attempt to integrate them. The key to such success as was achieved lay in the involvement of the concepts adaptation and integration in both sets and their relation to each other. Almost equally important, however, was the use of the analogy, which I noted in the General Introduction, put forward by the biologist Alfred Emerson [26] between "gene" and "symbol," as he called them, which phrasing I have modified to the "genetic heritage" of organic systems and the "cultural heritage" of action systems. Had I known at the time, which unfortunately I did not, of Ernst Mayr's concept of *teleonomy,*[27] as the "goal-directed" propensity of organisms, I would certainly have introduced this, as well, into the analysis.

The article reprinted in Part I, on the other hand, dealt with another aspect of the functional problem, which is logically prior to the one just outlined. This is the general problem, rooted in the philosophy of science, of the status of the concept function, above all in its relation to system on the one hand, structure and process on the other. My confidence in the soundness of the position taken here has been enhanced by a more recent "revisit" to L. J. Henderson's writings where, especially in *The Order of Nature,*[28] but also in *The Fitness of the Environment,* he puts the strongest emphasis on the critical importance of the concept system

[24] This was published in the volume, *Theoretical Sociology,* edited by John C. McKinney and Edward A. Tiryakian (New York: Appleton-Century Crofts, 1970), which issued from that conference.

[25] Cf. David Aberle et al., "The Functional Prerequisites of a Society," *Ethics,* Vol. IX (January 1950), pp. 100–111.

[26] Cf. Alfred E. Emerson, "Homeostasis and the Comparison of Systems," in Roy R. Grinker, Sr. (ed.), *Towards a Unified Theory of Human Behavior: An Introduction to General Systems Theory* (New York: Basic Books, 1956).

[27] Ernst Mayr, "Teleological and Teleonomic: A New Analysis," in Marx Wartovsky (ed.), *Method and Metaphysis: Methodological and Historical Essays in the Natural and Social Sciences.* Proceedings of the Boston Colloquium for the Philosophy of Science, 1969–1972, Vol. 6 (Holland: Brill, 1974), pp. 78–104.

[28] Henderson, *The Order of Nature, op. cit.*

and gives a most illuminating explication of what he means by it.[29] To sociologists who are worried about the "functional" problem and tend to think it is somehow "unscientific," I unreservedly recommend those two small books, which were published, without reference to social science, in 1913 and 1917, and his much later (also small) book, *Pareto's General Sociology* (1935),[30] which did stress the place of the concept system in social science.

The inclusion of the four papers just discussed thus seems to me to be justified, not only by their several independent contributions to theoretical development in this area, but by the fact that, coming as they did at a rather critical juncture in my theoretical career, they exemplified the interdependence of three particularly important themes of theoretical preoccupation, none of which has been in the center of at least explicit concern on the part of sociologists. They are all, in different ways, in line with the theme, stated in the General Introduction, of the progressive enlargement of theoretical concerns, starting with the step from the economy to the society, which has characterized my intellectual career as a whole.

Leaving aside the earliest preoccupation, which does not figure at this point, the first of these themes is that of the relation of the social system to the next order of more comprehensive system, which we have called the general system of action, including as it does behavioral, personality, and cultural systems. It has seemed to me that many problems which have often been conceived to be primarily "sociological" could only be satisfactorily approached by attempting to place their social system aspects in the setting of the more comprehensive general action system. Salient examples of different types are, first, the problem of the "socialization" of the individual personality, which surely cannot be adequately dealt with except in terms which include "psychological," precisely as distinguished from sociological considerations. The naiver apostles of Durkheim may disagree but that seems to me to be the situation. In another direction, I fail to see how the problems of the institutional status of intellectual culture, as these have come to be salient in connection with the educational revolution, can be adequately dealt with in the absence of *explicit* consideration of problems of theory at the cultural level. The first phase of this has concentrated above all on the cognitive aspect of culture, especially in the book, *The American University*. More recently, however, as will become more evident in the collection of essays which is to follow the present one, it has turned much more explicitly to the other branches of the cultural system, culminating with the relation of what we have called "constitutive symbolism" to the telic system at the level of the "human condition" as this concept will be explicated in that volume.

[29] L. J. Henderson, *The Fitness of the Environment: An Inquiry into the Biological Significance of the Properties of Matter* (New York: Macmillan, 1913).

[30] Henderson, *Pareto's General Sociolgoy, op. cit.*

The second primary theoretical theme is the extension of the attempt at systematic theoretical conceptualization beyond the system of action itself to the level of what we will call the human condition, but in this case with primary concern for one of the boundaries of the action system, namely the one of considerable previous concern, that vis-à-vis organic living systems, or more colloquially put, the "biological" world. After all, every living human being is a living organism, and collectively they constitute an organic species—though a system of actors as well.

This has above all been the context of the interest in problems of evolution which has become so prominent that it has been included in the title of this volume. This emphasis has been built on the growing conviction that there has been an underlying unity of the world of what we have called living systems, which must be better understood if the sciences dealing with organic life and those dealing with human action are to be satisfactorily articulated with each other. The field of evolutionary ideas and phenomena constitutes one of the primary fields in which this articulation is most strongly needed, and to which I have paid the greatest attention.

The second of the fields of articulation is that of the complex nature of the human "individual" who, as just noted, is at the same time both living organism and *actor*. The theoretical necessity of distinguishing these two "aspects" of the same concrete entity *analytically* from each other, has been a major theme of my whole intellectual career and one the centrality of which has grown more rather than less salient in its recent phases. This area of articulation above all involves problems of the relation of motivation of the individual and cognitive processes, treated both at the organic and the action levels in relation to each other. As suggested above they involve evaluation and interpretation of the work especially of Freud in the motivational context and that of Piaget, especially as treated by the Lidz brothers, in the cognitive. Substantially fuller consideration of these problems will be presented in the forthcoming volume to follow this one, but it is important to alert the reader to their importance on the present occasion.

Finally, the third theme which runs through Part II is that of the nature and importance of what we call "generalized symbolic media of interchange." As noted above and in the relevant places in the articles themselves, this conception originated in reference to the social system, being first developed in relation to money and then extended to political power, influence, and value-commitments. Then the idea emerged that the conception should not be confined to the level of the social system, but could be fruitfully extended to that of the general system of action. Perhaps the most important "gadfly" pressing in this direction was the problem of how to deal with the status of language, the importance of which has long been recognized but, like so many other things, the

specific meaning of its existence has been taken for granted rather than being theoretically analyzed.

As we have noted, Chapter 10 in this volume is a *first* attempt to explore these possibilities. A second, in my opinion greatly improved, attempt was made in *The American University* (Technical Appendix, Figure A–7). The present volume does not present any attempted further advances of this line of work; indeed, it does not even attempt to present the level worked out in *The American University*. Further developments have, however, occurred, some of which will be presented in the volume to follow. In particular, these will center about the attempt to take a further major step of extension, namely to the level of the Human Condition considered as a system. This statement, like others, is not meant to explicate these theoretical innovations, but only to alert the interested reader to take into account, in his judgment of the materials presented in the present volume, especially Part II, the fact that they are part of a larger conceptual scheme, further extensions of which unfortunately cannot be made available until some months after the appearance of the present volume.

7.   Social Interaction

IT IS ALMOST pure tautology to say that human "social" phenomena are cases of the *interaction* between two or more human beings conceived as "persons," "organisms," "selves," or "actors." Hence, it may be thought that what is meant and implied by the concept of interaction and its theoretical context is the sheerest common sense. However, this is not so. This theoretical complex has had a long, complicated history, and the outlines of its place in modern social science, which is our concern here, have emerged only gradually.

On reflection this should not be too surprising. After all, science is not common sense, and its most basic theoretical ideas and frames of reference require development through complex intellectual processes which involve not only interpretations of observation but also theoretical and partly philosophical conceptualization. Perhaps this process has been particularly difficult in the case of human social action, because the subject matter is so close to immediate experience that isolating a scientifically usable scheme from the matrix of common sense is particularly difficult. In any case, for the limited purposes of this article it seems useful to begin by sketching the historical background of the problem.

Early History of the Concept

From one point of view modern philosophy "got off on the wrong foot" for clarifying the nature of human interaction, while, from another viewpoint, it appears that indirectly this was fruitful over the long run. In any case, I think there is general agreement that of all the areas in

From the *International Encyclopedia of the Social Sciences,* David L. Sills, editor, Volume 7, pp. 429–441. Reprinted by permission of the Publisher. Copyright © 1968 by Crowell Collier and Macmillan, Inc.

which modern philosophy originated, the most relevant to the present discussion is the problem of knowledge.

The Cartesian Schema

The focal early statement of this problem was Decartes's *Discourse on Method*. This work is justly considered the basic philosophical charter of modern science, having posed the problem of the philosophical basis of empirical knowledge of the external world with the greatest clarity. This clarity, however, was bought at the price of assumptions and predilections which are central to our problem.

The first was the treatment of the significant "external world" as the *physical* world. This was natural, in that, among other things, the science of the time, which had recently made very striking advances, was overwhelmingly physical science. Consequently, the object of knowledge for Descartes was not conceived as "knowing" or "acting" (since physical objects do not act). Thus, his formulation blocked concern with the interplay between entities which are *both* subject and object at the same time and, hence, with the analytical distinction between these aspects of social actors.

The second was the treatment of the problem solely as one of *knowledge*. Presumably it was in order to facilitate this that Descartes treated his subject as a given—e.g., in the famous formula *Cogito ergo sum*— rather than analyzing it as a structured identity. In this respect the Cartesian analysis did not venture beyond asserting the existence of the "thinker" and the fact of his cognitive relation to objects in the external world.

Of course we can now say, almost at the level of common sense, that Descartes dealt with a limiting case of social action. First, he excluded the "inter" in our formula of interaction by assuming that there was no "action" on one side of the relation, i.e., that the object only came to be known and that "being known" was in no way a stimulus for the object to intervene in and possibly change the relation to the knower. Second, he excluded analysis of the complex nature of the "entity which" knows, which is part of the basic relational system of the subject–object relation. We would now hold that empirical cognition is an activity or "function" of persons, an understanding of which entails analyzing the structures and processes of personalities by virtue of which a variety of factors become so organized as to facilitate the "attainment of knowledge" as a goal output of personality systems. Furthermore, the recognition of complexity *in* the units on both sides of the relationship obviously entails complicating the conceptualization of the relation pattern between them. Here Descartes considered the relation merely one of the flow of "information" from

object to subject, resulting in consequent "understanding," or knowledge, with little specificity about how far and in what ways such understanding involved processes other than the simple input of information.

Differentiation of the Cartesian Object

The Cartesian schema may be regarded as the primary reference point for a process of differentiation. Because it formulated a relational scheme, its differentiation necessarily cut across all of its components, involving both subject and object *and* the character of the relation between them. Since we are concerned with science, it is easier to understand the differentiation on the object side, which entailed the first step away from the more purely physicalist predilection of Descartes.

The human object came to be regarded not merely as a "knower" but also as a physical organism "behaving" (to use a later term) in an environment and actuated by "wants"—or, as Hobbes said, "passions"—which accounted for its action. This differentiation appeared even in Descartes's own century, the seventeenth, notably in the writings of Hobbes and Locke. This development marked the beginning of utiltarianism, established the theoretical groundwork of both the discipline of economics and a major branch of psychology, and had important side effects upon law, political science, and sociology.

The Utilitarian Differentiation. The Cartesian pattern was maintained in the assumption that the individual's wants were given. Even though these wants were also assumed to be plural, the problem of how, specifically, they were patterned and organized was not dealt with. However, the analytical concern was now no longer confined to knowing the external world but included "rationally" manipulating it through goal-directed activities. The early modern social scientist, then, is conceived of as an observer of objects who are at the same time actors striving to satisfy their wants through action. Moreover, only in a limiting case does the observer confine his observation to single individuals; generally he observes an interacting plurality. Economic exchange, through barter or the more elaborate market systems, became a prototype of such interaction, but the men of Hobbes's state of nature, seeking to "destroy or subdue one another," were also conceived of as interacting in this sense. Clearly, trying to satisfy wants or seeking to destroy others involves action in a sense not attributable, for example, to celestial bodies. Such wants or passions are easily distinguished from the activities—to use a term later made much of by Alfred Marshall—intended to implement them. Problems of the nature of the interaction systems generated by action conceived within this framework and of the conditions on which such systems can

"function" become very important here. The nature and significance of "self-interest," in the classic modern sense, and the basis of normative order in social systems become very problematic in this frame of reference.

Thus, the "utilitarian" frame of reference can be said to have emerged from the Cartesian problem-statement through the inclusion in the schema of a class of objects which are not physical and which interact in a sense in which neither knowers nor physical objects do. Although this conception emerges by differentiation on the object side of the Cartesian scheme, it implicitly raises the question about the position of the observer. Very clearly, knowledge of the *situation,* of the wants and activities of others in the interaction system, itself becomes a factor in want satisfaction. The utilitarian actor, considered as an observer, is a Cartesian "knower," but he is more than that. Thus, introducing this additional element into the total scheme presents exceedingly important problems.

Idealistic Differentiation of Subject. As noted Descartes left the structure of his subject unanalyzed: the "I" which thinks, and therefore exists, is *given.* Very broadly, the idealistic movement was an attempt to analyze the content of this given entity. Most crucially in Kant, it took the content of knowledge as its primary reference point. Contrary to the views of the British empiricists, knowledge was considered to be patterned and organized according to the Kantian schemata of intuition and the categories of understanding and not derivable from the "intrinsic" properties of the object world itself as they impinged on the subject in the form of "sense impressions," or in Locke's term, "ideas."

As for Descartes, the idealists' reference here was the scientific understanding of the physical world. However, it had now been greatly "relativized"—in a special sense—because the major structure of empirical knowledge was attributed not only to the "nature" of the objects known but also to the "categories" in terms of which they are known. These categories could not be located in the objects of cognition, nor could they be treated basically as variant properties of the individual personalities of the knowers. In more modern terms, they constitute a *cultural* frame of reference which partly governs the whole action system so far as it is dependent on empirical knowledge. This raises a problem parallel to the utilitarian one concerning actors who are not only knowers.

It is fair to say that such a differentiation of the Cartesian subject, parallel to the utilitarian differentiation of the Cartesian object, was a principal consequence of Kant's analysis. Thus "pure reason" concerned essentially the epistemological grounding of physical science, whereas "practical reason" regarded the other, especially noncognitive, concerns of human "actors." Utilitarianism treated wants only as given and analyzed activities overwhelmingly by projecting a Cartesian rational knower into the role of the actor—hence the formula of rational self-interest. Kant

took practical needs, which he considered predominantly *moral,* as essentially given, and he heavily discounted the possibilities of solving intellectually the underlying problems. Here he came close to the view that the moral imperative is existentially given.

Hegelianism. The Hegelian movement attempted to fuse the cultural component of Kant's empirical epistemology, especially the "categories," with the sphere of practical reason, thereby developing a unified idealistic metaphysics built about the key concept of the "objective spirit" (*objectiver Geist*). It then conceived of the whole of history as the "unfolding" of the world spirit, human action being essentially an "acting out" or implementation of the spirt's "ideal" content.

Perhaps the primary disposition of the Cartesian phase of this broad intellectual development was to derive as much as possible from the inherent nature of objects; the conception of the "mind" as a *tabula rasa* which is only a recipient of sense impressions just carried this to an extreme. By contrast, idealism tended to attribute as much as possible to the creative activity of mind. On the one hand, this emphasized the importance in action of individual human agents as distinguished from the circumstances of their situations. But on the other hand, the problem of a cultural system, *transcending* (in the strict Kantian sense) the individual actor was necessarily extremely prominent.

Marxism. As the massive development of economics and, later, of psychology into firm disciplines led in the nineteenth century to the establishment of a strong intellectual tradition which positively institutionalized recognition of the wants–activities differentiation within human objects of scientific observations, so the idealistic conception of an "unfolding" *Geist* could not satisfy for long. It required a parallel to the utilitarian differentiation between wants and activities. Such theoretical formulation emerged most clearly with the conceptions of Marx, who set a world of "material" factors over against the "ideal" factors of the Hegelian tradition. The famous aphorism about "setting Hegel on his head" makes clear, I think, that on broader grounds Marx intended to stay within the idealistic framework. The Marxian category of "material" was therefore in no way identical with that of "physical," which had figured in Descartes and even Kant. It concerned, above all, those aspects of the human condition which are *conditional* to the attainment of human goals. The old primacy problem, which is inherent in the use of dichotomous conceptualization, came, in this case, to focus on whether primacy lay in the "ideal" realm or in the conditions necessary for their implementation. Marx's materialism consisted essentially in his confronting the "utopians" with the necessity to be "realistic" in taking account of such conditions. Importantly, his "material" system was not simply an "unfolding spirit" but a social system, in present terms an interaction system, however inadequately analyzed.

Modern Developments

There are two limiting boundaries of the "action" aspect of the human condition: the biological, conceived of in terms of heredity and environment; and the cultural, conceived of as a symbolically defined system of order with normative primacy, to which men are *obligated* to conform on pain of this-worldly—or otherworldly—sanctions. Both major trends of social thought have been under pressure toward a reductionism grounded at one of these two boundaries. The utilitarian tradition has tended to be biologized, and the Kantain tradition to be "Hegelianized"—if one may take Hegelianism as the relative extreme of idealistic reductionism. At the same time, considerations similar to those that gave rise to the Marxian revolt against Hegelianism stimulated movements from both traditions that have brought conceptual definiteness and clarity into the middle ground between these two extremes.

Freud and Personality Theory

On the utilitarian side, the development of biological science in the latter half of the nineteenth century and the fluorescence of varieties of "social Darwinism" acutely posed the problem of how the essential components of human social action could be treated in a manner that would be realistic about the continuity between "human nature" and the organic world. Here the most important single figure was Freud, who, as a physician, started with the conception of man as organism but, as a psychiatrist, became primarily concerned with man's behavior, not the internal state of his organs. Furthermore, the clinical method developed by Freud stressed the emotions and wishes and goals, rather than cognitive matters.

Freud started as an "instinctivist," in the familiar hereditarist sense. Although, of course, he never abandoned emphasizing the importance of instinctual needs, he developed the concept of instinct itself from the more conventional idea of a hereditarily given pattern of behavior "triggered" by environmental stimuli to that of a highly generalized motivational system involving a complex relation between basic instinctual energy and the mechanisms of its goal specification and its control. The erotic complex, the focus of the "pleasure principle," became a complex system which was by no means given and which was complexly integrated (or malintegrated, as the case might be) with the noninstinctual components of personality.

Relatively early, Freud gained the insight that the expression of instinctual need was regulated by the society's moral standards—often, but in no

simple sense always, in conflict with instinctual needs,—and that these standards were *introjected* into the personality itself, becoming components of its structure. The final form of this conception crystallized about the famous idea of the superego. Later this basic mode of conceptualization was extended to the social environment, conceived of as an environment much in the Cartesian—Durkheimian sense. The famous "reality principle" came to focus on "object relations," which for Freud meant relations to other persons, especially the parents, considered as agents of socialization. But these human objects were not only "adapted to" in the sense true for physical objects; they were also introjected—or, as we now usually say, internalized—to form part of the personality structure, particularly of the ego, in Freud's sense.

Thus, Freud brought the distinctive properties of the social, as distinguished from the physical, environment of the action of the individual to the forefront of analytical consideration in two connections: that of normative standards and that of the more empirical aspects of the social object world. Indeed, it can be shown that even the id, the third of Freud's primary structural subsystems of personality, is not purely "instinctual" but is organized about the "precipitates of lost objects," especially those salient in the earliest phases of a person's socialization experience (Parsons 1958).

Durkheim and the Content of Culture

Whereas Freud, from a biological starting point, arrived at the recognition of the distinctive properties of social systems, Durkheim began with the conviction that clear distinctions between social and personal systems were essential; in his famous phrase, society was a reality *sui generis.* In order to ground this, however, he had to escape the toils of utilitarianism. He chose to do this by harking back to the Cartesian frame of reference, including its cognitive primacy. Durkheim's basic difference from Descartes was his insistence on exploring the distinctive category he called *social facts,* the facts of the social environment of the actor of reference. However, Durkheim also recognized a strong need to consider the actor as something more than a "thinker." Furthermore, since the relevant environment was social, insofar as it included a plurality of individual actors they were all units of the same character as the original actor of reference and were conceived of as *interacting* with him.

From this start Durkheim came to converge with Freud at three essential points. The first was Durkheim's primary starting position, his analysis of the distinctiveness of the *social* object world. If we combine this analysis with that of Freud, we can confidently speak of its distinctiveness vis-à-vis not only the physical world in the narrower sense but also the organic

world. The second was the idea that an essential aspect of the social environment is that it imposes normative requirements on the individual and sanctions him for compliance and noncompliance. The third was that the structure of this social environment, particularly its normative component, comes to be internalized in the personality of the indvidual. Otherwise, the *moral authority* of "society" as an agency of the control of the individual's action—as an agency of constraint, in Durkheim's sense—could not be understood. Although Durkheim did not develop a technical theory of the personality of the individual as a system, clearly the structure of his theoretical scheme articulates very directly with the type of personality theory Freud developed and even demands such articulation for theoretical closure.

Durkheim's treatment of the normative components of social systems, however, went well beyond Freud, in a direction that brought him close to Kant. Since concern with the social system was primary for him (rather than residual, as for Freud), he was aware of the conception that normative components are part of a cultural system and in that sense transcend the individual. Durkheim developed this theme particularly well with his conception of "collective representations" and spelled it out in his analysis of religion in *The Elementary Forms of the Religious Life* (1912). He made it quite clear, as Freud did not, that systems of "representations"— no longer just a Cartesian mode of expression—were basically *symbolic*. In so doing, he took a most important step toward conceiving of the content of culture as consisting of codified symbolic systems and toward a general understanding of their articulation both with social systems and personalities.

Durkheim and Marx. Although this late development of Durkheim's work brought him into direct contact with the idealistic movement, he was no more an idealist than Marx. It is interesting to compare them in this connection. Marx represents, of course, a particularly notable reaction against the Hegelian extreme, and indeed his conception of social systems is closer to Durkheim's than has generally been believed. It can, however, be said that Marx was particularly ambiguous about the status of the normative components of social order. This ambiguity resulted from his scheme's being incompletely differentiated in two main respects. First, the ideological–evaluative aspect was not clearly differentiated from the scientific aspect. For instance, with reference to "capitalism," the moral condemnation of its normative structure tended to underrate its empirical importance in an analytical sense, suggesting that it merely cloaked exploitative interests. Second, Marxian thought shared with Hegelian and other postidealistic theories a commitment to *historicism*. This position denied the possibility, for the sociocultural field, of generalized analytical theory. Marxian theory is a theory of the development of a succession of dynamically linked *particular* socioeconomic systems, not an analytical theory

of society in general. Marx does not use Ricardian economic theory as economic theory in the general sense but as the theory of capitalist process within one historical economic system.

Durkheim was not caught in these difficulties. He assumed as a good Cartesian, that if social facts were facts, the general methodology of science, including general analytical theory, applied to them. And dealing with the problem of the "ideal" factors from a rather pre-Hegelian, Kantian viewpoint, he did not worry about the alleged dilemma of whether ideal or material factors determined human action "in the last analysis."

Max Weber and the Individual Actor

If Durkheim avoided the ideal-material dilemma, Max Weber, starting from reference points within the German idealistic tradition, worked his way out of it, in a manner converging directly with Durkheim's position. His crucial reference was the "motives of individuals"; only through understanding (*Verstehen*) of the *meanings* of motives of actual and typical individuals could the motives be used to explain empirical courses of action—in relation, of course, to the conditions of the action situation. These motives of individuals were by no means the same as the wants of the utilitarians, precisely because, instead of being taken as given, their structure was a matter of major interest. Indeed, cultural meaning systems constituted a primary focus of Weber's interest, as developed most clearly in his studies in the sociology of religion.

At the same time, Weber's position is by no means a Hegelian idealism or a post-Hegelian "gestaltism" in the manner of Dilthey. In these latter cases the principal relation of a meaning complex (*Sinnzusammenhang*) to material reality is simply that of "unfolding." Weber, however, made the crucial contribution of breaking down the rigid alternative of using *either* ideal *or* material *systems* as empirically closed, in that he developed a way of analyzing the complex interdependences between them. This is how Weber could become eminent *both* as a "sociologist of culture," e.g., of religion, and as a sociologist of economic and political phenomena (particularly the latter), with his analysis of the social significance of law providing the most important link between them (cf. Parsons 1965). Thus, he managed to emphasize the complete reality of the "material" interests of persons and groups, while avoiding the faulty assumption of the Marxian model that these interests constitute a closed system which can be broken through only by a total revolutionary transformation. In regard to the individual actor, Weber, rather than having to arrive at a conception of internalization—as did the utilitarians, as well as Freud and Durkheim—quite naturally took it for granted, on the basis of his general theoretical position.

This orientation can be detailed only through the systematic analysis of interaction. Unit-by-unit social systems must be analyzed as engaged in detailed interchanges with each other, interchanges which constitute performances or sanctions according to which unit, the "sender" or the "receiver," is the point of reference. Weber, more than any other figure emerging predominantly from the idealistic tradition, laid the groundwork and demonstrated the use of the more generalized schema toward which the movements of thought we are considering had been evolving. The relations of the authority of office to the use of power and of property to markets and exchanges were primary focuses of the vast range of his empirical studies. Power and economic resources, of course, constitute particularly salient sanctions and resources in the more-differentiated interaction systems, and Weber's work may serve us as a kind of charter for analyzing them in social-system rather than purely economic or political terms.

A Paradigm of Social Interaction

The broad outline of the present conception of interaction has emerged from the above movements. Its focus is a social system generated by and composed of the interaction of units which are "behaving organisms," personalities, or various levels of collectivity. Acting units, however, are always involved in cultural systems, which express, symbolize, order, and control human orientations through patterned meaning systems consisting of both codes of meaning and specific combinations of symbols in particular contexts. At a minimum, an interaction system in this sense involves four analytically distinguishable aspects or components: (1) a set of "units" which interact with each other; (2) a set of rules or other "code" factors, the terms of which structure both the orientations of the units and the interaction itself; (3) an ordered or patterned system or process of the interaction itself; (4) an environment in which the system operates and with which systematic interchanges take place. It can be seen that the various intellectual movements reviewed contributed one or another special emphasis or combination of components to this paradigm but that only at a late stage did anything like the complete paradigm emerge.

Pragmatism and the Nature of the Self

Before a fuller exposition of the paradigm is attempted, two further movements, which contributed less to its main outlines than those already reviewed but which have nevertheless been very influential, should receive brief attention. The first of these is primarily American and may be con-

sidered an aspect of the pragmatist movement. In a sense, James and Peirce cut through the structured rigidity of the European thought of their time to bring the whole self-object system into a new flux. Particularly in view of the "scientistic" trends in American thought, pragmatism raised questions about the self which were particularly important. James introduced a distinctively un-Cartesian pluralism into the concept: besides the *I,* which thought, there were an *I,* a *me,* and various other possible *selves.*

Symbolic Interaction—Cooley and Mead. One branch of the pragmatist movement made a special contribution to social interaction theory, namely, that associated with Charles Horton Cooley and George Herbert Mead, which eventuated in a special kind of social psychology. It was Cooley who first took seriously the truly indeterminate character of the self as a structure independent of others. This led to the idea that the self developed in the process of interaction with others. As Mead said, to Cooley the "other" belonged in the same field as the self and was just as immediately given (Mead 1930).

Cooley, however, despite some arresting insights about the "looking-glass" features of the self, adhered to a semi-idealistic, subjectivst concept of "mind" which, though no longer individualistic in the Cartesian or the utilitarian sense, achieved only a truncated conception of interaction systems. Mead, however, took the essential step of treating the individual as being both subject and object at the same time and in the same interpersonal system. Furthermore, he was far clearer than Cooley in showing that the personality of the individual emerges from the process we now call socialization precisely through the interplay between these subjective and objective aspects. This is not (as the idealists would have it) a process of the "unfolding" of the mind, individual or collective, but vitally includes the internalization of *objects.*

Mead also contributed a most important conception in his idea of the *generalized other.* Through symbolic interaction the individual learns to use and develop generalized codes that can interrelate a conception of the particular other with generalized categories and collectivities. This is the foundation, in the process of socialization, of the internalization of cultural, as well as social, systems, which in turn can come to be differentiated from each other. Mead took much longer steps than Cooley toward opening sociology and social psychology to the substitution of more technical research procedures for reliance on interpretative insight alone.

This was social psychology, in that it demonstrated and analyzed the intimacy of the relation between personality and social system by showing (in a way related to but different from Freud's) that the personality cannot be understood independently of its articulation, including its genetic involvement, with social interaction. Moreover, particularly in Mead, who was a kind of symbolic behavorist, there was an even fuller awareness than in Freud of the evolutionary continuity of phenomena between the

human levels of action and those of organic life more generally. Mead also surpassed Freud in beginning the exploration of truly symbolic processes and in building a bridge between behavior theory and linguistics. There was certainly impressive convergence between this version of "symbolic-interaction" theory and the ideas of both Freud and Durkheim on the internalization of social objects.

The Existentialist Tradition

German, or, more broadly, continental European, thought has for a considerable period involved a strand of thinking which has recently gained promience in analyzing interaction in a manner playing into a basic, if still relatively unclear, synthesis with the American tradition of social psychology. Perhaps it is most conveniently traced back to the Kantian phase in the development of idealism. Kant's sphere of "practical reason" was specifically unstructured, in any sense comparable to that of either the phenomenal or the physical world. It was the world of will, individuality, and what may be considered socially unorganized meanings. It is perhaps particularly important here that this tradition experienced great difficulty in making the crucial discrimination between the biological–environmental and the cultural–cosmological reference poles of action systems. It has tended to merge the two in speaking of the "deeper" human needs of motivations.

In the early phase, perhaps Schelling was the interpreter of the Kantian tradition who veered furthest in this direction. Later, various more or less definitely "existentialist" orientations, but particularly those of Kierkegaard and Nietzsche, seem to be most prominent. A rough continuum among three distinct emphases evidently characterizes the more modern and more sociologically oriented phase.

Weber is at one end, self-consciously analyzing the interdependence of "intended meanings" and situation, interaction and sanctions, and being less concerned with the "fate" of subjective fantasies and hopes themselves than with the nature of the interaction systems generated by the complex modes of their implementation (and the failure thereof).

Perhaps Georg Simmel, who has had a very important impact on American social science, can be placed in the middle. Simmel attempted to confine "phenomenal" determinacy to the "forms" of interaction, and he devoted his immense intuitive talents to the interpretative understanding of the meanings individual actors and types of action injected into interaction, thereby creating, in a broad and rather loose sense, the determinate framework of such interaction. Significantly, Simmel's influence came into American social science via the University of Chicago, which was also the home of Mead. Simmel's "forms of social relationship" were not ex-

planatory categories so much as a frame of reference for interpretive essays (see Naegele 1958).

The third movement, that furthest from Weber, is grounded philosophically in the phenomenological tradition of Husserl and, in part, Heidegger and has affiliations with existentialism. Less immediately, it is also certainly linked with the post-Hegelian historicism that was Weber's major critical foil. It focuses primarily on the most intimate experiences and feelings of the individual and from that vantage point mounts a relativizing criticism upon the more conventionalized and supposedly "superficial" structures of social life. At least certain elements in the movement stress individualism to the borders of a philosophical anarchy, running strongly counter to traditional sociological emphases on the grounding of basic order in social life.

Perhaps the most prominent writer in American sociology today strongly influenced by both a Meadian symbolic interactionism and a phenomenological viewpoint is Erving Goffman. Goffman's most distinctive line of thought is a stress on the discrepancies between the self-image which the actor presents to others in the interactive process and his underlying private attitude and preoccupations (Goffman 1956).

Empirical Approaches

Since World War II there has been an important movement in the United States in favor of the empirical study of interaction, especially in small-group research. Three aspects of this may be mentioned. The so-called group-dynamics tradition was founded by the social psychologist Kurt Lewin (1939–1947; Lewin et al. 1944; Benne et al. 1950). It has been relatively eclectic, with an emphasis on the malleability of human goals through interaction. This environmentalism has been associated with a strong "action" orientation, i.e., toward changing behavior in desired directions through group participation experience.

The second movement has been the experimental and laboratory study of interaction in small groups by Bales and his associates (cf. Bales 1950). This group has concentrated on technical observational and analytical methods and theoretically has strongly emphasized the concept of social system at this level, as well as that of larger systems; in this respect it may be said to be in the theory-of-action tradition.

The third type of work is that of Homans, which took its departure from the study of informal organization in industry by Elton Mayo and his associates (cf. Homans 1950). In his latest work, Homans (1961) has, broadly in what above has been called a utilitarian framework, attempted to derive the main features of what he terms "elementary social

behavior" from experimental psychology of Skinner's type and from certain postulates of the theory of economic exchange.

Interaction and the Social System

The remainder of this article will attempt a systematic outline of both the components of an interaction system and some major aspects of the interaction process itself. I shall try to show that the principal emphases of the historical theories outlined above figure somewhere in a more generalized and theoretically comprehensive scheme. This more comprehensive scheme is a "theory of action," in the sense long used by the author and also, in substance, by very many others, although their terminology may differ.

The concept of interaction is the first-order step beyond the action concept itself toward formulating the concept of social system. In speaking of action, we assume meaningful motivations and goal directedness. Motives, goals, and the like are expressed in, and hence must be interpreted as embodying, cultural-level symbolic form. There are infrastructures of all action systems which are not symbolically structured, but there is no *system* of action, in the present sense, which does not involve cultural symbolization—pre-eminently, of course, through language.

The concept of a dyadic interaction is convenient for clarifying certain fundamentals of interaction phenomena generally. But since it is a limiting case, general inferences from it should be made with care. This is true in the same sense that, although the unicellular organism is convenient for studying certain fundamentals of all organic life, alone it can scarcely provide adequate evidence for a theory of organic evolution.

The crucial reference points for analyzing interaction are two: (1) that each actor is *both* acting agent and object of orientation *both* to himself and to the others; and (2) that, as acting agent, he orients to himself and to others and, as object, has meaning to himself and to others, in *all* of the primary modes or aspects. The actor is knower and object of cognition, utilizer of instrumental means and himself a means, emotionally attached to others and an object of attachment, evaluator and object of evalution, interpreter of symbols and himself a symbol.

From these premises derives the fundamental proposition of the *double* contingency of interaction. Not only, as for isolated behaving units, animal or human, is a goal outcome contingent on successful cognition and manipulation of environmental objects by the actors, but since the most important objects involved in interaction act too, it is also contingent on *their* action or intervention in the course of events. The theory of games is perhaps the most sophisticated analysis of the implications of such double

contingency. Of course, the contingency factor multiplies with each addition to the number of interacting units (for my own earlier formulations, see Parsons & Shils 1951).

Double contingency and more complex contingencies have a crucial set of consequences. On the one hand, as analyzed pre-eminently by Hobbes in an interaction system the possibilities of instability far exceed those to which isolated actors are exposed in relation to environments containing only nonactors, e.g., physical objects, as the significant objects. On the other hand, if the autonomy possessed by each acting unit relative to its environment is *integrated* with that of the others with which it interacts, the interaction system as a whole can gain vastly in autonomy, or freedom of action. Moreover, under certain conditions this enhanced autonomy of the system can be shared by the units within the system. In this situation a unit within the "organized" interaction system has greater freedom to act autonomously than does a unit which has the same capacities but which is isolated in relation to its physical environment, in the manner of Robinson Crusoe. This is the analytical basis of the "institutionalized individualism" which Durkheim so clearly demonstrated to be a product of the division of labor, in his sense.

Conditions of Integration

The most important *single* condition of the integration of an interaction system is a *shared basis of normative order*. Because it must operate to control the disruptive potentialities (for the system of reference) of the autonomy of units, as well as to guide autonomous action into channels which, through mutual reinforcement, enhance the potential for autonomy of both the system as a whole and its member units, such a basis of order *must* be normative. It must guide action by establishing some distinctions between desirable and undesirable lines of action which can serve to stablize interaction in these fundamental senses. Whether the stabilized system is "static" or "dynamically changing" in one or more of many senses is another issue. The theory of games can be said to have proved that a complex interaction system with no rules, but in which each unit is supposed only to be "rationally pursuing its self-interest," *cannot* be stable in the above sense. This is a critical point for understanding the place of "rationality" in social behavior.

The concept of a shared basis of normative order is basically the same as that of a *common culture* or a "symbolic system." The prototype of such an order is language. A language involves a *code,* consisting of the generalized norms which define "correct" speech or writing, as the basis for using symbols to formulate and transmit messages. Although

there is considerable minor deviation, the massive fact is that *all* speakers of a language "observe" the norms of the code—"conform" to them, if you will—on penalty of not being understood.

Language, to be sure, is not a primary normative constituent of *social* systems in the sense true of the law in complex systems, but it is a primary normative constitutent of distinct *cultural* systems. However, the point I wish to make here is that *all* culture is a matter of normative control, or the "guidance" of action. This is one sense in which the dyad is clearly a limiting case of interaction. However isolated a dyad may be in other respects, it can *never* generate the ramified common culture which makes *meaningful* and stable interaction possible. A dyad always presupposes a culture shared in a wider system. Furthermore, such a culture is always the product of a "historical" process long transcending the duration of a particular dyadic relationship.

As Durkheim made clear, for actors in interaction this common normative culture has a double significance. On the one hand, for each actor it constitutes a primary part of the situation or environment of his action. Its existence and the ways in which it guides the actions of system members are social facts of which the actor must take account. These facts include the probabilities of the imposition of sanctions contingent on action relative to the norms: rewards for conformity and negative sanctions for nonconformity. On the other hand, the normative culture becomes, in the paradigmatic cases, internalized in the personalities of individual actors—and institutionalized in collectivities—and thereby comes to control action, in part, by *moral* authority. To this extent conformity is voluntary, and hence internal sanctions come into play.

The phenomenon that cultural norms are internalized to personalities and institutionalized in collectivities is a case of the *interpenetration* of subsystems of action, in this case social system, cultural system, and personality. Since these subsystems are defined analytically, not concretely, it is understandable that the concrete boundary of any one subsystem may include within it spheres or zones which require an especially intimate integration with part of one or more other subsystems. Here the critical proposition is that institutionalized normative culture is an essential part of *all* stable systems of social interaction. Therefore, the social system and the culture must be integrated in specific ways in the area of their interpenetration.

The dyadic paradigm of interaction also constitutes a special limiting case in regard to the way in which an interaction system constitutes a collectivity. This point deserves special emphasis. Treatment of the dyad as the typical rather than the limiting case tends to perpetuate the utilitarian view of interaction and to underplay both solidarity and the role of normative culture in favor of the "wants" of individuals—or any other version of individual "interests." Any given dyadic relation, as well as any given

"individual," should be seen in the context of a wider social system inter-penetrating with a broader, shared culture.

Role Pluralism and Personality

Relative stability of a significant level of integration over time implies both a common normative culture and rather definite criteria of member-ship status. Members share with each other a level of solidarity not ap-plying, in the relevant collectivity reference, to the relations between mem-bers and nonmembers. Solidarity involves some special quality and level of presumptive mutual trust and loyalty to the collective interest, on oc-casion involving the sacrifice of unit interests. In principle a collectivity is capable of "action in concert," in the sense of taking collective action toward goals defined in social process as those of the collectivity and resist-ing centrifugal forces which might reduce the collective involvements of member actors to pure self-interest. Indeed, the possibility of such action provides the primary basis for the boundaries between a social system and its environment, consisting of other social systems or other types of systems.

Dyadic interaction systems may constitute collectivities and be solidary in signficant degree, but they are always subsystems of more extensive social systems. One reason for this is the necessity of a common culture; thus, for example, the interaction possible without a common language is very limited indeed. A second reason invovles the relation of the inter-action system to the personalities of its members. A dyad, as a matter of empirical fact, never constitutes an independent society; a member of a dyad never interacts *only* with the particular role partner of that dyad. Hence, his *whole* personality, so far as it is engaged in social interaction, is never engaged only in a single dyadic interaction. Thus, although mar-riage is a particularly important dyadic relation, it is typical in *all* known societies that married couples have children and that the role of spouse is differentiated from that of parent; moreover, the nuclear family always constitutes a more inclusive collectivity in which each member plays *plural* roles.

The phenomenon of *role pluralism* is a central feature of all human societies, and this is more important the more highly differentiated the society. Therefore, the interactive spheres of different individuals, al-though overlapping and interpenetrating, are not identical. Any given individual participates in a considerable number of specific interaction systems, the more important and enduring of which are the stable col-lectivities in which he is a member. Thus, the unit of collectivity member-ship is not *the individual* in general but the *person in role*.

Two consequences follow from this. First, parallel to the interpenetra-tion between social and cultural systems noted above, there must be inter-

penetration between social systems and personalities. Concretely, just as normative culture is internalized in personalities as well as institutionalized, there must be institutionalized expectations about the particular role in the particular collectivity which are also interalized in the personalities of incumbents. Typically, of course, internalized expectations of reciprocity shade in varying degrees into alienation and propensities for deviance.

Second, however, the specifications of normative culture to the different collectivities in which the individual participates and the expectations about behavior in the individual's various roles must be integrated with each other *at the level of the personality.* One-to-one matching between the specific structures of particular personalities and the behavioral requirements of socially organized roles is precluded by, together, the pluralistic differentiation of subcollectivities in the social system and the plural role participations of individual persons. The sociological reason for this, which combines with genetic, psychological, and other kinds of reasons, is that no two persons have the same combination of role involvements—a circumstance greatly accentuated in societies where a substantial proportion of role involvements are nonascriptive—and, hence, role involvements are entered as a matter of, in some sense, voluntary choice. (Positing such a correspondence between the bases of social system and of personality integration has been a major fallacy in many theories of "culture and personality" and "national character.")

Here we encounter again Durkheim's analysis of the double relations between actor and normative culture. From the perspective of the social system the personalities of its participating members are at the same time, in different respects, *both part of the social system,* through interpenetration, *and part of its environment.* The zone of interpenetration is that of the expectations about role performance, since they are both institutionalized in the social system and internalized in individual personalities. Here it is particularly important that, where the roles of role partners are differentiated, expectations are, not for identical, but for *different yet complementary* performances. For instance, huband and wife, in their differentiated roles in the family, are generally expected to act, not alike, but differently, each having a distinct proper sex role. The differences between roles, as well as their common solidarity, are legitimized by the values shared between them.

Organism and Environment

The personality of the individual, as an analytically defined action system, is one major parameter, linked to the living organism, the two being, in our terminology, ascribed to each other. They must nevertheless be

distinguished analytically because the structure and mechanisms of the organism are physical, while those of the personality are psychocultural and learned. As with the personality and social system, there can be no one-to-one correspondence between the properties of an organism and the personality's internalized content of normative culture, and social role expectations. In certain contexts, this is very well known; thus, no expert contends that, in any but a "programmed" sense, there is specific anatomical or physiological structure distinguishing the speakers of a given language from those of another.

The organism is the link between action systems and the physical world. *All* concrete action is, in one aspect, the "behavior of organisms," but only in one aspect. Thus, all linguistic communication involves the speech organs, the auditory apparatus, and the brain (or alternative mechanisms, as in the case of writing and reading). Since organisms are always located in particular places at given times, all social systems have their ecological aspect, i.e., there is location, movement, and distribution of organisms and activities in space. Clearly, an individual's own body and the bodies of others are crucial objects of orientation to him in a wide variety of ways.

It seems to follow that the organism should be included in the physical environment of action systems and hence of social systems. In the light of our traditions of thought, the physical environment is clearly the least problematic of the environments of interaction systems. However, the old difficulties over the sense in which the individual as a whole (including his organic aspects) should be included in the concept of social system can be resolved with the same logic that has been used in relating social systems to the cultural and psychological systems of action.

First, there is a category of objects which are *only* physical, whether they be "natural" objects or artifacts. These cannot and do not interact in human social systems, animals being a marginal case. In this sense, human organisms not only are physical but also interpenetrate with the other action systems. They are environmental objects and also, through interpenetration, parts of the action (and interaction) system.

This dual relation to interaction, however, does not apply equally to all aspects of the human organism. The concept "behavioral organism" designates the components of the organism for which interpenetration with personality, social system, and culture is most important. Some (for instance, H. A. Murray) have used the concept "vegetative organism" to designate aspects, such as most of the metabolic processes and mechanisms, that are minimally involved in action. One should not, however, assume that the line is empirically fixed; action phenomena may shift (through stress or psychotherapy, for instance) to involve rather directly organic processes that ordinarily are insulated from them.

Certainly, the involvement of the organism in interaction comprises

all the modes of orientation and modalities of objects. The organism is perhaps particularly important as an instrumentality, but Freud's concept of primary narcissism rightly considers the child's love of his own body an authentic case of love. Similarly, there is an organic aspect interpenetrating with the nonorganic aspects in every subsystem of the orientation of actors. There has been considerable research, for example, on the organic "bases" of the emotions, starting with the well-known work of Cannon (1915).

Interaction as Process

We may conclude with a brief outline of interaction as process. First, we presume that whatever the intermediate stages in the course of evolution from simple animal behavior to human social interaction, the latter is couched primarily at symbolic-cultural levels, although it certainly has various "subcultural" underpinnings. The action process, then, can be analyzed into two phases: what happens *within* the acting unit (e.g., a person in role or a collectivity) and what happens *between* such units. It seems to be generally acceptable terminology to refer to the former process as "decision" and to the latter as "communication."

In decision processes, information communicated to the deciding unit (this is the interaction case, but environmental information may also be relevant) is "processed" in the light of the "dispositions," goals, sentiments, etc., of the unit. An *act* is then performed, which typically consists of a communication to other units in the system. Whether the communication is verbal or not is an open question, as it may consist, for example, in a gesture of the sort Mead analyzed so clearly. This communication then becomes an input to the receiving units, including the promulgator, who may be, in terms of a stock phrase for this type of situation, "appalled by what he just said."

Every output of communication involves crossing a boundary, as does its receipt as input. Its meaning must be interpreted and introduced into a combinatorial process, along with other inputs and with aspects of the internal structures and processes of the unit, whether a personality or a collectivity. This interpretive and combinatorial process constitutes "decision," from which emerges new communicative output.

The output must also undergo a process that involves an indefinite number of stages before the communication reaches the target unit, units, or categories of units. In a variety of ways this process involves media of communication, which expose the communication to a variety of influences, such as modifications or distortions or maintenance of its "message"

by special measures. Such influences are, of course, the outcome of decions made by units through which the communication passes.

Generalized Media of Interaction

Of the many aspects of the communication process in interaction, one may be singled out for special comment, namely, the role of *generalized* media. I have already mentioned language a number of times as the prototypical medium. At the cultural level it is clearly the fundamental matrix of the whole system of media. Large-scale social systems, however, contain more specialized media (if you will, specialized "languages"), such as money, power, and influence (see Parsons 1963a; 1963b). Such media, like language, *control* behavior in the processes of interaction. They do so, however, by *symbolic* means, i.e., by presenting the actor, not with an intrinsically important object, such as a food object, but with a symbolic "representation" of such an object. Symbols can arouse the expectation that a meal will be served; hence they prepare the communication's recipient for the experience of food-gratification and, within important limits, even substitute for the experience. The working of money in this regard is the best-understood example of a social system medium. It has, as the classical economists put it, no "value in use," but only "value in exchange." Possession of money symbolically concretizes expectations of access to gratifying objects of utility, but money is not itself such an object.

There are various other such media in human interaction. Freud's "erotic pleasure" certainly constitutes one, as do the phenomena referred to by such terms as "affect" and "social acceptance," and what W. I. Thomas called the "wishes" for response and recognition. The demonstration that such media are deeply needed by persons at a psychological level is excellent evidence of the phenomena of initernalization discussed above and, more generally, of interpenetration.

Bibliography

BALES, ROBERT F.   1950   *Interaction Process Analysis: A Method for the Study of Small Groups.* Reading, Mass.: Addison-Wesley.

BENNE, KENNETH D.; BRADFORD, LELAND I.; and LIPPITT, RONALD   1950   *Social Action.* New York: B'nai B'rith Anti-Defamation League.

CANNON, WALTER B.   (1915)   1953   *Bodily Changes in Pain, Hunger, Fear and Rage: An Account of Recent Researches Into the Function of Emotional Excitement.* 2d ed. Boston: Branford.

COOLEY, CHARLES H.   (1902)   1956   *Human Nature and the Social Order.*

Rev. ed. In Charles H. Cooley, *Two Major Works:* Social Organization *and* Human Nature and the Social Order. Glencoe, Ill.: Free Press. Each title reprinted with individual title page and pagination. Separate paperback editions were published in 1964 by Schocken.

DURKHEIM, ÉMILE (1893) 1960 *The Division of Labor in Society.* Glencoe, Ill.: Free Press. First published as *De la division du travail social.*

DURKHEIM, ÉMILE (1895) 1958 *The Rules of Sociological Method.* 8th ed. Edited by George E. G. Catlin. Glencoe, Ill.: Free Press. First published as *Les règles de la méthode sociologique.*

DURKHEIM, ÉMILE (1912) 1954 *The Elementary Forms of the Religious Life.* London: Allen & Unwin; New York: Macmillan. First published as *Les formes élémentaires de la vie religieuse, le système totémique en Australie.*

GOFFMAN, ERVING (1956) 1959 *The Presentation of Self in Everyday Life.* Garden City, N.Y.: Doubleday.

HOMANS, GEORGE C. 1950 *The Human Group.* New York: Harcourt.

HOMANS, GEORGE C. 1961 *Social Behavior: Its Elementary Forms.* New York: Harcourt.

LEWIN, KURT (1939–1947) 1963 *Field Theory in Social Science: Selected Theoretical Papers.* Edited by Dorwin Cartwright. London: Tavistock.

LEWIN, KURT et al. 1944 *Authority and Frustration.* Iowa City: Univ. of Iowa Press.

MEAD, GEORGE H. (1930) 1964 Cooley's Contribution to American Social Thought. Pages 293–307 in George H. Mead, *George Herbert Mead on Social Psychology.* Rev. ed. Edited by Anselm Strauss. Univ. of Chicago Press.

MEAD, GEORGE H. (1934) 1963 *Mind, Self and Society From the Standpoint of a Social Behaviorist.* Edited by Charles W. Morris. Univ. of Chicago Press. Published posthumously.

MEAD, GEORGE H. 1938 *The Philosophy of the Act.* Univ. of Chicago Press. This volume consists almost entirely of papers unpublished during Mead's lifetime.

NAEGELE, KASPER D. 1958 Attachment and Alienation: Complementary Aspects of the Work of Durkheim and Simmel. *American Journal of Sociology* 63:580–589.

PARSONS, TALCOTT (1958) 1964 Social Structure and the Development of Personality: Freud's Contribution to the Integration of Psychology and Sociology. Pages 78–111 in Talcott Parsons, *Social Structure and Personality.* New York: Free Press.

PARSONS, TALCOTT 1963a On the Concept of Influence. *Public Opinion Quarterly* 27:37–62. A comment by J. S. Coleman appears on pages 63–82; a communication by R. A. Bauer appears on pages 83–86; and a rejoinder by Talcott Parsons appears on pages 87–92.

PARSONS, TALCOTT 1963b On the Concept of Political Power. American Philosophical Society, *Proceedings* 107:232–262.

PARSONS, TALCOTT 1965 Evaluation and Objectivity in Social Science: An Interpretation of Weber's Contribution. *International Social Science Journal* 17:46–63.

PARSONS, TALCOTT; and SHILS, EDWARD A. (editors) 1951 *Toward a General Theory of Action.* Cambridge, Mass.: Harvard Univ. Press. A paperback edition was published in 1962 by Harper.

SIMMEL, GEORG (1902–1917) 1950 *The Sociology of Georg Simmel.* Edited and translated by Kurt H. Wolff. Glencoe, Ill.: Free Press.

SIMMEL, GEORG (1908) 1955 *Conflict; The Web of Group Affiliations.* Glencoe, Ill.: Free Press. These essays appeared originally as "Der Streit" and "Die Kreuzung sozialer Kreise" in Georg Simmel's *Soziologie.*

SIMMEL, GEORG *Georg Simmel, 1858–1918: A Collection of Essays.* Edited by Kurt H. Wolff. Columbus: Ohio State Univ. Press, 1959.

TIRYAKIAN, EDWARD A. 1962 *Sociologism and Existentialism: Two Perspectives on the Individual and Society.* Englewood Cliffs, N.J.: Prentice-Hall.

WEBER, MAX (1922) 1957 *The Theory of Social and Economic Organization.* Edited by Talcott Parsons. Glencoe, Ill.: Free Press. First published as Part 1 of *Wirtschaft und Gesellschaft*

8. Social Systems

"SYSTEM" is the concept that refers both to a complex of interdependencies between parts, components, and processes that involve discernible regularities of relationship, and to a similar type of interdependency between such a complex and its surrounding environment. System, in this sense, is therefore the concept around which all sophisticated theory in the conceptually generalizing disciplines is and must be organized. This is because any regularity of relationship can be more adequately understood if the whole complex of multiple interdependencies of which it forms part is taken into account.

Social Systems and the Action System

Methodologically, one must distinguish a theoretical system, which is a complex of assumptions, concepts, and propositions having both logical integration and empirical reference, from an empirical system, which is a set of phenomena in the observable world that can be described and analyzed by means of a theoretical system. An empirical system (e.g., the solar system as relevant to analytical mechanics) is never a totally concrete entity but, rather, a selective organization of those properties of the concrete entity defined as relevant to the theoretical system in question. Thus, for Newtonian solar system mechanics, the earth is "only" a particle with a given mass, location in space, velocity, and direction of motion; the Newtonian scheme is not concerned with the earth's geological or human social and cultural characteristics. In this sense, any theoretical system is abstract.

As a theoretical system, the social system is specifically adapted to

From the *International Encyclopedia of the Social Sciences,* David L. Sills, editor, Volume 15, pp. 458–473. Reprintetd by permission of the Publisher. Copyright © 1968 by Crowell Collier and Macmillan, Inc.

describing and analyzing social interaction considered as a class of empirical systems. These systems are concerned with the behavior, as distinguished from the metabolic physiology, of living organisms. Among the categories of organisms, our interest in this article centers on human social interaction, which is organized on the symbolic levels we call "cultural." However, one should remember that such interaction is a late evolutionary product and is continuous with a very broad range of interaction phenomena among other organisms. All bisexual reproduction, for example, requires highly structured interactive relations between the organisms of the two sexes. Various kinds of interspecies ecological relations constitute another example, one to which human relations wth domesticated animals are relevant.

The aspects of behavior which directly concern "cultural-level" systems I call *action*. Action in this technical sense includes four generic types of subsystems, the differentiation among which has gained fairly clear definition during modern intellectual history.

The first is simply the organism, which though quite properly treated as a concrete entity in one set of terms, becomes, on a more generalized level, a set of abstract components (i.e., a subsystem) in the culturally organized system of action.

A second subsystem is the social system, which is generated by the process of interaction among individual units. Its distinctive properties are consequences and conditions of the specific modes of interrelationship obtaining among the living organisms which constitute its units.

Third is the cultural system, which is the aspect of action organized about the specific characteristics of symbols and the exigencies of forming stable systems of them. It is structured in terms of patternings of meaning which, when stable, imply in turn generalized complexes of constitutive symbolisms that give the action system its primary "sense of direction," and which must be treated as independent of any particular system of social interaction. Thus, although there are many ramifications into such areas as language and communication, the prototypical cultural systems are those of beliefs and ideas. The possibilities of their preservation over time, and of their diffusion from one personality and/or social system into another, are perhaps the most important hallmarks of the independent structure of cultural systems.

Fourth, the analytical distinction between social and cultural systems has a correlative relation to the distinction between the organism and those other aspects of the individual actor which we generally call the personality. With the achievement of cultural levels of the control of behavior, the primary subsystems of action can no longer be organized—or structured primarily—about the organic base, which, in the first instance, is anatomical or "physical." Personality, then, is the aspect of the living individual, as "actor," which *must* be understood in terms of the cultural and social

content of the learned patternings that make up his behavioral system. Here, "learned" refers not only to the problem of the origin of the patterns in the heredity-environment sense, but also to the problem of the kind and level of their content. The connection between these two problems partly reflects the fact that we have no evidence that cultural content is, at what we call here the level of pattern, determined through the genes. Thus, there is no evidence of a hereditary "propensity" to speak one language rather than another, although the genetically determined capacities to learn and use language are generally fundamental.

Thus, we treat the social system, when evolved to the action level, as one of four primary subsystems of action, all of which articulate with the organic bases of life and with organic adaptation to the environment in the broadest biological sense.

There is a sense in which the social system is the core of human action systems, being the primary link between the culture and the individual both as personality and as organism—a fact for which "culture and personality" theorists have often not adequately accounted. As the principal source of the independence of cultural systems from restrictive organic and environmental conditions, it has been the primary locus of the "operation bootstrap" of human evolution. The secret of this evolutionary capacity evidently lies in the possibilities for "reverberation" among the intercommunicating members of a social system, each of whom is both an actor orienting himself to his situation in terms of complex, cultural-level, intended meanings and an object of orientation meaningful to orienting actors. Furthermore, each person is both actor and object to himself as well as to others. Interaction at the symbolic level thus becomes a system analytically and, very appreciably, empirically independent of its presymbolic bases (though still grounded in them), and is capable of development on its own.

Insigt into this basic complex of facts constitutes a principal foundation of modern social science theory. It has been attained by convergence from at least four sources: Freud's psychology, starting from a medical-biological base; Weber's sociology, which worked to transcend the problems of the German intellectual tradition concerning idealism-materialism; Durkheim's analysis of the individual actor's relations to the "social facts" of his situation; and the social psychology of the American "symbolic interactionists" Cooley and Mead, who built upon the philosophy of pragmatism. (*See* Chapter 7.)

In dealing with social systems, one must distinguish terminologically between an actor as a unit in a social system and the system as such. The actor may be either an individual or some kind of collective unit. In both cases, the actor *within* a system of reference will be spoken of as acting in a *situation* consisting of other actor-units within the same system of reference who are considered as objects. The system as a whole, however,

functions (but does not "act" in a technical sense) in relation to its environment. Of course, the system references are inherently relative to particular scientific problems. When a collective (i.e., social) system is said to act, as in the case of a government conducting foreign relations, this will mean that it and the objects of its action constitute the social system of reference and that these objects are situations, not environment, to the acting collectivity.

The Social System and Its Environments

A social system, like all living systems, is inherently an open system engaged in processes of interchange (or "input-output relations") with its environment, as well as consisting of interchanges among its internal units. Regarding it as an open system is, from some viewpoints, regarding it as a part of—i.e., a subsystem of—one or more superordinate systems. In this sense, it is interdependent with the other parts of the more comprehensive system or systems and, hence, partly dependent on them for essential inputs. Here the dependence of the organism on its physical environment for nutrition and respiration is prototypical. This is the essential basis of the famous concept of *function* as it applies to social systems, as to all other living systems.

For any system of reference, functional problems are those concerning the conditions of the maintenance and/or development of the interchanges with environing systems, both inputs from them and outputs to them. Functional significance may be determined by the simple criterion of the dysfunctional consequences of failure, deficit, or excess of an input to a receiving system, as asphyxiation is the consequence of failure in oxygen input, and so oxygen input is judged to be functionally significant for the organism. Function is the only basis on which a theoretically systematic ordering of the structure of living systems is possible. In this context functional references certainly need beg no question about how structural arrangements have come about, since the biological concepts of variation, selection, and adaptation have long since provided a framework for analyzing the widest variety of change processes.

Goal-attaining processes explicitly intended to fulfill functional requirements constitute a limiting, but very important, case. Outputs in this sense have primary functional significance only for the system which receives them and which is situational or environmental to the system of reference, although they have secondary functional significance to the latter. For example, although economic output ("produced" goods) goes to "consumers," the maintenance of certain levels of salable outpute clearly has great significance to producing organizations. It is its inputs that have

primary functional significance for any given system of reference. The "factors of production" of economic theory are classic examples, being the critical inputs of the economy.

In a crucial sense, the relation between any action system—including the social—and any of its environments is dual. On the one hand, the particular environment constitutes a set of objects which are "exterior" to the system in the Cartesian-Durkheimian sense. On the other hand, through interpenetration, the environmental system is partially and selectively included in the action system of reference. Internalization of cultural and social objects in the personality of the individual is certainly the prototypical case of interpenetration, but the principle it involves should be generalized to all the relations between action systems and their environments.

Thus, neither the individual personality nor the social system has any *direct* relation to the physical environment; their relations with the latter are mediated entirely through the organism, which is action's primary link with the physical world. This, after all, is now a commonplace of modern perceptual and epistemological theory (Ayer 1956, pp. 130–133). In essentially the same sense, neither personalities nor social systems have direct contact with the ultimate objects of reference, with the "ultimate reality" which poses "problems of meaning" in the sense sociologists associate above all with the work of Max Weber. The objects that personalities and social systems know and otherwise directly experience are in our terminology cultural objects, which are human artifacts in much the same sense as are the objects of empirical cognition. Hence, the relations of personalities and social systems with ultimate "nonempirical reality" are in a basic sense *mediated* through the cultural system.

Emphasis on their lack of direct contact with what is "out there" concerns in both cases certain qualities of the environing systems as objects. There is, however, important contact with the physical and supernatural environments through the interpenetration of the latter into action systems. Hence, such concepts as knowledge are not naive illusions but modes of the organization of the relations between the various action systems and their environments (Whitehead [1929] and Mead [1938] based their analysis of action on philosophical positions similar to that assumed here). We must regard the relations between the subsystems of action, and between the action system and the systems of nonaction, as *pluralistic*. That is, there will be no one-to-one correspondence between any two interdependent and interpenetrating systems, but there will be a complex relation which can perhaps be understood by theoretical analysis. This is true of "heredity and environment," "culture and personality," and the "ideal" and "real" factors in social systems.

It is necessary to consider the various environments of a living system, because each such environment is engaged in one of the interchange relations with the system, and the specialized natures of these relations serve

as the primary bases of the internal differentiation of the system. For instance, the nutrition and elimination systems, the respiratory system, and the locomotor system of an organism are differentiated from each other on this basis. This, as noted, is the essential meaning of the controversial (in social, not biological, science) concept of function. The basis of differentiation *is* functional, since it consists in the differing input–output relations of the system with its various environments and, following from that, the internal relations between the differing parts of the system itself.

Society and Societal Community

On the understanding that all social systems are systems of interaction, the best reference point among their many types, for general theoretical purposes, is the society. The definition of this concept presents considerable difficulties, the history of which cannot occupy us here. For present purposes, I shall define a society as the category of social system embodying, at the requisite levels of evolutionary development and of control over the conditions of environmental relations, the greatest self-sufficiency of any type of social system.

By self-sufficiency (a criterion which has figured prominently in Western thought on the subject since Aristotle at least), I mean the capacity of the system, gained through both its internal organization and resources and its access to inputs from its *environments,* to function autonomously in implementing its normative culture, particularly its values but also its norms and collective goals. Self-sufficiency is clearly a degree of generalized adaptive capacity in the sense of biological theory.

The term "environment" is pluralized here to emphasize the fact that the relevant environment is not just physical, as in most formulations of general biological theory, but also includes the three basic subsystems of action other than the social, which have been outlined above.

The core structure of a society I will call the societal community. More specifically, at different levels of evolution, it is called tribe, or "the people," or, for classical Greece, *polis,* or, for the modern world, *nation.* It is the collective structure in which members are united or, in some sense, associated. Its most important property is the kind and level of solidarity—in Durkheim's sense—which characterizes the relations between its members.

The solidarity of a community is essentially the degree to which (and the ways in which) its collective interest can be expected to prevail over the unit interests of its members wherever the two conflict. It may involve mutual respect among the units for the rights of membership status, conformity with the value and norms institutionalized in the collectivity, or

positive contribution to the attainment of collective goals. The character of solidarity varies with the level of differentiation in the society, differentiation which is evident in the structures of the roles in which a given individual is involved, of the system's subcollectivities, and of its norms and specified value orientations. The best-known basis for classifying the types of solidarity is Durkheim's two categories, mechanical and organic (see Parsons 1960*a*).

Both types of solidarity are characterized by common values and institutionalized norms. In the case of mechanical solidarity, however, the patterns of action expected from units are also uniform for all units in the system: relative to one another, the units are *segments,* since they are not functionally differentiated. Durkheim analyzed crime as the prototype violation of the obligations of mechanical solidarity. For full members of the community, no matter how highly differentiated the society, the treatment of the criminal should ideally be always the same, regardless of *who* commits the crime, even though this ideal is frequently and seriously deviated from. At the societal community level in differentiated societies, the core of the system of mechanical solidarity lies in the patterns of citizenship, in T. H. Marshall's sense (1949). These patterns can be conveniently subdivided into the components of civil–legal citizenship, political citizenship, and social citizenship. In modern American society, the bill of rights and associated constitutional structures, such as the fourteenth amendment, comprise the most directly relevant institutions in this field.

Organic solidarity concerns those aspects of the societal system in which roles, subcollectivities, and norms are differentiated on a functional basis. Here, though common value patterns remain of the first importance to the various subsystems at the relevant levels of specification, expectations of behavior differ according to role and subcollectivity. Solidarity, then, involves the integration of these differing expectations with respect to the various bases of compatible functioning, from mutual noninterference to positive mutual reinforcement.

Organic solidarity seems to be particularly important in three primary structural contexts. Most familiar is the one Durkheim himself particularly stressed, the economic division of labor, where the most important institutional patterns are contract and property. Second is what we ordinarily call the area of political differentiation, that of both the organization of authority and leadership and the various modes of participation in collective decision making, which involve the interplay of information and influence bearing on collective action. The third is the area of the society's relations with its cultural involvements. This particularly concerns the society's articulation with the religious system, but also (and the more so, the more differentiated both the society and the culture) with the arts, the system of intellectual disciplines and the relationship between the patterns of moral obligation and those of law.

Organic Solidarity and Pluralism

In all three contexts, organic solidarity is associated with the pheno-menon generally called pluralism. In none of these cases is the structure of a subsystem articulating with the social community ascribed to the structure of the latter. On the contrary, as a function of the level of dif-ferentiation among the articulating subsystems, there is an increasing flex-ibility that facilitates the concrete relations coming to be established by relatively specific processes. Thus, there is, first, a pluralism of economic interests which, if uncontrolled, would tend to destroy the solidarity of the societal community—indeed, it may be suggested that an exaggerated anxiety about this underlies much of the modern socialist dogma that only the central societal collectivity, the state, can be trusted with any interest which seems important to the public welfare. However, there is a second pluralism of "interest groups" in the political context which, though of course linked with the economic pluralism, is by no means the same. The political process, as that leading to collective decision making, is in part a "political struggle" among such interest groups. Thus, it has great poten-tial for disrupting societal solidarity. However, the latter can also not merely contain the struggle but, even more positively, further integrate the disparate groups by virtue of various mechanisms of integrative con-trol. Finally, the more differentiated societal community tends also to be culturally pluralistic. This is particularly conspicuous in the few Western societies which have attained a certain level of religious pluralism. Thus, at the very least, contemporary American society is a multidenominational, Judaeo–Christian society which also *includes* secular humanists who prefer not to affiliate with any explicitly religious association. In one sense, it has "transcended" the historic bases of religious conflict which prevailed in the Western world for centuries. The basis of this is genuine denomina-tional pluralism, not only before the law but also in terms of acceptance in the community.

Very closely associated with this is the pluralism among the intellectual disciplines which has gained institutionalization in modern society, espe-cially in the university system (Parsons 1965). The rise of the sciences was, in the first instance, a profound symbol of this pluralization. But it has now become a major factor in the future development of modern society in a variety of ways. The problem of "ethical" pluralism is analyt-ically more difficult and complex. The trend seems to be away from the special *kind* of moral uniformity which characterizes societies in which mechanical solidarity predominates. The essential point concerns the level of generality at which common moral standards are defined: if a pluralistic society is to integrate its many various kinds of units into a solidary so-cietal community, what counts as moral obligation cannot be defined in

terms specific to each kind of unit but must be sufficiently general to apply to the considerable range of differentiated classes of units. Moral*ism* ties morality to the specifics of a subgroup or a particular stage of social development and must be distinguished from concern with maintaining control of action in accord with more generalized moral standards.

Cultural System and Political System

The societal community in the present sense is articulated most directly with the cultural and political subsystems of the society. Furthermore, it is in these two relationships that the main connections between organic and mechanical solidarity are lodged.

The cultural (or pattern-maintenance) system centers on the institutionalization of cultural value patterns, which at the general cultural level, may be regarded as moral. Institutionalized societal values, and their specifications to societal subsystems, comprise only part of the relevance of moral values to action; moral values are also involved, through interalization, in structures of the personality and behavioral organism; and, more generally, they articulate with religion, science, and the arts within the cultural system.

Community in the present sense is never a simple matter of the "acting out" of value commitments. It also involves differentiated acceptance, in valuational terms, of the *conditions* necessary for the functioning of societies and their subsystems. Essentially this latter element draws the line between utopianism—making an imperative of "pure" value actualization—and realistic social idealism. Avoiding the uptopian dilemma involves organizing the value system so as to include the positive valuation of social relationships for their own sake, not only as being rigidly instrumental to specific value patterns.

But this is not the whole story. In addition to a general "set" establishing a presumption of legitimacy for the social system as such, there must also be a more flexible set of mechanisms providing for adaptation between the cultural subsystem of the society and the societal community itself. These mechanisms concern the capacity for handling the changing needs and exigencies of various associational relationships in the light of both their developing interrelations and their relations with the value system; the more particularized commitments must be a function of changing conceptions of the imperatives of relationship, as defining the nature of "valued association." The commitment to the societal community is, so far as this interchange develops flexibility, no longer ascriptive but dependent on the need for such commitment and on an evaluation of its compatibility with deeper moral commitments at the cultural level. One aspect of this flexibility is the individual's enhanced moral independence from impera-

tives of unquestioning obligations to conformity. But the obverse aspect is the "right" of the community to expect appropriate flexibility in the adaptation of moral demands to exigencies of realistic implementation.

The minimum imperatives of specified *common* value commitment define one pole of the structures of the societal systems organized with mechanical solidarity. There is a place for organic solidarity in this context so far as such commitments are so firm as *not* to be "negotiable" and so general as to permit the kind of flexibility in adapting to particular "exigencies" which has just been discussed. What I above called moralism is the limiting case where lack of generality (and perhaps firmness of commitment) forecloses such flexibility. The basic rights of members in the societal community constitute, in negative definition, the limits of application of these value commitments. Members' complementary obligations to the societal community constitute the obverse expectations of contribution to the functioning of a social system to which they are committed.

In a sense, the "payoff" on such obligations comes in the relation between the societal community and the political subsystem, since the latter is concerned with collective goal attainment as a function of the total society and, *pari passu,* of each subsystem grounded in communal solidarity. This relation between the societal community and the political subsystem concerns a further step toward mastering exigencies in the interest of the implementation of values. It is a matter not just of establishing particular relationships of solidarity as the "setting" for value implementation but, further, of committing the interests of that community to particular collective goals—which involves dealing with the exigencies of particular environmental conditions. For the individual, then, this concerns not merely his personal commitment to the goal but his obligations as a member of the community. Committing the community implies a solution to the problem of integrating the community with reference to the "policy" in question, whether this involves developing a broad consensus or ruthlessly suppressing minority, or even majority, views. As a somewhat extreme case, entering a war commit the national community, whatever various membership elements think about it, short of their mustering a resistance which would favor the enemy cause.

Here, as in the relation of the national community to the "cultural" subsystem, two importantly different levels are involved. One concerns the general "authority" of differentiated elements in the society to commit or bind the collectivity as a whole in the pursuit of particular goals in particular situations. One extreme in this context would be an absolutist or despotic "government" which presumed to act as it pleased, regardless of consent or opposition in the broader societal community. An opposite extreme would be a community which made any collective action dependent on virtually unanimous and explicit consent.

By differentiating the two levels, modern governmental systems avoid being caught in the above dilemma. They set up procedural rules defining

the level of support needed to authorize collective action binding the collectivity as a whole, including minorities that dissent in various contexts. For this to work, the minorities must be committed to the legitimacy of the governmental system, even though they refuse to support particular policy decisions of the moment.

For the individual (or political minority groups), however, such situations may present a moral dilemma. In his role as a responsible member of the societal community, which includes an obligation to support its government (not particular decisions or parties) the member of a minority subgroup is, up to a point, obligated not only to accept but often also to cooperate actively in implementing a policy of which he disapproves. There may, however, be a point beyond which his conscience will not allow this. He will then be driven into various levels of resistance, ranging from withdrawal of active participation, through public protest, conspicuous noncooperation, and militant attempts to prevent or sabotage its implmentation, to revolution.

The development of political differentiation and pluralism, including the generalization of the crucial levels of political obligation, tends to broaden the range of individual freedom for dissent and also to draw the lines between politically institutionalized—as distinguished from moral—rights of dissent and opposition and those institutionally defined as illegitimate. The basic independence of the cultural-moral and the socially institutionalized systems, however, precludes *any* social community from being completely immune to the kind of political opposition which can lead to the disruption of its basic solidarity.

The element of mechanical solidarity here concerns the *legitimation* of collective decision-making authorities. Such legitimation must derive from common value commitments to the societal community and, hence, to the kinds of collective action considered legitimate, including the identification of the agencies entitled to take such action. Obversely, this also concerns the rights of membership elements to give or withhold support for particular policies and, more generally, particular claims to leadership status. The appeals for such support, however, must be on grounds of organic rather than mechanical solidarity. The procedural rules become the focus of common commitments, while particular outcomes become matters for legitimate contest.

Solidarity and the Economy

At this point, we may recall that Durkheim introduced the concept of organic solidarity in analyzing the division of labor in the economic sense. This was quite logical in the light both of the utilitarian theories to which he was critically orienting himself and of the economy's relative remoteness from the setting of the system of mechanical solidarity as that which

was just discussed. Focus on the economic system was the most convenient way to set up a clear conceptual dichotomy.

Nevertheless, it now seems better to approach the problem of the economic system indirectly, through its relations to the other aspects of a social system. We conceive of the economy as the functional subsystem of a society differentiated about producing and allocating fluidly disposable resources within the society. As put in a quite familiar paradigm, it operates through combining the factors of production—e.g., land, labor, capital, and organization—to produce the two primary categories of output: commodities and services. The economic categories are not the physical objects or the physical behavior involved as such, but certain ways of controlling them: in the case of commodities, essentially property rights; in the case of services, the kind of authority or power over the performer we associate with the status of employer.

The actual combinatorial processes, which we call economic production, take place in goal-oriented organizational units that economists call firms. The strictly economic functions concern the management of the boundary relations of these units through what is ordinarily called the market system, and should be distinguished from the technological functions. The economic functions involve procuring control of the factors of production (including determination of requirements for them) and disposing of the outputs of production through marketing. These processes operate by adjusting relations between supply and demand through establishing terms for the transfer of control that equate quantity and price for both parties to the exchange.

Here the primary institutional focus of organic solidarity is the institution of contract, which is essentially the set of procedural rules regulating transfers of both factors of population and economic outputs. This institutional complex not only regulates the actual settlement of contracts but also defines what types of contract may—and may not—be entered into, how agreements may be arrived at, their bearing on the interests of third parties, and the obligations of parties under various special contingencies, such as the development of unforeseen obstacles to the fulfillment of terms.

The institution of property, then, is the normative system regulating acquisition, disposal, control, and use of physical objects in relation to the contractual system, whether the objects be factors of production or commodity outputs. And the institutional complex we call employment regulates the acquisition and utilization of human services, either as factors of production or as ultimate agents of valued consumption.

Generalized Media of Interchange

In sufficiently developed and differentiated systems, a central role in economic process is played by money, as both a symbolic medium of ex-

change and a measure and store of value in the economic sense. Money may be defined as the capacity of a societal unit to command economically valuable resources through the exchange process, i.e., through contractual agreements, without giving commodities or services in return. The payment of money constitutes the transfer of such capacity from one unit to another. In most transactions in a developed economy, entities that have "value in use" figure on only one side of an exchange relationship, being balanced by a monetary "consideration" on the other. To "pay" money is to accept certain economic obligations, defined by a proportionate diminution in one's capacity to command economic "values" in other transactions. To accept money in payment, on the other hand, is to gain the right to an expectation that others will make economically valuable goods and services available at the times and places of one's own choosing, within the limits defined in the market nexus. It has long been a commonplace of economics that only a far-reaching institutionalization of the monetary mechanism can make an extended division of labor possible (see, for example, Adam Smith's classic statement in 1776, book 1, especially chapter 3), though it is known that politically controlled administrative allocation of resources can substitute for the contractual–monetary mechanisms up to a point, as in the "command" economy of the Soviet Union, which reached its highest development in the late Stalinist period (see Grossman 1962). Nevertheless, the extent of an economy's "monetization" is undoubtedly the most important single index of the mobilizability of its resources and, hence, the flexibility of their allocation, at all combinatorial stages, from ultimate natural resources and human energies or skills, to finished consumption goods and services.

Money is also important theoretically as the best-understood member of the family of generalized symbolic media of interchange involved in social interaction processes. Political power and influence as used in political leadership processes certainly belong to this family (Parsons 1963*a*; 1963*b*).

The economy, as here conceived, articulates with the societal community primarily through the institutional complex of contract, property, and the employment–occupation system. Its solidarity is maintained by keeping its transactions in line with certain integrative imperatives, e.g., by protecting the interests both of parties to contractual relations and of third parties and by providing a basis in solidary relations for effective collective action, especially through making economic resources available to collective units, including particularly the government.

Money, like the other members of the family of media, is a *symbolic* medium which, without being too farfetched, we may call a specialized language. Like all such media, it expresses and communicates messages having meanings with reference to a *code*—that is, a set of rules for the use, transformation, and combination of symbols. (The theory of the operation of such types of messages and codes of rules has been developed

in the field of linguistics by, particularly, Jakobson & Halle 1956; Chomsky 1957; 1964). In the case of money, as institutionalized, it is highly important to recognize that the relevant code is part of the *legal* system; this is most clear in societies having a sufficiently high level of differentiation. As we have put it, the institutions of contract, property, and employment, as parts of the legal system, constitute the code in terms of which transformations between money and commodities or services and among different forms of monetary assets operate. Financial transactions, therefore, constitute a certain type of "conversations."

This paradigm is also applicable to relations between the societal community and the other primary functional subsystems of the society. In the case of the polity, the medium which corresponds to money is *power*. This I conceive as the generalized medium of mobilizing capacities for effective collective action, utlizable by members of collectivities to contribute toward binding the collectivity to particular courses of action, either determining or contributing to the implementation of specific policy goals. (This usage of the concept of political power is clearly different from those most common in both sociology and political science; for a discussion of the issues involved in the usage of this concept, see Parsons 1963*b*.) The code within which power as a medium operates centers about the institution of *authority,* which in turn articulates with the patterns of institutionalized leadership and administrative responsibility for maintaining regulatory norms.

In the sphere of articulation with the cultural system, the operative medium is what I call commitments. This concerns the specification of the general value patterns to the levels necessary for their workable combination with the other factors requisite to their implementation in concrete action. Commitment to valued associations of the societal community type is the prototype here analyzed in "On the Concept of Value-Commitments," *Politics and Social Structure,* Chapter 16. The relevant code is the set of institutions which constitutes the underpinning of society's mechanical solidarity—in American society those formulated in the bill of rights, etc., as noted. Within this context, the *civil* component holds precedence, because it formulates the valuational basis of community membership.

Finally, the societal community itself is the focus of operation for a fourth generalized medium which I have called, in a special technical sense, *influence* (Parsons 1963*a*). Here the relevant code is comprised of the norms underlying organic solidarity, as they relate to the pluralistic structure of differentiated societies. Since their primary context is that of the solidarity of the society, we may consider their major focus to be *justification* for the allocation of loyalties. Here justification must be carefully distinguished from legitimation. Justification is less absolute and operates

at a lower level in the cybernetic hierarchy. The *system* may well be legit-
mated while questions of the justification of certain choices between alternative subsidary solidarities are still left open where actual or potential
dilemmas are posed.

These different code components are more or less adequately integrated
in a going social system, where they constitute its basic normative structure. They should be distinguished from the primary normative components of a pattern-maintenance system, since the latter are made up of
value patterns and their specifications, not of differentiated norms. The
integratively oriented code of the societal system must be anchored in a
value system if it is to have a basis of legitimation. But its structure is
determined not only by value specification but also by adjustment to the
exigencies of the other functional subsystems. But in this process of adjustment the integratively oriented code still maintains a certain level of integrity with respect to the value commitment and solidarity of the societal
community. In highly differentiated societies, this basic code system is the
core of the legal system.

Societies and Their Environments

We may now return to the problem of the relations of a society
as a social system with its environments. The basis of the differentiation
between the societal community and the other three primary subsystems
of the society should be sought in the basis on which they in turn are
differentiated from it and from each other. In general, it can be said
that the reason for the existence of these patterned differentiations is
that they help the social system to cope with the exigencies imposed on
it by its environments.

The Organic–Physical Environment

In dealing with this problem, perhaps we had best begin with the
economy, partly because the relevant theoretical analysis is most highly
developed there. In the terms of our general paradigm, the intrasocial relation between societal community and economy is paralled at the level
of the general action system by the relation between the social system and
the behavioral organism.

First, it should be emphasized that all relations between the social
system and the *physical* environment are mediated through the behavioral
organism. The perceptual processes of the organism are the source of

information about the physical environment, which gains cultural organization from its conceptual and theoretical components. The organism is also the source of the "instinctual" components of the motivation of individuals' personalities.

The relation between the organism and the society's economic subsystem, which is of direct concern here, constitutes the *technological* system. This involves the utilization of empirical knowledge, structured by perceptual feedback through the cultural system, for the design and production of commodities having utility for human social functions. *What* is to be produced, in what quantities relative to alternative uses of the factors of production (cost factors), is economically determined; *how* it is to be produced is a technological problem. Technology involves not only the use of ultimate "natuural" resources (analytically a "land" factor) and "equipment" (a benefit from previous production) but also labor—a factor that, sociologically speaking, takes the form of service. This is a particularly important category of the interpenetration of the economy with other parts of the societal system. We conceive of service as an output from the economy which "corresponds" to labor as a factor of production but which should definitely not be identified with labor. Very importantly, however, service is a crucial factor in technological efficiency. This apparently paradoxical conception derives from the fact that technological processes always occur within a framework of *social* organization, never as "purely physical" phenomena. This means that the physical, behavioral operations of persons in technological settings are a function of their commitments, as members of the societal community and its relevant subsystems, to devote their energy and skill to productive uses in the economic sense. This human component is then combined, at the general action system level, with empirical knowledge of standards of socioeconomic utility to produce facilities which can be relatively freely allocated to the various functional needs of societal units. Analyses in these terms can contribute much toward resolving the old controversy about whether the material basis of a complex societal system is "ultimately" economic or technological, or whether the distinction between these categories should be abandoned.

Physical location is a particularly important involvement of technological systems, deriving from the necessity to bring together physical materials, plant, equipment, and organisms as performers of service. Role differentiation between the occupational and residential units tends to involve physical separation of workplaces from places of residence, although, the involvement of the same persons in both units sets certain requirements for the physical interrelations of the units' locations. In particular, the modern urban community is very largely built about the relationship between these two sets of locations.

Residence, like occupation, also articulates physical location and the

organism into the social system. But it operates in the context of the organic rhythm, such as sleep, nutrition, and sexual activity, to which human beings are bound. Another limiting factor is that the household (which, in spite of many exceptions, remains the usual unit of residence), has at its core kinship units centering on one or more nuclear families. The place of residence is the human individual's residual location, the place where he is likely to be, and is often normatively expected to be, when he is not engaged in such other specific activities as work and special recreation.

Communication and transportation—of both goods and persons—therefore require physical media and must be involved in the physical world, perhaps especially in its spatial aspects. The actual communication of a message from a sender in one physical location to a receiver in another is always problematic, even if the two are engaged in face-to-face conversation in the same room. The same is true of broadcast communication—newspapers must get from the printing plant to the readers, radio and television broadcasts must be transmitted through the "air"—and of the conveyance of persons and goods from place to place.

In certain senses, though, the most fundamental problem here is that the normative orders constitutive of social systems must "apply" to categories of persons and their acts in ways that include specifications of where the persons or acts are located. Very generally, then, the societal community and various of its subsystems "claim jurisdiction" over persons and their acts with reference to particular territorial areas. A most important reason for the prominence of territoriality is that normative obligations, if taken sufficiently seriously, must on occasion be somehow enforced, and this involves resort at some point to physical negative sanctions, which can only be applied to the noncompliant individual where he is. This, in turn, obviously includes enforcing claims to the jurisdiction over, and the utilization of resources within, an area and, hence, a readiness to enforce respect for such control upon outsiders, i.e., the function of defense (Parsons 1960*b*).

Thus, spatial location is involved in all the functions of social systems. Its articulation with social processes is what we ordinarily call the ecological aspect of the system—the distribution of its various activities in physical space and their orientation to spatial considerations. In principle, all other analytically distinguishable aspects of physical systems are comparably involved with social interaction, but the foregoing will have to serve for illustration.

The core of the social system, the societal community, relates to the physical environment primarily through two mediating systems: the economy, which is primarily social but which interpenetrates with the technological system, and the technological system, which is primarily organic–physical but which interpenetrates with the economy. Organic–physical

factors, then, operate in all the other primary subsystems of the society, each of which has its technological and economic aspects, although they are subordinated to other considerations, such as the political.

The Cultural Environment

There is parallel complexity at the other end of the cybernetic heirarchy, in which action and, hence, social systems are involved. A society, or any other type of social system, has a pattern-maintenance subsystem, the units of which (once the system is sufficiently differentiated) have *cultural* primacy. These social system units, then, interpenetrate with both the societal community (and other societal subsystems) and with the cultural system proper. With progressing differentiation, they tend to become distinctively different according to whether their primary concern is cultural or social.

Religion comprises the matrix from which cultural institutions in general have become differentiated and remains the "master system" in the cybernetic sense. But secular intellectual disciplines (science), arts in the expressive–symbolic sense, and normative disciplines (e.g., ethics and law) have gained differentiation from it.

This formulates very briefly the main line of internal differentiation of a cultural system. The pattern-maintenance system, however, is not a cultural system in a strict sense (though for simplification the distinction has not always been made in this article), but the subsystem of the social system articulating most closely with the cultural system. Religion as a *cultural* phenomenon is not part of the pattern-maintenance system. Rather, the relevant structure is the collective organization of religious orientations, e.g., in churches or in prophetic movements. Science as a body of knowledge is cultural; universities as collectivities organized about the development of science through research and about its communication through teaching are parts of the society. Pattern-maintenance structures in this connection have cultural primacy only in that their societal functions concern interchange with the cultural system and in that they interpenetrate with the latter. Thus, religious orientations or scientific "systems of knowledge" are constitutive parts of churches and universities, not only "environments" to them.

Just as man has no direct contact with the physical world independent of the organisms (which, however, is itself part of that world), so he has no direct contact with the ultimate nonempirical "grounds" of his existence, what Weber called the world of "ultimate realities." His *objects* in this realm to which he orients himself are not ultimate entities as such but his representations of them. They are cultural objects—parts of the cul-

tural system in the action sense—and hence interpenetrate with all the other subsystems of action.

As structures of such interpenetrations, "theological schools," or "prophetic movements," though quite distinct from religion as a component of the culture, are cultural subsystems of the society that have religious primacy but also interpenetrate with churches or other forms of the social institutionalization of religion. In the same way, law schools, as companies of legal scholars, are cultural subsystems, whereas courts of law are the social-system units in which legal doctrines are applied to social situations. In the more strictly cognitive disciplines, "companies of scholars" constitute cultural subsystems, which often involve "schools" at the level of cultural content, whereas universities and other educational collectivities constitute the articulated social system units.

For certain purposes, we may, as above, legitimately equate the pattern-maintenance subsystem of a society with the cultural system, since its primary function is articulating the social system as such—the system constituted by social interaction—with cultural patterns and norms. This, however, is elliptical. In the first instance, there are the more complex relationships just sketched, but there is also a further complication. Any system of cultural content, particularly a value system, must be specified from the most general relevant levels to levels relevant to the highly particular functions and exigencies of many and various subsystems. For instance, every technological system producing a particular commodity has special exigencies that the general principles of the relevant science cannot handle alone; similarly, every medical case is in some sense unique, and the physician must tailor his general medical knowledge to its specificities.

One set of exigencies of human societies has a special bearing here. It concerns the consequences of the fact that culture is *learned* by the human being; it is not part of his hereditary equipment. If a given society is defined by its institutionalization of certain cultural patterns, then the necessity of internalizing those patterns in the oncoming generation is second in functional importance only to maintenance of the adult levels of differentiation, of many kinds and levels of formal education.

This whole subsystem of institutions, as well as those involved with cultural innovation (e.g., research organizations), should be included in the pattern-maintenance subsystem of a society, characterized by primary interpenetration with the cultural system of action. Kinship, however, having special reference to child care, is the substructure of the pattern-maintenance system that operates at the farthest remove from the considerations of the general culture; at the appropriate level of specification of values, however, it *has* cultural primacy. Furthermore, it also relates quite specially not only to the society but also to the exigencies of both organism and personality, about which a few words must now be said.

The Psychological Environment

The personality, as analytically distinguished from the organism, constitutes the third primacy environment of a social system. It interpenetrates with the individual organism in the obvious and fundamental sense that the storage facilities of learned content must be organic, as must the physical mechanisms of perception and cognition, of the control of learned behavior, and of the bases of motivation.

At the level of this discussion, however, the personality forms a distinct system articulated with social systems through their political subsystems, not simply in the sense of government but of any collective ordering. This is to say that *the primary goal output of social systems is to the personalities of their members.* Although they interpenetrate crucially with social systems, the personalities of individuals are not core constituents of social systems (nor vice versa) but precisely environments of them. Freud, especially in his later work, was quite clear about the obverse relationship: namely, that the individual personality's primary environment consists of the social systems into which it becomes integrated. Freud's famous "reality principle" is the principle of ego adaptation to the social environment.

I am treating the personality last among the primary environments of the social system because, of the three, it is the least commonly conceptualized as such. This conceptualization directly counters the long tradition that a society is "composed" or "made up" of "individuals." The latter may be true if the society and the individual are conceived of as concrete entities. Here, however, social system and personality—the concrete term "individual" is avoided in this context—are used as abstractly defined systems which are distinguished analytically, though allowance is made for the crucial relation of interpenetration. The unit of interpenetration between a personality and a social system is not the individual but a *role* or complex of *roles.* The *same* personality may participate in *several* social systems in different roles.

From the viewpoint of the psychology of the personality, the positive outputs from the social system are rewards. Indeed, I would even say that, at the level of cultural symbolization, except for intermediate cases specially involved at the crux of differentiation between organism and personality (notably, erotic pleasure), all rewards are social system outputs. Conversely, outputs from the personality to the social system are personal goal achievements which, from the viewpoint of the receiving social system, are *contributions* to its functioning, insofar as the two systems are integrated with each other.

The focus of such integration is the phenomenon of "identification," through which the personality acquires a motivationally and cognitively

meaningful role set and the social system acquires a member who can make meaningful contributions. Malintegration means that this matching relationship has failed in one way or another—"deviance," "alienation," and a variety of other phenomena fit in this category. It is also crucial to allow for personal creativity in relation to the social system. The analytical independence of social system and personality is the basic origin of both the prevalence of deviant behavior and the openings for creativity. The frequent allegation that sociology teaches the necessity of flat "conformity" is a conspicuous case of the fallacy of misplaced concreteness. If our analytical generalizations about social systems "applied" without qualification to all the member personalities, this would be the case. The mutual independence of the two categories of system—though accounting for their interdependence and interpenetration—is the theoretical basis for the fundamental and general phenomenon of the autonomy of the individual, so far as the social system is concerned.

Two important considerations reinforce this assertion of the reality of personal autonomy, the degrees and kinds of which must be seen as varying with different types of social system. First, analytically and apart from its direct relation to the social system, the personality system is the *primary meeting ground* of the cultural system, the behavioral organism, and secondarily, the physical world. Although there have been serious theoretical difficulties with the "culture and personality" studies of the last generation in behavioral sciences, they did focus upon a crucial relationship here, as did the "behavioristic" traditions of psychology in studying the interrelations of personality and organism. Hence, it can be said not only that the personality is autonomous *as* a distinct subsystem of action, but also that this autonomy is importantly grounded in the personality's interchanges with the cultural and organic levels of the organization of action. These three sets of considerations (plus the uniqueness of the genetic constitution of practically every human organism) as far in explaining the *irreducibility* of the distinctiveness of all human personalities, as well as their autonomy.

The second consideration derives from an internal feature of social systems that is generally called "role pluralism." That is, not only do individuals have plural role involvements, but also different individuals' *combinations* of role participations vary widely. Such variance includes complexes of differing roles which are often categorized together for limited purposes. Thus, one "middle-class suburban mother" may have one child, another three, and another five, and the assortments of the children by age and sex may vary, so that even "being a mother" is not an identical thing for each member of that category, even sociologically. To this we can add differences in occupation of husbands, religion, ethnicity, participation in community affairs, etc.

When so many mutually independent—though also interdependent—

factors are operating, anyone familiar with the logic of combinatorial variability should find it difficult to maintain that a modern, highly differentiated society is incompatible with individuality. Of course, there are also matters of the *specific kinds* of autonomy and individuality which are at stake. However, the arguments alleging that modern societies are repressive of all autonomy and stifling of all individuality are frequently so overgeneralized that they appear to deny altogether the combinatorial argument just outlined. Furthermore, a strong case can be made that the trend of *modern* society, because it has become so highly differentiated and pluralistic, is positively to favor individuality rather than to suppress it in favor of conformism.

We have confined our attention here to human-level social systems and have emphasized the importance of the symbolic systems, which we call cultural, that become constitutive of them through being involved in action and interpenetrating with social systems. Perhaps the most general matrix of these symbolic systems is language. On various levels, there is great familiarity with the concept of symbolic systems, e.g., of "ideas" having a predominantly cognitive focus and of "expressive symbols" in the arts and in ritual.

The Media of Interchange Revisited

In conclusion, we may carry a little further the discussion, introduced above, of another category of symbolic systems that emerges into great prominence in highly differentiated social systems: the media of interchange. Attention was called above to money as the medium of exchange in economic transactions. Though the science of economics has gone far in understanding the vastly complex phenomena of monetary systems, they have generally been considered as unique. I have suggested that money is not unique in either of two senses.

First, it can be considered a special case of a very general phenomenon: language. It is in fact a very highly specialized language. Crucial here is the recognition that it operates at the *symbolic* level and that its primary function is commuunication, though of a special normative sort. The "monetary system" is a *code,* in the grammatical–syntactical sense. The circulation of money is the "sending" of messages which give the recipient capacity to command goods and services through market channels. The recipient gains the *expectation* that he can "request," by virtue of his holding money, access to goods and services of a given value. There is an institutionalized obligation on those receiving such requests—if they are "in business"—to comply. But the process of money circulation in-

volves literally nothing except communicated messages. A check is only a filled-in form letter to the bank on which it is drawn.

Second, money is not the only specialized language of this sort operating in social systems. Political power is certainly another. It centers on the use of discretionary authority in collective organizations to make decisions which, as binding on the collectivity, require performances of those who are obligated to further their implementation. Not only executive decisions continue uses of power in this sense, but also the exercise of franchises in many connections, from voting in governmental elections to voting as a member of a small committee.

A third generalized symbolic medium is influence. By this I mean, quite technically, the capacity to achieve "consensuus" with other members of an associated group through persuasion, without having to give fully adequate reasons (an adequate reason, in this sense, would be one that gave the recipient sufficient information for making a rational decision himself, or one that was at least fully understandable to him). Thus, a physician, as a technical specialist, may persuade a patient to follow his advice even when it is out of the question that the patient is competent to understand its technical grounds. The patient must, as members of the profession often put it, have "confidence" in his physician.

Fourth is the medium of generalized *commitments* to the implementation of cultural values, at the level of the social system as such. It is the most difficult to conceptualize, and the least can be said about it.

The need for generalized media of interchange is a function of the differentiatedness of social structures; in this sense they are all partly integrative mechanisms. The relations between markets and money and the division of labor are well known, but similar considerations apply in the other cases.

In the political case, the necessity for the mechanism of power stems from the social "status distance" between the loci of decision making and the loci of the performances necessary for the implementation of the decisions. In complex organizations, it is not realistically possible for decision makers to consult in detail with every person upon whose compliance effective implementation of their decisions depends. This may involve reasons of time and urgency, technical considerations, access to special information, or various exigencies of coordination. Thus, elections must lead to a concentration of power in the hands of the candidates elected. There cannot, however, be a simple consensus between all the members of the electorate and the preferred candidate—this would be incompatible with the voter's freedom of choice. Hence, the individual voter must agree to make a binding decision that he prefers candidate X over Y. If enough voters do likewise, X will be elected. The electoral authorities are obligated to comply with the aggregate of decisions of the voters.

In the case of influence, the functional need involves bridging certain

gaps between the bases of accepting "advice" (in the sense of attempts to persuade without either situational inducements or threats of coercive sanctions) and the intrinsically cogent "reasons" for such acceptance. Complex communities cannot wait for fully rational demonstrations of the advisability of all commitments. Therefore, they must rely on influence or, as we sometimes say, prestige, as utilized by persons in responsible roles. The user of influence create a *presumption* for the reasonableness of his case, so that the object of his attempts at persuasion feels, in the integrated case, reasonably sure in trusting him.

Similarly, commitments are given to others when an individual enters into a situation (i.e., makes or, more appropriately, gives a commitment) without in fact being fully able to ensure that the process of action implementation will be carried out in a manner conducive to preserving or enhancing the integrity of his values. Thus, in a sense different from that of the influence context, he has either to trust others or to sacrifice the prospect of successful implementation. In turn, others must trust him to gain fulfillment of *their* commitments. It is in this sense that commitments may be considered a "circulating" medium.

These media appear in generalized and differentiated form only when relatively high levels of differentiation in the relevant spheres have been attained. Primitive societies never have money and market systems, and many archaic societies have them only rudimentarily, if at all. What Weber called "patriarchal" political structures do not have power as a *generalized* medium, and "patrimonial" regimes show only its first emergence.

Other generalized media seem to operate in the zones of interpenetration between the social system and the other primary subsystems of action. As already noted, what Freud called erotic pleasure is at the same time both organic (i.e., a component of the personality) and, because of its involvement with interpersonal relations, a component of certain elementary social systems. What psychoanalytic and other social psychologists have called *affect* is probably another such mechanism, operating among persons in the interchange between the personality and social systems rather than in direct relation to the organism. The two famous "wishes" for recognition and for response discussed by W. I. Thomas perhaps designate still another medium which, however, may be a subdivision of the more general mechanism of affect. In the organic- physical set of relations, technological "know-how" and skill are probbaly well regarded in this way.

Another set of media operate in the zone of interpenetration between the social and cultural systems. Ideology is a conspicuous example. The concept *conscience,* as used in Puritan traditions especially, seems to belong in this category. *Reputation,* as that term is used in discussing the social structure of scientific communities, is probably another case. The

concept *faith,* as used in Christian tradition, especially Protestantism, probably refers to a generalized mechanism peculiar to the cultural level of action organization.

The relative salience of the various generalized media of interchange (and of particular cases within them) *for* specific structures is a useful guide to the structural arrangements among and within the subsystems of more generalized social systems, notably societies. We have also claimed that the core of a society is the societal community, which, functionally regarded, is the integrative subsystem. It interpenetrates and interchanges directly with each of the other primary subsystems: the pattern-maintenance or cultural-primary subsystems; the goal-attainment subsystem, or polity; and the adaptive subsystem, or economy. The medium focal to the societal community is influence, which is interchangeable for power, money, and value commitments.

Each of the other three subsystems constitutes a zone of primary interpenetration and interchange between the social systems and one of its intra-action environments. The economy interchanges with the organic–physical environment; and money, in a sufficiently differentiated economy, can be used in exchange for the factors of production, which are then also technologically combined. Though a modern economy is structured primarily about financial institutions and market systems, these latter interpenetrate, in turn, with the technological organization of production.

The polity interpenetrates, in the first instance, with the personality. Power, as the medium having political primacy, can be used to acquire both human servcies and the demands for collective action which justify leadership initiative. Underlying these two forms of "mobile" human resources are the processes that generate and stabilize them. Here the interpenetration between social system and personality leads toward both the psychological "depths" of the personality and the relational contexts articulating the basic integration of social systems. Above all, family and kinship, as well as neighborhood and education, fit this context but so do complexes such as recreation. These operate, however, at a level quite different from the direct interchanges between personality and polity. For *macrosocial* purposes, therefore, they should be treated as pattern-maintenance processes.

Finally, the interpenetration between social and cultural systems concerns, most saliently, the place of religion in relation to social structure. Indeed, the primary structures of the most primitive societies fall almost entirely into the two basic categories of kinship and religion. With further differentiation, however, religion becomes more and more clearly distinguished from political organization. It also tends to become distinguished from economic structuring, while the latter remains ascribed to both kinship and, above all, to the polity (in the broad, analytical sense).

In relatively advanced societies, the cultural system itself begins to

differentiate, particularly through the appearance of secular cultural disciplines. Thus, law, in close relation to ethical philosophy; the arts, as something other than direct handmaidens of religion; and, generally last, science have become independent cultural realms—though they are always *also* interdependent and interpenetrating with each other and with the social system. Value commitments constitute the principal *societal* medium operating in this realm, though society, then, contains a considerable number of structural units having cultural primacy. Religious collectivities need hardly be mentioned, so conspicuous are they from any comparative point of view. Increasingly, modern societies have universities, which institutionalize the intellectual disciplines that are in some sense sciences, various organizations focusing upon the arts, and the very crucial institutions of highly generalized law, with their articulations to ethics.

The social system is, thus, a very complex entity. As an organization of human interests, activities, and commitments, it must be viewed as a system and in functional perspective. This is the key to its lines of organization, its modes of differentiation, and its integration. Such a system may be considered as *both* structure and process, in different aspects and for different scientific purposes. Structurally, we have suggested that there is a double basis for systematizing differentiation and variation: that internal to the primary social system itself and that involved in its relations to its primary environments, as analyzed with reference to the general system of action. Processually, the categories of analysis must follow from and integrate with those of structure. I suggest that, given the central position language as definitive of human society, the more differentiated and specialized symbolic media of interchange constitute the master scheme for the systematic analysis of social system processes.

Bibliography

AYER, A. J.   1956   *The Problem of Knowledge*. New York: St. Martin's. A paperback edition was published in 1962 by Penguin.

CHOMSKY, NOAM   1957   *Syntactic Structures*. The Hague: Mouton.

CHOMSKY, NOAM   1964   *Current Issues in Linguistic Theory*. The Hague: Mouton.

GROSSMAN, GREGORY   1962   The Structure and Organization of the Soviet Economy. *Slavic Review* 21:203–222.

JAKOBSON, ROMAN; and HALLE, MORRIS   1956   *Fundamentals of Language*. The Hague: Mouton.

MARSHALL, T. H.   (1949)   1964   Citizenship and Social Class. Pages 65–

122 in T. H. Marshall, *Class, Citizenship, and Social Development: Essays.* Garden City, N.Y.: Doubleday. The essay is based on the Marshall lecture delivered at Cambridge in 1949. The collection of essays was first published in England in 1963 as *Sociology at the Crossroads.*

MEAD, GEORGE H. 1938 *The Philosophy of the Act.* Univ. of Chicago Press. Published posthumously.

PARSONS, TALCOTT 1960*a* Durkheim's Contribution to the Theory of Integration of Social Systems. Pages 118–153 in Kurt Wolff (editor), *Emile Durkheim, 1858–1917: A Collection of Essays With Translations and a Bibliography.* Columbus: Ohio State Univ. Press.

PARSONS, TALCOTT 1960*b* The Principal Structures of Community. Pages 250–279 in Talcott Parsons, *Structure and Process in Modern Societies.* Glencoe, Ill.: Free Press.

PARSONS, TALCOTT 1963*a* On the Concept of Influence. *Public Opinion Quarterly* 27:37–62. A comment by J. S. Coleman appears on pages 68–82; a communication by R. A. Bauer, on pages 83–86; and a rejoinder by Talcott Parsons, on pages 87–92.

PARSONS, TALCOTT 1963*b* On the Concept of Political Power. American Philosophical Society, *Proceedings* 107:232–262.

PARSONS, TALCOTT 1965 Unity and Diversity in the Modern Intellectual Disciplines: The Role of the Social Sciences. *Daedalus* 94:39–65.

SMITH, ADAM (1776) 1952 *An Inquiry Into the Nature and Causes of the Wealth of Nations.* Chicago: Encyclopedia Britannica. A two-volume paperback edition was published in 1953 by Irwin.

WHITEHEAD, ALFRED N. (1929) 1957 *Process and Reality: An Essay in Cosmology.* New York: Humanities.

9. Social Structure and the Symbolic Media of Interchange

IN RESPONSE to Peter Blau's invitation to me to participate in this major symposium on the theory of social structure, it seemed to me that it would be appropriate to take as a subtopic within that field an outline of a development which has been of very great importance to me and a few other associates for a number of years now. This is the analysis of what we have been calling generalized symbolic media of interchange as components of social systems and other systems of action.

The Properties of Media

For me, the primary model was money,[1] but another which has been conspicuous in recent years and has recently been much further studied by Victor Lidz,[2] is language. There has, however, been a tendency to treat each of these phenomena as unique in itself and not related to other

---

[1] Cf. John Stuart Mill, *Principles of Political Economy*, edited with an Introduction by W. J. Ashley (London: Longmens, Green and Co., 1909). First published in 1848.

[2] Victor Lidz, "Blood and Language: Analogous Media of Homeostasis," Paper submitted to a *Daedalus* Conference on the Relations between Biological and Social Theory, Cambridge, Mass., 1974, and "The Analysis of Action of the Most Inclusive Level: An introduction to Essays on the General Action Systems," in J. Loubser, R. Baum, A. Effrat and V. Lidz (eds.), *Explorations in General Theory in Social Science: Essays in Honor of Talcott Parsons* (New York: Free Press, 1976).

phenomena in the action system. This postulate of the uniqueness of money on the one side, language on the other, is one of the traditions which some of us have been challenging. Our attempt has been to treat each of them as members of a much more extensive family of media. So far we have explored intensively the family, which is anchored in the social system, where, in addition to money, we have dealt at some length with political power, influence, and value-commitments as such media.[3] We have also extended the analysis to the level of a general system of action where the anchor concept has been intelligence, unconventionally conceived not as a trait of personality but as a generalized medium. We have tentatively worked out a four-fold scheme for the general action level. We have also made beginnings with respect to the personality of the individual, but this is only a beginning and will need much further work.

The foundations of this development lay in two major steps of my own theoretical development, specifically, of the four-function scheme. Its first version was published in *Working Papers in the Theory of Action,*[4] in which I collaborated with Robert Bales and Edward Shils. The second, somewhat later foundation was the substantially revised version of my views of the relation of economic and sociological theory which was published in the small book *Economy and Society,*[5] in collaboration with Neil Smelser. Subsequent to these works, however, the development of the idea of generalized media took a few years. The first venture beyond money was the analysis of the concept of political power[6] and the second was the concept of influence.[7] It was in connection with the latter that I first encountered James Coleman in this context, when at the meeting of the Association for Public Opinion Research at which I presented my paper he was one of the main commentators.[8]

With respect to money, three of its functions which were clearly stated by the classical economists relatively early in the last century stood out as salient. Money, that is to say, was (1) a medium of exchange which had value in exchange, but in the pure type case, no value in use. (2) Money

[3] Cf. Talcott Parsons, *Politics and Social Structure* (New York: Free Press, 1969), Chapters 14–16.

[4] Talcott Parsons, Robert F. Bales, and Edward A. Shils, *Working Papers in the Theory of Action* (New York: Free Press, 1953).

[5] Talcott Parsons and Neil J. Smelser, *Economy and Society* (New York: Free Press, 1956).

[6] Cf. Talcott Parsons, "On the Concept of Political Power," *Proceedings of the American Philosophical Society*, 107 (1963). Reprinted in Talcott Parsons, *Politics and Social Structure, op. cit.*, pp. 352–404.

[7] Cf. Talcott Parsons, "On the Concept of Influence"; "Rejoinder to Bauer and Coleman," *The Public Opinion Quarterly*, Vol. 27 (1963), pp. 37–62 and 87–92. Reprinted in Parsons, *Politics and Social Structure, op. cit.*

[8] Cf. James S. Coleman, "Comment on 'On the Concept of Influence,'" *The Public Opinion Quarterly*, Vol. 27 (1963), pp. 63–82.

functioned as a measure of value, as they put it, in that it makes goods and services and factors of production, which in other respects such as physical properties are incomparably heterogeneous, comparable in terms of an economic measure, that of utility. And (3) money served as a store of value in that if it were accepted in exchange for possession of concrete commodities or access to concrete services, apart from phenomena of inflation, retaining possession of money does not lead to loss over time; on the contrary, it leads to gain in the form of interest.

The endeavor in extending the theoretical model of money as medium to other media was to match these traits with cases which, though formally similar, had a different content. The first criterion or property of a medium was the symbolic character which was stated by the classical economists for money in the proposition that it had value in exchange, but not value in use. Such a criterion applies to linguistic symbols, e.g., the word "dog," though signifying a species of mammalian quadruped, can neither bark nor bite, though the concrete dog can do both. Under this general rubric of symbolic character, we have stressed four further properties of such a medium as money. First comes *institutionaliszation,* especially in relation to property. We thus held such a medium to be characterized by a state of institutionalization, one aspect of which for the case of money is its backing by governmental authority through the status that is technically called legal tender. In the case of power this criterion led us to focus on what Weber [9] calls legitimate use of power as distinguished from a Hobbesian capacity to gain one's ends through having "what it takes." [10] Money can, of course, be used illegitimately through such channels as political bribery, and similarly power and influence can be used illegitimately; but these are special cases rather than constitutive criteria of the phenomena.

Second, there must be *specificity* of meaning and efficaciousness in both evaluation and interchange. As we put it in the case of money, it is the medium which can operate in economic exchanges, but many other interchange relations among humans cannot be mediated by money.

The third property may be called *circulability.* Money, like possession of commodities, changes hands. Any other medium should be subject to transfer of control from one acting unit to another in some kind of interchange transactions.

A fourth property, which proved of particular importance in bringing political power within this context, was the contention that a medium *could not have a zero-sum character* attributed to it in all contexts. Most political scientists dealing with political power had either explicitly stated

[9] Max Weber, *The Theory of Social and Economic Organization,* ed. by T. Parsons, trans. by A. M. Henderson and T. Parsons, "Power, Authority and Imperative Control" (New York: Free Press, 1947). pp. 152–153.

[10] Cf. Thomas Hobbes, *The Leviathan: or the Matter, Form and Power of a Commonwealth, Ecclesiastical and Civil* (London: Crooke, 1651).

or tacitly assumed that it was a zero-sum phenomenon, that is, that an increase in the amount of power held by one group in a system *ipso facto* entailed a corresponding decrease in the amount held by others.[11] This patently was not the case with money because of the phenomenon—well known to economists—of credit creation. And we went to considerable trouble to show that it need not be assumed to be a characteristic of power systems.[12]

The Institutional Contexts of Media

It is an exceedingly important point that the theoretical articulation of social system media with the social structure should be conceived at what I should call the institutional, precisely as distinguished from the collective, level. Unfortunately, sociological terminology has almost from the beginning tended to confuse the two. We speak of organizations and other collectivities as institutions (note McGill University or the Université de Montreal), but we also speak of property, contract, and authority as institutions. In the collective sense, of course, the concept of membership in an institution makes sense; in the latter context, membership is simply nonsensical—one simply cannot speak of being a member of the institution of property. Institutions in the latter sense, the one relevant here, are complexes of normative rules and principles which, either through law or other mechanisms of social control, serve to regulate social action and relationships—of course, with varying degrees of success. Each medium then is conceived to be articulated in a functionally defined institutional complex.

For the economic case, it would seem that the central institution is that of property. The underlying concept of property rights centers on rights of possession, which in turn can be broken down into disposal-acquisition, control, and use. In legal history there has been endless discussion and analysis of the nature of property. The objects of rights of possession are broadly classifiable into the three categories of (1) commodities or physical objects; (2) services, that is, human performances evaluated as having utility in the economic sense; and (3) financially significant assets where the economic value is abstracted from any particular characteristics in other respects, such as corporate or government securities, bank accounts, or insurance policies, all of which constitute rights to money payments under specifiable conditions.

[11] See C. J. Friedrich, *Man and His Government: An Empirical Theory of Politics* (New York: McGraw-Hill, 1963); H. Lasswell and A. Kaplan, *Power and Society* (New Haven: Yale University Press, 1950); and C. Wright Mills, *The Power Elite* (New York: Oxford University Press, 1956).

[12] Cf. Talcott Parsons, "On the Concept of Political Power."

The other principal economic institutions are occupation and contract. I conceive occupation essentially to be the institutionalized rubric under which rights to services as an output of the economic process, as distinguished from goods or commodities, are, as rights, transferable from performers to recipients. Seen in this context, a commodity is a physical object of output, possession in which can be transferred without the involvement of human agency beyond the settlement of terms; whereas services require that the performer stand in continuing relation to the recipient throughout the duration of the process.

We think it exceedingly important to make a distinction between services and their occupational organization as categories of economic output on the one hand and labor as a factor of production in the sense of economic theory on the other hand. Labor becomes service only when it has been combined with the other factors of production, and thereby its value has been added to.

Contract we conceive to be the primary integrative reference of the institutionalization of the economic complex. It is the institutional nexus which defines the conditions of legitimate exchange and possession in a sociological as distinguished from either a specifically economic or legal context. I would consider Durkheim [13] to be the preeminent sociological theorist of the nature of contract.

Other media, of course, function in complexes of institutional norms which are different from those of primarily economic significance. In the political context the paramount institutional complex is what we call authority. This may be defined as the legitimized capacity to make and to contribute to the implementation of decisions which are binding on a specifiable collective unit or class of them, where the holder of authority has some kind of right of speaking in the name of the collectivity. A typical case is that of a duly legitimized official of a unit of government. The principal modes of institutionalization under authority are the familiar executive, legislative, and judicial categories.

Even within the restricted framework outlined so far, it can, I think, be seen that the conception of generalized media and their articulation with structural components at the institutional level introduces an element of dynamic into the analysis of social relationships and processes. The broadest formula is that, in sufficiently highly differentiated systems of interchange, the principal processes, whether they be those of equilibration or of structural change, are mediated by the interchange of media for intrinsic outputs and factors and conversely of intrinsically significant outputs and factors for media. In this process the media provide or perform regulatory and integrative functions in that the rules governing their use

---

[13] Cf. Emile Durkheim, *The Division of Labor in Society*, trans. by George Simpson (New York: Free Press, 1964), Book 1, Chapter 7. Originally published in French in 1893.

define certain areas of legitimacy and the limits of such areas within which extension of systems of transaction can develop and proliferate. The introduction of a theory of media into the kind of structural perspective I have in mind goes far, it seems to me, to refute the frequent allegations that this type of structural analysis is inherently plagued with a static bias, which makes it impossible to do justice to dynamic problems. Let me, then, again insist that under the category of dynamic I mean to include both equilibrating processes and processes of structural change.

Having reviewed certain features of money as a medium and its institutionalization, let us now say something about the first major extension beyond money which we undertook, namely fitting a revised concept of political power into the idea of media of interchange. This was substantially more difficult than the analysis of money because in the latter case we were aided by the fact that the economic theorists have handed us a monetary concept which, with certain adaptations, could be treated as ready-made for sociological purposes. As I have noted, this has not been the case for the concept of political power, most conspicuously owing to the explicit or implicit assumption of a zero-sum condition. There are, however, also certain other difficulties. One of the most important of them has been the lack of specificity of the concept of power. This goes back to the great tradition of Hobbes, which most political theorists have followed, as have such sociologists as Max Weber. Hobbes' [14] famous definition will be remembered: "The power of a man . . . is his present means to obtain some future apparent good." Power, this is to say, is *any* capacity for an acting unit in a social system to "get what it wants," as Weber [15] said, with or without opposition, in a nexus of social relationships. By this definition, money clearly is a form of power, as also are influence and a number of other entities.

A theoretically satisfactory solution of this problem proved difficult, but I think it was finally arrived at. Two essential features of this solution are its collective reference and its rooting of power in legitimacy. It is first our contention that the concept of political power should be used essentially in a collective context to designate capacities to act effectively with reference to the affairs of a collective system, not necessarily of government. The Hobbesian version of individualism, to talk about relations among individuals independent of their collective affiliations, has been one source of lack of specificity.

The second essential ingredient is the concept of *blindingness*.[16] This

<hr />

[14] Hobbes, *The Leviathan.*

[15] Max Weber, "Class, Status and Party," in H. H. Gerth and C. W. Mills (eds.), *From Max Weber: Essays in Sociology* (New York: Oxford University Press, 1946), p. 180.

[16] On the concept of bindingness, see Parsons, "On the Concept of Political Power," pp. 381–382.

bindingness definitely rests on a conception of legitimacy. That is, people who have power have legitimated rights to make and implement collectively binding decisions. The role of coercion can be dealt with from this point of view in that coercive sanctions are important in the follow-up of binding decisions. The most general formula is that in the case of a decision which is politicially binding in the present sense, noncompliance on the part of those to whom it applies will in general evoke coercive sanctions. Physical force is not so much the prototype of such sanctions as the limiting case whereby the symbolic elements of social interaction are reduced to a minimum in favor of measures which either compel or strongly motivate to submission independent of questions of legitimacy.

It is assumed throughout this analysis that the category "political" is analytically defined and not the label for a concrete set of phenomena. In this respect it is parallel to that of "economic," which deals, at a technical theoretical level, with an analytically defined set of aspects of concrete behavior, and not, except secondarily, with a concrete type of behavior. Thus, to cite an example, Chester Barnard's famous book *The Functions of the Executive* [17] deals overwhelmingly with action in business firms. This, however, does not make it a theoretical treatise in economics; I would consider it one of the classics of political theory. The firm as collectivity, that is to say, performs political functions in the analytical sense, even though, since it is a firm, these functions are subordinated to economic organization, purposes, and goals—in Barnard's case, the purveying of telephone service under the imperative of financial solvency and profit.

Before leaving the subject of political power, a few further words should be said about the zero-sum problem in that context. As I mentioned, there was a particularly sharp difference of opinion between economic theorists dealing in the monetary area and political theorists dealing in that of power to the effect that, of course, money was not subject to zero-sum conditions, whereas power almost "of course" was. This dichotomy did not seem to make sense, and I think the claim can be made that the issue has been resolved, at least in principle, in favor of the economic non-zero-sum model, as generalizable to the power case.[18] The essential question seems to me to be whether there are processes, and what they are, by which power, as defined, can be newly introduced into a power system without a corresponding dimunition of the power in the hands of other elements.

In the case of money the classical instance is the creation of new money in the form of credit by banks. This is to say that bankers lend

[17] Chester I. Barnard, *The Functions of the Executive* (Cambridge, Mass.: Harvard University Press, 1938).

[18] Cf. Parsons, "On the Concept of Political Power."

funds which are the property of their depositors to borrowers on terms that involve an inherent risk to the depositors' financial interest but are nonetheless both legally legitimized and relatively safe under "ordinary" circumstances. There is a fundamental asymmetry in the relations of a bank to its depositors, on the one hand, and its borrowers, on the other. Depositors are entitled to the return of their deposits in full on demand; the bank, however, makes loans which are not repayable before the expiration of the stated terms of the loans. In a certain technical sense, therefore, any normally operating bank is inherently "insolvent," but entering this condition of insolvency is a condition of its being an economically productive institution in a sense other than being only a custodian of deposited funds.

We would contend that the—or one—political analogue of the banking function in the lending context is to be found in that of political leadership. Political leadership will make promises, fulfillment of which is dependent on the implied consent of the constituencies of the political leaders who have given them a grant of power under institutionalized authority, most obviously in cases of election to office. Once in office, however, such power holders may introduce extended plans which can be implemented only through new political power. As in the case of bank loans regarded as funds for investment, it is expected that they will pay off over time, but any immediate stringency which calls for immediate repayment can ordinarily not be met. Essentially, what this type of leadership is doing in our opinion is to use its fiduciary position to extend credit to politically significant enterprises which are not at the time of these decisions in a position to present complete pay-off in political effectiveness. We think that this is a process which is rather strictly analogous to that of credit creation on the part of bank executives.

In the case of credit creation through the legal bindingness of loan contracts, power is mobilized in support of economic investment. Similarly in the case of power creation, the influence of leadership may be mobilized in support of the expansion of power. In both cases this support comes from calling on the medium next higher in the cybernetic order. It need not, however, follow that *only* this next higher medium is involved in such cases. It seems more likely that various cybernetically higher forces, in combinations that vary from case to case, are mobilized in such a way that the total effect is "funneled" through the next higher medium.

The next step beyond establishing, in what seemed to us to be a relatively satisfactory theoretical manner, a status of the concept of political power as a symbolic medium, was to explore the possibilities of finding still other members of the family of media anchored in social system functions. The obvious focus of this next step concerned a medium which was primarily anchored in integrative functions of the system. This led

into a complex set of ramifications of considerations of sociological theory. The paths were even less clearly marked than in the case of political power. An index of this indeterminancy was the fact that there was no obvious single term such as power, to say nothing of that of money. We, however, thought that the use of the concept influence in much sociopolitical discussion made it worth exploring as a possible symbolic label appropriate to this particular context.[19] As the crucial differentiating criterion between power and influence, we took that of collective bindingness in the one case and its absence in the other. The essential problem was what was going on in the context of a unit or class of units trying to get something of collective significance "done," and what, if anything, was the difference between the two cases. In the case of power we used the criterion of the bindingness of their decisions on the collectivity as a whole as the primary criterion. If, however, they were using influence, their decisions and recommendations would not in this sense be binding, that is, noncompliance with them would not result in coercive sanctions. We have treated influence as a medium of *persuasion*.

Persuasion here should be regarded as only a partially adequate term. The place assigned to it in the sanction paradigm [20] is to our mind clearly justified by the contrast with the relevance of the two sategories of negative sanctions, namely, deterrence and activation of commitments.

The mode of persuasion that is particularly relevant for influence entails invoking collectively relevant *justifications* of the course of action recommended by the agent of influence. This in general invokes considerations of *collective* interest transcending those of the particular units involved and usually includes the call to what is at some level defined as a matter of moral obligation.

There are a number of different contexts of social interaction in which this problem could be worked through. One that has turned out to be particularly important to me and my colleagues is that of the performance of professional services, which for us came to a head in the medical world. When, however, such a term as "doctor's orders" is used, it clearly is not binding on the patient to comply with those orders at the penalty of some kind of coercive negative sanctions. The penalty will probably be health disadvantages to the patient, but he can make his own decision without exposing himself to "punishment" for noncompliance, that is, punishment administered by the physician or by some collective agency of health care which he represents. Thus a heart attack is not imposed by the medical profession on patients who disregard warnings about overexertion.

At the same time, it was difficult to clarify the implications of the fundamental distinction about media that influence should not be interpreted to

[19] *Ibid.*

[20] Parsons, *Politics and Social Structure*, pp. 412, 413, 415 ff.

be a matter of conveying specific information but rather of using a position of prestige which might be based, among other things, on specialized knowledge and experience, to persuade objects of interaction, in the medical case patients, that it was in their interest and that of the relevant collective groups to accept what was often called the "advice" of a physician.[21] The costs of such non-acceptance, however, would be assumed directly by the patient and not imposed through the means of coercive sanction. We came to feel that influence in this sense is a deeply important mode of the regulation of communication in systems where neither economic interests nor politically binding considerations are paramount.

A particularly significant empirical finding came in some of the work on academic systems in which I have participated.[22] We felt that we were able to make a pretty clear discrimination between positions or the components of positions predominantly involving power in our technical sense and involving influence within the academic context. For example, in an as yet fragmentarily published study of academic roles, we used the question whether the respondent would prefer to function as a department chairman or as an influential senior member of the department.[23] We found our respondents, on the whole, highly sensitive to this distinction and, especially at the institutions of higher prestige, a substantial majority preferred to be influential members of their departments. We thought we could draw the line between the fact that the chairman, by virtue of his office, exercises certain capacities to make power decisions binding on the department and that fact that an influential member cannot do this except through the collective process of departmental decision-making through voting or "persuading" the chairman and other colleagues. We suggest, therefore, that independently of specific expertise, which, after all, cannot be generalized in a highly differentiated system, persons occupying positions of prestige in the system could function effectively to persuade their colleagues and the collectivity without having coercive sanctions at their disposal.

Parallel to property and authority we conceive prestige to be the primary institutional category focussing on the integrative system, or societal community. It operates primarily under the legitimation of the value-pattern of solidarity, similar to utility in the economic sphere and collective effectiveness in the political.

Under the authorization of relative prestige, then, we postulate the

---

[21] Parsons, *Politics and Social Structure*, pp. 430–438.

[22] See Talcott Parsons and Gerald M. Platt, *The American University*, in collaboration with Neil J. Smelser (Cambridge, Mass.: Harvard University Press), 1973.

[23] Cf. Talcott Parsons, "Considerations on the American Academic System," *Minerva*, Vol. 6, No. 4 (Summer 1968), and Talcott Parsons and Gerald M. Platt, "The American Academic Profession: A Pilot Study" (Cambridge, Mass.: multilith, 1968).

institutionalization of capacity, through influence, to mobilize commitments of units to what we have called valued association, and to regulate the interplay between political support and identification through membership in (plural) solidary involvements.

Intelligence and Affect

The roster of primary media anchored in the social system is conceived to consist of the three that have been briefly discussed, namely, money, political power, and influence, and a fourth we have called value-commitment, which is anchored in the fiduciary system.[24] It has, however, become increasingly evident that the same general mode of analysis ought to be extended to other systems of action than the social. The example that has been most fully worked out is that of what we have been calling the general system of action. This is interpreted to comprise the social system, the cultural system, the personality or motivational system of the individual, and what currently I have started to call the behavioral system, omitting earlier reference to the organism. (This change has been under the influence of a paper by Victor and Charles Lidz which relates the conception to the cognitive psychology of Jean Piaget.) [25]

To my mind, an important line of development of the theory, which has occurred essentially since my original book, *The Structure of Social Action,*[26] has sought to clarify the nature of the general action system. The first major step in this direction was achieved in the volume *Toward A General Theory Action,*[27] but it has been quite substantially extended and revised since that time.[28] A particularly significant distinction—on a strictly analytical level, of course—is that between the social system and the cultural system, in our technical sense of the terms. The recent program of study on the university in which I have collaborated with Gerald Platt [29] involves these problems, because one cannot deal theoretically with the university without taking into account systematically both its characteristics as a social system and its involvement with a cultural system.

[24] See Talcott Parsons, "On the Concept of Value-Commitments," *Sociological Inquiry,* Vol. 38 (1968). Reprinted in Parsons, *Politics and Social Structure.*

[25] Victor Lidz and Charles Lidz, "The Psychology of Intelligence of Jean Piaget and Its Place in the Theory of Action," in J. Loubser, R. Baum, A. Effrat and V. Lidz (eds.), *Explorations in General Theory in Social Science: Essays in Honor of Talcott Parsons* (New York: Free Press, 1976).

[26] Talcott Parsons, *The Structure of Social Action,* (New York: McGraw-Hill, 1937). Reprinted by The Free Press, New York, 1949.

[27] Talcott Parsons and Edward A. Shils, *Toward a General Theory of Action* (Cambridge, Mass.: Harvard University Press, 1951).

[28] Cf. Parsons and Smelser, *Economy and Society.*

[29] Parsons and Platt, *The American University.*

The focus of the university's involvement in the cultural system lies epecially in its concern with knowledge. This concerns the transmission of knowledge, notably from faculty members to students through the processes of teaching and learning, but also the advancement of knowledge which is particularly concentrated in the research function. From the point of view of researchers and their collaborators, research is also a learning process since a research program whose outcome is known in advance would be pointless. The researcher has to *learn* the answers to the problems posed in a research project.

Knowledge we have treated as the primary cultural component of a larger complex involving all of the subsystems of the general system of action. In this connection we have treated rationality as predominantly a phenomenon of the social system, as competence is anchored in the personality system; and we have adapted the concept of intelligence to the role of a generalized symbolic medium as anchored in what Lidz and Lidz [30] call the behavioral system. The most important link between the cultural and the social systems we treat as the commitment of the university as a whole to the value of cognitive rationality. Rationality, as noted in this context, we conceive to be basically a social category, whereas the term "cognitive" formulates the relation of rationality to the prevailing concern with knowledge in the two primary modes of transmission and advancement just mentioned. The individual's capacity to handle cognitive problems we have called competence, which we conceive as established in the personality through processes of socialization which constitute an essential part of the experience of participation in academic communities, especially, though far from exclusively, in the role of student, whether graduate or undergraduate.

Let me now elucidate a bit how we have tried to adapt the concept of intelligence to the rubric of generalized medium of interchange. The simplest definition we would give is that intelligence may be considered to be the capacity of an acting unit, usually an individual, effectively to mobilize the resources requisite to the solution of cognitive problems. This definition is conventional enough. The unconventionality of our treatment lies in our conception of the conditions and processes involved in its operation as such a capacity. First, we conceive of intelligence, though of course greatly affected by genetic components, to be predominantly acquired through socialization and learning processes. However, we conceive it not only possible to acquire intelligence but also to spend it through use in problem-solving activity.

Perhaps it will be helpful to explicate what we mean by the circulation of intelligence. If the human individual be taken as the primary point of

---

[30] See Lidz and Lidz, "The Psychology of Intelligence of Jean Piaget and Its Place in the Theory of Action." See also Parsons and Platt, *The American University*, pp. 33–102.

reference—as seems appropriate for most purposes—we conceive that the level of intelligence of such an individual as an adult, let us say, is the outcome of combinatorial confluence of factors which have operated on him in the course of his life history. Among these factors clearly must be included the relevant aspect of the genetic constitution with which he was born. But the genetic factor does not stand alone. It is combined with cognitive learning experience and with a primarily noncognitive framework of socialization expectations.

Intelligence as cognitive capacity may then be conceived as capable of growth for long periods. Once available it can then be "used" in a wide variety of ways, notably in the solution of specific cognitive problems. The question then becomes whether and how such an actor of reference can recoup expenditure of intelligence on problem-solving activity. The answer seems to be that he "learns from experience" and the next time around can—on a certain average—do better than he could have without the experience.

Thus, rather than treating a person's intelligence as something he simply "has," we treat it as a fluid resource which can be acquired and enhanced in the course of action and effectively used by being "spent." [31]

There is a primary line of distinction between intelligence as medium and intelligence as trait. Our model here for intelligence as medium is that of other media, notably, money. We can speak of an individual as wealthy and in one linguistic usage his level of wealth is a trait of the individual; on the other hand, we know that his wealth was not part of his hereditary constitution, in the organic sense, and that the possession of wealth, that is, of economically valuable assets, places the individual in a network of interchange transactions where he can not only acquire such assets but also use those he has in the further interchange system.

We therefore posit that intelligence, considered as a medium, must meet the criteria of circulation. Its relative specificity seems scarcely to be in question, and the fact of the mode of its involvement in the cognitive complex, including the various levels of education, points to the primacy of the factor of institutionalization, which we also have stressed for media in general. I will not try to enter into an analysis of the non-zero-sum properties of intelligence conceived in this way, but will assert most emphatically that it fits the model of money as essentially a non-zero-sum phenomenon, and not the more traditional one of power as bound by zero-sum limitations. Indeed, I think one of the most serious objections to the conventional psychological conceptions of intelligence lies in the tendency to subject it to the zero-sum condition.

The relation to social structure comes from the fact that we think of the entire cognitive complex as institutionalized at the social system level.

[31] *Ibid.*

Without this state of institutionalization there could be no such thing as the modern university. As institutional type, we think of the university as belonging to a distinctive category of social organization which, unfortunately, has not in our opinion been adequately stressed in most recent sociological writing. The technical term we choose to refer to it by is a "collegial association." This should clearly be distinguished from a market system on the one hand, from a bureaucratic type of organization on another, and within the broader category of associational types, from purely democratic associations. It is distinguished from the last by a fiduciary component, in this case responsibility for the complex of cognitive interests and their involvement in certain respects in the larger action system, and a related pattern of stratification.

As concrete organization, the modern university has, of course, a bureaucratic component of considerable magnitude; and it is involved in the market nexus through its multifarious economic transactions. But the core, in our opinion, consists in the faculty–student collectivity which we define as predominantly a collegial association. Perhaps the most telling structural criterion of this is the fundamental equality of the status of membership at each of a number of graded prestige levels. The highest we conceive to be senior faculty status, which has traditionally come to carry full tenure; we have, however, extended the concept of tenure to include not merely senior faculty but also junior time-limited faculty membership and membership in student capacities, both graduate and undergraduate. At any given level of tenure we conceive members of the same university to be equals of each other, but the system as a whole is stratified on the basis of levels of commitment to and competence in the implementation of the value of cognitive rationality. Thus it can scarcely be conceived that the average undergraduate freshman is the equal in these two respects to the career-committed senior professor. We thus treat the tenure levels as the main framework of its stratification pattern.[32]

The academic version of the collegial association belongs to a larger family of such associational structures in modern society. To us the most notable others are the kinship association, especially in the form in which it has developed in the more recent phases of modern society, the national or societal community, and the predominantly religious association. If space permitted, the similarities and differences among these four types could be considerably elaborated.

All of these major types of fiduciary association tend to have a collegial character and some concept of membership of which in a certain sense prototypical is that of citizenship, as that idea has been defined and developed by T. H. Marshall.[33] All are social structures within which certain

---

[32] Parsons and Platt, *The American University*, pp. 103–162.

[33] T. H. Marshall, *Class, Citizenship and Social Development* (Garden City, Anchor Books, 1965).

functions can be performed with relative success and which are to important degrees insulated from the generally recognized "play of interests" which in a society like ours focuses at the economic and political levels From the point of view of the more simplistic conception of the determination of social phenomena by interests in this sense, they are relatively useless from a utilitarian point of view. Perhaps a classic statement of this point of view is the one attributed to Stalin, I believe at the Yalta Conference, in which there was some reference to the Pope. Stalin's query in evaluating the importance of the Pope was alleged to be, "How many divisions does he have?" Quite clearly neither the military nor the economic significance of universities, of families, of religious bodies, and indeed, of communities in the sense of this discussion are the primary criteria of their importance. They are not primarily characterized by sheer control of means or coercive sanctions by political power or wealth.

This, however, is not a criterion of their lack of importance as components of the social structure. As I have several times said in print,[34] I concur with Daniel Bell [35] in the judgment that the university has become stratgeically the most important single category of structural collectivity in modern society, especially in what Bell refers to as its post-industrial phase. This is not because it has become the center either of wealth or of power, though it must participate in both of these interchange systems. It is rather because it is the center of the mobilization of a type of resource which has acquired a quite new level of significance in the more recent phases of social development which Bell characterizes, correctly I think, as focusing on the importance of "theoretical knowledge."

In order not to leave the concept of intelligence as a generalized medium functioning at the level of the general system of action entirely alone, perhaps it would be appropriate at this point to introduce a brief discussion of another medium which I have been calling *affect*.[36] Whereas I conceive intelligence to be anchored in what the Lidz brothers [37] call the behavioral system, I conceive of affect as anchored in the *social* subsystem of the general action system. It is, however, conceived to circulate not only within the social system but between it and the other primary functional subsystems of action, namely, the cultural, personality, and behavioral subsystems. Affect thus conceived is the generalized medium most

[34] Cf. Parsons and Platt, *The American University*, pp. 1–7, and Talcott Parsons, "Social Stratification" in *Encyclopedia Italiana*, Vincenzo Cappelletti (ed.) (Rome: Instituto della Enciclopedia Italiana, 1976).

[35] Daniel Bell, *The Coming of Post-Industrial Society* (New York: Basic Books, 1973).

[36] Cf. Parsons and Platt, *The American University*.

[37] Lidz and Lidz, "The Psychology of Intelligence of Jean Piaget and Its Place in the Theory of Action."

definitely concerned with the mobilization and control of the factors of solidarity in Durkheim's sense.[38]

Solidarity as a primary property of social collectivities grounded in a value category is dependent on factors mobilized from all four of the primary subsystems of action. These factors include the cathectic commitments of individual persons to participation in solidary collectivities; the moral standards which underlie social order as this concept was employed by Durkheim, which is a contribution from cultural sources; and finally, rational grounds for the allocation of affect as between the societal and nonsocietal commitments and within the latter as between plural memberships in different societal subcollectivities.

Back of this way of looking at affect as a generalized circulating medium lies a Durkheimian conception of the social system as playing a dual role in action. On the one hand, from the point of view of the acting individual, it is an environment which constitutes the focus of the individual's primary adaptive orientations. On the other hand, it is not part of the "natural" environment, which is analytically separate from the field of human action, but is itself part of the system of action and a creation of past processes of action. As such, its constitution consists of action components, of which a particularly important aspect is provided by the element of moral order which is a primary regulator of solidary relationships within the same social system.[39]

Affect we conceive to be the medium through which the stabilities essential to the moral order of a social system are adjusted to the ranges of variation that occur in the more concrete social environment in which the individual acts. We have stressed that the level of the general system of action must be intimately articulated with that of the internal imperatives of the social system. We would like, therefore, to draw a parallel between the functions of intelligence and the functions of affect as media which are involved in these processes of articulation. In fact, affective attachment of individuals to the collectivities which are constitutive of the structure of the social system and to the other individuals who share membership status with them are at the center of the mechanisms by which general action factors can achieve the status of institutionalization in de-

[38] Among those concerned with media theory at the general action level there has been a disagreement with respect to the placement of affect. Notably, Mark Gould and Dean Gerstein have opted to use it as the medium anchored in the first instance in the personality system and to introduce an alternative concept for the social system medium. My own preference is definitely to use it in the social system context, but I do not feel dogmatic about it and hope that it will eventually prove possible to reach terminological consensus in this important area.

[39] Cf. Talcott Parsons, "Durkheim on Religion Revisited: Another Look at *The Elementary Forms of the Religious Life*," in Charles Y. Glock and Philip E. Hammond (eds.), *Beyond the Classics? Essays in the Scientific Study of Religion* (New York: Harper and Row, 1973).

fining the structure of social units. We have already illustrated this in the case of the modern university considered as a social system. These considerations can and should be generalized to a wide variety of other types of collective structure which play a part in social systems, particularly of the modern type characterized by an advanced division of labor.[40]

Social Stratification

In this last section, I want to return to the social system level to outline briefly a use of the conception of generalized media of interchange in relation to social structure in dealing with a very central problem which has concerned sociological theorists for a long time, namely, the nature of social stratification.

Perhaps as good a starting point as any is to make clear that the older organization of stratification systems about the institution of aristocracy may for most practical purposes be considered to be dead. It has not, however, been replaceed by a pattern of flat equality, though pressures in the direction of equalization have been very powerful in recent times. What we seem to have, however, is a complex balance between trends to equality on the one hand and the kinds of opportunities and freedoms that make for considerable inequality on the other.

It has frequently been noted that modern society has been characterized by a growing trend to pluralization which is very much in accord with Durkheim's [41] conception of the progressive growth of the social as distinguished from the purely economic division of labor. Of course, the scale of organization has continued to grow; and many observers, particularly those with a neo-Marxist bent, seem to feel that the nineteenth-century characterization of the stratification structure of industrial society, especially in the Marxian tradition, is still fully adequate. There is a sense in which this characterization has been held to be reinforced in the later stages of "capitalism" by the concentration of managerial authority and

---

[40] We consider the process of institutionalization, as previously referred to, to be the action-system equivalent of natural selection as that concept has come to be an integral part of biological theory, that is, the theory of the nature and functioning of organic systems. The general action system, and particularly its cultural component, we conceive to be analogous to the genetic constitution of species and the primary source of genetic variation. As such, the cultural system promulgates patterns of what at the value level may be characterized as desirable modes of action. By no means all of these, however, become institutionalized as operative characteristics of going social systems. The intervening process is one of selection according to which some such patterns prove to be favorable in meeting the conditional exigencies of more concrete societal functioning, whereas others prove to be less successful. There develops, that is to say, a differential survival probability among those that are better and less well adapted to coping with such exigencies.

[41] Durkheim, *The Division of Labor in Society*, Book 1.

power in large organizations and by the growth of big government which has maintained close liaison with the private-enterprise business world.

We would like, however, to direct attention to a somewhat different aspect of development. Bell has strongly emphasized the growing importance of the university in modern society, and this growing importance cannot be explained mainly by the transfer of very large shares of the control of economic resources and of political powers to it. As Bell [42] puts it, it rests mainly on the university's role in the mobilization of a newly important resource, namely, theoretical knowledge. Another straw in the interpretive wind has been the contention of Jencks and Riesman [43] that the line between the college-educated sector of the population and those who lack this level of education has come to be the most important single line in the stratification system. We may perhaps put these two sets of considerations together in their relation to another phenomenon, which, for example, has recently been emphasized by Eliot Freidson,[44] and which he refers to as the trend to professionalization of modern society. Many social scientists have been aware of the major shifts that have taken place in the nature of the labor force, notably through the relative decline of agriculture, the decline of the role of unskilled labor, and the concurrent rise of what are ordinarily designated as service occupations. Freidson in particular stresses the rise of the technical and professional occupations in relative size and importance and their requirements of specialized training in institutions of higher education, that is, institutions that are by and large outside the spheres of control of the employing organizations and their managerial components. Freidson, quite correctly I think, strongly emphasizes the penetration of large organizations both in government and business as well as in the private nonprofit sector by professional components and in particular the impact of this on the postion of management in the traditional sense. One way of putting it is to suggest a substantial decline in the relative importance of bureaucratic authority of the traditional sort in modern organizations and a far greater autonomy in the hands of the trained and technical occupational groups. Such groups, however, have been organized more according to associational than to bureaucratic patterns.

It was Durkheim [45] above all who, in sharp disagreement with Spencer,[46]

[42] Bell, *The Coming of Post-Industrial Society.*

[43] Christopher Jencks and David Riesman, *The Academic Revolution* (Garden City: Doubleday, 1968).

[44] Eliot Freidson, "Professions and the Occupational Principle," in *The Professions and Their Prospects* (Beverly Hills: Sage Publications, 1973), pp. 19–38; and Eliot Freidson, "Professionalization and the Organization of Middle Class Labour in Post-Industrial Society," *The Sociological Review* Monograph No. 20, pp. 47–59.

[45] Durkheim, *The Division of Labor in Society*, Book 1.

[46] Herbert Spencer, *The Principles of Sociology*, 3 Volumes (New York: Appleton, 1925–1929). Originally published in 1876–1896.

held that the concomitant development of an economy made up of independent units, in something like a so-called free enterprise systems, and of the state and government, could be regarded as a normal development. It seems to me that in some of the developments we have just mentioned, still a third more or less independent set of structural components has risen to a new order of prominence, namely, those having to do with a certain cultural primacy. The case of the system of higher education, which should be understood to include the research function, is probably only the most conspicuous single case. Again, as Freidson [47] points out, professionalism permeates the structures of large business enterprise and governments, but its significance is by no means confined to this penetration. Besides institutions of higher education, we can think of the immense proliferation of health care organization and the other so-called helping professions, and as another particularly important case that of the mass media, in which we could include the press, television and radio, book publishing, and a variety of other modes of organizing broadcast communication.

I would like to suggest that a structural pattern which Gerald Platt and I [48] utilized in our analysis of the university can be generalized to help understand the nature of the changes that have been occurring in the general stratification system. For the case of the university we were struck by the persistence under the same organizational tent, as it were, of a number of apparently heterogeneous elements. Thus, for example, universities have come to include the whole range of intellectual disciplines, the teaching function and the research function, both graduate and undergraduate versions of the teaching function, and professional schools, along with the core arts and sciences faculties. We called this combination the "bundle." [49]

We think that the wide scope of this conspicuous bundle, which stands in contrast to the much touted tendencies to specialized separatism, has to do with an analogy to Adam Smith's [50] conception of the relation of the division of labor and the extent of the market which clearly includes level of productivity as well as quantitative extension. We think, however, that the effectiveness of the combination of academic functions through their being in this sense "bundled" together is highly dependent on new levels of the development of generalized media. In the case of the university we have stressed two levels, intelligence as we have outlined its nature operat-

[47] Freidson, *The Professions and Their Prospects* and "Professionalization and the Organization of Middle Class Labour in Post-Industrial Society."

[48] Parsons and Platt, *The American University.*

[49] Cf. Talcott Parsons, "The University 'Bundle': A Study of the Balance Between Differentiation and Integration," Epilogue in N. Smelser and G. Almond (eds.), *Public Higher Eductaion in California: Growth, Structural Change and Conflict* (Berkeley: University of California Press, 1974). See also Parsons and Platt, *The American University,* pp. 346–388.

[50] Adam Smith, *An Inquiry Into the Nature and Causes of the Wealth of Nations,* edited by Edwin Cannon (London: Methuen, 1950). First published in 1776.

ing at the general action level, and influence operating internally to the social system aspect of the organization of higher education and mediating its relations to other sectors. We suggest that such coherence as exists in the upper sector of the modern system of stratification might also be considered to be integrated especially through bundle mechanisms.

In order to make clear what we mean by such a statement, it would seem best to outline very briefly what components go into such a bundle and how they are related. The two most obvious dimensions are a "horizontal" one (for purpose of diagramming) and a "vertical" one. The former may for our purposes be designated as the "range" of extension of a bundle, whereas the latter may be designated to refer to the "levels" at which various components of the bundled complex are held to stand. In the academic case referred to previously the range is constituted by the spectrum of intellectual disciplines, which ranges from mathematics and physics through the biological and the social sciences into the humanities, perhaps ending with the critical analysis of the arts.

What, in *The American University,* Platt and I have called the "cognitive complex" invovles in the first instance a cultural level which comes to focus about valid and significant knowledge, considered as a primary output of cognitive processes (notably research) but, at the same time, as a central condition for the further development of cognitive processes. At another level the cognitive human interest comes to be embodied in a variety of social organizations—in higher education, colleges and universities, faculties and departments, administrations, research organizations, and schools for professional training. We hold quite specifically that it is not fruitful to confuse the cultural and the social organization levels. Finally, at both levels, the cognitive endeavor is one actively participated in by various categories of human individuals, as personalities and as behavioral systems. At the sociological level they are in such roles as faculty members, graduate and undergraduate students, research workers, and administrators.

Two further ranges, related to but not identical with the primary academic one of the intellectual disciplines stand respectively above and below the latter in level terms. The first of these may bec alled the range of "research problems," which often stretch across parts of several disciplines.

The second range arises primarily for the applied professions. Platt and I [51] have called it the "clinical focus." The prototype example is the frequently referred to "science of medicine," which is not a discipline in the Arts and Sciences sense at all but a way of mobilizing knowledge in terms of its practical bearing on the tasks of the health professions in dealing with problems of health and illness.

[51] Parsons and Platt, *The American University,* pp. 225–266.

For the case of a stratification bundle, clearly the principal range axis concerns the variety of what in a broad sense are "social" types which have some standing in the higher prestige levels. Though kinship heredity has not altogether disappeared—*vide* the Kennedys and the Rockefellers—by and large eligibility is gained mainly by achievement, not kinship ascription. There has been, in the middle third of the present century, an enormous access of new groups, such as Jews and more recently blacks. We may conceive a continual process of competition for prestige status, among those already "there" and between them and aspirants for inclusion.

The weakening of the hereditary principle is conspicuous, but even more so perhaps is the wide variety of types which must now be included. It used to be said that the businessmen were the "natural leaders of the community." That a good many prominent businessmen are among such leaders today few would doubt, but equally few would doubt that a considerably broader group, or rather set of groups, would now need to be taken into account. I would not conceive such a set of "upper" groups to constitute a neatly structured symmetrical pyramid but rather a variegated complex of types of "influentials" who would be regarded, with an approximation of consensus, as having relatively high prestige.

In a rough way these groups can, I think, be arranged along a spectrum which is not as such a rank order of prestige. At one end of the spectrum I should place groups whose claims to prestige could be grounded in cultural—shading into moral—bases of status. This "wing" of the spectrum would include, first, the academics, the more professional types rather than top administrators such as presidents; second, that rather vaguely defined category called "intellectuals" who are found both inside and outside academia, third, the clergy of various denominations; and fourth, the artists, including the literary contingent. The final, fifth, principal subgroup I would assign to this wing are the "professionals" in the traditional sense, distinguished from the academics. This group comprises those engaged in "practical" pursuits but with major academic training, such as lawyers, physicians, increasingly some "para-medical" health personnel, engineers, and representatives of some of the newer professional groups.[52]

In what may be called the "middle" sector of the spectrum I would include some of the higher reaches of the political and the business worlds. There is, however, an important if not fully clear line which cuts across these categories, namely, that between proprietors or politicians "in their own right" and "administrators" who, at least nominally, are "employed" by the former. It is here that most of what has sometimes been called the "power elite" is to be found, but it is itself a mixed bag and internally very heterogeneous. Also, though less prominent, I think the leadership of labor unions should be included here.

---

[52] Cf. Parsons and Platt, *The American University*.

Finally, the third sector will include the leadership of movements which have gained some importance and usually some "political clout" but which are not yet fully integrated in the larger stratification system. Most conspicuous among these are leaders of various "rights" movements, of which two of the more massive recently have been "civil rights" and women's rights. Certainly such leaders are very much in the public eye, and some of them have become national heroes.[53]

It should be made clear that most of the occupational categories mentioned above comprise a range of prestige status such that only their higher-prestige subgroups can qualify for inclusion in an "upper" stratum of the society. Thus members of the faculties of small community colleges have clearly a different status from those of leading universities, officers of small local businesses from those of major national and international firms, politicians in minor local offices from national political figures, and so on. The cutting points, however, are by no means rigidly defined.

Another relevant basis of differentiation is that defined by Merton,[54] Gouldner,[55] and others as that between "locals" and "cosmopolitans," which has to do with the range of salience and influence.

The second major dimension of variation is that which we have called *level,* using that term to refer to the cybernetic heirarchy of components of systems of human action. We have referred above to the increasing prominence, within the present century, of groups the prestige of which is grounded in primarily *cultural* competence and achievements, such as the rise in relative standing of scientists and other masters of "theoretical knowledge" as compared to the promience of "practical" men of business at the turn of the century. Another example is the rise in the relative prominence of the arts and the groups involved with them. The relations between adcademic intellectuals and the arts are highly complex. I think Bell [56] goes too far in speaking of a nearly total dissociation between the "cultural," as he calls it, and the institutionalized aspects of culture in science and technology.

---

[53] There is something to be said for the view that some students should be included in this higher-prestige range, not so much because of high academic achievement, to say nothing of kinship ascription or eliteness of institution attended, but by virtue of leadership in one or a set of "movements."' Certainly in the disturbances which culminated in the late 1960's a good many student leaders gained national prominence. The great structural difficulty of including such a group in a national "elite" lies in the age-boundedness of student status and hence the short period in which any given individual remains a student. High academic achievers will have a chance to become prominent academics or professionals, especially, but the future of student leaders, after their student days are over, is more problematic.

[54] Cf. Robert K. Merton, *Social Theory and Social Structure* (New York: Free Press, 1957).

[55] Cf. Alvin W. Gouldner, "Cosmopolitan and Locals: Toward an Analysis of Latent Social Roles," *Administrative Science Quarterly*, Vol. 2 (1957–1958), pp. 211–306 and 444–480.

[56] Cf. Bell, *The Coming of Post-Industrial Society*, especially the last chapter.

A further prominent shift is in the rise of a very diverse category of predominantly secular "intellectuals," writers and communicators on many different levels on many subjects, among which subjects problems of public policy figure prominently. There is a partial but by no means simple sense in which these have displaced the more traditional clergy as the intellectual–moral leading element.

By contrast to the just-listed groups, with the practicing professions standing somewhat in the middle, we may place the groups with leading positions in practical affairs—in the business, labor, and political worlds, including those in administrative rather than proprietary or elective positions who work at rather high levels of responsibility in organizations in these sectors.

Finally, as noted, the more prestigeful elements identified with "movements" should be placed in a somewhat different category because of their only partly institutionalized status. For individuals and subgroups of course this status can shift. Thus Thurgood Marshall as lawyer made his primary reputation as attorney for the NAACP in the legal phase of the black movement's battle for improved civil rights. On his elevation to the Supreme Court, however, Mr. Marshall came to occupy one of the most fully institutionalized statuses in the higher echelons of the society.

The two dimensions which we have called range and level have never stood alone in bundle phenomena. Thus in the academic case we have stressed the importance of what we have called the socialization function, analysis of which Platt and I [57] concentrated on in our chapter on the undergraduate aspect of the university system. There is a sense in which socialization is a set of processes which help to integrate a complex and tension-prone institutional system along the age gradient of the life course. In this case the primary reference points are the generation groups incorporated in the statuses of student and faculty member respectively. We have stressed that, though necessarily faculties exercise more "influence" on their students than vice versa, the process is clearly not merely a one-way affair but a two-way one with built-in reciprocities. The primary interacting groups, however, are not simple "equals" of each other because of the double difference of stage in the life course and levels of competence and commitment in the academic culture.

Perhaps the most closely analogous function of the stratification bundle concerns the part it plays in the integration of the society across lines of actual and potential conflict. That such lines should be both "vertical" and "horizontal," in our metaphorical language, is, of course, commonplace. They of course include but are not confined to "class" conflicts, latent and overt, which I conceive as vertical in the sense that they concern different statuses within given sectors of what we have called the

[57] Parsons and Platt, *The American University*, pp. 163–224.

relevant ranges. For present purposes, however, I should place greater stress on the other axis of conflict, namely, that of qualitative differentiation, which has arisen in the course of the division of labor as well as certain "historical" factors such as religious and ethnic diversity grounded (for the United States) in the history of immigration. This is to an important degree the context which has often been referred to as the "pluralism" of modern societies, especially perhaps the American. Much more circumstantial investigation of the range dimension and that of levels, as well as that of lines of conflict, is greatly needed but cannot be undertaken within the confines of this rather brief paper.

In conclusion only two more topics can be all too briefly dealt with. The first concerns the probability that in spite of the growing pluralism to which reference has just been made, one or a few particular groups may acquire a special salience in the stratification and integrative functions of such a society. I should like to suggest that this is the case in the recent and present junctures, for certain leading elements of what may be called the legal complex in American society. In the recent dramatic processes leading to the forcing of a President from office for the first time in American history, a special role has been taken by lawyers, in and out of public office. In the latter context the courts of law have, of course, played a special role, both the Federal district courts as the trial courts for grand jury investigations and actual trials of indicted persons, and the Supreme Court, especially in its unanimous decision on Presidential prerogative.

Legislative bodies have always had a major participation of lawyers, and in both Houses of Congress recently they have played an especially prominent part, notably the House Judiciary Committee, the whole membership of which consists of lawyers. Then, in spite of their vicissitudes, the role of two special prosecutors and their staffs should not be forgotten.

Of course these "in office" actions of lawyers could not have taken place without the existence and position in the society of a much larger pool of lawyers who have shown a special concern for the "public interest," as it has often been called. There is a sense in which the current era has been one of resurgence of the significance of "the law," including not only the body of norms but also the groups with special responsibilities for their implementation. It seems to us that this special role of the legal complex operates in part because it can mediate between the normative and cultural orders which have become so important to a complex society and the vast complex of especially economic and political interests which are the primary focus of centrifugal pressures. This is a topic meriting much more sociological attention than it has received.[58]

---

[58] This is partially remedied by the dissertation of John L. Akula: "Law and the Development of Citizenship," unpublished dissertation, Department of Sociology, Harvard University, 1973.

The final topic for brief mention is the role in this integrative process of the media themselves. Because of the complexity of the problems only a few bare indications can be given here. First, it seems to me that the central role must be given to *influence* as a medium and that this connects especially with the role of the legal complex, but also the intellectuals and the media people, as I have called them. Lawyers, through legislative enactments and court decisions articulate with the power system and its coercive sanctions but its main members are not primarily "men of power" but rather of influence, as trustees of an especially important aspect of the normative order of the society. In such capacities their role is much more to define, interpret, and advise than it is to issue "orders." They are, above all, regulators of the power system and, in somewhat different ways, of the economic system.

In the other cybernetic direction, "upward," the influence complex is articulated with that of values, which overlaps especially into the constitutional aspects of the legal system itself. Here one of the most important functions of the members of the legal complex is to activate the consideration of the relevance of general moral and institutional principles which have been central to our societal history and to help bring them to bear on the specific problems of the day. Here the academic branch of the legal profession is of paramount importance and, through it especially, the articulation in the larger university system and the culture of intellectuals.

Finally, one generalized medium operating at the level of the general system of action, affect, belongs in this context. If we are right about its special relation to solidarity, we may suggest that it functions above all to help to mobilize the factors in generation and renewal of the larger solidarities which have been imperiled by recent developments. This, however, opens up complications which far transcend the scope of this paper; the problem could only be mentioned.

I hope it has been possible to present a brief outline, in this concluding section, of how, through a recently emerging "stratification bundle," a set of integrative mechanisms has begun to take hold in our society, which can easily be overlooked because of our preoccupation with the more specific phenomena of economic and political interests. If this is indeed developing, its understanding will centrally involve what we have been calling the generalized media of interchange in relation to the social structure.

10. Some Problems of General Theory in Sociology

My ASSIGNMENT as a participant in the symposium on the state of theory in sociology was to contribute something about *general* theory. The difficulty of the assignment lies nearly as much in its definition as in its execution. There is danger of being primarily programmatic, failing to confront genuinely substantive problems; and there is danger of being parochial, dealing with matters of more personal than general professional concern.

In this instance it seemed better to lean more in the latter than the former direction, dealing with a problem area which has been central to my own work for a good many years, but which has bearings of general concern. I am referring to the concept of function, which has been close to the center of the stage of general theoretical controversy for a long generation now. While much of the previous discussion—for example over the more naïve forms of functional teleology—is now only of historical interest, the general problem area is very much alive. An attempt to formulate the best statement of which I am capable in this general area should prove useful.

Furthermore, I have in previous work specified a paradigm of functional analysis considerably more circumstantially than has generally been the case, and claimed that this specified version has a high order of general theoretical significance. This, of course, refers to the four-function paradigm of adaptation, goal-attainment, integration, and pattern-maintenance which has been used in a variety of contexts as a theoretical reference point. I should like, then, first to consider the general status of the concept function in sociological theory and then to discuss the justifications for the four-function scheme.

The focus of this paper is on problems of general theory in sociology, but this cannot reasonably be isolated from other branches of general theory. Within the province of the social system this must include economic and political theory, at the very least, and beyond that, in the sphere I have called *action,* it must include psychological and cultural theory, the latter in the anthropological rather than the humanistic sense. In the relevant sense action is, except for protophenomena, specifically human, and concerns those aspects of human *behavior* which are involved in and controlled by culturally structured *symbolic codes;* language is an obvious prototype. "Acts" in this sense are behaviors to which their authors and those who significantly interact with them attribute, in Weber's phrase, a "subjective," which is to say cultural or symbolic, meaning. This implies that the process of interaction takes place within a framework of *common* cultural codes: a conversation requires a common language.[1]

Action systems in this sense are a subclass of a broader set, which may be called *living* systems, as such a conception is used in the biological sciences. The subcultural behavior of organisms, their metabolic processes, and biological evolution are all important aspects of the latter category. For reasons of theoretical parsimony, I will not consider the extent to which other systems, for example physical–chemical ones, share the properties of living ones.

I wish to argue that the concept function is central to the understanding of all living systems. Indeed, it is simply the corollary of the concept living system, delineating certain features in the first instance of the system–environment relation, and in the second, of the internal differentiation of the system itself. This proposition is based upon a dual consideration. First, as has been clear at least since the great contributions of Bernard and Cannon,[2] a living system is one which maintains a pattern of organization and functioning which is both different from and in some respects *more stable* than its environment. Secondly, the maintenance of this specific and relatively stable pattern occurs not through total isolation or insulation from the environment but through continual processes of interchange with it. In this sense, all living systems are "open" systems. From this perspective, the functional problems of a living system concern the maintenance of its distinctive patterns in the face of the differences between internal and environmental states, the greater variability—in some respects —of the latter, and the system's own "openness."

Thus there would be a functional problem even if there were a single

[1] See Talcott Parsons, "Social Interaction," in David L. Sills, ed., *International Encyclopedia of the Social Sciences* (New York: Macmillan, 1968), reprinted as Chapter 7 in this volume.

[2] Walter B. Cannon, *The Wisdom of the Body* (New York: Norton, 1932). Very little of Bernard's pioneering work in physiology has been translated into English, but some is available in Claude Bernard, *An Introduction to the Study of Experimental Medicine* (New York: Dover, 1957).

unified environmental condition of system-maintenance. In fact, however, there are always plural conditions which vary more or less independently of each other, but which often have complementary significance for the system. For example, in the animal world, in which oxidation is the basis of metabolism, the ingestion of oxidizable materials from the environment and the intake of oxygen are both necessary, and the two must be in proportion to each other. However, there is no reason to assume that the organically optimum combinations of these two in the environment will vary together. Furthermore, oxidation produces waste products, and their disposal without injury to the organism presents another partially independent functional problem. Hence the necessity of functional differentiation of different system–environment exchanges, which is fundamental to all living systems.

This differentiation of system–environment interchanges has implications for the internal state of the system. Insofar as the exchanges must be differentiated, so must different parts of the system be differentiated. Thus, to return to our example, alimentary and respiratory systems are structurally distinct in higher zoological organisms. Given internal differentiation, the relations among the parts within the system cannot be assumed to be stable on given bases, but must involve processes of mutual adjustment. There must be, in addition to processes which mobilize inputs and outputs across the system–environment boundary, different processes which mediate the combination of inputs within the system and the genesis of a differentiated plurality of outputs.

Thus, the kind of difference between system and environment which was postulated as basic to all living systems implies that within the living system itself there will be two distinctive types of mediation: mediation of external interchanges and mediation of internal combinations. This differentiation of the system along the axis of external relations to the environment and internal relations of the components to each other is one of the two primary axes on which the four-function paradigm is built.

The second axis is based upon the consideration that a living system not only is different from its environment in various respects at any given moment, but *maintains* its distinctive organization over periods of time (which need not be unlimited—witness the phenomenon of biological death[3]). In circumstantial detail, the processes which maintain this distinctiveness cannot be presumed to involve only instantaneous adjustment, but *take time*. If a postulated state of affairs is to be maintained in a variable environment, its underlying conditions must be involved in processes of complex sequence. To use our previous illustration, the intake of nutritional materials must precede the internal process of oxidation which

---

[3] The late Professor E. B. Wilson once remarked to me that the process of disappearance of the difference between the internal state of the organism and the environment was the best biological definition of death.

produces organic energy. Output to the environment in the form of behavior which requires energy must therefore at some time have been
preceded by both nutritional intake and oxidation.

There is a fundamental basis of differentiation along the range of temporal sequence which consists in the fact that there is not a simple one-to-
one relation between conditions necessary for the attainment of a given
goal-state and its attainment. The same conditional state of affairs (the
establishment of which may itself constitute a goal) can often be a condition of the attainment of a plurality of different goal-states, some of
which are alternatives to each other in that, given a set of conditions, only
one of a pair of goal-states is realistically attainable. Therefore the processes involved with establishing conditions of future goal-states, and the
more ultimate or "consummatory" processes of approaching such goal-
states, tend to become differentiated in living systems. At the action level
this is very much involved with the means–end relationship. Activities
concerned with the procurement of means not only may be logically distinguishable from those concerned with goal-attainment, but are in many
cases realistically different.[4]

This distinction has become increasingly prominent in the course of
evolution because adaptive capacity has become increasingly generalized
and goal-attainment capacity increasingly flexible. This is one of the bases
of the "activism" which is far more prominent in the sphere of behavior
than in that of metabolic or vegetative functions. Here it has become established usage—after much controversy—to speak of an organism as
engaged in goal-seeking behavior. This may be defined as behavior which
has the "meaning" (or possibly the intention) of altering the otherwise
obtaining organism–environment relationship in a direction more favorable
than otherwise to the maintenance of the pattern of the organism. This
might be manifested, for example, in food-getting activities, where the
procurement of food would constitute the attainment of a goal.

A similar distinction holds for the processes of internal mediation
namely between processes which preserve and protect the system's potential for actualization of its pattern, and those which "mortgage the future"
in some kind of consummatory interest. We may thus take this axis of
differentiation, of the establishment of general conditions for the attainment of system ends on the one hand, and action on the basis of such conditions on the other, as the second basic axis of differentiation of living
systems, cross-cutting the first.

In a sense, both the system–environment and the temporal pattern
maintenance–goal attainment axes are foci of continuous variation. The

---

[4] To take a familiar apposite case, the acquisition of a typewriter as a personal
possession is clearly not the same as the use of it to write a particular letter or manuscript. A typewriter is a *generalized facility*, the properties of which do not determine
the particular use to which it may be put.

case for dichotomizing is more immediately clear in the former context. The differential between internal system states and those of the environment in general is not continuous but involves *boundaries*. In higher organisms, potential food in the environment is not the same as digested nutritional material in the blood stream; the former, among other things, is much more diverse. In the temporal axis, there is, however a parallel in the "turn" from a system's "interest" in the "stock" of instrumentally utilizable facilities, and of their consummatory utilization for specific ends.[5] There are, then, boundaries of the meaning of temporal selection—on the aciton level "choice"—which in certain respects correspond to the boundary between system and environment. In both cases they constitute something akin to "watersheds." On one side of the boundary, processes work to produce one kind of result; on the other side, quite another kind. It is a qualitative distinction, not a question of position along an unbroken continuum. It should be made clear, however, that the distinctions being drawn do not imply that a structure in a living system cannot be involved in processes on both sides of either of the two "boundaries."

The logical outcome of dichotomizing on both of the two primary cross-cutting axes of differentiation is a four-fold classification of function. In terms of previously established usage, the four functions are referred to as pattern-maintenance (internal–means), integration (internal–ends), goal-attainment (external–ends), and adaptation (external–means).

Among the four, pattern-maintenance occupies a special place in that it is the focus of stability in *both* of the two main respects. It is internal rather than external, in the sense of being insulated from the more fluctuating processes of the environment, and it is associated with the long run and insulated from the continuing adjustments which the adaptive and goal-oriented processes on the part of plural units bring about in the internal subsystems. The distinctive features of this greater stability are formulated as constituting a pattern which is distinctive of this system or type of system, and which may be presented to be, or to have a tendency to be, maintained in the face of fluctuations in the relevant environmental conditions and over time.[6]

---

[5] In modern economic theory, which grounds in this general conceptual scheme, this is broadly the line of distinction between production and consumption.

[6] This proposition, which has been stated in many variants, is perhaps the focus of the accusation of "functional teleology." The distinction between the teleological position and the functional one concerns the question of fact, whether indeed such a pattern exists for a certain class of systems. For example, Cannon begins his treatment of homeostasis in *The Wisdom of the Body* with the observation that certain higher organisms tend, *in fact*, to maintain a constant body temperature. The question then becomes *how* this pattern is maintained, which is not a teleological question. The answer includes delineation of the conditions under which it will *not* be maintained. The question of the functions of the pattern itself involves shift to a different level of theoretical system reference, in the body temperature case, that of evolutionary theory, not, as Cannon treated it, of physiology.

This basic asymmetry is the main ground of the teleological character of living systems, and of the theory of living systems. It is reflected in the reversal of the direction of explanation characteristic of functional analysis. A functional explanation begins with a postulated state of affairs, and refers *back* to the necessary antecedent or underlying conditions. Such teleology must of course be conditional, couched in the form that *if* certain patterns are to be maintained, or certain goals achieved, certain conditions must be fulfilled.

It is a common experience in the history of science that the purely empirical assertion that a state of fact exists (for example, that certain species tend to maintain a constant body temperature) is later explained by understanding the processes at work. For a long time, biological science has stressed the importance of the distinction between the genetic factors in the functioning of organisms and the somatic or physiological factors, between genotype and phenotype, between germ plasm and somatoplasm. On the level of factual propositions in the action field, as well as in the organic field, there has long been a good case for singling out the function of pattern-maintenance as concerned with the mechanisms in the basic asymmetry of living systems. In relatively recent years, developments in both general and biological science have strengthened the basis on which it is reasonable to assert continuity in this respect across the class of living systems. These are the developments, first of cybernetic theory, and second, of the "new genetics" by virtue of which the genes are asserted to be a system of codes whose functions and operating processes are analogous to those of symbolic systems.

The general principles of cybernetics and its close relative, information theory, are now well known. A system, which may be mechanical or electronic and need not be living, is conceived as "programmed" to behave in a planned way wthin a range of developing contingencies, without the necessity of predicting the specific contingencies in advance. As the process of "behavior" of the system develops over time, there is a feedback of information about developments in the environment, including the consequences of the preceding operations by the system. This feedback information is evaluated in its relation to the program, and the outcome is the setting in motion of a new set of operations which are "adapted" to the new situation.[7]

For the simplest cybernetic systems, such as the thermostat, there is

[7] One of the simplest cybernetic mechanisms is the theromstat, a special type of thermometer which will turn on a heating apparatus when the temperature falls below a certain point, and turn it off above a certain point, thus keeping the relevant space at a relatively constant temperature. The "program" or "goal" of the system is the temperature range for which the thermostat is set. There *must* be a goal-attainment mechanism if the temperature of the relevant space is to be kept constant under fluctuating environmental conditions.

only one goal-state and perhaps the possibility of positive and negative deviation from it, and hence a simple single either/or choice involved in operations to maintain the goal-state. In our terminology such a system has only pattern-maintenance and goal-attainment functions, performed respectively by the cybernetic mechanism (the thermostat) and the operative mechanism (the heating apparatus). For more complex systems, however, there may be many mechanisms which perform different kinds of operations and there may be many linked cybernetic submechanisms. It is such complications which necessitate functions of generalized adaptation (such as the processing and integration of several sorts of feedback information) and of integration (the coordination of many different information processing systems and many "operative" mechanisms).

From our present point of view the great significance of the new genetics is two-fold. First of all it strengthens the evidence that living systems generally, in the sense of Cannon's homeostasis, maintain their stability through cybernetic control processes; and secondly it shows that the most far-reaching stabilities of all, those of species genotypes, are maintained by such mechanisms, the biochemical properties of which can now be understood in some detail. These turn out to have formal properties identical with those of symbolic codes, with their extraordinary combination of stability of pattern but with an indefinite variety of possible operative outputs and an indefinite capacity to make these outputs adaptive in the sense of maintaining the patterns—and perhaps, in a higher order of system reference, the functions—of the programmed system. Thus, given the functions of a language as communication among human users, the code elements of the language (its syntax, grammar, vocabulary) make possible an indefinite variety of specific utterances, which are adaptive in the sense that they are intelligible—they convey meanings which are or can be shared by both speakers and hearers. "Conversation" then carries such processes to a higher level in that there is mutual feedback among the speakers, who are also listeners.[8]

There is an important sense in which the above developments indicate that the properties of culturally ordered and controlled systems of human action, if properly interpreted, throw more light on the processes of subhuman organisms than, conversely, the properties of mechanical systems (in the sense of the older scientific materialism) throw on the operation of human societies. However important this may be, it does not follow that specific theory in the latter field is in some simple sense deducible from the continuities we have claimed. It does, however, suggest that there

---

[8] The eminent biologist Alfred Emerson has spoken of the functional equivalence of gene and "symbol," by which he meant that for culture-level systems of behavior, which we here call action systems, symbolic systems have the same *order* of functional significance that genetic systems have at the organic level.

are sound scientific grounds for exploiting fully for our theoretical purposes the cybernetic, information processing, and communication aspects of human culture.

The central thrust of the argument then, is that the four-function scheme is grounded in the essential nature of living systems at all levels of organization and evolutionary development, from the unicellular organism to the highest human civilization. This holds true for the two basic axes of differentiation and for the significance of treating them, for analytic purposes, as dichotomous. The contributions of homeostatic physiology, the new genetics, and cybernetic and information theory lend strength to the view that in these basic respects there is strong continuity over the class of living systems, especially with regard to the central role of the processes we have characterized as pattern-maintenance.

A common complaint about such a scheme is that it is *too* simple, and thus cannot account for the complexity of the real world. In light of the history of science, this is not a very convincing criticism, since very generally simplification through abstraction has been a central feature of empirically fruitful theory. The fruitful path has not been to avoid simple schemes but to use them to define elementary systems, and then to treat more complicated systems in terms of combinations of more elementary components on various different levels. For example, in mechanics, anything is a particle from a subatomic particle to the largest known celestial body, a simplification certainly as radical as any proposed here. Thus the issue turns on the usefulness of the abstractions proposed, and I hope to establish in the following discussion that the four-function paradigm is a powerful analytic tool.

Before we turn to the use of the paradigm, something needs to be said about the two essential categories of structure and process. For a considerable time it has been common to refer to structural-functional theory, even as constituting a "school." It has become my increasing conviction that this is not a proper designation. The concept *function* is not correlative with *structure,* but is the master concept of the framework for the relations between any living system and its environment. Functions are performed, or functional requirements met, by a combination of structures *and* processes.

The distinction and relation between the latter terms are essentially familiar. A structure is any describable arrangement of a system's elements which are distinguishable from each other, and the properties and relations of which can be presumed to remain constant for purposes of a particular analysis. A structure is not an ontological entity but is strictly relative to the investigatory purpose and prospective. It is continuous in the organic and the action sciences. Thus the anatomical structure of the organism is constant for purposes of most physiological investigations, but not over the life cycle, and not in the genesis of many pathological conditions.

Similarly the structure of a family may be treated as constant for purposes of the study of behavior of its members over short periods, but not through the phases of the family cycle.

Process, then, consists in the theoretically significant aspects of a system which undergo "change of state" within the time period of significance for a given investigatory purpose. It is structure and process which are correlative, not structure and function. *Both* structure and process are analyzed in functional terms.

It follows from our conception of action that the most important structural components of *any* action system are the symbolic codes by the use of which detailed adaptive activities take place.[9] Process, then, is of two orders. The more obvious is communication, the transmission of information or meaning from one acting unit to another in terms of a code, the rules of which are commonly understood and accepted. Communication is inherently *inter*unit and indeed, in action terms, a unit may be defined as a structural entity which functions as the sender or receiver, or both, of communicated meanings.[10] Where, as is prototypically the case, communication is not one-way but mutual between two or more acting units— the basic case of *interaction*—communications sent may be treated as outputs and those received as inputs.

Insofar as there is some kind of relationship between these inputs and outputs for a given unit, we must postulate a second order of process which occurs inside the "black box," the acting unit which relates antecedent inputs of communication to subsequent outputs. From the point of view of the process of determination of the relevant output or outputs, we may speak of this process as *decision*. This conception implies that only in limiting cases would the inputs completely determine the output. Something is conceived to be contributed by the deciding unit itself. Furthermore, it is only a limiting case where an output is related to only a single category of input. The general case is the occurrence of a set of combinations of input-contributions to bring about the output. The logic can easily be extended one step further to say that very frequently plural inputs are combined to produce not one but a plurality of outputs.. In either case the acting unit is a node at which processes of sorting and combination take place, so that in a variety of respects what comes out is different from what went in.

---

[9] It is probable that at least the most important components of the structure of the behavioral organism as an action system—not the total concrete organism—are given through organic hereditary processes. In the case of personality and of social and cultural systems, however, they are *learned* by the individual.

[10] The unit does not need to be an individual. Intrapersonal communication is well established; the idea of James's plurality of selves implies this, as does Freud's personality theory. Social systems, as collectivities, communicate with each other, though through the agency of individuals who can "speak" for them. The same applies to cultural systems: I as an "agent" of sociology, am engaged in a "dialogue" with the discipline of biology.

Social Systems

Let us now consider the use of the four-function paradigm in the analysis of social systems. In the sense in which I have previously used the term, a social system is that aspect of a general action system organized about the patterns of interaction of the individual actors. In this sense it is an analytically abstracted subsystem of a general action system.

In the development of my work, a particularly strategic line of thought was a reconsideration of some of the main features of economic theory specifically in terms of its relations to the rest of the theory of social systems, but within the action frame of reference. The approach taken to this problem was that of the paradigm outlined above. Thus it assumed the relevance of the four-function scheme to any highly generalized theoretical task, and conceived of pattern-maintenance as having a special stabilizing and organizing significance. Furthermore, it assumed that action systems, like other living systems, tend to differentiate along functional lines. Interaction was conceived of as taking place at different levels between units, and taking the form of communication. Also important was the conviction that, although the significance of decision and communication in human action processes has long been recognized, there have been great difficulties in introducing a combination of true theoretical specificity and generality into the utilization of such knowledge, and the four-function paradigm might prove of value in this context.

On this basis, it made sense to treat the factors of production of economic theory as a classification of inputs, and the shares of income correspondingly as categories of output. But inputs from and outputs to what? If production in the economic sense could be treated as a differentiated function within social systems, then perhaps they could be treated as inputs from and outputs to *other* functionally differentiated subsystems of the same social system. A critical question here was whether it was the same *social* system or the same general action system. Thus it would be very easy, in the factor-of-production sense, to treat labor as an input from personalities of individuals, and land as an input from the physical environment. Any solution to questions such as this required highly generalized theoretical analysis.

I have elsewhere given in detail the justifications for treating the economy as the adaptive subsystem of a societal level social system, and will not repeat the arguments here.[11] However, it should be noted that the economy as conceptualized here is *functionally* defined. Thus it is not coterminous with the business sector, although there is a fit between the

[11] See Talcott Parsons and Neil J. Smelser, *Economy and Society* (New York: Free Press, 1956).

two in that I would argue that the functional significance of the business sector for a society is primarily adaptive.

However this may be, a striking set of numerical relations emerged as soon as the problem was put in these terms. If the productive system, the "economy" in the technical sense of economic theory, could be treated as one primary functional subsystem of a society, it should, according to the paradigm, be one of four on a cognate level. Then there might well be input-output interchanges between it and the other three in a social system. Now modern economic theory, since Marshall and Schumpeter, has utilized a scheme of *four* factors of production—land, labor, capital, and organization—and four corresponding shares of income—rent, wages, interest, and profit. But interchange within a four-fold system called for three, not four, categories of each. In this dilemma a feature of economic analysis from the classical era came to mind, namely that land, and with it rent, constituted a special case. Its distinctiveness lay in the fact that the quantity of land in the system was, unlike the other three factors, not a function of its price. At the aggregate level of resources available to the system as a whole it could not be "bought" but was "given," and hence not involved in an interchange. This being the case, it made sense to assign each of the other three remaining categories to interchange with one of the three other primary functional subsystems of a society, which Smelser and I called the polity (or goal-attainment) system, the integrative system (or, recently, the societal community), and the pattern-maintenance system. The interchanges seemed to be, specifically, labor–wages between the economy and the pattern-maintenance system, capital–interest between the economy and the polity, and organization–profit between the economy and the integrative system.

At least to our satisfaction, this strategy seemed to work, as did the decision to treat all these interchanges as intrasocietal and not as between the social system and other primary subsystems of action. This left the problem of the status of the category "land," which traditionally had been treated as belonging to the physical environment. Our theoretical decision was to treat this physical aspect of land as derivative, and to redefine that category as the unconditional commitment of economically significant resources to the function of economic production, thereby withdrawing them from other potential uses. "Land," in this redefined sense, then became a primary case of the application of a set of societal value-commitments in social action. In its special function among the factors of production, land paralleled the pattern-maintenance function in action systems generally.

This line of theoretical codification implied that, in the relevant respects, traditional economic theory could be regarded as a special case of the theory of social systems in the action sense, that is, the theory of the functioning of one primary, analytically defined subsystem of a highly

differentiated society. This in turn, raised the question of whether codification could be matched by generalization, so that, with appropriate modifications, the theoretical resources of economic theory could be utilized for the analysis of the other subsystems of societies. The first major attempt in this direction, to resolve some of the old problems of the political aspect of social systems, succeeded so well that I have made the task of generalized codification one of my main lines of work ever since. Indeed, one of its first fruits was a departure from the view, stated in some length in *The Social System*,[12] that economic and political theory could not be treated as logically parallel.

The codification of the four-function scheme with economic theory seemed a major step in the development of general theory, especially insofar as the scheme is grounded in the general nature of living systems. To my knowledge, no economic theorist has contended that the four factors of production and corresponding shares of income had any generalized significance beyond the economic field.[13] Since economics is theoretically the most highly developed discipline in the action field—except perhaps, recently, linguistics—its conceptual fit with sociological theory and that of other disciplines seemed to be of high significance.

On this background, there developed leads into another aspect of action systems which had a grounding in economics but also linked up in exciting ways with the general field of symbolic codes and mechanisms. The main point of reference is the very simple consideration that with a high degree of division of labor, exchanges cannot be carried on simply on a barter basis, but must be mediated by some generalized mechanism. For the economic case, this medium is money. Thus in the classic case, labor is not remunerated in kind, by specific consumer goods, but by money, which in turn is used by household members to purchase needed goods. This line of reasoning raises two basic questions, namely, What is the nature of money as a medium of exchange, and Is it an isolated phenomenon or one of a "family" of such media?

The key to answering the first question lay in a distinction insisted on by the classical economists and taken for granted ever since, namely, the distinction between value in use and value in exchange. Money differs from commodities and services in possessing the latter and not the former —in the "pure" case, *only* value in exchange. It was not a very long step to the insight that money is not a "thing" in the usual sense, but is a mode of symbolic communication. An offer of money is literally a proposition:

[12] Talcott Parsons (New York: Free Press, 1951), especially chap. 12.

[13] There have been attempts to apply the economic perspective directly to noneconomic domains, without the necessary prior generalization of economic theory. See, for example, Thomas N. Carver, *The Essential Factors of Social Evolution* (Cambridge: Harvard University Press, 1935); or, more recently, Anthony Downs, *An Economic Theory of Democracy* (New York: Harper, 1957). These attempts, it seems to me, have not succeeded—nor could they.

"If you will give me what I want—for example, possession of some physical good—I will give you a certain sum of money." The mood of the proposition is conditional. Money, then, not only resembles a language, but *is* a very specialized language through which intentions and conditional consequences of actions are communicated. If this is true, then a whole range of considerations about the nature and operation of symbolic media should apply to money. The working out of these connections has been a complicated task, but I can see no reasonable doubt about the fit.

The answer to the second question, about the uniqueness of money, was then strongly indicated. If money is a language, then it would not likely be a totally isolated case except for what are usually called general languages. It would, for example, be possible that certain specialized uses of "ordinary language" could be functional analogues of money. This turned out to be the case for the first major extension of this analysis outside the economic field, which was to the concept of political power and its field of application.[14] Power is defined as the capacity of a unit to mobilize obligations of the unit-members of a collective system in such a way as to make decisions binding on the collectivity and ensure their implementation through the performance of those obligations. The mobilization of such obligations, the promulgation of relevant decisions, and explication of their consequences for performance of obligations, all occur through ordinary processes of linguistic communication.

The distinctiveness of a power system, as analogous to a market, is the kinds of content communicated, and the conditions on which there will be, as Weber put it, a probability that they will be acted upon in certain ways. Here it is particularly important to make the distinction parallel to that between value in use and value in exchange. Many students think of power as capacity to exert an intrinsically effective sanction on the action of others, a line of thought which leads to special emphasis on coercion and ultimately to physical force. This would make power equivalent to a class of commodities, not to a medium of exchange. Hence working with the parallel to money entails a rather sharp break with much of the usage of political theorists. One must abide by the consequences of the assumption that the use of power, as a medium, asserts only expectations and claims, and is not intrinsically effective.

Besides definitional and categorical symmetries, what are the advantages of such a break with tradition? They must lie in the grounding of

[14] Talcott Parsons, "On the Concept of Political Power," *Proceedings of the American Philosophical Society*, vol. 107, no. 3 (June, 1963); reprinted in Talcott Parsons, *Sociological Theory and Modern Society* (New York: Free Press, 1967), chap. 10, and also in Reinhard Bendix and Seymour M. Lipset, eds., *Class Status and Power*, rev. ed. (New York: Free Press, 1966). A further discussion of this subject can be found in my article "The Political Aspect of Social Structure and Process," in David Easton, ed., *Varieties of Political Theory* (Englewood Cliffs: Prentice-Hall, 1966).

theoretical propositions which otherwise would not be "seen," or be passed over as trivial, or might indeed be declared to be untrue. Let me illustrate with one case. Many of the most prominent users of the concept of political power have, explicitly or, more often, implicitly, used it in such a way as to build in the assumption that, in the language of the theory of games, power is a "zero-sum" phenomenon. This would mean that in a power system any gain in power by one unit or a class of possessing units would always have to be balanced by an equivalent loss on the part of other units. If this is correct, it is an exceedingly important property of power systems. We know, however, that it is not true for monetary systems. The phenomena of increase in amount of money through credit creation, and of inflation and deflation as processes of increase and decrease of this amount not strictly linked to distribution, are well established and well understood in economics. Parallel to this, I assert with some confidence that, under specifiable conditions, the power equivalent of the creation of credit by banks can and does occur, and that there are, in political systems, phenomena strictly parallel to—though of course not identical with—inflation and deflation in the economic sense. The specific consequences of such a difference surely are not trival.

Once an extension beyond the monetary case works out, as I think it has for the case of power, then the logic of the four-fold paradigm raises further questions. One concerns generalizing to all four subsystems the input-output pattern utilized in the case of the economy. This would entail identifying for each subsystem three mobile categories of resources which could be treated as inputs, one from each of the other three subsystems, and correspondingly, three categories of output, one destined for each of the other subsystems. A reasonable assumption here is that there is a complementary relation between the outputs or products from the point of view of one functional subsystem, and the transmission, in the opposite direction, of resources or factors from the point of view of its recipients. This clearly is the case for the exchange, fundamental to economics, between the aggregate of households and firms, namely, output by households of labor capacities, and by firms of commitments to provide consumer goods.

In working out this concept for the system as a whole, the considerations important to the nature and role of money become relevant. The proposition is that, in general, from the point of view of any given system unit, the sources of its most essential resource-inputs and the destinations of its product-outputs are not the same unit. Exchange therefore cannot proceed on a barter basis but must be mediated in ways analogous to that in which money mediates economic exchanges. This means that, between any pair of functional subsystems, there should be not one but *two* primary types of interchange; namely, from the point of view of one unit, an interchange of resource for medium, and one of output for medium.

For the pair of subsystems this would constitute a double interchange. If these theoretical "expectations" can be realized, it should be possible to work out a system of four primary functional subsystems, adequately differentiated from each other, and linked by six double interchange systems involving four generalized media. The four media would be, in addition to money and power, one for the integrative subsystem, which we have called "influence" in a special technical sense, and one for the pattern-maintenance subsystem, which we have called value-commitments.[15] Each of the media should be involved in three of the six interchange sets, mediating interchanges from the subsystem in which it is "rooted" to the other three.

This theoretical program clearly involves many further complications, one of which we will mention. Each of the media apparently can be exchanged either for "intrinsic satisfiers" as in the prototypical case of money for the possession of concrete physical commodities, or for one of the other media, as when an employing unit through the contract of employment gains the specification of the employee's value-commitments to "work faithfully" for the employing organization within the terms of the contract. Since details of work obligations are not usually specified long in advance, what the employer acquires is an expectation of service of a certain kind and within certain limits, thereby transferring the interchange out of the market into one internal to the organization of requesting and performing the fulfillment of commitments.

After much revising over several years, I worked out a complete interchange paradigm for the social system, at the level of *media,* and published it as such,[16] leaving the systematization of the relations of the media to the control of intrinsic gratifiers to be worked out in more ad hoc fashion for more particular subsystems. The form of this media paradigm has proved, now, to be relatively stable over a considerable period.

What has been accomplished by working out such a paradigm? Given, as I think can reasonably be claimed, its embodiment of certain fundamentals of the theory of living systems generally, and the conjunction of these with the somewhat different theory of cybernetic control in its relation to symbolic systems, the paradigm is, *at a certain level,* a deductive propositional system. Furthermore, its empirical relevance has been strongly evidenced at a number of points, some of the most conspicuous of which have been reviewed, notably in general biological theory, including genetics; in linguistic theory and more generally in the theory of

[15] Talcott Parsons, "On the Concept of Influence," *Public Opinion Quarterly*, vol. 27 (Spring 1963); reprinted in Parsons, *Sociological Theory*, chap. 11; Talcott Parsons, "On the Concept of Value Commitments," *Sociological Inquiry*, vol. 38 (Summer 1968), reprinted as chapter 16 of *Politics and Social Structure*, 1969.

[16] Parsons, "On the Concept of Political Power." The interchange paradigm is in the Technical Note appended to the article.

symbolic systems; and in economics. Considerations such as these make it virtually certain that it is neither purely speculative nor simply arbitrary.

If this is, however partial, a deductive system, it clearly is not a closed one. It is correct, as has often been said, that it is highly general and abstract, though this is by no means necessarily a fault. The fault lies rather in that at the many levels and in the many contexts where it is inherently relevant—if its general claims mean *anything*—the terms cannot be precisely defined, nor can they yet be adequately operationalized. It should not, however, be assumed that this is true across the board but rather that the situation is spotty, in that in some areas, such as the economic, there is a great deal more precision than in others such as in the "theory of social movements."

Action Systems

We have used the involvement with cultural level symbolic systems as the distinctive feature of the subclass we call *action* systems, within the larger category of living systems. The question now is how the general framework of functional analysis is to be applied and how its implications and uses are to be spelled out in this area. But this is a formidable task. It is necessary to designate correctly the lines of differentiation of the general system of action and the primary functional subsystems into which it comes to be differentiated.[17] Beyond that, it entails analyzing the input–output interchanges among these subsystems. Since, furthermore, they are both highly differentiated and their interchanges operate at the cultural-symbolic level, it is necessary to identify generalized symbolic media of interchange and to work out the principal contexts in which they operate as media.

For delineating the primary functional subsystems, the three-fold scheme of social system, personality (or more correctly, psychological) system, and cultural system was extremely helpful, but the scheme was rounded out only when it became clear that the "behavioral organism," as it has come to be called, should be included as a fourth primary subsystem. The significance of this addition is enhanced by the continuities between action theory and that of other types of living systems, which have made direct theoretical articulation with these others through specification of the significance of organisms even more important than before.

In this way it has proved possible to treat action systems at the most general level as differentiated on the basis of the four-fold scheme, with

---

[17] Others have been interested in the place of the social system in a more general framework. Cf. Pitirim Sorokin, *Society, Culture, and Personality* (New York: Cooper Square Publishers, 1962).

quite clear identifications of cultural systems as pattern-maintaining, social systems as integrative, psychological systems as goal-attaining, and behavioral-organic systems as adaptive in their primary functions for action as general systems. Each of these primary action subsystems is defined on the basis of theoretical abstraction. Concretely, every empirical system is all of them at once; thus, there is no concrete human individual who is not an organism, a personality, a member of a social system, and a participant in a cultural system. The basis of the abstraction is function within a more broadly defined system. Similar considerations are involved in defining the boundaries vis-à-vis nonaction systems.

The total concrete organism is not an action system in our sense. On one level it can be identified with the "individual," but on another level (for example, with respect to the metabolic processes, which Murray has called visceral) it is not a system of action, because only very indirectly, if at all, is it controlled by symbolic mechanisms. A further very important consideration about the organism is that human relatedness to the physical environment exists *only* as mediated through it. For information, this involves the mechanisms of sense perception, while in the motor context it involves the processes of physical behavior. Even the most predominantly "cultural" activities such as speech are, in *one* primary aspect, organic.

Before considering the problem of generalized media of interchange at the action system level, we should note an important clarification of the four-function paradigm which resulted from systematizing its relationship to the pattern variables. Our point of departure is the conception that the structure of action systems consists in normative culture, internalized in organisms and personalities, institutionalized in societies and cultural systems. This proposition may be interpreted in terms of the code aspect of symbolic-cultural systems, which undoubtedly constitutes a structure (in the sense of "structural linguistics," for example). If this proposition be accepted, the pattern variable scheme should constitute a classification of the basic components of such code systems in the action area. These components would not comprise codes for understanding the physical world, or subaction types of living system, although there should be clear relations to the latter.

The pattern variable scheme was originally worked out as a way of categorizing the structure of social systems, mainly at the role level, but it eventually developed that this was a special case, and that the more general statement should be couched at the level of the general system of action.[18] Reconsideration of certain aspects of the pattern variable scheme should then throw considerable light on the problems of the present paper.

Here it is worthwhile to recall that I personally arrived at the four-

---

[18] Talcott Parsons and Edward Shils, eds., *Toward a General Theory of Action* (Cambridge: Harvard University Press, 1951), especially the essay by Parsons and Shils, "Values, Motives, and Systems of Action."

function paradigm by establishing a new connection between the orientation and the object modality "sides" of the pattern variable scheme, and seeing that this converged with the functional analysis presented by Robert F. Bales in his *Interaction Process Analysis*.[19] Some years later, in "Pattern Variables Revisited," [20] I was able to show that this synthesis concerned the integrative standards of the general action system. In response to Dubin, I attempted to treat these as the principal components of the integrative subsystem of the general action system and to round out the other three in a set of logically determinate relations to this one.

The next step rested upon the assumption that the original distinction between the modality set and orientation set of the pattern variables could be formulated as the L-G [21] axis of the system, with the orientation variables in the pattern-maintenance position and the modality variables in the goal-attainment position, since *relations* to objects constituted the content of goal-striving.[22] Then the question arose as to whether sense could be made of an adequate subsystem which was logically symmetrical to the integrative.

In the synthesis reported in *Working Papers in the Theory of Action*,[23] Bales and I had postulated a primary combination of two pattern variable components characterized each functional cell, and a secondary combination which seemed related to the phase movements of system change, namely the phase out of which it came to enter the phase of reference, and the one into which it was tending to move. In "Pattern Variables Revisited" I suggested that the significance of these secondary combinations might be adaptive, and that they might therefore be put into the adaptive subsystem of the more general pattern variable paradigm. At that time, conceptualizing the adaptive subset in this way did not seem completely justifiable. Now, however, I think a good case can be made for using this formulation to characterize and distinguish the generalized media of interchange, both at the general action level and at that of the social system. I shall not take space here to spell out the fit for the much more fully

[19] Cambridge: Addison Wesley, 1950.

[20] Talcott Parsons, "Pattern Variables Revisited: A Response to Robert Dubin," *American Sociological Review*, vol. 25, no. 4 (August, 1960); reprinted in Parsons, *Sociological Theory*, chap. 7.

[21] I am using here the established "short-hand" for the four functions, which is: L for pattern-maintenance, I for integration, G for goal-attainment, and A for adaptation.

[22] This way of arranging the components almost certainly would not have occurred to me had it not been for a thorough reconsideration of Durkheim's theory of solidarity, and new understanding of the relationship between mechanical and organic solidarity, the former being interpreted in terms of the L–G axis, and the latter in terms of the I–A axis. See Parsons, "Durkheim's Contribution to the Theory of Integration of Social Systems" in Kurt Wolff, ed., *Emile Durkheim, 1858–1917* (Columbus: Ohio State University Press, 1960), reprinted in Parsons, *Sociological Theory*, chap. 1. This paper was written before "Pattern Variables Revisited."

[23] Talcott Parsons, Robert F. Bales, and Edward Shils (New York: Free Press, 1953).

analyzed social system media reviewed above,[24] but I will use these criteria in setting forth a newly revised scheme of media for interchanges at the general action level.

Perhaps the best place to begin is with a famous concept-pair, namely two of W. I. Thomas's four wishes, for response and for recognition.[25] I have vacillated as to the placement of these two categories—though I have long assumed that they, or some semantic variant of each, can be characterized as generalized media at the action level. The connection with personality makes it plausible that the wish for response, or mutuality of affect, should be the medium focusing at the personality system (the *G*-subsystem of general action), and recognition at the social system level. Recent reconsideration, however, has convinced me that the reverse is the appropriate placing.

Affect, as the term was used in the later Freud and in subsequent psychoanalytic literature, seems to be the most appropriate term of which Thomas's response may be regarded as the alter-to-ego variant. According to the general pattern variable paradigm, the integrative medium should be affective, as distinguished from neutral. The most obvious specific reference is to the motivational base of loyalty or collective solidarity. For the individual personality the reference is to the relation to positively cathected objects, not to the objects themselves.[26] The medium is, however, also defined by quality—as contrasted with performance—which is appropriate because a relation involving cathectic attachment is, once formed, a *given* one, involving mutual adaptation or adjustment.[27] The inclination to place affect at the personality level seems to me to have arisen largely from confusion between the general action and the social system levels. The impersonal normative order involving neutrality of attitude is part of the social system, not a general action grounding of it, unless it be at the level of moral authority rather than of societal norms.[28]

Thomas's category of recognition seems most relevant to the general-

[24] Thus, following a logic parallel to that used in defining the integrative standards, affective neutrality and performance should categorize money, which seems reasonable, since money is a way of "getting things." Particularism is relevant to power in that power operates to activate collective obligations; so is specificity, in that this is for specific goals, and is not an appeal to diffuse loyalty. Quality and affectivity categorize influence, in that it is directed to persons with common membership status, and in terms of their diffuse loyalty to the collectivity. Universalism and diffuseness characterize commitments, in that commitments invoke universalistically defined values on a diffuse basis not restricted to specific goals or interests.

[25] William I. Thomas, *The Unadjusted Girl* (Boston: Little, 1923).

[26] This focus on relationships to objects parallels the conception of values as used in the general scheme of action: values are not conceived of as aspects of *objects*, but as aspects of an actor's *relation* to objects.

[27] This interpretation closely fits the excellent analysis of the code of the American kinship system as presented in David M. Schneider, *American Kinship: A Cultural Approach* (Englewood Cliffs: Prentice-Hall, 1968).

[28] See Victor M. Lidz, "The Functioning of Secular Moral Culture: Steps toward a Systematic Analysis," Ph.D. dissertation, Harvard University, 1976.

ized medium of the personality system. For this medium the pattern variable components are specificity and particularism, and the medium is an analogy to power at the social system level. If recognition is taken as the way of rewarding socially valued achievements, then the pattern variable components would seem to underscore the fact that achievement involves specific actions toward particular goals. A further analogy to power is that recognition of achievement would seem to be subject to a kind of "bindingness" not connoted by affect, with its overtones of spontaneity. Probably the best term to designate the generalized medium is "performance capacity."

If we turn to the adaptive category, the starting point is the fact that the actor-type reference is to the behavioral organism. The pattern variable components are neutrality and performance. On the analogy of money we may say that, if the hereditary component is not too highly stressed, something like "intelligence" fits very well. Money should function as a generalized resource in action processes or, conversely, as a generalized medium for the mobilization of resources, of which knowledge and achievement motivation may be treated as the most significant.[29] Perhaps the other two of Thomas's famous categories, the wishes for new experience and for security, can be fitted in here. I suggest that they may be considered as the positive and negative references of the medium intelligence which, among other things, is involved in the balancing of innovation and its risks against preservation of secure statuses and its costs in lost opportunities.

The last of the four media operating at the general action level should be rooted in the cultural system. Its pattern variable markers are universalism and diffuseness. This suggests a generalized code through which action is oriented; Thomas's other famous concept of the "definition of the situation" seems appropriate here. One crucial property is that it is generated in the process of interaction itself—"a situation defined as real is real in its consequences." It is not specific to any particular goals of acting units—it is diffuse; and as cultural, it is not particular to any system of social inclusion or solidarity but is universalistic.[30]

Perhaps the main thesis of the last few pages is that if the four-function

[29] For a considerable time, I tried to deal with erotic pleasure as the generalized medium of the behavioral organism in the general action paradigm, but abandoned it. Erotic pleasure, rather, is the "security base" of affect as a medium, in a sense analogous to that in which gold is a base for money, and coercion a base for power.

[30] As components of a culturally structured code system, the pattern variables in this connection may be compared to the "distinctive features" which play such an important part in linguistic theory. Their "function" is to select, among a wide variety of plausibly significant bases of difference, those which have special *theoretical* significance. Thus Schneider, in *American Kinship*, suggests that the basis on which one of a spouse-pair does the cooking is sex role rather than marriage membership. A wife cooks because she is a woman, not because she is married, but she cooks for her husband rather than for other men because they are married to each other.

paradigm is linked in systematic ways with the pattern variable scheme, it should be possible to systematize the relations, not only between the two, but also between the social system level, with which the present paper is primarily concerned, and that of the general system of action.

Given a formulation of the generalized media at the action level, it still remains to specify the input–output relationships among the different subsystems of action. Here it should be kept in mind that the ideal case is one involving six double interchanges among the four subsystems, with each medium involved in three of the six. After previous unpublished attempts I have essayed a new formulation in this direction. In an Appendix, I have made a very schematic and tentative statement of this formulation, which delineates the interchanges on the level of the general action system, as has already been done for the level of social system theory.[31] It should be clear that in order to develop a complete paradigm of the general action system even at this elementary level, it would be necessary to present three further interchange systems, namely for the behavioral organism, for the personality system, and for the cultural system—and to coordinate all five satisfactorily.

The Strategic Use of the Four-Function Paradigm

Since the present paper is concerned with general theory in sociology, I shall, in the space remaining, consider the advantages to social systems analysis that derive from systematizing both general action theory and sociological theory in terms of the four-function paradigm. The central problem here, of course, is to determine the best strategy for dealing theoretically with empirical complexity. Clearly the solution preferred here is the construction, at the general theoretical level, of a relatively simple system. From that starting point one deals with complexity beyond the capacities of a single empirical reference of the simple theoretical system by treating the empirical phenomena—with adequate empirical justification, of course—as resultants of the involvement of a plurality of systems which are variants of the generalized system. The theoretical scheme must therefore distinguish between primary categorizations, distinctions, and relationships on the one hand, and on the other, those which derive from involvement of multiple subsystem relationships as defined at this level.

However, the implementation of such a strategy is difficult. It requires specification of the proper level or levels for dealing with a given problem, and furthermore presumes a clear understanding of the level at which a given theoretical contribution is valid. For example, it is significant that

---

[31] Parsons, "On the Concept of Political Power."

Thomas is generally categorized as a social psychologist. If it turns out that his influential scheme of categories can be fitted with the present one as characterizing the level of the general system of action, this confirms an impression I have long had, namely that the concept of psychology has not, frequently or even most generally, been used to designate, as I have generally used it, the theory of personality (the G-subsystem of general action) or even the combination of the G and A systems, as in the common formula of psychology as the science of the behavior of organisms. I do not have a very strong feeling about which usage is correct, but it does seem to me important that in our usages we should be clear what our designative references are.[32]

From this perspective it is also important to note that perhaps the Achilles' heel of Bales's postulation of social psychology as the truly "fundamental" behavior science lies in the implicit claim that the theory of cultural systems is a branch of "psychology." It is essentially for this reason that I prefer to use the term general action rather than psychology, because the latter usage runs a double risk, namely of neglecting the analytical independence of cultural levels, and of introducing a psychological type of reductionism into the treatment of the social system. Similarly, it is clear that the "psychological laws" of Homans's "elementary behavior" lie at the general action level.[33]

I should now like to discuss briefly two areas of interrelation of the theory of the social system with that of general action, the first having to do with the classical Durkheimian problem of solidarity in relation to the societal community, the second with the "achievement" complex in its relation to the occupational role system of modern societies, and in its relation to education as a component of capacity to achieve.

The societal community, conceived as the integrative subsystem of a society as social system[34] has long been understood to be the primary focus of articulation between a system of values and norms, deriving from the cultural system of general action, and the motivational attachments to social collectivities and to the normative system, relating to personality systems in particular. Durkheim was undoubtedly the classic theorist of the institutionalization of the normative component. A notable recent contribution has been T. H. Marshall's analysis of the three components of what he calls "citizenship" for modern societies: the legal (or civic), the

[32] My colleague Bales has said that, to him, social psychology is the most fundamental discipline in the behavioral sciences, and is not interstitial between sociology and general psychology or correlative with sociology. It seems legitimate to interpret this view as locating social psychology as the theory of the general system of action in my terminology. On that interpretation, his assertion is correct.

[33] George C. Homans, *Social Behavior: Its Elementary Forms* (New York: Harcourt, 1961).

[34] See Talcott Parsons, *The System of Modern Societies* (Englewood Cliffs: Prentice-Hall, 1971), chap. 2.

political, and the social.[35] The first of these components is central to the sociology of law, and a good deal has been learned in this area in the last generation.[36] The content of the political component has been elucidated by political sociologists, notably Lipset and Rokkan.[37] The third, the social component, belongs mainly to the area of economic sociology and is quite well understood.

The relatively satisfactory state of theory with reference to the normative aspect of the integrative system is not, on the whole, matched on the motivational side. There has, of course, been a great deal of work done on deviant behavior, and on the alienation which underlies phenomena ranging from vague and diffuse discontent to violent protest and militant movements for change; but an adequate basis of generalization seems to be lacking.

As I have already suggested, I am increasingly convinced that part of the difficulty has lain in a confusion of "levels" of system reference, marked by vaciliating tendencies to define the problem as sociological on the one hand, and social psychological on the other. My suggestion is that alienation and its opposite, motivational integration of the personality in the soical system, should in the first instance be explained at the level of the general system of action rather than the social system, and only then should a careful theoretical articulation between them be worked out.

In my own previous thinking on this question, one factor which now appears to have been an obstacle to understanding was the inclination to consider *affect* as the generalized medium rooted in the personality subsystem of action. Reconsideration of the motivational bases of social solidarity has led me to the view that it is rooted in the social, or integrative, subsystem. This position seems defensible in light of the significance of affect for object relations, to use Freud's terms, and more specifically for the attachment of one person to one or more others and to the collectivity constituted (in part) by their mutual attachments. Mutuality of affect then may be considered to be a bond which unites two or more units of a social system, especially personalities, in a solidary or harmonious relationship—in the Confucian sense.[38]

Affect is obviously particularly relevant to what sociology calls "asso-

---

[35] T. H. Marshall, *Class, Citizenship, and Social Development* (Garden City: Doubleday, 1964).

[36] This has been an area of special recent concern to me, reflected in a collaborative seminar given for two years with Professor Lon L. Fuller of the Harvard Law School. Fuller's book *The Anatomy of the Law* (New York: Praeger, 1968) is an excellent introduction to the kind of sociologically relevant approach to law I have in mind.

[37] Seymour M. Lipset and Stein Rokkan, eds., *Party Systems and Voter Alignments* (New York: Free Press, 1967), especially the editors' introduction.

[38] The mutual solidarity of collectivities must be mediated by the affective orientations of individual persons.

ciational" relationships, based upon equalitarian value patterns. Such relationships have become increasingly salient with the evolution of modern societies, and the citizenship complex, which seems central to the modern societal community, is one of them. This suggests that one fruitful approach to understanding the motivational integration of the personality in the social system could begin, for modern societies especially, with analysis of the development and generalization of affective associational ties.

The modern kinship pattern is an obvious departure point. Marriage is probably *the* prototypical associational relationship, especially by contrast with primordial ascription in terms of biological descent. It is true that in primitive and indeed in all nonmodern societies, the ascriptive element in marriage has been very prominent, but it is distinctive of modern societies that entry into it has become, very much in principle, *voluntary*. The modern pattern of marriage is not only voluntary, but in principle *affective*. The justification for establishing the tie is in the first instance that the partners are "in love." Among many other aspects of the definition of the situation, this legitimates their erotic relation to each other.[39]

From the perspective of the development of the individual's personality, involvement with and sensitivity to affect are rooted in the socialization experience in the family. The stage of "mother–child identity" is that in which no generalization, or differentiation as a medium, has occurred. However, the attitudinal foundations are here. As is generally said, a good mother loves her child and the child learns to love her. By the time the parent—child "love–dependency" stage is reached, affect has become generalized to the level of what Schneider calls "diffuse, enduring solidarity." It is then, and on this basis, that the child becomes a full member in his family. The crutch of erotic attachment to the parents has been discarded (during latency), and motivation to participation and fulfillment of expectations is grounded in the love relationship reciprocal among all members.

From the point of view of children, though not of parents to each other, this family membership is ascribed by "blood" ties, as Schneider calls them symbolically. The next major step of generalization of the affective medium for the child is to the context of *voluntary* association. The setting for this is in all modern societies provided by the relation of elementary formal education to residential community structures, and by the formation of peer or friendship groups among contemporaries. This new affective focus involves tension-laden reactive relations for the child. On the one hand, he begins to feel emancipated from the family, and attempts to escape its control. On the other hand, his peer group is an affective counterpoint to the pressures of school achievement and its competitive

[39] The intricacies of this affective-erotic complex have, from a cultural perspective, been enormously elucidated by Schneider, *American Kinship*.

dimension. Since such groups are ascriptively composed of age-peers, and antagonism in both contexts is directed towards adult-controlled systems, it is not surprising that the autonomy linked to voluntary participation is colored by a generation conflict.

The voluntary peer association is in many ways analogous to a market, in that there is a considerable range within which the individual can exercise options of giving or withholding his participation in such relationships, and can regulate its intensity. The extent of the "market" is considerably enhanced when both sexes are included by virtue of coeducation, which in turn has many repercussions on the internal structure of family.

Pursuing the market analogy further, we note that perhaps the most decisive step in the industrial revolution was to put the factors of production on the market to an unprecedented extent. Similarly in the family, and in much of premodern *Geminschaft,* the objects of cathexis have been prescribed: the child is *expected* to love his parents and siblings. Beginning with the modern peer group, however, there is a much broader choice of objects and of collectivities in which to participate and with which to identify. In a strict theoretical sense this shift parallels the differentiation between households and producing–employing units which made labor a marketable factor of production.

Analogous to the use of capital as a mobile factor of production, we find the development of what I shall call (in the Appendix to this chapter) the "moral sanction of association." This is to say that, within the framework of a highly generalized value pattern, there develops a greatly enhanced autonomy of unit choice with respect to associational participation and to moral sanction of such choices. Freedom of choice of a marriage partner is a first prototypical instance, but a great many other associations belong in this category. In this respect, modern society has been moving in the direction of greatly increased associational pluralism, with the possibility of moral justification for increasingly broad ranges of acceptable choices.

This view casts serious doubt on the allegation that functional analysis of social systems implies an imperative of conformity. We must keep in mind that we are here speaking of the general action level, and that the term "moral" refers to any culturally grounded justifications of selection among alternatives for action, whether they be for sustaining a given social system, or for its revolutionary overturn, or for any of the wide variety of withdrawing or otherwise deviant modes of association. The essential point is that the affective exchange system is extended into the realm of moral questions and thus moral decisions come to be, in a new sense, contingent. From the societal point of view this means that legitimacy is not ascriptively given, but must be competed for. Among the bases of such legitimacy is the capacity to command, through moral assertion, *affective* response.

It should be clear by this point that the kinds of coordinative linking of the motivational "investments" of individuals (somewhat in Freud's sense of cathexis) with the moral imperatives of a culture and society, and with the needs and expectations of human organisms, could not operate without the functioning of generalized media of interchange. Affect is the medium of most direct interest in the present analysis.

The extension of exchange relationships in which affect is involved to include the "factors of solidarity" clearly implies that the system of reference must become more differentiated; there is a plurality of more or less distinct "markets." It is noteworthy, in this connection, that adolescent peer groups in secondary school are generally segmented rather than differentiated, in that membership patterns are ascriptive by age and heavily influenced by the social class of the members' parents.

A major step in the process of differentiation occurs at the level of higher education, which by now is generally available to all. This does not eliminate ascriptive segmentation by social origin—which operates above all through the kinds of colleges attended—but it does considerably reduce it.[40] It seems reasonable to suggest that the system of higher education is particularly important in the development of mobile "markets" for the factors of solidarity. The paradigm of the Appendix calls attention to two particularly important processes, namely (1) the $I-G$ interchange where affect is articulated with the performance capacity medium, one version of which is Thomas's recognition, and (2) the $I-L$ interchange where the affective system articulates with the definition of the situation, particularly in its moral aspects.

The significance of higher education in these respects is enhanced by its relationship to the general pattern of solidarities and stratification in the society at large. In modern societies higher education has become the most important pathway to all higher occupational statuses and, for women, the road to the "best" marriage opportunities. It is also important to note in the present context that the company of educated men (and, of course, women) is rapidly becoming the most important prestige and leadership element of the societal community, and thus central to the system of stratification.

However, the affective bases of participation by students within the academic community itself is not unproblematic. The worldwide phenomenon of student unrest—in communist as well as noncommunist countries—in which affective factors seem to have such a salient role, is clear evidence of this. We might begin by noting that, from the point of view of the social system, higher education is a mechanism of socialization. In this respect, it is comparable to the family, although far more complex and differentiated. The two are also analogous in that the family is interstitial

[40] See Christopher Jencks and David Riesman, *The Academic Revolution* (Garden City: Doubleday, 1968).

to the social and psychological systems, and higher education is interstitial to the social and cultural systems, most notably with regard to the complex focused on the values of cognitive rationalilty. In both cases there are certain roles which reflect this duality especially clearly: the father, who leaves the family to pursue his occupation; and the teacher, who is not only teacher but also researcher and author.[41] Structurally, then, the modern university "marries" agents of socialization and agents of socially important cultural functions, and students are in a position of partial and equivocal inclusion in some ways parallel to the status of children in the family.

Insofar as modern systems of education have become the center of a societal storm of sorts, affective factors have clearly been prominent. The attitudes of student activists are highly impassioned, and the symbolic themes prominent in the movements fit with the paradigm we have been discussing. Student power and oedipal aggression are similar in their implicit if not explicit claim to a right to "take over." [42] On the other hand, "student power" has strong overtones of moralism, manifest above all in the students' attempt at politization of the academic system and in their claim to the right, not only to condemn on moral grounds those exercising authority—the "fathers"—but to define for themselves the morally acceptable functions of the university. We can therefore see student discontent as a second oedipal crisis which could fully emerge only with the kind of development of higher education which modern societies have experienced, just as the full impact of the original oedipal problem could not have occurred before the industrial revolution.[43]

It should be clear that, for our purposes, the old Burgess formula that the family is a "set of interacting personalities," with the implication that its significance lies primarily in psychological factors, is inadequate for sociology. The family is part of the structure of society, with essential functions at the social system level, notably the socialization of children. Similarly the system of higher education is not simply a set of interacting personalities of students, faculty members, and administrators, to be understood psychologically. It is a particularly crucial part of the *structure* of modern societies, with very important functions at that system level: the appropriate part of the socialization function, the allocation of personnel

[41] See Talcott Parsons and Gerald Platt, "Some Considerations on the American Academic Profession," *Minerva*, 6, 4 (Summer, 1968), 497–523, and *The American University* (Cambridge: Harvard University Press, 1973).

[42] There may be an analogue of the incest taboo here. Students, while students, do not replace their teachers, nor achieve full equality with them with respect to the professional functions of the teacher role. They achieve the equivalent of adulthood in general, but in contexts *other* than that in which they have been students. They do not "marry" their *alma mater*, but by graduating they become eligible for a teacher or other fully adult role.

[43] See Fred Weinstein and Gerald Platt, *The Wish to be Free* (Berkeley and Los Angeles: University of California Press, 1969).

in the occupational system, the "advancement of knowledge," and, most important in the present context, the generalization of the factors underlying affective participation in modern social structures.

The preceding discussion originated in the general problem of understanding the modern type of societal community in terms of what we have called the citizenship complex. We were searching for an underpinning on a basis different from the role of law, democratic political organization, and social welfare; in particular, one which seemed more relevant to the motivational concerns of the individual. Given the natural inclination of a student of the sociology of higher education towards trying to understand the very salient phenomenon of student unrest,[44] certain aspects of the problem came to focus on the kind of community participation involved in the academic world and the peculiarities of the students' transitional status. This has proved to have implications for the more general problems of societal community.

It is our contention that the significance of these themes would not be understandable without reference to the general action level, and especially to the role of affect as a generalized symbolic mdium and its articulation with the achievement and control system on the one hand, and with the moral aspects of the definition of the situation on the other. This relevance of general action, however, must be carefully articulated with analysis at the level of social systems as such. It would not be wise to treat these issues as wholly those of "social psychology" in the general action sense, or as sociological in the stricter sense of social system theory.

I should like to parallel this fragmentary analysis with a still briefer account of a closely related aspect of modern societies, that of the institutionalization of an achievement complex in the occupational system. This problem has become caught up in the nexus of socialization theory, extending with increasing intensity into the realm of higher education. It has become clear that, in this field also, puristic social system analysis is not adequate. Explicit concern for both motivational and cultural problems involving not only values, but also cognitive aspects of the definition of the situation, are indispensable.

This problem, of course, goes back to the implications of Weber's analysis in *The Protestant Ethic and the Spirit of Capitalism* and the difficulties this occasioned for the more naïve versions of the doctrine of the "rational pursuit of self-interest." One of the main difficulties in discussing Weber's analysis has been the tendency to assume that the religious orientations he was concerned with transformed themselves *directly* into motives for concrete action in concrete situations. This is tantamount to

[44] See Parsons and Platt, *The American University, op. cit.*, chap. 7, and my article, "Higher Education as a Theoretical Focus," in Herman Turk and Richard L. Simpson, eds., *Institutions and Social Exchange*, chap. 15 (Indianapolis and New York: Bobbs-Merrill, 1971).

assuming that a cultural component, defined as such at the general action level, could be presumed to institutionalize itself without regard to the conditions of institutionalization in the structure of the society—as well as the conditions of internalization in personality systems. Such an approach begs too many fundamental questions.

For Weber, the typical entrepreneur was still the selfmade man whose socialization took place mainly in the context of family and diffuse community setting, including, of course, a church. One important phase of the process of institutionalization of the achievement complex involved the phenomena with which Weber was primarily concerned, namely the rise of the bourgeois classes and their involvement with what he called "rational bourgeois capitalism."

Presently, however, the institutionalization of the achievement complex has been broadened and deepened all over that part of the world which is now building on the industrial revolution, and relatively independently of the current specification of ascetic Protestant values.[45] The relevant values have, by specification, come to be differentiated from their religious matrix and institutionalized in particular in the occupational system. Furthermore, the managerial stratum no longer consists primarily of selfmade men in the old sense, and the relevance of higher rational achievement has been immensely broadened, above all to include a proliferation of many types of professional roles.

The occupational system in turn has come to be integrated to an unprecedented degree with higher education and its accompanying institutions for the advancement of knowledge. From the point of view of the social system, the functional problem is, on the one hand, to anchor the individual in a sufficiently solidary community which, in the circumstances, centers on the age-peer group. On the other hand, it is the guiding of the motives of the achievement complex into meaningful channels which establish some kind and degree of coherent integration between the demands of society for labor force services and the choices of individuals within the manifold of opportunities offered by the educational system, in a sense of the word choice which includes commitment and not just preference. Assuming, as I do, that the American value pattern of instrumental activism (I deal here only with the American case) is in general intact, and further assuming a sufficient anchorage in socialization at the family level, then the educational system from elementary school on constitutes a far more effective mechanism for the socialization of *differentiated* achievement motivation than had been the case for an earlier period. Above all, its broad extension to the level of higher education has opened up an immense manifold of new opportunities for specific function, differentiated

---

[45] This was the most salient "spearhead" of the development of a value system, but was by no means isolated. See my article "Christianity," *International Encyclopedia of the Social Sciences.*

achievement, which in its rationality has a special affinity for this value syndrome.

Let us briefly examine the educational system from this perspective. If we approach the problem from the point of view of socialization, the most decisive development is entry into the system of formal education. This is now cushioned by kindergarten and, increasingly, nursery school, but its full impact comes with the standard elementary grades. It is crucial, as I have elsewhere argued [46] and many others have realized, that in a radical departure from the organization of the family, in the school class a group of age-peers who are presumptively equals are differentiated on the axis of personal achievement. There are, of course, two aspects of this differentiation. On the one hand, individual pupils fare unequally on the axis of valued performance. On the other hand, the class as a collectivity comes to be differentiated, and most obviously bifurcated, into groups of high achievers and low achievers. Furthermore, for our purposes, it is critical that the achievements with respect to which this differentiation is defined and legitimated are achievements of cognitive mastery, defined by standards of cognitive rationality.

It was an unexpected but very significant finding of a research project in which I was involved that the record of the elementary school period is—and I think this can be generalized—the primary basis of the expectation of going to college.[47] Though secondary education intervenes, it seems that—at least in New England circumstances—the winners of the elementary school competition, by being chosen for college preparatory programs, on the high average actually attend college. The relevance of these considerations to the preceding discussion of peer groups must be relatively obvious. The elementary school phase is one in which peer groups are in process of formation, stimulated partly by reaction against the pressures of school-performance competition. They are, however, particularly blocked by the imperative of sex segregation imposed by the social psychology (I use the term advisedly) of the latency period. With the emergence of adolescent cross-sex attractions, which we may assume are affective before they are erotic, an affective basis for comprehensive peer group structure can be attained. The suggestion is that for the individual the imperative at the secondary school level is to *maintain* his level of performance, established earlier, and of course its motivational underpinning.[48] It is thus in a sense a moratorium.

[46] Talcott Parsons, "The School Class as a Social System" in *Social Structure and Personality* (New York: Free Press, 1963).

[47] Ibid.; see also Talcott Parsons, "General Theory in Sociology" in Robert K. Merton, Leonard Broom, and Leonard Cottrell, Jr., eds., *Sociology Today* (New York: Basic Books, 1959).

[48] As internalized in the personality, this motivation to perform seems to me to be essentially what McClelland has had in mind as need-achievement. See David C. McClelland, *The Achieving Society* (Princeton: Van Nostrand, 1961).

The college experience starts a new cycle. The emergence of mass higher education is of special importance in this context, as it was for the question of solidarity discussed above. Well into the present century, higher education everywhere was reserved to a small elite of the age cohort, whose status was for the most part ascribed by hereditary class status, though membership in this elite has been open to a minority of outsiders through channels of mobility. Now, despite the retention of an elite component in the older sense, the character of the system has been changed by its vastly extended inclusiveness. One consequence is an intensification of the competitive aspect which, in turn, is one cause of the emergence of intense affective concerns.

The college experience seems to further the processes of internalizing motivation to the higher levels of achievement which have come to be institutionalized in modern societies. These motivations center about the two primary areas of competence and responsibility, both of which are linked to autonomy. Hence the college experience may be considered to be, among other things, a major extension of the syndrome of "independence training" which has been such an important feature of the last generation's views on pre-adolescent child training. Certainly a primary focus of the restlessness of students is any restraint on their autonomy which they feel to be unjustified, but which may often be at least partially justified by the necessity of learning not only independence, but competence and discipline. Only the graduate ideally can be fully free from the tutelage of his teachers, and there are many problems of defining the nature and boundaries of justified tutelage, and they necessarily change with changing circumstances.

By contrast, for the cohort *not* going to college, the socialization system is and was in an important sense truncated. Termination of education with graduation from high school, if even that is achieved, means the beginning of adulthood, including entry into the labor force and eligibility to marry. Thus, the processes of internalizing higher levels of achievement motivation do not go so far in developing competence and responsibility, nor, indeed, so far as to produce certain additional strains.

The extent to which the occupational system has become linked to higher education represents a major change in the society. College education has become almost a binding prerequisite for virtually all of the higher occupational roles. Furthermore, the higher professional complex, entry into which typically requires postgraduate training, has become much more important in the total system. This development brings increased pressure to bear on those who aspire to some kind of—to them—meaningful career, and at the same time provides them with a range of opportunities which, compared to earlier conditions, is immensely expanded.

The fact that the current phase of development centering on the occupational and educational systems is one of considerable alienation

and unrest does not by itself negate the soundness of the above analysis. My broad interpretation is that this constitutes a phase of development of the total system in which integrative problems have, for the time being, assumed primacy. This is a sequel to a preceding phase in which goal-attainment processes, at both societally collective and many other levels, have undergone an unprecedented development. It is particularly striking that the malaise of our time does not seem to have its internal focus in the structure of the industrial economy as such—it is not a period of major labor unrest—but in the generation structure with its close relation to the system of higher education, and in the status of those population groups who are, relative to the societal community, the most marginal.

Whatever the case may be, the essential *theoretical* point is that, here again, any adequate analysis in this field requires consideration of social system theory on the one hand, and of the general action level theory, including its nonsocial subsystems, on the other. Not only have we been discussing the institutionalization of a cultural value system, the primary analytic origins and anchorage of which must be extrasocial, but we have found that another cultural syndrome, concerned with cognitive rationality, is of paramount importance. Similarly it seems clear that neither institutionalization, which includes socialization in terms of these values, nor its opposite, alienation, can be adequately analyzed without consideration of the psychology of personality. It is as a demonstration of these analytical necessities that these two examples from the dynamics of modern society have been introduced.

Conclusion

In embarking on this paper my primary object was to refine the grounding of the four-function paradigm, that part of the scheme of general theory in sociology with which I have been working and which has for some years served as perhaps the most central reference point for a wide range of more restricted theoretical enterprises. I hope that I have made a more cogent case than in any previous discussion in print that it is deeply grounded in the intellectual exigencies of the analysis of living systems generally.

This grounding seems to have been strengthened by theoretical development in biology and general science during roughly the last generation. These have clarified the conceptions of the mechanisms of "control" of the processes of living systems in relation to their environments. The earliest and more restricted of these conceptions was that of homeostatic mechanisms, associated above all with the name of W. B. Cannon. A more general and more radical conception then emerged in terms of cybernetic

controls in relation to information theory, with its almost obvious relevance to culture. The relation of this theoretical complex to linguistics has also been notable. A particularly salient synthesis has been the emergence of the new genetics with its treatment of genetic mechanisms as "codes" carried by very complex biochemical substances which are capable of reproducing their patterns in successive generations of concrete organisms and parts of them.

The conceptions of homeostasis and cybernetic control pose problems of understanding the mechanisms of the integration of living systems. It thus seemed significant that the four-function paradigm proved useful in integrating economic theory within that of the social system, and in particular by analyzing money as a mechanism of integration—indeed a cybernetic mechanism at the symbolic cultural level—through ramified systems of market exchange. Even more important has been the possibility thus suggested of using both the four-function analysis of the primary subsystems of societies and the mechanisms involved in their integration as the framework for developing a more sophisticated analysis of the total society as a system, including its integration through the interchange of generalized media of interchange and control among the different subsystems. The first step of generalization beyond the economy to the polity, and the attendant analysis of political power as a generalized symbolic medium, was decisive to me in showing the soundness of this extension.

The four-function paradigm had originally been grounded in the pattern variables. The demonstration that these were in turn grounded at the general action level, and not only at that of the social system, raised again the question of the relations between the social system and that of general action. In the third section of this chapter we carry the analysis of this relation further than before by attempting to lay the groundwork for a paradigm of interchange mechanisms at the general action level. The main reference point has been the adaptive sector of the paradigm set forth in "Pattern Variables Revisited." A complete paradigm of interchanges has been worked out, but because of its highly tentative nature, it has seemed best to present it in the Appendix to this article, rather than in the main text.

Finally, this paper has attempted to demonstrate the point, so central to its theoretical argument, that sociological theory with its concern for social systems as such needs to be systematically articulated with the general system of action. I have, therefore, in the final section presented a condensed account of two major processes of development in modern societies, both related to changes in the system of higher education. The first of these concerns the development of the matrices of solidary association in which modern individuals are socialized. It has seemed justified to interpret some of the phenomena of modern youth culture, and in particular the recent waves of student disturbances, at least partly in these terms.

The second context is the more familiar one of the development of achievement motivation as this issue was raised by Max Weber in his famous thesis about the implications of the Protestant ethic for occupational behavior. Both of these phenomena come to focus in very salient processes and problems of the social system. Yet, I have argued, they are not understandable without careful consideration of both the cultural and the psychological, or personality, components in their genesis. I hope that even these sketchy discussions make clear that not only are these general action considerations programmatically essential, but the theoretical scheme with which we have been working makes possible going beyond programs to substantive explanations, however incomplete.

Appendix

This Appendix [49] will follow the same format as the Technical Note to my paper "On the Concept of Political Power." The paradigms presented in the Technical Note applied to the social system, which is conceived to be *one* primary functional subsystem out of four of the general system of action. This Appendix is a very tentative delineation for the general action system of the categories of symbolic interchange, and the corresponding symbolic media and value and coordinative standards. The four-function scheme underlies the treatment of the general action system, as it did that of the social system.

The primary functional subsystems of action have been stably decided upon for some time. In order of descending position in the hierarchy of cybernetic control, they are: pattern-maintenance (L), the cultural system; integration (I), the social system; goal-attainment (G), the psychological (personality) system; and adaptation (A), the behavioral organism.

We follow the general principles used in the analysis of social systems which assert that, at a sufficiently high level of differentiation of the general action system and its respective primary subsystems, a *generalized symbolic medium* of interchange will be anchored in each of the four primary functional subsystems and involved in interchanges with each of the other three. Thus, if we include only the media and not the intrinsic valuables

[49] In this whole enterprise I owe an immense debt, and to some degree an apology, to Victor M. Lidz. We have discussed these problems over a period of several years, and he first suggested that intelligence and the definition of the situation might be considered generalized media. We still differ over the latter: he would place it in the integrative system, and consider affect as the personality system medium. The apology I owe him is for rushing into print with this formulation before he has had an opportunity to mature his own views fully. My excuses are that the scheme belongs in the context of this paper, and that I have been responsible for holding up the publication of the volume for as long as my conscience will allow.

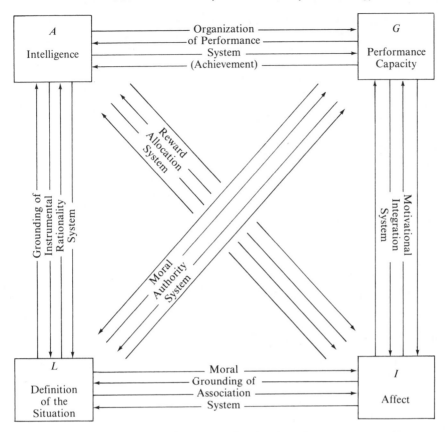

Figure 1. Format of the general action interchange system.

which they are able to command in exchange, at the level of differentiation of the whole system which is of theoretical interest here, there should be six double interchanges, as in the case of the social system paradigm. These will involve each of the four media in three interchanges. This will mean that each medium is involved in one double interchange with each of the other three. Since the media have above all integrative significance in the system as a whole, this is necessary if the integrative processes are to pervade the whole system.

Figure 1 simply presents the format of the four media and the six double interchange systems and, for convenience, gives a label to each of the latter. The most difficult and uncertain task has been to identify the four media and to place them correctly. Ever since first working on the problem I have thought that *affect* belonged in the list and that it was a variant, because of system-perspective, of W. I. Thomas's famous category of response, thereby linking a psychoanalytic type of theorizing with that of American social psychology. If response were to be included, it

seemed logical that recognition also ought to be—here I differ from Victor Lidz. This left the problem of placing both categories and designating the proper more generalized term of which recognition is a variant. The best terminological solution I have come upon so far is *performance capacity*. The appropriateness of this term depends on placing affect in the integrative position and performance capacity in the psychological system. Here the analogue of performance capacity to power at the social system level works out well, since power has been defined as a capacity to implement *collective* goal interests, whereas performance capacity may be conceived to anchor in individual performance.

It was only with Lidz's introduction of definition of the situation into the discussion that it occurred to me that perhaps Thomas, in his famous paradigm, had gotten hold of the whole roster of the general action media, though his terms were chosen from more particular and less theoretically generalized perspectives than the present one. In any case, definition of the situation seems to fit well as the culturally anchored medium.[50]

The pattern-maintenance system has a dual character which is related to its general stabilizing function in living systems. This has, in previous analyses, taken the form of distinguishing its lower and higher level references.[51] It seems to me that the concept of definition of the situation fits this theoretical requirement, and the clue to its interpretation lies in the relatively early Durkheim. This is to say that society, which most directly interacts with the cultural system, is for the participant individual at the same time an empirical entity which is to be cognitively known—in Durkheim's phrase, a *milieu social*—and a source of moral authority, the content of which is morally binding rather than situationally conditional. The relations between these two levels, and those of both of them to the other functional exigencies of action, can be stated in logical terms in the formula that the upper and lower levels of the pattern-maintenance system define the limits of the system of reference, in this case general action, with reference to its upper and lower environments respectively in the general cybernetic hierarchy. Thus, the lower limit concerns the subaction components of the organic world and the physical environment as its impact is mediated through the organism. The genetic constitution of the organism constitutes a set of givens from the point of view of action. At the upper limit it is some such category as "ultimate reality" [52] which is

[50] Thomas singled out the definition of the situation as a special case, set over against the "four wishes." If, as we suggest, two of the latter, the wishes for security and new experience, both refer to adaptation, we can regard the definition of the situation as the same kind of special case that all pattern-maintenance factors have within a fourfold scheme.

[51] Cf. Parsons et al., *Theory of Action*.

[52] Cf. Talcott Parsons, *Societies, Evolutionary and Comparative Perspectives* (Englewood Cliffs: Prentice-Hall, 1966), chap. 2.

mediated through cultural symbolic systems, the kind of reality postulated in many if not all religious systems, but also metaphysical cognitive grounds such as the Kantian *Ding an sich.*

Finally, we suggest that *intelligence* is an appropriate designation for the adaptive medium at the level of general action. It has been evident that there is a relation between economic resources at the societal level and cognitive resources at the general action level.[53] Intelligence, especially since we link it to the organism, may be presumed to have a centrally important hereditary component, but to be by no means only hereditary, as is indeed the prevailing psychological opinion today. Indeed, its L factor may be presumed to be hereditary. Intelligence seems to be particularly well suited to link the cognitive aspects of the cultural system with the ego-function, achievement-oriented aspects of the personality system.

Figure 2, as in the social system interchange paradigm, places the six double interchange sets of the general action system on a horizontal axis for convenience of reading, though in the more generally used convention they should be placed in the format of Figure 1. Figure 2 gives names to each of the twenty-four input–output categories involved, specifies by directional arrows sources and destinations, identifies which medium each exemplifies, and designates whether, from the point of view of the function of the subsystems, the input or output is a factor or a product. Since it has been necessary to select twenty-four verbal designations, there is likely to be an even greater factor of arbitrariness than in the selection of terms for the four symbolic media, and the present formulations are tentative.

Since the primary interest of this article is in linkage with the social system, we may begin with the interchange systems most directly concerned with it, and with affect as a medium. The first of these, the *I–G* system, has been called the system of motivational integration. The first interchange category, a factor of solidarity, is the well-known Freudian category of *cathexis of objects,* which comes very close to the definition of role expectations. This is treated as an input of performance capacity rather than affect, whereas the other input from personality to social system, called *identification,* is designated as involving the medium of affect, thus endowing it with a *collective* reference along the lines of my earlier analysis of the object relations syndrome.[54] The primary output from the social system to the personality, then, is *recognition of achievement,* again a form of performance capacity, whereas the related affective category is the place for Thomas's *response.*

In the *L–I* interchanges, which we have called the *moral grounding of association system,* the primary input of a factor of solidarity concerns the moral *sanction of association,* which was discussed on p. 253 of this paper,

[53] See Parsons and Smelser, *Economy and Society.*

[54] Cf. Talcott Parsons, *Social Structure and Personality* (New York: Free Press, 1964), chap. 4.

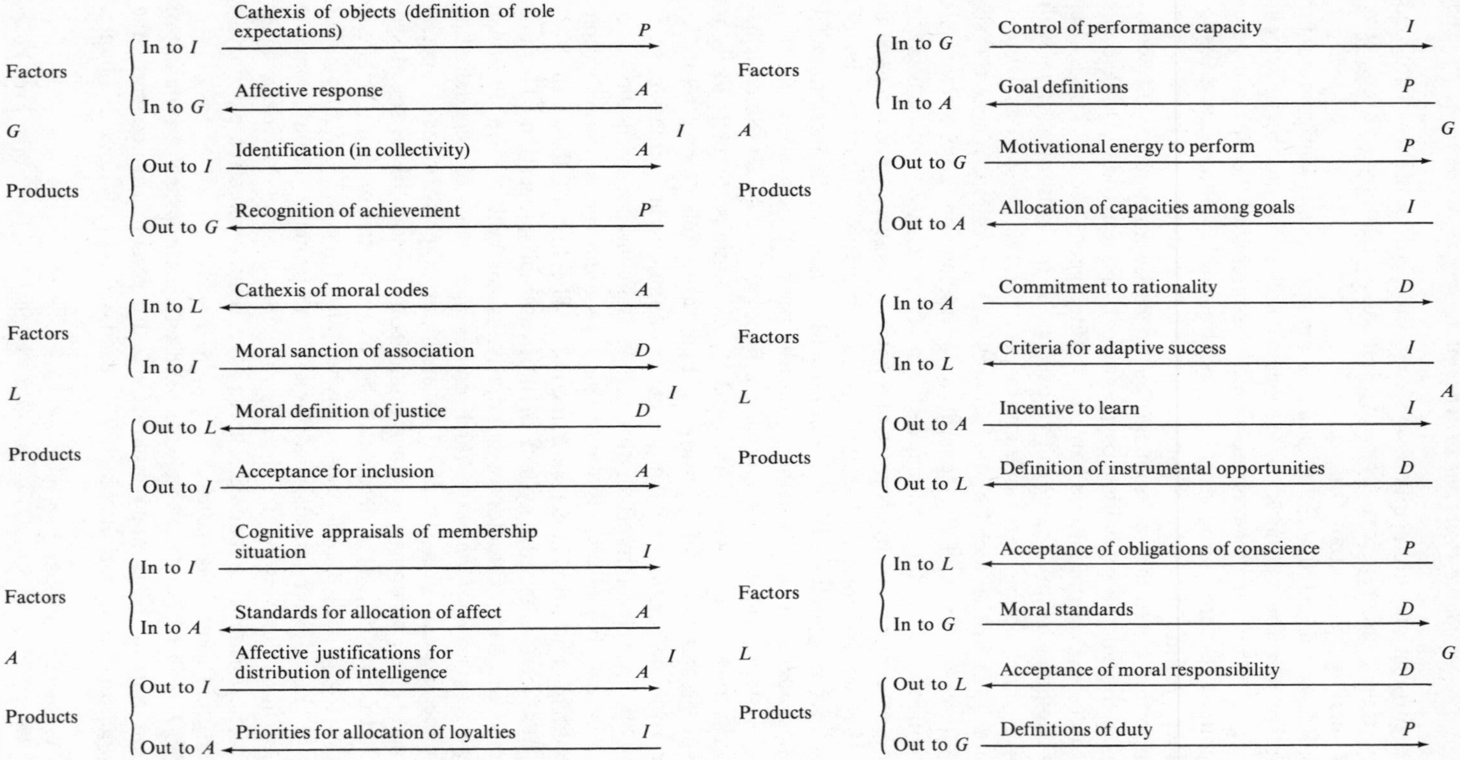
Factors
In to I
Cathexis of objects (definition of role expectations)
P
In to G
Affective response
A
G
I
Products
Out to I
Identification (in collectivity)
A
Out to G
Recognition of achievement
P
Factors
In to G
Control of performance capacity
I
In to A
Goal definitions
P
A
G
Products
Out to G
Motivational energy to perform
P
Out to A
Allocation of capacities among goals
I
Factors
In to L
Cathexis of moral codes
A
In to I
Moral sanction of association
D
L
I
Products
Out to L
Moral definition of justice
D
Out to I
Acceptance for inclusion
A
Factors
In to A
Commitment to rationality
D
In to L
Criteria for adaptive success
I
L
A
Products
Out to A
Incentive to learn
I
Out to L
Definition of instrumental opportunities
D
Factors
In to I
Cognitive appraisals of membership situation
I
In to A
Standards for allocation of affect
A
A
I
Products
Out to I
Affective justifications for distribution of intelligence
A
Out to A
Priorities for allocation of loyalties
I
Factors
In to L
Acceptance of obligations of conscience
P
In to G
Moral standards
D
L
G
Products
Out to L
Acceptance of moral responsibility
D
Out to G
Definitions of duty
P

Figure 2. General action system interchanges. The medium exemplified by each category of input or output is indicated as follows: *D*, definition of the situation; *A*, affect; *P*, performance capacity; *I*, intelligence. For a comparison with a somewhat later

and the primary product output of the integrative system is the *moral definition of justice* (perhaps similar to Homans's category of distributive justice). Both of these are forms of the definition of the situation as a medium. They are balanced in the two interchanges by another form of cathexis, this time *cathexis of moral codes,* and the *acceptance for inclusion,* both of which are forms of affect.

Because of their special status I shall leave the two "diagonal" interchange systems to the last. Turning to the *A–G* interchange, the *organization of performance* system, we consider the factor input to *G* to be the *control of performance capacity,* of which perhaps the most important intrinsically valuable items controlled are knowledge and skill. This we interpret to be an input of intelligence, which is balanced by the output of intelligence from personality to organism of *allocation of capacities among goals.* The corresponding transfers of performance capacity are *definitions of goals* and *control of motivational energy to perform.* The latter is a particularly important category in that it corresponds to the category of service as an output of the economy at the social system level. It seems close to the need-achievement which McClelland and his associates have studied so intensively.

The last schematically peripheral interchange system is that of the *grounding of instrumental rationality,* between *L* and *A*. We consider *commitment to rationality* as a factor output from cultural to organic system— for example, controls over emotions. The reciprocal input to the culture, corresponding to goods in the social system paradigm is the *definition of instrumental opportunities,* with their clear dependence on capacities of the organism. The intelligence interchanges, then, corresponding to the monetary interchanges in the societal labor-consumption system, are *criteria for adaptive success* (corresponding to wages) and *definitions of incentives to learn* (corresponding to consumer spending).

We have held that the diagonal interchange systems should be placed at the *code* level in the analysis of symbolic systems, rather than, to use a term from linguistics, that of message. In this sense they are integrative in significance. The *L–G* case seems to be the easier to define in terms of the appropriateness of the categories. The higher-level, "internal" pair we interpret as cases of definition of the situation, on the one hand *moral standards,* from *L* to *G,* and on the other, *acceptance of moral responsibility* from *G* to *L*. The lower-level, "controlled" categories are *acceptance of obligations of conscience* and *definitions of duty.* These last two, which involve performance capacity, define more particular duties and obligations.

We generalize from the social system paradigm that the *I–A* interchange system has primarily allocative functions. Since the integrative medium is affect, we suggest that the output of this medium to *A* consists in *standards for the allocation of affect,* and the input of affect to *I* is *affective justifications for distribution of intelligence.* The corresponding

transfers of intelligence consist in *cognitive appraisals of membership situation* and the setting of *priorities for allocation of loyalties.*

Figure 3 presents the generalized media in terms of the relations between the code and message components, and the significance of the latter as sanctions controlling both factors essential to the various functional subsystems and product outputs from these subsystems. The rows are arranged from top to bottom according to the hierarchy of control, each row designating one of the four media. The columns designate components into which each medium needs to be broken down if some of the basic conditions of its mediating interaction are to be understood. As in the social

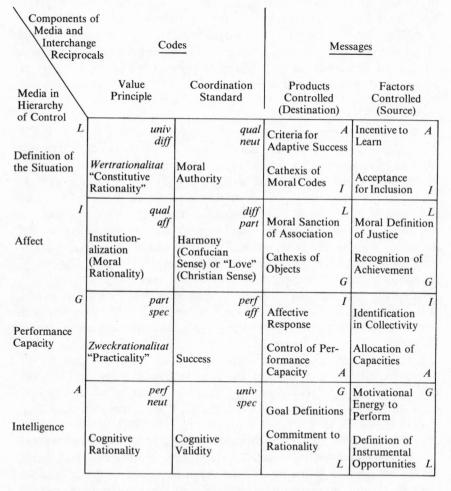

Components of Media and Interchange Reciprocals	**Codes**		**Messages**	
Media in Hierarchy of Control	Value Principle	Coordination Standard	Products Controlled (Destination)	Factors Controlled (Source)
L Definition of the Situation	*univ* *diff* *Wertrationalitat* "Constitutive Rationality"	*qual* *neut* Moral Authority	Criteria for *A* Adaptive Success Cathexis of Moral Codes *I*	Incentive to *A* Learn Acceptance for Inclusion *I*
I Affect	*qual* *aff* Institutionalization (Moral Rationality)	*diff* *part* Harmony (Confucian Sense) or "Love" (Christian Sense)	Moral Sanction *L* of Association Cathexis of Objects *G*	Moral Definition *L* of Justice Recognition of Achievement *G*
G Performance Capacity	*part* *spec* *Zweckrationalitat* "Practicality"	*perf* *aff* Success	Affective *I* Response Control of Performance Capacity *A*	Identification *I* in Collectivity Allocation of Capacities *A*
A Intelligence	*perf* *neut* Cognitive Rationality	*univ* *spec* Cognitive Validity	Goal Definitions *G* Commitment to Rationality *L*	Motivational *G* Energy to Perform Definition of Instrumental Opportunities *L*

Figure 3. The media as sanctions. The pattern variable components, designated by abbreviations in the code columns, are: universalism—particularism, specificity—diffuseness, performance—quality, and affectivity—affective neutrality.

system case, it is necessary to distinguish two components of the code aspect of each medium, namely the relevant value principle, which is the pattern-maintenance component not directly involved in interchange processes, and the coordinative standard, which regulates the diagonal interchanges (as represented in Figure 1).

The value principles for the different media are differentiated variants of the general pattern of rationality. It seems to me that Weber's famous concept pair *Wertrationalität* (translated as "constitutive rationality") and *Zweckrationalität* (translated as "practicality") should be placed in the L and G boxes respectively of the left-hand column. (It may be said that Weber was in some respect primarily a theorist of the $L–G$ relationship, whereas Durkheim concentrated on the $I–A$ relationship.) *Cognitive rationality* in relation to intelligence as a medium seems to fit the A cell of this column. For the I cell it was tempting to move the concept solidarity from the social system paradigm, but Lidz's suggestion of *institutionalization* (moral rationality) is more appropriate. This is a form of rationality in the sense that consistency between value commitments and beliefs on the one hand, and practice in going social systems on the other, is a central value.

The integrative column, labeled "coordination standard," is clearly related to the value principles. In the L cell the obvious entry is *moral authority* in Durkheim's sense, as grounding in social solidarity. In the integrative cell, perhaps the concept of *harmony* somewhat in the Confucian sense is appropriate, though some usages of the term *love* would fit. For the G cell, I have taken the concept *success* from the social system paradigm. I have not felt easy with its usage there and the individual performance emphasis of general action fits it better. Finally, the standard spelling out the value of cognitive rationality is *cognitive validity*.

The pattern variable components of the two code columns are taken from the paradigm presented in my article, "Pattern Variables Revisited." Briefly, the pattern variable components for the value principle column represent the adaptive subset of that paradigm, and those of the coordination standard column represent the integrative subset.

The other two columns are virtually self-explanatory. They arrange the input and output categories from Figure 2, except those of the diagonal interchanges, as factors and products of the functional processes of the subsystems of reference, indicating also their sources and destinations.

The reader who wishes to secure a clear understanding of this Appendix will undoubtedly find it helpful to compare it carefully with the Technical Note of my article on power.

Part **III**

THE EVOLUTION
AND INTEGRATION
OF MODERN SOCIETIES

Introduction

IT WAS NOTED in the General Introduction that one major trend of my theoretical thinking in recent years has been an increasing concern with problems of evolution in the human action system, particularly societies and cultures, and the relation of this to the nature and problems of organic evolution. This began before any of the essays included in the present collection were written [1] but came to an important stage of crystallization in the later period. The present volume does not, however, contain my most important attempts at formulation in this field; they are to be found in the two small volumes contributed to the Prentice-Hall Foundations of Sociology Series, namely *Societies: Evolutionary and Comparative Perspectives* and *The System of Modern Societies*.[2]

It is quite clear that a major reference point for this work on the theory of sociocultural evolution has been the problem of attempting to interpret, as a social scientist, some of the primary characteristics and trends of change in modern societies. Indeed, this focus of interest went back in my own experience even behind the influence of Max Weber to that of Hobhouse and Ginsberg at the London School of Economics. It was, however, powerfully stimulated by Weber's influence; it will be remembered that I wrote my Heidelberg dissertation on the "Concept of Capitalism in German [social science] Literature," dealing mainly with Marx, Sombart, and Weber.[3]

[1] Cf. Talcott Parsons, "Evolutionary Universals in Society," *American Sociological Review*, Vol. 29 (June 1964), pp. 339–357. Reprinted in Talcott Parsons, *Sociological Theory and Modern Society* (New York: Free Press, 1967), Chapter 15, pp. 690–520.

[2] See Talcott Parsons, *Societies: Evolutionary and Comparative Perspectives* (Englewood Cliffs, N.J.: Prentice-Hall, 1966), and *The System of Modern Societies* (Englewood Cliffs, N.J.: Prentice-Hall, 1971). These are about to be republished in a single volume, without major alterations, but carefully edited by Jackson Toby, entitled *The Evolution of Societies*.

[3] This dissertation was written in German and was never published as such. Two articles in English, on Sombart and Weber respectively, were, however, published—thereby fulfilling the Heidelberg publication requirement. (Talcott Parsons, " 'Capitalism' in Recent German Literature: Sombart and Weber, I" and " 'Capitalism' in Recent German Literature: Sombart and Weber, II," in *Journal of Political Economy*,

This concern with the institutional charactertistics of modern societies—and by logical extension their historical–evolutionary antecedents—has indeed been career-long. All three of the articles in Part III are concerned with formulating some of the essentials of the nature of modern societies, but at the same time in an evolutionary perspective.

The first of them, "Comparative Studies and Evolutionary Change" (Chapter 11), is much the most theoretically generalized of the three. It is a general statement of a paradigm of a phase of "progressive" change, which has been developed in connection with the above set of interests. Its conceptual roots lie in the four-function paradigm, not as applied to a "statically equilibrated" system, but specifically adapted to the analysis of processes of social change. From one point of view, it is a revision—a substantial one—of an earlier paper, "Some Considerations on the Theory of Social Change," published in *Rural Sociology*.[4] The paper here reproduced was written as a requested contribution to the volume edited by Ivan Vallier, *Comparative Methods in Sociology* (University of California Press, 1971), thus several years after the earlier formulation.

The phrase "progressive change" used in characterizing this paradigm is meant to indicate a process contributing to "evolutionary advance" as evaluated by the criterion of "enhanced adaptive capacity" as that concept has been adapted from the theory of organic evolution, especially in the post-Darwinian tradition.[5] In the light of the prevalence in our social science background of extreme skepticism about *any* idea of evolutionary "advance," it must be recognized that this conception involves manifold problems. These cannot be analyzed in this brief introductory statement. The skeptical reader, in this context, must be referred to the much wider discussion of the relevant problems in a literature to which various references have been given here, including references to the biological literature, e.g., in the question of whether and in what sense the organic species "man" is or is not, for example, an advance in this revolutionary sense, on insects, birds, or such mammals as rats, dogs, or horses, but also such "sociological" literature as that of Condorcet, Hegel, Comte, Marx, Spencer, and Hobhouse, to name only a few.[6]

Vols. 36 and 37 [1928 and 1929], pp. 641–661 and 31–51). The original document is preserved in the Library of the *Institut für Sozialwissenschaft* at the University of Heidelberg. (*Mirabile dictu*, it was not burned by the Nazis.)

[4] Talcott Parsons, "Some Considerations on the Theory of Social Change," *Rural Sociology*, Vol.. 26, No. 3 (September 1961).

[5] See especially Ernst Mayr, *Populations, Species and Evolution* (Cambridge, Mass.: Harvard University Press, 1970).

[6] Certainly one of the few most extensive and thoughtful discussions of the problems of evolution by a social scientist is that by Donald T. Campbell, "On the Conflicts between Biological and Social Evolution and between Psychology and Moral Tradition." This was his Presidential Address to the American Psychological Association in August 1975, which was published in the *American Psychologist*, December 1975.

The article here reproduced takes as its point of departure the very old concept of differentiation, which, it is well known, that Spencer took over from biological theory and attempts to redefine it in its relation to processes of change in systems of human action. The assumption is that, in the complex of goal-directed "thrusts" in a system of action, there will on the one hand be some kind of balance between internal pressures toward innovative change and factors of situtional and/or environmental opportunity for it. If the combined "pressure" of these factors is sufficient they will bring about some kind of "outlet" for the tendency to change. For this to happen new structures and processes are necessary. These, however, are unlikely to be maximally unrelated to those already existing. Hence the most likely outcome, other than the inhibition of the movement for change, is the "splitting off" of new structures from some already present and the performance of old, but newly emphasized functions, which were part of the functions of old structures, in new structures.

A classic example in the background of modern societies is the differentiation of structural units specially organized for economic production, the factory and the office, from kinship constituted households. The first primary consequence is that, through the freeing of resources by differentiation and the organization of new social units, there is a substantially enhanced output of more generalized resources made available in the larger system—in the above example, of economically usable products. Consequences, however, are not confined to this level but must include pressures to reorganization of the class of units from which the new ones have differentiated, in this case kinship households.

The first of the further processes following on differentiation we have called *adaptive upgrading,* as exemplified by the enormous increase of economic productivity following the industrial revolution.[7] The second is an aspect of integration which we have chosen to call *inclusion.* The new and the old units must somehow be integrated with each other, e.g., the persons employed in productive units still remain members of households, but since needs are much less met by production within the household, the money earnings of employed people enable them to fill their household needs through purchases on the market. There must, in that sense, be more *inclusive* mechanisms and structures, which foster integration as between productive units and households, than operated before the change within households.

Finally, we have maintained that changes such as those just outlined generate pressures to change in the value patterns on which they impinge. This change need not be one of primary direction of orientation, though

---

[7] Cf. David S. Landes, *The Unbound Prometheus, Technological Change and Industrial Development in Western Europe from 1750 to the Present* (London: Cambridge University Press, 1972), and Neil J. Smelser, *Social Change and the Industrial Revolution* (London: Routledge and Kegan Paul, 1959).

this *may* occur. The change to which we wish to direct attention, however, is a different one, namely in the level of generalization at which value-commitments are adhered to and influence action. Before the process of differentiation just illustrated, these commitments might simply be to the welfare of households, whereas after, they must be both to households and to the efficiency of producing units. Since the same people, notably employed adults, participate in the functioning of both types of organized units, the integration of their own personalities as well as that of the included social system demands that they can conscientiously approve both. To do this requires a level of the generality of value-commitments higher than that needed to approve either one but not the other. This is what we mean by a change in the level of *value-generalization* as the fourth primary constituent process of a phase of progressive change.

Each of the other two papers (Chapters 12 and 13) in Part III spells out the analysis of one primary axis of the structural differentiation of modern societies. The two have been called, for present purposes, stratification and ethnicity. It is indeed difficult for a sociologist with strong macro-sociological, evolutionary, and comparative interests *not* to become seriously interested in both of these topics. I have maintained [8] that neither is significantly developed internally to the most primitive societies, with the implication that both are the products of important steps in the evolutionary process.

Of the two themes, that of stratification has been the more prominent in the literature of sociology, in part because ethnicity through its close relations to nationalism and nationality has been partly preempted by politicial scientists, and also by historicians. The article on stratification reprinted here was written for a special issue of *Sociological Inquiry,* edited by Edward O. Laumann (Vol. 40, Spring 1970). As such, it was my third attempt at a general theoretical statement. The first was published in 1940, the second, a "Revised Analytical Approach. . ." in 1953.[9]

Published concern with these problems thus extends over a period of thirty years, so comparison of these essays should provide good evidence on the question of how static or how developing my theoretical thinking has been.

The most important new note in the third essay reprinted here seems to me to be, as I said in its opening statement, that the focus of interest was no longer, to quote Rousseau, on "the origins of inequality," but on the *balance* between equality and inequality in human affairs, especially

[8] Parsons, *Societies: Evolutionary and Comparative Perspectives,* Chapter 3.

[9] Talcott Parsons, "Analytical Approach to the Theory of Social Stratification," *American Journal of Sociology,* Vol. 45 (1940), pp. 841–862, and "A Revised Analytical Approach to the Theory of Social Stratification," in Reinhard Bendix and Seymour M. Lipset (eds.), *Class, Status and Power: A Reader in Social Stratification* (New York: Free Press, 1953), pp. 92–129. Both articles are reprinted in Talcott Parsons, *Essays in Sociological Theory,* revised ed. (New York: Free Press, 1954).

in the structure of modern societies. It seems to me that this permits a broader perspective on the problem. Strong social movements in relatively recent years pressing in egalitarian directions have heightened our awareness of these problems in the context of social justice.[10] The stress for present purposes, however, is not on national ideals, but on the problems needing to be understood by social scientists and on the theoretical resources they have and need to achieve this understanding.

Clearly the egalitarian "thrust" is not merely a passing ideology, but one of the most deeply grounded components of the cultural heritage, not only of the United States but of Western, and indeed other, societies. It does not and I think cannot, however, stand alone in that heritage or radically dominate other components. As far as the relative status of individuals is concerned, perhaps the most important other component is what Lipset,[11] among others, has called the achievement complex. The valuation of high achievement, which by definition has a differential reference, in cultural fields, such as intellectual or artistic, and in organizational fields like politics, administration, and economic production, cannot simply be dismissed as unacceptable "elitism." Nor can we deny legitimacy to all forms of effective large-scale organization in spite of the fact that these seem always to generate various kinds of inequalities. As in so many fields of social science the problem is "balance," but this term is mainly a name for the problem area, not a solution of the problems.

The other structural axis has here been called ethnicity. This may be thought of as the extension of diffuse solidarities beyond the boundaries of traceable and institutionalizable kinship *nexus*. As I pointed out in *Societies*,[12] in most primitive societies the boundaries of what constitutes the "society," from the point of view of membership, seem to be at most vaguely defined. Even languages seem to shade off into each other as dialects do in modern societies. The development of a "community" of people who have a sense of "belonging together" and sharing a common fate is a long and complicated process.[13]

The most prominent aspect of this in the modern world has been the development and consolidation of "nations," where above all ethnicity has ideally tended to coincide with territorially sovereign government. This coincidence has, however, never been as far-reaching as nationalistic

[10] As if this were not enough, I am writing this introduction very shortly after July 4th in the Bicentennial Year and hence scarcely need to be reminded of Thomas Jefferson's use of the statement, "All men are created equal . . ."

[11] Seymour M. Lipset, *The First New Nation* (New York: Basic Books, 1963), and "Values and Entrepreneurship in the Americas," Chapter 3 in *Revolution and Counterrevolution, Change and Persistence in Social Structures*, revised ed. (Garden City, N.Y.: Doubleday, 1970).

[12] Parsons, *Societies, op. cit.*, Chapter 3.

[13] Cf. Edmund R. Leach, "Legitimacy of Solomon," in *Genesis as Myth and Other Essays* (London: Jonathan Cape, 1969).

ideologies would like, and a certain process of differentiation has been taking place. Whereas the unity of Medieval Europe broke down into a set of national states, in the cases where the states were ethnically pluralistic, with the different groups territorially consolidated, there have been strong tendencies to political separatism, as in the case of the old Austro-Hungarian Empire, which collapsed in 1918, more recently in Belgium, and in North America in Canada.

Some modern societies, however, have become ethnically pluralistic without the situation's generating strong movements of political separatism. The most prominent of these has been the United States, and here we speak of problems of "ethnic" diversity, conflict, and integration, rather than of "nationalism." Though remarking briefly at the end on other situations, the article here reprinted (Chapter 13) is mainly concerned with the American situation and its recent development, with respect first to the relations between so-called white-Anglo-Saxon-Protestants (WASP's) and other groups who came in mainly from Europe by immigration, but also referring to the changing status of the black group in American society.[14]

This paper was written for a conference, and a subsequent volume, on the study of ethnicity, sponsored by the American Academy of Arts and Sciences. The volume, entitled *Ethnicity,* edited by Nathan Glazer and Daniel Patrick Moynihan, was published in 1975.

To use a spatial metaphor, stratification and ethnicity, respectively, may be said to constitute the axes on which the system of modern societies has most prominently tended to manifest "horizontal" and "vertical" cleavages. The former tendency has of course most prominently been expressed in the doctrine of "class conflict," with the common allegation both that this line of cleavage was overwhelmingly dominant and that the conflict element was overwhelmingly central until resolved by revolution. Somewhat parallel, however, has been the belief that in the first instance international conflicts constituted the main basis of cleavage in modern societies. Prominent corollaries have been that one nation state would tend to try to dominate the world, and more recently that within nations dominant ethnic groups tended to strive for unequivocal superiority of power.

It is our view that there is much exaggeration in such views of the power structure of modern society and that the history of the present century does not bear out any of the extremer versions. In any case, the social scientist can surely try to mobilize such theoretical and empirical knowledge as is available to help toward considered judgment in such matters.

---

[14] Thus the very recent election of Jimmy Carter of Georgia to the presidency, with strong black support, surely makes a notable change from conditions of, say, thirty years ago.

11. Comparative Studies and Evolutionary Change

PROFESSOR VALLIER has suggested that in this chapter I attempt to sum up some of the principal ideas about comparative studies which have emerged as significant to me out of my rather long experience with them.

I was really introduced to such studies in my first year of graduate work in London in 1924–1925. The dominant figure in the field there was L. T. Hobhouse, who was very much an evolutionist. I of course read his work, but my first systematic introduction was through Morris Ginsberg who, in Hobhouse's absence on account of illness, gave the course of lectures of *Comparative Institutions*. A year later at Heidelberg I began my acquaintance with a rather different orientation to these problems—that of Max Weber—which has been of central significance to me ever since.

Another significant early experience lay in the fact that, with the establishment of a Department of Sociology at Harvard in 1931, I was asked, as a very junior member, to serve as "coordinator" of an omnibus collaborative course called Comparative Social Institutions in which a rather distinguished group of faculty members in historical fields and disciplines related to sociology participated. These included, for example, Charles H. McIlwain, William S. Ferguson, Walter E. Clark, Arthur D. Nock, A. M. Tozzer, Edwin F. Gay, and Arthur M. Schlesinger, Sr. Though it proved not to be feasible to hold such a team together for many years, Comparative Social Institutions has been a continuous teaching venture for me ever since, the title of the course having been pared down eventually to simply *Institutional Structure*.

A major antecedent influence on me was my exposure, as an undergraduate (at Amherst College), to biological thinking. Since the conception of evolution has been so very central in that field, I started with a pre-

From *Comparative Methods in Sociology: Essays on Trends and Applications,* Edited by Ivan Vallier. Copyright © 1971 by the Regents of the University of California; reprinted by permission of the University of California Press.

279

disposition in favor of it, for the socio-cultural field as well as the organic. At the same time, my early intellectual maturity coincided with a major wave of reaction against evolutionary thinking in favor of the idea of cultural relativity. This response was especially strong among anthropologists but also appeared among sociologists. The Hobhouse–Ginsberg type of evolutionary thinking was one of the most widely attacked and, in large measure, I tended to "go along with" the attack. Nevertheless, I was never convinced that the anti-evolutionists had in any way seriously damaged the evolutionary components of Weber's historical-sociological analyses, nor those of Durkheim as I came to appreciate their nature better.[1]

Seen in the framework of the sociology of knowledge, it is clear that the anti-evolutionist wave was a partial manifestation of the social sciences' need to assert their independence from the biological. The original anthropological meaning of the word "culture" was thus that class of determinants and/or products of human action which were not "reducible" to terms of biological heredity. By and large, however, this "independence" movement in the social sciences has now long since succeeded, making it possible to acknowledge kinship—a little like the rebellious adolescent who, after having established his independence, can again acknowledge some genuine kinship with his parents in more than a biological sense.

It was in that frame of mind that I found myself, a number of years later, more and more positively concerned with evolutionary ideas. This interest led me back to biological reference points and to an attempt to understand some of the newer developments in biological science. Out of this I emerged strongly convinced about the basic continuity of the evolutionary development of all classes of living systems, including a continuity between the organic level and the socio-cultural.[2]

One particularly important point regarding the biological and socio-cultural levels may be noted immediately, though others will be developed as we go along. This is the "analogy" or functional similarity between the role of the genetic constitution in the organic world and that of the cultural system in the world of human action systems, an insight I owe especially to the biologist Alfred Emerson, who spoke of the parallel between "gene" and "symbol." This idea linked up in a special way with the "four-function paradigm" with which I have worked since 1953. Among the four functional categories, namely, those of adaptation, system goal-attainment, integration, and pattern maintenance, the last occupied a special place as relatively invariant, i.e., changing by something like "evolutionary" processes on a long-time scale, rather than by short-run "adjustive" processes.

---

[1] Robert Bellah, "Durkheim and History," *American Sociological Review*, 24 (August 1959), 447–461.

[2] The more autobiographical aspect of this development has been recounted in my article, "On Building Social System Theory: A Personal Account," in *Daedalus* (Fall 1970), and need not be repeated. It is reprinted as Chapter 1 of the present volume.

During about the same period it also became clear that the fourfold paradigm could be used at the "general action" level as distinguished from that of the social system, with which I had worked most intensively. At this level the four "primary subsystems of action" were clearly the "behavioral organism," the psychological or personality system, the social system, and the cultural system. The special position of the pattern-maintenance system was the primary key to another major insight, namely, that the fourfold scheme fitted the economic classification of the factors of production and the shares of income, and that within that "land" clearly belonged in the pattern-maintenance position.[3]

Soon after that I became aware of certain developments outside my own field which went far to give a deeper theoretical rationale to Emerson's "equation" between the gene and the symbol. One of these was the development of linguistics in ways which connected it with cybernetic and information theory, treating language as organized about "symbolic *codes,*" and the emergence in the new "microgenetics" of essentially the same conception, most dramatically set forth in the discovery of the chemical structure of DNA and the subsequent development of the conception of the "genetic code."[4] One might say, if language, the status of which as a central aspect of culture was scarcely in doubt, and the biochemistry of the genetic process were organized in terms of "codes" the main structure of which was resistant to short-run change, why should not the aspects of culture with which sociologists had been more concerned fit broadly into the same conception?

Some Relevant Sociological Theory

I do not mean to suggest that all of this perspective was borrowed from models of biological theory. There has been, over the years, on my own part and based on an impressive growth of the social science literature, a considerable accumulation of knowledge and insight at social science levels, the digesting and organizing of which, for me, revolved above all about two foci. One was my continuing concern with Max Weber's pattern of comparative and historical analysis of societies and their cultural traditions. The other was the "pattern-variable" scheme, which had "fathered" the four-function paradigm of which I have spoken. Perhaps this is sufficiently familiar to most readers so it is not necessary to outline it here, especially as it was used as the main organizing conceptual framework of my book *The Social System* (1951).

[3] Talcott Parsons and Neil Smelser, *Economy and Society* (New York: Free Press, 1956).

[4] Gunther S. Stent, "DNA," *Daedalus* (Fall 1970).

Another very important leading conception does, however, link directly with biology, namely that of *differentiation*. This conception and its complement, that of integration, have of course figured very prominently in social as well as biological science—perhaps most notably in Herbert Spencer. Among its various aspects, it seems appropriate first to emphasize that differentiation is a *directional* process, it has a starting point, namely an "un" or "less" differentiated state of a system and, at a later time, a differentiated or a more differentiated state.

An important point about differentiation as a process is that in living systems it follows, very generally indeed, the *binary* principle. What begins as one unit or subsystem divides into two. Perhaps the best known case in the organic world is the process of cell division. If there is at least a presumption in favor of the binary principle, this fact introduces among other things a very welcome element of both simplification and symmetry. It has been particularly congenial to me through its connection with the logic of certain aspects of the theoretical scheme with which I have worked, such as the dichotomous character of pattern-variable pairs and the conception of the four primary system functions. Furthermore, in tracing developmental processes this presumption may be a very useful guide in any attempt to identify stages.

The concept of differentiation is a basic unifier of the evolutionary and the comparative perspectives. A process of differentiation proceeds in a temporal sequence of "from–to." In the process it brings about *differences* among parts of the system which did not previously exist. Furthermore, since these differences are conceived to have emerged by a process of change in a system, which I interpret to mean in some sense within the "framework *of* the system," the presumption is that the differentiated parts are comparable in the sense of being *systematically* related to each other, both because they still belong within the same system and, through their interrelations, to their antecedents.[5]

The term "systematically related" as used above of course needs to be defined. Here my assumption is that *function* is the master concept for analysis of the organization of living systems.[6] As such it is superordinate to both "structure" and "process." That structures and processes should be differentiated along functional lines within the same system implies their *comparability*. If they were in principle incomparable, first the nature of the system could not be rationally understood, and second, it would not be possible to account for its integration as a system. Integration is an

[5] Talcott Parsons, "Pattern-Variables Revisited," *Sociological Theory and Modern Society* (New York: Free Press, 1951, 1967).

[6] Talcott Parsons, "Some Problems of General Theory in Sociology," in John McKinney and Edward Tiryakian (eds.), *Theoretical Sociology and Perspectives and Developments* (New York: Appleton-Century-Crofts, 1970), reprinted as Chapter 10 of this volume.

essential concept for living systems, even though in another sense and at another level a parallelogram of forces may be treated as a system without any assumption of integration, at least as the concept of integration is being used here.

This approach poses the question of comparability in a somewhat unusual way. The more usual way is to seek out "similars" which resemble each other in that they can be subsumed under the same logical "class" but are also significantly variant. From this starting point one could proceed to the building up of a "taxonomic" scheme in terms of the definition of more general classes, and various orders of subclasses, without reference to the question of whether the instances are or are not included in the same system.

If we are to take the "system" approach, rather than that of "similarity and difference," two dimensions become relevant to comparative studies which are not found at the taxonomic level. These are the nature and implications of the belongingness of compared items within the same system and, second, the genetic dimension of relatedness, namely, with respect to differentiation in what respects from what common origin. In this connection it is also essential to recognize the importance of the pluralism of systems. In the organic world the individual organism looms particularly large especially at the higher evolutionary levels. But the main genetic heritage is "carried" at another level, namely, that of the species, which is the primary system of reference for the subscience of genetics and for evolutionary theory. There is a variety of other system references at the organic level, such as that of "ecosystems."

At the human level, organism and personality are especially intimately linked system levels. An older generation of anthropologists tended to set both of these, more especially personality, over against "culture," as the other crucial reference, which is in some ways comparable to the species. Here, however, in a rather special way a fourth system reference, the social, i.e., the system constituted by the interaction of a plurality of organism-personality units within a cultural framework, becomes very central. The is true in a way which does not probably apply directly to subhuman species, even to the famous "social insects." The salient difference, of course, lies in the mediation of human social interaction by cultural level communication, which is unique to the human world, even though it has some antecedents.

At first glance the approach to comparability through common system-belongingness may seem to be a very limited one. This would indeed be the case if we were to accept the extreme "cultural relativity" view, complete with its German "historic'" antecedents, and maintain that meaningfulness of characterization of a structural unit or process could be defined only within *one* very specific system. If human "history" consisted of a population of essentially unique "cultures," as has been alleged, this con-

sideration would indeed virtually eliminate the relevance of "comparative method." But empirically, this simply is not the case; history consists rather, like the system of organic species, of an immensely ramified "inverted branching tree" of forms at many levels of system reference.

What ties the "branches," forms, and levels together into a macrosystem, is in the first instance common genetic origin. This is to say that differences among subsystems have, by and large, arisen through processes of differentiation from what in some sense have been "more primitive" forms. The human socio-cultural universe is by no means so variegated as, at least superficially considered, the organic seems to be, but it is by no means narrowly constricted.

Socio-Cultural Development from a Single Origin

A particularly important point here concerns a dual thesis. The first is that the organic development of man as species must have been essentially coincident with that of what we know as society and culture. The second is that the evidence seems to point to a *single* evolutionary origin of man. If this dual thesis is correct, the problem of comparability can in principle be held within the framework of differentiation and continuing inclusion within the same system. Furthermore, differences can be referred back to those emerging through processes of differentiation from a common origin.

If these two propositions are correct, then Durkheim's search, in forming the plan for his last major work, for the "most primitive" type of society and its religion, was sensible. However difficult it is to define and to find specific empirical evidence of such primitiveness, and however unsatisfactory Durkheim's attempt may appear in the light of both empirical and theoretical evidence which has become available in the sixty years since he wrote, this proposition concerning the importance of primitiveness remains valid. Moreover two major things can be said about such a primitive "society." At the action system level it must be the least differentiated which can be found. Secondly it must comprise all of the essential components of a social system of action, not in "rudimentary" form but in an important sense as "fully evolved." That the organic basis capable of "carrying" a cultural system must be present, goes without saying. We know something about the organic prerequisites involved, notably the capacity to "process information" through a special kind of central nervous system, to "deal with" the physical environment especially through hands and arms, and to form trans-organism solidarities, the latter emerging in the first instance, I suggest, through the potentialities of the erotic components of motivation.

"Culture" must be involved, first of all, through language as a genu-

inely symbolic medium of communication and expression, and also through what Durkheim, in a deliberately undifferentiated sense, called "religion." This latter must include a system of "constitutive symbols," which Durkheim, perhaps in an overly rationalistic way, called "beliefs," and a set of "practices" which above all are "symbolically significant" acts. These latter are generally called "rituals" and are performed for the most part by groups in organized social settings. Religion serves above all, at this level, to give cultural "meaning," both to the "society" and its principal substructures, seen collectively, and to the individual personality and organism as they bear on acting in social relations and in the context of cultural symbolization.

If religion is the primary cultural "glue" which integrates such an action system, it is kinship—a set of relations of social solidarity organized about the two foci of "blood"— which integrates action at the social system level. That these two foci of kinship organization are related to each other in complex ways is attested by the fact, which should be theoretically derivable, of the universal existance of an "incest taboo," i.e., the limitation of sexual unions, especially those legitimized by prospective parenthood, to certain subgroups of the membership of the society. These relations are defined both positively and negatively, i.e., by rules of endogamy and of exogamy.

Finally, society, personality, and organism are related, in ways always also involving culture, by two complexes concerned with human relations to the physical environment. The first of these is primarily economic, concerning man's relation to the environment as the location of resources necessary to meet his needs for food, shelter, clothing, and the like. The other is the organization of social relations with respect to the territorial location of behavior, which concerns place of "residence" but also concerns the territory within which groups may carry out their activities. This territorial focus may also regulate the involvements between society's members and nonmembers. The functional complex referred to as territoriality includes control of the use of physical force. In this and other respects it can be thought of mainly as a "political" complex.

I may now consider the question of what may reasonably be meant by the concept "undifferentiated" in this context. It clearly must be defined relative to system reference and not equated with simplicity in some vaguely general sense. Thus the kinship systems of the Australian aborigines are notoriously complex. Similar things can be said about primitive languages, and the length at which Durkheim found it necessary to discuss Australian totemism could certainly suffice as the basis for an adequate analytical treatise on a major branch of Christianity, which is certainly a more highly differentiated religion.

One major point is that differentiation is not only internal complicatedness, but differentiation *from*. The word "from" then must be defined as

meaning differentiated from other components of what is treated as the same system. Thus even though Australian kinship is highly complex, it is not highly differentiated from structural components with primarily economic, political, reglious, and other functions. This is very unlike kinship in modern societies which in one sense is much "simpler" but in another is much more highly differentiated from other structures with different functions. In a society like the Australian the *whole society* is a single nexus of kinship relations which then constitutes a structure which, in the nature of the case, is to a high degree "functionally diffuse."

If function is, as I suggested above, the master-concept for the analysis of living systems, then the criterion of high vs. low levels of differentiatedness must be differentiation with respect to kinds of functional importance or "contribution" to the functioning of the specific system, or class of systems, of reference. By this criterion, kinship, religion, economic, and political organization are far more highly differentiated from each other in modern than in any less "evolved" type of society.

Modes of Social Differentiation

Two problems open out from here. One concerns the axes on which differentiation may be expected to occur or, conversely, can retrospectively be interpreted. If we work with a very simple basic scheme, in this case one involving only four functions, then the cases that are too complex to fit directly into such a scheme must be dealt with in terms of plural system-references, which is in the nature of the case a difficult enterprise. The second problem concerns the delineation of some scheme of evolutionary stages in the realm of human action systems.

With respect to the first problem, a "landmark" insight occurred which was nearly contemporaneous with the emergence of the four-function paradigm and had much to do with it, namely that of the highly generalized significance of the lines of differentiation of the nuclear family on the axes of generation and sex roles. The nuclear family is, of course, a social grouping which is in a special sense "biologically based" and hence may have special significance for the problem of continuity and articulation between the organic and the action level of living systems. It became evident that these two axes of generation and sex were, on a general theoretical level, essentially the same as those which Bales and his associates had found in the experimental study of small groups, whose members were essentially uniform by sex and age, and were without the "diffuse enduring solidarity" which ideally characterizes families. These two axes constitute what is, in some sense, an hierarchial status-difference: in the familial case

as between the parental and the filial generations, and in the case of the experimental groups, a leadership–followership differentiation. The other axis is that of a differentiation between qualitative "types" of function in the system: in the family case, the sex-role; in that of the experimental groups, the distinction formulated as that between primarily "instrumental" and primarily "expressive" functions.

The first or generational axis, which I would postulate as not characteristic of the most primitive societies, is that on which systems of stratification are built. As I have noted in *Societies,*[7] stratification entails the rupture of the "seamless" nexus of kinship relations, so that the emerging "classes" become exogamous to each other. At both ends, however, the principal kinship units, notably lineages, remain to a high degree functionally diffuse, not only with respect to the "personality-focused" functions of the modern family, but economic, political, and religious functions as well.

However this rupture of the kinship nexus cannot occur without segmentation of the former society into at least two, unless there is a basis of solidarity which is not fused with kinship ties and which crosses the class line. It would, I think, be very generally agreed that such solidarity in the early stages is political and religious. It very generally involves the emergence of "centers" in Shils' sense [8] and frequently the kind of chieftainship which merges into monarchy. Military functions, oriented both toward effectiveness in relation to other societies and toward maintaining order and control within the population and area of the society, are likely to be prominent, just as they are in more complex societies. However, religion, with the development of genuine cults and with them more or less definitely specialized priesthoods, tends also to be very prominent. Any very considerable differentiation of economic institutions tends to come later.

The analytical interpretation of these generally accepted facts raises certain questions. Clearly the second, "horizontal" or "instrumental-expressive," axis is involved. In spite of there being stratification, centralization, and an "elite," there is a pronounced tendency at the very top for the political and religious components to be combined, most strikingly in the institutions of a "God-King," even though lower down political functionaries, like the military and civil "administrators," will be differentiated from predominantly religious personnel, usually called "priesthoods." The principle of the heredity of status through kinship, however, remains very strong for both political and religious groups. Such social mobility as there is operates either through such mechanisms as favoritism—e.g.,

[7] *Societies: Evoluntionary and Comparative Perspectives* (Englewood Cliffs, N.J.: Prentice-Hall, 1966), ch. 2.

[8] Edward Shils, "Centre and Periphery," *The Logic of Personal Knowledge: Essays Presented to Michael Polanyi* (London: Routledge and Kegan Paul, 1961), 117–131.

"adoption" into kinship status, and merging into "patrimonialism"—or through the consequences of political overturns, conquests, and coups.

It seems most reasonable to treat this massive set of phenomena, within the simple four-function paradigm, as the differentiation of the system along one "diagonal," namely that of pattern-maintenance and goal-attainment as distinguished from adaptation and integration. The functional reasons for this asymmetry seem to concern the strains incident to the combination of major new steps toward collective effectiveness—in the "political" context—and at the same time from the problem of maintaining the kind of solidarity which would at least contain centripetal tendencies, especially as between elite and "common people." Here Weber's very fundamental analysis of the *legitimation* of political authority is central. This legitimation must at some level be conceived and institutionalized in religious terms.

It will be evident to many readers that this is the axis which Durkheim classically formulated as that of "mechanical solidarity." He did not, however, I think, sufficiently emphasize its connection, at least in early societal evolution, with the emergence of stratification and the simultaneous functional imperative of promoting collective effectiveness and legitimizing the agencies of that effectiveness in ways which asserted solidarity *across* the lines of stratification.

The suggestion then is that stable differentiation on the more or less "pure" instrumental–expressive axis depends on some kind of prior "solution" of the problem of legitimizing politically oriented stratification and its relation to a cultural base. Here a fundamental point concerns the differentiation of the legitimation of inequalities from that of qualitative functional contributions. There are innumerable concrete contexts in which this problem has arisen, but one which has been perennial right down to the present is that of the roles of the sexes, which as I suggested, seems to be in some sense "prototypical" of this instrumental–expressive axis. In spite of the nearly obvious qualitative basis of the differentiation of role-function, there has been a very persistent tendency at the same time to define it as a superiority–inferiority relationship. In an important sense a new phase of strain over this problem has very recently arisen in modern societies.

Durkheim again suggested a line of analysis which seems to be of central importance here. This is, if I may interpret freely, the development of "organic solidarity" as the essential condition of institutionalizing the *combination* of instrumental–expressive differentiation and equality of status. Put in analytical terms, this means that the egalitarian component must be not only a "value" pattern, but that it must also be rather firmly institutionalized in the integrative sector of the social system if it is to be capable of resisting the pressures toward inequality that stem both from the urges toward collective political effectiveness and from the recognition

of competent achievement. This institutionalization must be reinforced by autonomous control of adequate economic resources.

Only in the broadest sense can an ultra-simple fourfold scheme like that with which I have been working deal with such problems as the delineation of the main structural outline of the earlier phases of socio-cultural evolution. Even if the exceedingly schematic pattern just outlined is in any sense acceptable, there are immense complications and difficulties in dealing with the details of internal structuring of particular societies and the ranges of variation among them, even at what, by analytical judgment, may seem to be "about the same level of differentiation."

Systems of Societies

Perhaps, in view of the limitations of this discussion, I may be permitted to bypass these many complications and "cut through" to a consideration which I think has by and large not received sufficient attention among comparative sociologists. For understandable reasons we have tended to assume the system-reference of a "society" to be the relevant one, and to speak of differentiation, integration, and the other functions in this context. The concept of *a* society, is by no means a simple and obvious one, and I have found myself forced to attempt to clarify and refine it considerably.[9] One of the important outcomes of these attempts has been the emergence of the conception of a *system of societies,* precisely as a social system, with all its cultural, psychological, and environmental concomitants.

Perhaps the most obviously tangible criterion of a society here is that it is a relatively autonomous territorially organized unit, the members of which on the whole display a relative solidarity and sense of identity— i.e., constitute a "social community"—though of course this solidarity need not be exclusive. Relative "autonomy" in these senses, is however, by no means incompatible with, not only interdependence of various sorts with other societies, but also systematic differentiatedness relative to certain of the societies with which the one of reference stands in relations of interdependence. Here a highly important consideration is that there should be evidence that the system of societies had, in the course of its history, undergone a process of differentiation, the main steps of which can be traced. Of course other processes of change are also implied, some of which will be discussed presently.

The small book—the sequel to the one entitled *Societies: Comparative and Evolutionary Perspectives*—with the title *The System of Modern*

[9] Parsons, *Societies,* ch. 2.

Societies,[10] uses the plural form of the word "society" in the title quite deliberately. We can of course meaningfully speak of "modern society" as a type, but I do not think it would be useful for sociologists to speak of the Soviet Union, Britain, France, the Scandinavian countries, and the United States—to name a few of the most important—as constituting *one society.* But if they are many, it does not follow that their differences from each other follow a pattern of random variation, explained in each case by unique "histories."

The broad pattern of analysis which I have followed for modern societies first crystallized for me in reading Marc Bloch's *Feudal Society,* particularly his characterization of differences in the extent and characteristics of "feudalism" in the high Middle Ages among Italy, France, England, and Germany. The variations he outlined seemed definitely to fit into a four-function pattern.[11]

When, however, from these clearly "premodern" background considerations, I came to try to characterize the first main emergence of the modern system, this type of functional classification became even more important as a framework for systematization. It became clear that the first "truly modern" phase should not be placed, as so many have, in the late 18th century signalized by the industrial revolution, but in the 17th. It was also clear that, with respect to the centrally important institutional developments like the legal system, governmental organization, parliamentarism, religion, secular culture, and economic innovation, there was clearly a "lead sector" of the European system in that period, namely, the Northwest Corner" including England, Holland, and France, even though France was quite different in certain respects from the other two.

The same period saw the emergence of Prussia as a major political unit on the Northeastern Corner of the system, as well as a good deal of political and military ferment involving above all Poland and Sweden. Then the "Southern tier," comprising the two "great powers" of Austria and Spain, united for a time under the House of Hapsburg, and a changing post-Renaissance Italy, all on the background of the Counter-Reformation, could be regarded as constituting the more ascriptive, pattern-maintenance and integrative base of the system. For special reasons, which I cannot enter into here, I assigned the goal-attaining role to the Northwest corner, the adaptive role, to the Northeast.[12]

At a much later phase, that of the present century, the same paradigm seemed to be usable again, but in terms of an expanded and northward-moving central system. The "lead sector," I have contended, had become North America, especially of course the United States, and the Northwest

[10] *The System of Modern Societies* (Englewood Cliffs, N.J.: Prentice-Hall, 1971).

[11] Marc Bloch, *Feudal Society,* trans. by L. A. Manyon (Chicago: University of Chicago Press, 1964), 2 vols.

[12] See *The System of Modern Societies,* ch. 4.

frontier role had come to be played by the Soviet Union, while the center of gravity of the pattern-maintenance base had moved clearly to continental Europe north of the Alps, including I thought both France and Germany, with England and the smaller Northern countries assuming primarily the integrative role.

There is a further very essential aspect of this paradigm of a modern system of societies. This is the insight—I think it is more than a "contention"—that the modern type of society has had a *single* evolutionary origin. This is a crucial fact parallel to that of the unitary origin of the human species, and with that, of human culture, society, and personality. The older social evolutionists in one sense held this view, but they were not at all clear about the line between modern and premodern. My own appreciation of it came above all from Max Weber, most succinctly stated in his Introduction to the general series on the Sociology of Religion, the first volume of which he himself prepared for press in the last year of his life.[13]

What I have just said about 17th-century Western society implies that by that time the system was already differentiated to the point of involving at least four distinguishable types of society, with perhaps certain further complications such as the status at about that time of the "city-state belt" rather closely following the Rhine river, and the still somewhat peripheral Northern sector.

As part, then, of the task of comparative systematization, these primary social types acquire, in their differentiatedness from each other and from their place in the system, a certain level of sociological meaningfulness. This, however, can be considerably reinforced by following the problem of comparability and comparison back in the development sequences. In the same third chapter of the *System of Modern Societies* I have attempted to outline what seem to be the most important considerations. My reference to Bloch makes clear that I think a major structural differentiation of what at least were partially subsocieties had already begun by the high Middle Ages. They existed, however, still within the framework of a formally common religious culture, namely Roman Catholic Christianity, and one which at the political level had not yet clearly broken up into "national states," even though the Holy Roman Empire was very loosely organized. The fact that England and France were at best only equivocally incorporated into the Empire was of course one of the starting points for their lead position at the decisive period.

The Reformation period clearly involved the breaking up of what was

---

[13] As early as 1930 I was sufficiently impressed with the importance of this statement to translate it and include it with the essay on the *Protestant Ethic,* though it was not part of that study, having been written more than fifteen years later. It was, however, not many years later that the full significance of social and cultural development in the "west," as he called it, gradually became clear to me.

the previous Mediaeval unity, both through the split in formal religious organization and through the relation of this to national political organization. It is particularly important that the two themes cross-cut each other. Thus England, Holland, and Prussia became Protestant powers, whereas France, after a near-miss of Protestant ascendancy, became a Catholic power, but one which allied itself with Protestant powers against the Hapsburgs and others. Of course the cultural ferment of the Renaissance was very important in the background.

The development of the European system seems to me to have depended heavily on the inheritance of certain elements of common culture and institutions from the ancient world. These were both religious and secular in the usual senses. The Church, however, not only incorporated certain crucial elements of the Jewish religious tradition, and the Christian innovation itself, but certain structural patterns which derived from the Greek polis and from Rome, especially at the legal level. Similarly Roman law was so widely influential that through its incorporation into Canon Law, the broad ideal of a "roman" state never died, and the institutional traditions of the polis survived in the traditions of "municipal" organization, including the Italian and Rhenish "city-states." Clearly, as the recent "Ecumenical" movement makes clear, the Reformation was a process of differentiation *within* Western Christianity, not the introduction of a "foreign" element into it, nor a total "segmentation" of the religious sysem.

These combined cultural and institutional commonalities, however, were clearly, in the European case, related to an underlying "variegatedness" of subsocieties and cultures, varying most broadly on a regional basis. This was substantially less variegated than the Roman empire, but of the same general character. The crucial early "segmentation" was the split between the Eastern and Western territories, reflected above all in the usage of the Greek as distinguished from the Latin language, and the "orthodox" as distinguished from the "Catholic" church. Only in the later modern phase did the question of the inclusion of the "East" in this sense arise seriously again, focusing of course on Russia, since the "Middle East" was for long Islamic, then socio-politically quite chaotic.

This regional difference then had to do with such factors as, first, the old locus of culture and political authority (Italy) and the movement of the center of gravity of both economic and political interests north of the Alps—starting with the definition of the Holy Roman Empire as the "German Nation." Then the difference between the currently opening sea frontier, ranging from the Iberian Peninsula to Scandinavia, as distinguished from the land frontiers, of which Austria and Prussia were the prototypical guardians, became another major focus of differentiation. The integrative role of France was very directly associated with its location at the intersection of the processes of religious and political differentiation.

It is my view that these foci of variation have come gradually to be

built into the structure of the modern system. The fact that these foci represent a very broad pattern of internal functional differentiation may be taken as one of the principal conditions of the development of the modern system. This broader, more variegated set of components is a condition that the Roman Empire even at its height could not, I think, have satisfied. That it was satisfied in later times set the stage for a process which I should treat as being probably as important as that of differentiation, namely, what I have been calling *inclusion.*

The Process of Inclusion

I think of inclusion as the process by which structural components which have been either peripheral to a social system, or on its boundaries but "outside," are brought into a status of fuller integration *in* the system and hence *with* its other components. This integration can be defined either with respect to the dimension of stratification, i.e., in some sense the hierarchical dimension, or that of qualitative functional differentiation, or of course some "diagonal" combination of the two. Inclusion may also refer to continuing retention in the system of elements which have become separated from others by segmentation or differentiation, as distinguished from their "extrusion."

The process of inclusion stands in a kind of "dialectical" relation to that of differentiation. Thus, in the temporal perspective I am emphasizing, the line along which inclusion processes have taken place in a previous time period may become, at a later stage, an axis of differentiation. Thus perhaps the most massive inclusion process underlying the European system of modern societies was that of the "Germanic" world which was sufficiently broad to comprise not only "Germany" but the Anglo-Saxon and Scandinavian complex, i.e., in a very broad sense those peoples speaking languages not of Latin derivation, nor of Slavic, nor the residual Celtic, or Finnish, or Hungarian enclaves.

In the Roman imperial period, the Roman "colonization" of these areas that did take place consisted mainly of establishing frontier outposts, such as the line along the Rhine, and Vindobonum near Vienna. Britain was far more fully "colonized" than other areas, and there is a highly significant relation between its early Roman occupation and the "conquest" by the Normans nearly a millennium later. Hence, there is a sense in which it can be said that France—"Gaul"—was predominantly "Latin" with a non-Latin substratum, and that Britain was predominantly "Germanic" with a Latin substratum. This balance seems to me clearly to relate to their capacities to assume "lead" functions in the modern system.

However, when the basic processes of differentiation that destroyed

the "Mediaeval" system crystallized, the great religious division broadly followed the earlier ethnic–regional lines. The Reformation was clearly a predominantly "Germanic" movement, whereas the Catholic Church, especially in the Counter-Reformation, was predominantly Latin. Indeed, as I have suggested, this differentiation goes back to the Middle Ages, in that the Church at that time was mainly Latin in orientation, while the Empire was of the "German Nation." With the migration of political power and economic development north of the Alps, a "material" underpinning of the Reformation was clearly present.

These lines of differentiation are still important in the political party alignments of European countries.[14] This ethnic–regional inclusion process was predominantly "lateral" in terms of our main functional paradigm, and helps to explain the nature of East–West differentiation within the modern system. Since a major development of the early modern period was also that of territorially independent political units, the process of inclusion on the vertical or stratification axis was not so visible as a phenomenon of the system as a whole. That the main structure of European society inherited a "class" axis of differentiation goes almost without saying. As Bloch noted, the crucial phenomenon was the institution of aristocracy, which became the main focus of European "feudalism" even in the sense in which Marx, rather vaguely, formulated its characteristics.

It can then be said that the "core" of the emerging modern system consisted in the combination of "church and state" but with the church focused in the *first* instance on the religious orders, and the "state" on the aristocracies, with monarchs in the position above all of *primus inter pares*—after all the heads of aristocratic lineages were very generally called "peers," not only of each other but of royalty itself. From this reference point on, we can speak on a grand scale process of inclusion of the "common people" into statuses of "full" membership in their respective societies. There have been a number of aspects of this process, too complex to follow here. However, let me mention that, in English development, the concept "common" emerged at two particularly strategic points.

The first of these is in the conception of the *Common Law*, which was, as distinguished from "manorial" law, common to the whole realm, but also defined the rights of "Englishmen" whether they were aristocrats or not, i.e., it was law for "commoners." This development was clearly one in the direction of institutionalization of a "societal community" which was not confined to aristocrats. The second development was the conception of the British Parliament as consisting of two "houses," a House of Lords (Peers), and very significantly, a *House of Commons*. It is of course true that in the early periods most of the members of the latter

[14] Seymour Lipset and Stein Rokkan, "Cleavage Structures, Party Systems and Voter Alignments: An Introduction," *in* Lipset and Rokkan (eds.), *Party Systems and Voter Alignments* (New York: Free Press, 1967).

House were members of the "gentry" rather than of the "common people" in the more radical democratic sense, but its composition was open-ended in the downward direction of the social status scale, and it was capable of evolving into a legislative assembly representative of the "people" as a whole.

In a more dramatic way the "democratic revolution" came to focus in France with an abrupt shift from a monarchical-aristocratic regime to one which represented the "people" as *citizens—Citoyen* was the central symbol of the French Revolution. In those aspects of the process of inclusion which have come to be called the "democratic revolution," England and France performed one of their most important "lead" functions in the earlier phases of the modern system of societies, England, significantly, coming first since the two basic developments just noted occurred preeminently in the 17th century.

Two other modes of inclusion, which have figured prominently in the modern development, but also elsewhere, should be briefly discussed. The first is the process of reintegration that occurs after a process of differentiation which, in the nature of the case, generates such high tensions that the system seems to be undergoing destruction. The Reformation was such a development and seemed to many for a long time to have created two quite independent "civilizations" that, among other things, engaged in bitterly destructive wars with each other. Even the truce under the formula *cuius regio, eius religio,* seemed to confirm this. As early as the 17th century, however, England and Holland introduced limited *internal* religious toleration. A major step was taken with the separation of church and state—as distinguished from their differentiation—in the American Constitution. From negative toleration of the right of religious dissent, then, there has been a gradual process in the direction of what today is usually called "ecumenicism": the positive inclusion of plural religious groups in a single "moral community" (in Durkheim's sense) which comprises the societal communities of most of the societies which are members of the modern system.[15] This inclusion has led widely to a process of differentiation whereby "church" religion has become differentiated from what Robert Bellah,[16] in his very illuminating conception, calls "civil" religion. The latter can, of course, be shared by members of plural denominational groups.

The second type of inclusion process has been intimately associated with the reintegration just discussed, but is in certain respects different. In the case of the inclusion of the "Germanic" world discussed above, whole societies were "brought into" the European system by processes which

---

[15] A qualification must be made for the societies under the control of Communist parties which, with varying degrees of rigor, recognize the moral legitimacy only of the "political religion" of Marxism–Leninism.

[16] "Civil Religion in America," *Daedalus* (Winter 1967), 1–22.

comprised both military conquest and political consolidation, as well as religious proselytization. The case in which this has occurred on the largest scale is the United States, wherein mostly unorganized population elements with differing religious and ethnic heritage have immigrated into a host society. Then, provided they are not to be temporary visitors, the question naturally arises as to what their status and that of their descendants is to be in the host society.

In the American case it seems to be clear that there has been an important interactive process involved. Though most immigrants, starting with Negro slaves, have entered the society in relatively low status positions, the presence of very large immigrant groups and the fact of the society's relative openness to social mobility have encouraged a general trend to pluralization of the social structure. Religious ecumenicism is one of the main outcomes; indeed it is at least probable that the American example has accelerated this process for Western society as a whole. There has also been ethnic pluralism which is related to religious ecumenicism in complex ways. Thus the predominant elements in the U.S. Roman Catholic religion are highly diverse ethnically, and these groups, e.g., of Irish, Italian, Polish, French-Canadian, Latin American origin, have been juxtaposed with each other in a way quite different from the European situation involving the same ethnic groups. The "pull" of this ethnic ecumenicism has at last begun powerfully to put pressure for the enhanced inclusion of the Negro minority.

Such pressures toward pluralistic inclusion could not, however, have operated as effectively as they have, had the more general social structure not, in certain respects, favored such inclusion. Not only did the United States have a very liberal immigration policy in the decisive period, but it did not exert the strongest conceivable pressure toward full "assimilation"—though many have asserted ideologically that it did. Not only was there relative religious freedom, but also freedom for private educational programs and other organizational initiatives based on ethnic lines.[17] However this may be, the American societal community which has emerged is, though uniformly English-speaking, no longer a WASP (white, Anglo-Saxon, Protestant) community, but an ethnically and religiously pluralistic community, however important the remaining "discriminations," notably by race, may be.

Dealing with certain phases of the problem of analyzing the processes of inclusion has led us to shift attention from the level of the system of societies to that of the internal processes of particular societies. Before taking up the important question of the more general relation between the

[17] It is interesting to note that the policy of requiring almost all Catholic parochial schools to use the English language was not enforced by government, but by the Church itself, which was dominated in *its* government by English-speaking Irish bishops.

two levels, however, it is well to discuss briefly the other two categories of the paradigm of a phase of progressive developmental social change with which I have been working in recent years, namely what I call "adaptive upgrading" and "value-generalization."

Adaptive Upgrading in Relation to Integration

By adaptive upgrading, I mean enhancement of the capacity of an action system—in this case a social system—to maintain and generate resources which can serve to improve the system's level of adaptation to the environments in which it is situated. Relative to the attainment of system-*goals* the adaptive function is generalized; it involves resources which are relevant to the attainment of plural and alternative goals. At the social system level economic resources are prototypical in this sense, as fluidly available through the use of money and the market mechanism.

In the above characterization of the adaptive function I have deliberately used the word environment in the plural. The common sense of social science is still deeply imbued with the conception that there is one environment and it is "obviously" the physical environment. As human beings, however, we are very much involved in interaction, not only with the physcial world in the narrower sense, but with the nonhuman part of the organic world. At the action level, then, the *social system* must treat human behavioral organisms, including those of its own members, as environmental objects. The same kind of reasoning leads us to treat the personalities of individuals, including societal members, as environmental to the social system, and finally also the cultural systems with which it is involved. Of course a social system must also include other social systems in the environmental category of the society, especially other societies.

Certain imperatives of the human relation to the physical and nonhuman organic environments have clearly given a certain premium to the economic aspects of adaptation, which has a special relation to these environments. However, the prominence, on occasion, of the health complex should warn us that the adaptive function in relation to our own organisms is far from negligible, and the prominence of education has emphasized even more the importance of personalities. Such considerations suggest that the very special prominence of economic considerations which has characterized the period of the industrial revolution, extending in some respects into our own time, is a function of a special combination of circumstances rather than of a universally "inherent" relation between man and his physical-organic environment. Such a point of view relativizes the "economic interpretation of history" in a double sense: First, it challenges the generalized predominance of "economic factors" in the determination

of human action and, second, it suggests that such predominance as economic factors have varies as a function of a complex constellation of circumstances, many of which are predominantly noneconomic in character.

Indeed I suggest that Western society has been to a high degree adaptively oriented. This means above all two things. First, it has been oriented toward the management of its relations to its environments, i.e., their "control," if this concept is properly understood. One aspect of this is the concern for active adaptation as distinguished from passive adjustment, the latter being that which was very prominent in the earlier discussions of organic evolution. Secondly, however, as between the two basic functions involving stress on orientation to the external, environmental world, priority has tended to run in favor of the adaptive as distinguished from the system-goal attainment complex—of A over G in our functional shorthand. Thus my suggestion has been that the "lead" has been taken by the relatively "decentralized" societies—England and Holland at one period, North America on the other—rather than the highly centralized, hierarchical ones, e.g., Prussia and the Soviet Union.

Within this framework there has been not one but a series of environmental foci of adaptive processes, with corresponding variations in the structures and processes of the internal system. The process which is here called "upgrading" includes a trend toward the salience of environments progressively higher in the cybernetic scale. It is apparent, however, that this trend has not been fully uniform because it has been intertwined with nonadaptive functional exigencies, notably the integrative.

Within the cultural framework of which Roman Catholicism and the recently differentiated Protestantism were the main features, the first major adaptive process which belongs to the complex of modern societies seems to have been "political" in a special sense, namely the emergence of the territorial states from the matrix of the Empire. This placed a heavy adaptive-goal attainment stress on foreign affairs which has in certain respects persisted ever since, though just what the continuities and changes have been raise complex questions.

It seems that this political focus brought the functional problems of societies sufficiently "down to earth" so that, at a societal rather than only a local level, a much more differentiated concern with strictly *economic* exigencies could develop. This development, again very broadly, may be said to have occurred in the two main stages of the "commercial revolution" which was part of the efflorescence of the 17th century and came to be centered in the Northwest corner after initial developments during the Renaissance in Italy and the Rhineland. The great "issue" at this stage was that of "mercantilism," namely the role of government in the control of economic interests and processes.

These adaptive processes soon came to be balanced by somewhat corresponding ones in the integrative sector. The developing symbolization of

statehood, including palaces, the trappings of courts and the like, certainly belong in this category. But probably the most important process in the early modern era was the development of legal systems, mainly a modernized Roman law on the Continent of Europe, but a more distinctive system in the English Common Law which, however, developed continuously from Roman Law origins. These developments laid the foundations of what T. H. Marshall called the "civil" component of the modern institution of citizenship which he particularly exemplified by the "rights of Englishmen." [18]

The second main stage of economic upgrading was the "industrial revolution," gathering force in the later 18th century and penetrating much more deeply into the social structure, especially through the enormous spread of what we now call "occupational" roles and the organizations in which they function.

I think that what is ordinarily called the "democratic revolution" should be considered to be in the first instance a new set of repercussions centering in the integrative sectors of modern societies, following the immense changes in the relations of these societies both to the other societies that impinged on them and to their physical-organic environments. The latter relational changes took place primarily through technological and economic mechanisms. The relation of the "democratic revolution" to the process of inclusion as discussed above is nearly obvious. Characteristically the English version involved a rather gradual movement of the inclusion process downward in the social scale from the aristocracy— T. H. Marshall's account of the British growth of the citizenship complex admirably exemplifies this.[19] By contrast the French development was much more oriented to foreign relations and hence "patriotism"—thus the *Marseillaise* remains to this day as the symbolic song both of the Revolution and of French nationalism. This is not true in the same sense of "God Save the King."

The democratic and the industrial revolutions, taken together, raised acute problems about the integration of modern societies, the first centering almost directly on the question of what constituted a "member" of such a society, i.e., a citizen; the second centering more directly around the question as to what the allocation of *human* resources to economic production meant for the other aspects of the status of the "labor force." These two functional problem complexes clearly dominated societal "concern" through most of the 19th century and into the present one.

Another integrative thrust, connected especially to the adaptive developments of the industrial revolution and surely importantly related to political democracy, is that which Marshall has called the development of

[18] *Class, Citizenship and Social Development* (New York: Doubleday Anchor, 1965), esp. ch. 4.

[19] *Ibid.*, esp. ch. 4.

the "social" component of citizenship, eventuating in what is often called the "welfare state." [20] This is essentially the public guarantee of minimum standards of access to the conditions of "welfare" for the whole population of a modern society, especially protected against destitution through unemployment and through the social and organic disabilities of old age. However, access to health services and to educational opportunity, which will be discussed presently, have also figured prominently.

These integrative strains operating in modern societies clearly have had something to do with the emergence of three new adaptive concerns relative to three of the social system's environments. These are respectively the "human-organic," the cultural, and the psychological or the level of the personality.

It is surely significant that the second half of the 19th century saw an altogether new level of concern with problems of health, mostly at the level of the organism. This of course was bound up with the new potentialities which grew out of the extension of the science and technology, which had "worked" in relation to the physical environment, to the emergence of the "life sciences" and with them new technologies for dealing with the somatic problems of health. The most sensational development in this connection was Pasteur's discovery of the role of bacterial infection and the opening up of major possibilities of its control.

The Educational Revolution

By this time, however, the "educational revolution" was well under way. This can be considered to be a dual process. One side of it, taking root a little before mid-century, was the process of universalization of formal education, beginning with simple literacy and gradually moving up the educational ladder. It is of course well known that early in this century in most of the modern societal world, elementary education had been nearly completely universalized. Russia of course lagged but has caught up rapidly. In the middle third of the present century, especially in the United States, a relatively analogous pattern in the universalization of secondary education has gone far, and starting near the middle of the century we have seen the beginning of mass higher education which seems to point in the direction of universalization.

It does not seem necessary to elaborate further on this much-discussed development. From the present, formally analytic point of view, it may be interpreted to be a highly active process of adaptation between the social system and the personalities of individuals; in that sense it is part of the

[20] *Ibid.*, esp. ch. 4.

"socialization" process about which much has been said in recent years. It is thus by no means simply a process of "adaptation to" personalities on the part of social systems, but first, of modification of them in directions of functional significance to the social system of reference. This involves a process analogous to the "mastery" of the physical environment by technology and the "conquest" of disease by modern medicine and public health measures at the somatic level.

There is, however, another and subtler aspect of the process, and one in which the concept of "mental illness" provides a better model than does that of somatic illness as indicated in the classical meaning of "scientific medicine." Indeed the mental illness case is actually intermediate. This has to do with the fact that the process of modification of personalities involves the *interpenetration* of social and personality systems through the "internalization" of the normative structures and symbols of culture and of "social objects," both collective and individual. Of the many complex consequences of such a development, a particularly salient one concerns the undermining of many of the traditionalistic and ascriptive components of social status and "security" in such statuses. These processes occasion still another complex of integrative problems, about which something will be said presently.

Before entering into that, however, I want to emphasize that the educational revolution, if I may call it that, has not been an isolated phenomenon but has developed, especially at the levels of higher education, in very close relation to a "cultural revolution" which has centered in the area of *cognitive rationality,* namely, the growth and other forms of development of philosophy and science. It seems to be significant that the two great phases of the development of the system of modern societies, the 17th century and the 19th to 20th, have been integrally connected with major developments in both philosophy and science, perhaps particularly the latter. In the case of the second of these main phases there have been, of course, major new developments in the area of physical science, but also for the first time a high peak of development of the biological sciences with their medical and other applications, and a not yet so impressive, but still far from negligible development of the action, behavioral, or social sciences as they are variously called.

In a sense including empirical validation, theoretical sophistication, and differentiatedness, we can speak of a modern system of the *intellectual disciplines* which, however impressive its antecedents may have been, is a *new* phenomenon of the cultural world. This of course has become basically "international" and is not bound to any particular national unit of the system of societies, nor is it bound to any particular "ideological" position.

Elementary, and for the most part secondary, education should still utilize essentially the received cultural bases. There was a process of

societal adaptation going on in that these "given" cultural factors came to play a new role in the personal orientations and societal concerns of modern societies. At the level of higher education, however, the educational process as such came to be involved most intimately with major processes of cultural innovation, especially those usually categorized under the rubric of "research.'

We might, in a certain sense, suggest that these circumstances established a special kind of society–environment relationship. It is generally true that, from both the perspective of the social system and that of the personality, the cultural environment is a "man-made" environment, and becomes problematical to the degree that those aspects which center on the intellectual disciplines constitute a "special" kind of societal–environment relationship. Thus under the heading of "charisma" there has been much discussion of the process of change at both the levels of constitutive symbolism and moral-evaluative symbolization.[21] Here perhaps Weber's comparative studies in the sociology of religion constitute the prototype analytical statement of the problem. Weber's "exemplary prophet" seems to typify the creator of new constitutive symbolism; his "ethical prophet," that of new moral imperatives. Distinct in important ways from both of these have been the concentration on what I have called "expressive symbolization" which in its most differentiated form concentrates in what we know as the "arts." It is perhaps significant that the term "creative"— which in our religious history was a special prerogative of the divinity— has settled more on the artist than any other order of cultural specialist, even the religious. Certainly there is far more resistance to characterizing a scientist as "creative" than an artist. The fact that the scientist is bound by obligations of fidelity to the "constraints" of environmental considerations—sometimes called "the facts"—while the artist is permitted to be much more freely "imaginative," may have something to do with this intriguing linguistic usage.

However this may be, what I count to be the fourth main category of content of the cultural system, namely that centering on "empirical cognition" and its products, has come to occupy a special place in both the cultural environment and the cultural constitution of modern societies. The sense in which this place is special may in the first instance be looked at in terms of the pattern of cultural differentiation. The most important single step in this differentiation has been the "secularization" of various branches of culture, among which the intellectual disciplines loom very large.

In the first instance it may be noted that empirical cognition is the adaptive subsystem of cultural functioning and that for this reason it can be expected to play a special part in processes of adaptive upgrading.

[21] Talcott Parsons, "Culture and the Social System: Introduction," in Parsons and others (eds.), *Theories of Society* (New York: Free Press, 1961), 963–997.

Furthermore its focal position in the system of formal education generally suggests that there has been a kind of "spiral" of development from the commercial and industrial revolutions (the "counterpoint" in the integrative context being the democratic revolution and the rise of nationalism) to a new predominantly adaptive phase, in which a new level of empirical knowledge and its utilization by a highly educated population has assumed a central place.

For this reason the strong stress on adaptive function in the value systems of modern societies is clearly significant—and I have called this primary value pattern, with special reference to the American case, "instrumental activism." The combination of the development of science and of higher education has given rise to an immense new proliferation of technologies, very conspicuously in the physical-engineering fields, but also in fields of applied biological science and partially of behavioral science. It has also given rise to an immense increase in the numbers and the relative importance of the professions in the occupational structure, including of course the "academic" profession.

This complex within the professions has come to embody, although with structural variations in the different societies, the dual functions of teaching at levels of higher education and of "research" or institutionalized provision for the continuing advancement of knowledge. Even where a large proportion of relatively "basic" research is done in specialized institutes, this development has elevated the institutions of higher education, especially the universities, to an especially salient position in the most recent phase of the development of modern societies. This is perhaps particularly true of the United States where, on the one hand, the research and the teaching functions tend to be combined in the same groups and where, on the other hand, mass higher education has extended furthest.

The impact of the educational revolution has of course been spreading through sectors of the society other than the primary centers of innovations involved in it, as happened also with the industrial and democratic revolutions. The contributions of recent technology to the standard of living are clear as well as more recently in the context of the salience of the problem of environmental pollution. The growth in importance of the professions has also brought about a major change in the nature of instrumentally oriented collectivities, notably in industry and government, in such a way as to make obsolete, in important respects, not only Marx's picture of the "capitalistic" firm, but also Weber's of bureaucratic organization and its predominance in both business and government. Related to this of course is the general upgrading of the labor force, very conspicuously by the elimination of very large numbers of unskilled tasks through mechanization and automation.

Two further sets of repercussions, however, are of special interest here. The first concerns the relation of the educational revolution to the inte-

grative function, while the second set of repercussions will serve as a transition to a brief discussion of the fourth of the central processes of structural change which I have been reviewing here, namely, value *generalization.*

Both the industrial and the democratic revolutions occasioned major social disturbances. The events in France in the Revolutionary period, from 1789 at least to the ascendancy of Napoleon, as well as those that occurred in many other counties for several decades are familiar.[22] In the case of the industrial revolution, various kinds of "labor" disturbances took place, the most important developing toward the middle of the 19th century.[23] These included not only "protests" and movements toward unionization, but also the political labor movements, including the socialist parties.

The reasoning and evidence which connect these two sets of disturbances with the democratic and industrial revolutions respectively would lead one to expect that the educational revolution, if its consequences are as important as we have suggested, should also be the storm center of comparably severe social disturbances which are mainly generated by it and, though linking up with other sources of strain in the society, center more in it than at any other point. These disturbances should also have a special relation to problems concerning integrative functions because of the specially important dynamic relations between adaptive and integrative processes.

Clearly the most likely parallel phenomenon is student disturbance. There are two especially interesting features of this parallel. In the educational system, students clearly constitute, relatively speaking, a low-status group, as compared to members of faculties and adminstrative officers. In this respect they have had positions in some ways analogous to those of commoners by contrast with aristocrats, and of workers by contrast with owners and managers. Secondly, however, it has become increasingly and widely recognized that the spearhead of such protest or radical movements has not come from the most disadvantaged groups. Thus in the democratic revolution it has been the "bourgeoisie" rather than the lower class which has been in the forefront. Even the Parisian "sansculottes" were predominantly what we would call "lower-middle-class" people rather than the "poor." Similarly in the labor movement it has been the relatively skilled workers that have led rather than the mass of the unskilled laborers. Two considerations then apply to the student disturbances. First, it is college and university students who are the focus of disturbances, not those in secondary schools, to say nothing of primary schools. Second, it is students

[22] R. R. Palmer, *The Age of Democratic Revolutions* (Princeton: Princeton University Press, 1959).

[23] Neil J. Smelser, *Social Change in the Industrial Revolution* (Chicago: University of Chicago Press, 1959).

in the institutions of higher standing rather than the more disadvantaged sectors of the system of higher education, who have been most disturbed.

There is, however, one particularly salient difference. While the "bourgeoisie," including the sansculottes, and the "proletariat" could be categorized as "classes," this designation is not appropriate for students, for the simple reason that, increasingly with the spread of mass higher education, they constitute a category of the stage-of-life course rather than one of ascription to lifelong status. Clearly, there is a complex of "mobility problems" for students, both with respect to access to higher education at various levels, and with respect to prospects following the educational process,[24] but in its primary "meaning" student status is not one of presumptively permanent inferiority. As a major focus of structurally conditioned disaffection, hence, it may be regarded as essentially a new phenomenon in the developmental pattern of modern societies.

Erikson has made a particularly illuminating suggestion [25] about the symbolic meaning of student status. For the democratic revolution, the focal context of evil was subjection to arbitrary "authority," notably that of monarchical regimes which denied the legitimacy of citizen participation.[26] Secondarily, the focus was "privilege" with special reference to the status of aristocracies. In Marxism, and the socialist movement more generally, it was "exploitation," usually defined primarily in an economic sense but including the conception that economic advantage was reinforced by political power.

Erikson's suggestion is that the current focus is neither of these, but "dependency." Thus he says that the common theme which links dissident students with the groups which they seek as allies in the United States— notably the "blacks," the "poor," women, and the "third world" as putative victims of "colonialism"—is their perception of common dependency on presumptively illegitimate organs of control.

I suggest that the following are the main structural background developments underlying these three dominant themes. The authority theme mainly concerned the process of differentiation between the polity and the societal community. The focal concern was that persons and groups exercising authority, hence, using power, ostensibly in a collective interest, should be accountable to the membership of the societal community as a constituency—eventually on a "fully democratic" basis, though this took a long time to develop.[27] The theme of "exploitation," in turn, has con-

---

[24] Christopher Jencks and David Riesman, *The Academic Revolution* (Garden City: Doubleday, 1968).

[25] Erik H. Erikson, "Reflections on the Dissent of Contemporary Youth," *Daedalus* (Winter 1970): 154–177.

[26] Fred Weinstein and Gerald Platt, *The Wish to be Free* (Berkeley and Los Angeles: University of California Press, 1969).

[27] Stein Rokkan, "Mass Suffrage, Secret Voting and Political Participation," *European Journal of Sociology,* 2 (1961): 132–152.

cerned primarily the differentiation of economy from polity. Of course, there have been important complications connected with this process. In the earlier phase, that of the "commercial revolution," the "business" community felt constrained by the power of government. The classical statement of this feeling is perhaps Adam Smith's famous attack on mercantilism. In the later phase, the "workers" felt constrained by the economic and, I think, in a more analytical sense, by primarily the political power of the "capitalists."

In the current rhetoric, focusing around student disaffection, these themes of attack on allegedly illegitimate authority, exploitation, and combined power, continue to reverberate. At the same time I think that Erikson is correct that there is a new and different note sounded by the dependency theme. This concerns the process of differentiation in the first instance between the personality of the individual and the social system. By contrast with the authority context, students feel not so much "dominated" as "constrained," and by contrast with that of economic class, not so much "exploited" as "alienated."

Put in formal terms, this "disturbance" constitutes a new point on a "spiral" of societal community development which is parallel to that which shifted emphasis from the economic function to that of empirical cognition on the adaptive side. It constitutes a shift of focus from the level of the social system alone to that of the general system of action. Here the crucial medium is not authority-power, but the relation between the performance capacity and *affect,* i.e., the individual's attachment (cathexis and identification) in the social systems in which he participates. The primary trend, looking toward resolution of these severe conflicts, I should expect to lie in the direction of the conception of "institutionalized individualism" which leads to enhancement of the autonomy of the personality, but in the context of certain types of institutionalized structure. In relation to these problems, Durkheim has been the preeminent theoretical forerunner.

The knowledge side of the educational revolution derived from cultural developments, in the first instance in interaction with the social system in the areas of the social organization of education itself and of research. The developments of which we have just been speaking, on the other hand, derive mainly from developments in the system of personalities, in interplay with social system agencies of socialization, in the earlier phases primarily the family of orientation, but then with the system of formal education, and its closely associated peer group cultures, playing a prominent part.

However, we feel that the phase which has just been outlined is new in that a special set of processes, having to do with socialization as well as predominantly cognitive learning processes, have developed at the level of *higher* education. It has been customary for sociologists and person-

ality psychologists to terminate the main process of socialization with the transition from adolescence. We feel, however,[28] that mass higher education and attendant structural changes have brought about a new process centering about the status we call "studentry." This has very much to do with socialization for universalistically evaluated achievements, of which performance of the professional type of function is prototypical, but also for responsible membership and leadership roles, especially in associational types of collectivity, which includes the acceptance of authority both on the "receiving" end and in psychological capacity to exercise leadership and authority.

The Process of Value-Generalization

For a very long time I have treated institutionalized value-patterns as a primary, indeed in one special respect the most important single structural component of social systems. What is often called the "content" aspect of a value system would concern the balance among the broadest type of orientation alternatives, such as between instrumental and consummatory emphases and between religious and secular emphases. In these respects the broadest evidence seems to indicate that the most firmly institutionalized value systems have considerable stability transcending the shorter-run change in the structure of particular societies—meaning time periods up to several centuries. Thus I should argue that the system of modern societies has had a broadly stable pattern of value-orientation, which derives in the main from the "marriage" of Israelitic and Greek components in the Christian movement, notably as this became institutionalized in "Western" society.[29]

The dimension of concern here, however, is a different one. It in-involves the primary point of articulation between the differentiatedness of a social system and its values. The basic proposition is this: The more differentiated the system, the higher the level of generality at which the value-pattern must be "couched" if it is to legitimate the more specified values of *all* of the differentiated parts of the social system. Thus in the background of modern societies the differentiation of church and state, whereby the "state" or secular society acquired religious legitimation, was fundamental, as was the Reformation and later, in the early modern period, the first phases of "secularization."[30]

[28] Talcott Parsons and Gerald Platt, "Higher Education, Changing Socialization, and Contemporary Student Dissent," *A Sociology of Age Stratification,* Vol. 3 of *Aging and Society* (New York: Russell Sage Foundation, 1972).

[29] Parsons, *The System of Modern Societies,* 1970.

[30] Parsons, "Conference on the Culture of Unbelief: Commentary," in R. Caporale and A. Grumelli, eds., *The Culture of Unbelief* (Berkeley and Los Angeles: University of California Press, 1971).

Perhaps the crucial point here is the institutionalization, in Durkheim's sense, of a "moral community" which both cuts across "denominational" lines—in the more narrowly religious sense—and those of ethnic culture, but also includes legitimation of structures which are both "sacred" and "profane." Here I use "cutting across" to mean the inclusion, *under* a single legitimizing value-pattern, of components which are not only diverse and differentiated from each other, but many of which have, historically, claimed some sort of an "absolutistic" monopoly of moral legitimacy. Thus clearly at one stage only "good Catholics" could be full citizens of many Western societies; at the height of nationalism, e.g., only "good Frenchmen," understood in an ethnic-cultural sense, could be full citizens; or, more recently, only "good members of the working class," with a presumptive eligibility for membership in the Communist Party, could be full citizens. In this context value-generalization is of course intimately associated with the structural "pluralization" of modern societies. A major component of what Karl Mannheim called "utopias" may be considered to mark steps in value-generalization, such as the liberal-democratic and the socialist-communist utopias.[31]

What, then, can we say about the *process* of value-generalization? First it must be conceived as involving the zone of interpenetration between cultural and social systems—as well, especially, as personalities—in such a way that a significant change in the social structure must at the same time comprise cultural change. The stimulus for such change can come from a wide variety of sources, most of which can be categorized under the heading of "strain" in the social system, including for example the strain over the problem of "usury" in the period of the commercial revolution [32] and the strain over the problem of clerical celibacy in the Catholic church at present.

To state a framework within which further clarification can be sought, three primary stages of specification of value-institutionalization can be stated. The first is what may be said to precede secularization of any serious sort, namely where values are directly ascribed to specific religious commitments or orientations. This is the familiar case of either a predominantly "traditional" situation or one dominanted by an established religion where subscription to its tenets at all levels provide the criteria of moral acceptability as a member of the society. In the modern societal systems this position was under severe attack in the early phase and had already begun to give way.

The second stage is the one outlined above where "denominational pluralism" has become more or less fully established and religious partic-

---

[31] Karl Mannheim, *Ideology and Utopia*, tr. by Louis Wirth and Edward Shils (New York: Harcourt, Brace, and World, 1936).

[32] Benjamin Nelson, *The Idea of Usury*, 2d ed. (Chicago: University of Chicago Press, 1969).

ularism is transcended by a "moral" unity by virtue of which the society becomes a "moral community," in Durkheim's sense, and which is also characterized by an "ecumenical" civil religion. The third stage or level concerns transcending this primacy of societal commitment in favor of a new kind of "moral autonomy" of the societal unit—in the "last analysis" the individual person, but within a framework of the sort referred to above as "institutionalized individualism." Here both of the other levels "survive" in the total pattern of value-orientation, and above all imply the second level as the term institutionalization has just been used. There is, however, a new element in that the individual or other unit comes to be "free" within ascertainable limits, to define his own value-commitments, independently either of a received religious base or of the imperatives of societal moral authority.

What I have called the second level comprises the main pattern of differentiated societal functions—such as economic production, contribution to political effectiveness, or even to societal solidarity—but goes beyond this to sanction spheres of autonomy and intiative whether or not they "contribute" in the above sense. The familiar strictures on mutual compatibility of the modes of exercise of such autonomy of course apply, i.e., remaining within the limits both of compatibility with the interests of the societal system and not too greatly injuring the interests of other units of the system.

It is my view that a principal source of the turmoil in which modern societies are involved in their current phase has to do with the initiation and spread of this extension of legitimate value-commitments to a new level of generality and hence inclusive tolerance of variation. If the "absolutizing" of the societal moral community, which I take to be characteristic of the Communist societies, is no longer legitimate, the question becomes urgent of the basis of which a viable mode and level of societal community solidarity can work out. The current mood seems to be one of loudly asserting claims to freedom *from* societal obligations, but these assertions, for which there are many historical precedents, will not just make the problem "go away." Perhaps the problem of violence, when and how it is justified, how it shall be controlled, is in course of becoming the focal center of the *value* problems involved in this transition.

Any such threefold classification of levels must of course, on a more general theoretical basis, be considered to be relative. Thus one could, I think, fairly argue that within small limits the third level was briefly attained in the male citizen body of the more advanced Greek *poleis* in their culminating period—only very marginally for a few women. The conditions of consolidating this institutionalization, however, were not present, to say nothing of its immediate extension, though some of the best features of Roman Imperial society may be said to have constituted a partial institutionalization of it on a broader basis than in any previous case. In the

modern world it is unevenly institutionalized in particular "national" societies, and to a considerable extent in "international" contexts, but its current status is both highly incomplete and precarious. A major extension beyond particular societies seems to me to depend on the institutionalization of a firmer and broader system of societies than we have yet seen. Such a process would entail a repetition of the stage-process on a wider set of system-reference bases. The general conceptual structure of the series I conceive to be a "spiral," which is parallel to that involving the adaptive factors in the technological, economic, and scientific series, on the one hand, and the integrative factors in the field of the generalization of affect, on the other.

To return to the problem of process. A first point concerns what I have called "value-pressure." Assuming that a value-pattern has in fact become internalized and institutionalized to a significant degree, discrepancy between the valued "ideal state" and the actual state of affairs becomes a source of strain. The commitment to the ideal then constitutes a set of factors exerting pressure toward changing the actual state in the direction of conformity with normative standards. This pressure is likely to be stronger in proportion as the value-pattern is "activistic," i.e., calls for positive goal-attainment and active adaptation rather than more passive "adjustment" to the system's environments.

A value-pattern, no matter how firmly institutionalized, constitutes only one major factor in the determination of social process, though in cybernetic terms it is placed at the highest level. The factors of "interest," notably in the economic and political categories, are analytically independent as, when properly understood, are norms as distinguished from values. Moreover the value-*system* itself is not simple but complex. It consists not only of a "master pattern," but also of many levels of subvalues, specified both in terms of level of the functions in the system which they regulate, and of qualitative differentiation among such functions—e.g., the subvalues governing a business firm are different from those of a university. Nonvalue factors can, of course, operate in interdependence at every level and type of specification. This is one of main reasons why maintenance of the "integrity" of the value-pattern, as I have called it, is empirically problematical.[33] This complicatedness of the value-system itself is clearly a function of the pluralism and differentiatedness of the social system of reference.

Very broadly we may say that the "pressure" of interests tends to be "centrifugal," with a built-in tendency to escape the "control" of values, whereas the tendency of the value-pattern's pressure is obversely "centripetal." Among action components and types other than values themselves, then, the effect of the value-pattern tends to be selective in the sense of

[33] Parsons, "On the Concept of Value Commitments," reprinted in my collection of essays, *Politics and Social Structure* (New York: Free Press, 1969).

creating various difficulties for the types of actions which do not fit, and advantages for the ones which do. This is a process which is in certain respects, though by no means all, analogous to the process of natural selection in the organic world. There is also, of course, collective action directly oriented to the implementation of values, most conspicuously shown in crisis situations, though not always. Hence both the selective and the directly implementive aspects of value-institutionalizations must always be considered.

The maintenance of what I have called the integrity of a value-pattern can occur in more than one way. Besides "implementation" in the most direct sense, which is the "moral" equivalent of "law-enforcement," it can occur through two other primary processes, namely specification, as just referred to, and value-generalization. The two are, of course, concretely interdependent with each other, as well as with other factors in concrete social process.

I have suggested that differentiation is in part a consequence of value-pressure. At the same time it creates problems from the point of view of integrity, namely, will the value-pattern, as institutionally "conceived" in Kluckhohn's term, legitimize both parts of the newly differentiated complex, rather than only the one which existed prior to the step of differentiation? Thus in a classical example, when occupational roles came to be differentiated from those in kinship-based households, massively through the industrial revolution, a value-problem was created, which has reverberated for a long time, essentially around the question as to whether work outside the household is basically legitimate. The Marxian concept of the "alienation" of labor is clearly a negative answer to this question. Similarly when the societal community became differentiated from a religiously sanctioned collectivity, a process, often called "secularization," gave rise to the question of whether it did not constitute "simple" abandonment of religious commitments.

The pattern of specification constitutes a meaningful linkage between more generalized and more particular levels of generality. Hence, it is nearly obvious that, in order to bring new particulars together with old under a common general rubric, the general rubric may be redefined at a higher level of generality than before. The problem of integrity here concerns the question of whether, in being generalized, the pattern does or does not maintain the same "orientational" character, i.e., whether the change is one of generalization to include new modes of implementation of the "essential" pattern or represents a step in the direction of "eclecticism," namely, willingness to tolerate types of action which are in fact incompatible with the value-pattern. The concept of value-generalization in my sense excludes the "eclectic" alternative.

The process of institutionalizing a new level of value-generality is very often fraught wth conflict in concrete situations. Those genuinely com-

mitted to the old, and now inadequate, level are very likely to feel that *any* alteration of their concrete commitments is a surrender of integrity to illegitimate interests. This I have called the "fundamentalist" reaction. Along the lines of Smelser's analysis of collective behavior it may be said that strain tends, in proportion to its severity, to propagate defensive reactions upward in the cybernetic order, and that the appearance of conflict at what ostensibly is the level of values, is the "end of the road" at least within the social system as distinguished from other subsystems of action.

The tendency to "de-differentiation" among groups motivated to innovative social change is essentially another aspect of the same basic phenomenon. It is the attempt to legitimize the innovations by appeal to a more "primordial" level of values than can fit the newly possible structural manifold; it is also a resort which is very generally motivated in substantial part by an attempt to "discredit" the fundamentalists. The result tends to be a polarization of conflict at the value level, with both "poles" assuming a position of "value-absolutism." The conflicts attendant on the Reformation, the French Revolution, and the socialist opposition in the industrial revolution all exemplify this polarization. This pattern of polarization is also prominent in the conflicts of our own time.

In most cases it is intrinsically possible, though never inevitable, that such polarizations should be resolved by redefining the relevant value-patterns on a level of sufficient generality to include *both* sides of the previous polarity. Thus we now have an "ecumenical" conception of basically Christian religion which includes both Catholics and Protestants, to say nothing of others. We have a legitimation of "liberal democracy" which includes both "elite" classes and the common people—with all the difficulties of legitimizing "what elites?" On somewhat similar grounds I should argue that the old polarization between "capitalism" and "socialism" is in process of attenuation. If these historical interpretations are correct, a process of value-generalization has been occurring as an essential ingredient of these processes.

Most generally, I should say that without a process of generalization at the value level, the other processes of basic and potentially "progressive" social change which have been outlined here cannot eventuate in a stable new state of a social system. It is particularly important to distinguish between value-generalization and inclusion, which is the version of the more general imperative of integration which has figured in the present paradigm. Too low a level of value-generality tends to impede inclusion and to favor polarization over that issue. Thus many innovative trends, particularly in our own time, press for new inclusions. Fundamentalists, in the above sense, tend to resist, and the proponents of change reciprocally, tend to assert value-positions which cannot be generalized to include both. Indeed this combination of inadequately generalized value-

commitments, with the "sponsoring" of our resistance to important new inclusions, is perhaps the most important formula for defining a "revolutionary situation." Such conflicts may be resolved without actual revolution; or they may lead to revolution, with an eventual resolution which both includes and legitimizes what originally were both "sides"; or, of course, they may not be resolved at all—one possibility in this category being segmentation: they simply go their separate ways. The realistic possibilities in this latter direction are, however, clearly limited.

Particular Societies and Systems of Societies

In the above discussion I have stressed the concept of system of societies rather than that of the particular society, because it is considerably less familiar than the latter and also because of its special relevance to the evolutionary perspective. Though I had intended, when I began the discussion, to devote more attention to premodern societies as systems, it seemed better to concentrate on the modern system as I got into the matter. Even so, within the limits of this paper, I have been able only to single out a few illustrative themes and problems rather than presenting a systematic survey.

In my own experience the emphasis I have used here is a product of a kind of three-stage, if you will in a rough sense, "dialectic" development of interest and theorizing. It began, as I stated, with exposure to the Ginsberg–Hobhouse version of comparative analysis. This was continued in the early Harvard course which, within a theoretical framework that was very loosely structured, attempted on the one hand to deal comparatively with functional complexes of "institutions" in terms of the then current classificatory rubrics such as economic, political, religious, kinship, and the like, and, on the other hand, to deal in a brief synthetic way with a series of "total" societies, e.g., European Feudalism, Greece, Rome, Ancient China, India. However rough and crude, this pattern of organization did contain the main axes of later, more sophisticated conceptualizations.

It was perhaps a not unusual experience for sociologists with macrosocial interests to become rather especially concerned with problems of the nature of their own society. In the very early 1940's, just as the crisis of Western society over Nazism was coming to the climax in the generalized Second World War, I introduced a course under the title "Social Structure of the United States," which, with a few interruptions, I have continued to teach ever since.[34]

[34] The two fields, "Comparative Institutions" and the course of American society, have for thirty years now been the mainstay of my teaching of substantive sociology, excluding courses in theory as such and in certain topical fields, such as sociology of religion or the professions.

I have very explicitly used my comparative interests as a means of trying to gain an improved perspective on the problems of American society—a task of particular difficulty for a student of it who is also directly involved in it at a time when its state has been one of rapid change and relative turbulence. Conversely, the relatively greater intensity and depth of study of American society has raised many problems and suggested interpretations which were relevant to a broader comparative perspective.

Over the years it has become increasingly clear that to achieve genuine perspective on more or less contemporary American society there had to be "historical depth" not only in the history of the United States, but of the wider "Western" system of which it was a part. To this may be added the consideration that America and other Western societies were coming into increasingly significant contact with other societies which were not, except remotely, genetically derived from the same sources, notably of course those of Asia. Considerations such as these have led me to attempt, increasingly, to generalize from the more useful kinds of "historical" concerns to those which can be called evolutionary. This trend of thought coincided with a set of developments within biological theory and in general science—notably the "new genetics" and cybernetic theory—which indicated a far greater continuity between human socio-cultural evolution and that of the organic world than had been at all widely appreciated, especially after the social science revolt against evolutionary ideas to which I referred earlier.

My own specific work within this framework has involved two phases of foci, exemplified by the two small volumes referred to in the *Foundations of Modern Sociology* series. The first of these is the very sketchy attempted codification of comparative-evolutionary ideas for premodern societies, including those outside the "Western orbit" which have remained pre-modern, in the theoretical sense, well into the modern age.

I may perhaps single out two interpretive conceptions which have been central to that work, not for careful development, but illustrative mention in the present context. Some years ago I concurred with Robert Bellah in trying to work with a very tentative five-stage paradigm of societal evolution, as presented by him in his notable paper "Religious Evolution." [35] This scheme has constituted an important part of the analytical framework used in the two small volumes referred to. Apart from the kind of concerns with the structure of the modern system which have been discussed above, there were two especially important theoretical pay-offs for me which clustered about Bellah's conception of the stage of "historic" religion.

The first concerns a remarkable historical situation in which apparently the main outline of the process of differentiation between the great civilizations of the Orient and of the Western world, in the broadest sense, took

[35] *American Sociological Review*, 29 (June 1964): 358–374.

shape. Considering the primitive character of communications at the time, it is remarkable that near the middle of the first millennium B.C. there developed nearly simultaneously four very major cultural movements: Confucianism–Taoism in China, Brahmanism in India, the Prophetic movement in Israel, and the emergence of "philosophy" in Greece. What seems to be common to them is a much sharper level of differentiation between cultural and social systems—and somewhat less directly between both and personalities and organisms—than had been the case for "archaic" levels. The theme of rejection of the world appeared, something which Weber analyzed in his well-known essay and to which Bellah brings a new sense of interpretation. This theme was most pronounced in Brahamanism, but also prominent in the Taoist countercurrent to Confucianism, in the "Dionysian" countercurrent to the main Greek trends, and in the mystical undercurrents which became prominent in post-Prophetic Judaism.

Weber never attempted to systematize the pattern of differentiation of these four main cultural movements, all of which were either very specifically religious or included a major religious aspect. If, however, as Weber did not do, the four mid-millennium movements are treated together and separated from Christianity, it seems that they can at least plausibly be fitted into the four-function paradigm, namely, Brahmanism in the Pattern-maintenance cell, Confucianism in the Integrative, Greek classical in the Adaptive, and Prophetic Judaism in that of Goal-attainment. The system-reference here must be societal-cultural as a whole, though the movements were clearly associated with the process of differentiation on the social-cultural axis also. All four, taken together, constituted a cultural-social *system* at the most general level.

The two Oriental systems were clearly concerned with the emphasis on "immanence" of principles of divinity and related themes, as compared with the theme of "transcendence" in the Western cases. There is, however, another interesting difference. Both the Indian and the Chinese cultural developments arose within what were probably in their day the most "advanced" large-scale societies, and did not establish clearly differentiated subcollectivities with religious primacy within them. This is to say there was no structural situation at all closely analogous to the Medieval differentiation between Church and State which underlay the modern development. The largely, though not wholly, "traditional" order—in Weber's sense—was "sacralized" by Brahmanic and Confucian constitutive symbols: the conceptions of transmigration and Karma and their relation to ritual purity on the one hand, and those of Tao, Yang, and Yin and their relation to "propriety" on the other.

In addition to this "sacralization" of traditional social orders—a phenomenon which was quite new compared to cases like ancient Egypt—there was in both cases a more or less "monastic" safety valve for persons who were more radically committed to new religious patterns: the Taoists

in China; the Brahmanistic "mystics" and the Buddhists in India. However for many centuries in both cases the sacralized traditional order prevailed, though this seems to have come into flux in the most recent period.

In the West, however, the two main culturally innovative movements arose, not in the principal large-scale societies, notably those of Egypt or Mesopotamia, but in small "marginal" societies, or, as in the case of the Greek Poleis, systems of societies, namely Israel and Greece. Partly because these societal systems were small in scale and marginal [36] to the "big" political systems, the *whole* socio-cultural system in each case could come to be differentiated from its neighbors in line with the cultural innovation. Thus Israel became, as "People," the societal institutionalization of a distinctive "historic" religious orientation—the "religion of Jahwe"—in a sense that had not occurred in any archaic society. In parallel, the system of Greek Poleis could become the institutionalized embodiment of the new culture of the "corporate rationality of a citizen body in accord with Nature," to put it in a very awkward and complex phrase.

As it happened, neither of these radical cases of institutionalization of a new cultural orientation turned out to be politically viable, in the sense of any realistic prospect of maintaining their independence relative to the "great powers" of the time. Indeed, both came to be absorbed into the growing Roman Empire. In the process of this absorption, however, the main cultural component came to be differentiated from the structure of the host society and, I think, largely *because* there had been a societal carrier in the background, i.e., the "people" of Israel and the Greek "Polis." Thus it was possible for a basis to develop in social structure which could exert societal and not only cultural "leverage" for further

---

[36] When I say "marginal," I would like that to be interpreted to mean that they were both "member societies" in a system of societies, or possibly more than one. This seems to be true in a sense of which I was not fully aware at the time of writing *Societies*. Probably the correct statement is that both belonged in the same system of which the political center was the Empire of Mesopotamia. There was clearly a time when Israel was in the Egyptian orbit, but the whole story leading up to the Exodus and the prophetic role of Moses seems to constitute a basic breakaway from thát orbit. The later conquest by the Babylonians and the "exile" in Babylon does not contradict the suggestion of Israel being a "satellite" society in the Babylonian system, and later of course part of the Hellenistic and Roman successors of Babylonia.

It is quite clear that there were important structural continuities, in somewhat different directions, between the society of Mesopotamia and that of the Northeast corner of the Mediterranean. (Compare chs. 4 and 6 of *Societies*.) In particular a "city-state" component was common to both. From the Greek point of view the Mesopotamians were not quite complete "barbarians" in the sense in which the "Scythians" were.

Both of these seedbed societies, however, enjoyed for a critical but brief period a special order of independence relative to the political center of the Mesopotamian system and, though the societal aspect of the independence was lost in both cases, the cultural innovation was not reabsorbed along with much of the political and social structure.

development. The maintenance of precisely the *societal* integrity of the Jewish communities in the Diaspora is the outstanding "interim" example, but considerations of this sort underlay the crucial significance of the Christian Church.

As I put in *Societies*,[37] Israel and Greece constituted "seedbed" societies, from the point of view of their impact on the future. Precisely because they became differentiated so far "out of line" with the main societal system of the time, they could not maintain their independence. But their cultural innovations survived. The Christian "breakthrough" was clearly a major cultural innovation beyond either the Judaic or the Greek. Part of its distinctiveness consisted in the cultural "marriage" between these two patterns. At the same time, however, both seedbed societies offered models of societal organization which could be synthesized within the conception of the Church as an entity set over against the Roman Empire of the time, involving a special combination of a "people" in the Judaic sense and of a "citizen body" in the Greek sense.[38]

The "syncretism" which constituted this crucial cultural "marriage" was part of a very broad welter of syncretisms occurring decisively about this time, which notably included Egyptian and Persian themes—e.g., the cult of Isis and Osiris and Mythraism.[39] It thus seems reasonable to suggest that a decisive advantage of the Christian synthesis lay in the fact that it carried with it the Value and, even in part, the Norm basis for a pattern of firm collective organization, independent of the society within which it developed. It is of course quite clear that without the individualism and universalistic cosmopolitanism of Imperial Roman society, it could not have survived, to say nothing of being able to proselytize. Equally essential was the break with the Israelitic ethnic community since even a restructured "Judaism" could not have become the official religion of the Roman Empire.

Subject to conditions such as these, however, the makings of the social institution which became the Christian Church constituted a set of decisive factors in making not only the survival and spread of early Christianity within Roman society possible, but in making it possible, at a much later

---

[37] Parsons, *Societies*, ch. 6.

[38] This duality seems to be symbolized in the Eucharist, the basic ritual of the Church. The wine, as symbolizing the "blood" of Christ, seems to connect with the Judaic background, the "people," whereas the bread, symbolizing the "body" of Christ, seems to derive from the conception of the polis as a collective body in which the individual participates as a "member." There is a very striking parallel here to David Schneider's analysis of modern kinship, with his categories of the importance on the one hand of "blood" relationships, and of those involving "law" as prescribing relatedness through observance of a "code of conduct." Schneider, *American Kinship* (Englewood Cliffs, N.J.: Prentice-Hall, 1968).

[39] Franz Cumont, *Mysteries of Mithra*, tr. from 2d rev. French ed. by Thomas J. McCormack (New York: Dover Press, 1956), and A. D. Nock, *Conversion* (London: Oxford University Press, 1933).

time, for Christianity to become the main cultural base of the unique development of modern society.[40] The above very sketchy discussion of the differentiation among the "historic" religions, in Bellah's sense, and the special circumstances in which two of them in combination laid the cultural foundations of modern society will illustrate, I hope, the utility of the particular version of comparative and evolutionary conceptualization for the analysis of certain crucial features of premodern socio-cultural development which has been discussed here. In this connection, again, the conception of a system of societies (and cultures) has been of critical importance.

In conclusion I should like to sketch out one more illustration, this time with reference to modern, up to very recent, developments. This concerns the problem, noted above, of perspective on the development of American society. It may be pertinent first to remark that my earlier predilections were, in line with the main intellectual currents at the time, first to emphasize the decisive importance of economic emphases, not only in the descriptive characterization of modern and especially American society as "capitalistic," but to carry through to the conception that this was not only a characterization but an explanation. Max Weber cast considerable doubt on the latter set of inferences, but introduced still another note, namely, that of the prevalence of "bureaucracy," not only in government but in the field of economic organization.

In the sense in which Weber's essay on the *Protestant Ethic* proved decisive for me in beginning to question the adequacy of the prevalent "economic interpretation" of social processes, if not of "history" as a whole, my beginning concern with the significance of the professions in modern society contained the seeds of a questioning of the thesis of the all-pervasive "dominance" of bureaucracy,[41] a thesis which has received massive ideological reinforcement in recent years from the "New Left."

By that time I was thoroughly acquainted with Durkheim's work. Moreover, a fact that was particularly significant was that within the framework of the convergence of theory between him and Weber, which was so important to me, Durkheim was giving an emphasis in his interpretation of some of the main trends of modern society that was different from Weber's emphasis on bureaucratization. It gradually became clearer that this pattern identified by Durkheim was closely associated with that of the professions and, up to a point, also with that of the economic market, precisely in contrast with the predominantly hierarchical stress of bureaucracy.

---

[40] For my views on these matters see my article "Christianity" in David Sills, ed., *International Encyclopedia of the Social Sciences,* vol. 2 (New York: Macmillan, 1968).

[41] James L. Peacock and A. Thomas Kirsch, *The Human Direction* (New York: Appleton-Century-Crofts, 1970).

The conception, however, of a system of modern societies, which has been discussed at some length in the present paper, helped greatly to focus and crystallize views on this issue, with special reference to the "diagnosis" of American society in its recent phases of change. A certain pattern of continuity, as discussed above, was particularly clear, beginning with the case of England and Holland in the 17th-century phase of modern development, in contrast both with Prussia in particular, and with the older Counter-Reformation powers, notably Austria and Spain.

In this respect, then, the "hierarchical" aspect of British society, centering above all on the institution of aristocracy, could be seen as relative; and in the system as a whole, one giving way gradually to a new level of "egalitarianism" in America, especially perhaps in the phase described by Tocqueville. This theme, however, not only connects with democracy in a political and a perhaps vague "social" sense, but also with the implications of the new levels of development of education and of the professions, as again broadly outlined above.

It has become my view that a highly bureaucratized social system, like that of the Soviet Union, can borrow and utilize such cultural and social components often, from certain points of view, more effectively than the societies which favored their original creation, but that, since the Middle Ages at least, the more creative centers of structural innovation of modern society have remained and are likely to remain in the future in the less "highly" and hierarchically organized subsocieties of the system. The very fact that the United States has recently become a center of conspicuous turmoil, which many interpret as heralding its early decline, may on the contrary be a sign that it continues to harbor the seeds of major sociocultural innovations which will be decisive for the future. The analogy to the turbulence of the 17th century in the European Northwest Corner is evident.

However this may be, I think it is correct that American society is in many respects the most individualistic, the most "collegial," and the most univeralistically oriented of the major units of the modern system, and that the accusations that it is uniquely "repressive," far from being true, constitute simply a case of a familiar ideological "reversal." The best previous case perhaps is that of the "liberation" of productive capacity, through the industrial revolution which was, in the socialist movement interpreted to be mainly a process of "exploitation" of the workers.

Whatever the merits or demerits of such perspectives, I think I can say that without the evolutionary and comparative frame of reference, I could not have remotely approached satisfying my intellectual conscience with respect to a sociological view of my own society. To me the intellectual need to understand what is going on in one's own social milieu and how it fits in a broad spectrum of antecedent structures and processes, and

of similarities and differences with other currently extant social systems, are correlative and mutually imply one another. I do not think one can be a first-rate interpreter of any current social situation without comparative and evolutionary perspective nor, vice versa, that one can be a good comparativist or evolutionist without the deepest concern for one's own society and the "meaning" of its characteristics and trends of change.

12. Equality and Inequality in Modern Society, or Social Stratification Revisited

The editor of this issue has suggested that I attempt to reconsider my "generalized analytical approach" to the theory of social stratification after a first attempt, published in 1940 [1] and a second attempt published in 1953. In between, I have dealt with the topic in an essay on Marx's views of stratification (cf. Parsons, 1954: Chapter XV). Naturally problems of stratification have also been touched upon at many other points in my published work.

Both of the two earlier papers were rather directly concerned with the problem of stratification in the sense of the bases of hierarchical status or rank among societal units. This time I should like to attempt to broaden the base and speak of the problem of the nature and determinants of the balances between trends and forces making for equality and inequality in society—for current purposes, essentially modern society.

A strong stimulus in this direction was given a few years ago by Seymour Martin Lipset when he wrote, first in *Political Man* and then, with greater elaboration, in *The First New Nation,* of the problems in American society of balancing equality and what he called "elitism" (cf. Lipset, 1960, 1963, 1966). In this connection Lipset made the suggestion that this dichotomy might be defined as a pattern variable. This suggestion did not appeal to me on grounds that it did not seem to fit in the pattern variable scheme. A suggestion of how it may relate to the scheme will, however, be made at the end of this paper.

In terms of empirically substantive significance, however, the Lipset formulation was much more appealing and has been a focus of considera-

---

From *Sociological Inquiry,* Toronto, Canada, Vol. 40 (Spring 1970), pp. 13–72. Reprinted by permission.

[1] Both are reprinted in Parsons (1954: Chapter XIX).

tion for some time. If my interpretation is correct, the concept of "elitism" in the modern, especially American, setting, refers primarily to what has been called the "achievement" complex—which as a focus of inequality has tended to replace aristocracy and other ascriptive bases during the last few generations. For purposes of the present paper, I should like to try to balance my concern with the factor of stratification as inequality, with an equivalent concern for the factor of equality.

Sociological interest has tended to focus on inequality and its forms, causes, and justifications. There has been, however, for several centuries now, a trend to the institutionalization of continually extending bases of equality. This came to an important partial culmination in the eighteenth century, which happened to be the founding period of the politically independent American variant of Western society. Such cultural influences as the conceptions of natural rights or the rights of man had a profound effect on the normative definition of the nature of the new society and received a particularly important embodiment in the Bill of Rights, which was built into the United States Constitution as the first ten amendments. The egalitarian focus of this system of "rights" was unmistakable. It was also, however, closely associated with the nearly contemporary emphases of the French Revolution on the concept of citizenship. In the United States this could, to a degree impossible in the Europe of that time, be dissociated from religious and ethnic bases of the solidarity of societal communities, since the pattern of separation of church and state and denominational pluralism in the religious sphere was already well launched. This "liberalizing" tendency was reinforced by the beginnings of the attenuation of the assumption that the new American societal community was "essentially" Anglo-Saxon. Though English remained the common language for the whole society, the ethnic and religious diversity of the elements entering the society by immigration strongly reinforced the pluralistic potentials which were present in the cultural tradition. Indeed, the Negro, recently the most difficult element to include, has, after a long and tragic history, begun to change status quite markedly in the direction of equality. Though there is a good deal of scepticism on this score, the indications of the trend point, in my judgment, to broadly successful inclusion after much further tension and struggle over a protracted period. Thus we can say that two of the most deep-seated ascriptive bases of inequality, religion and ethnicity, have lost much of their force in a society which in both respects has become notably pluralistic in composition.

There are two further contexts in which historically central foci of ascription have come to be greatly modified, namely, local and regional particularism and social class. Both present very complex problems which can only be alluded to here. With respect to the first, I may quote Daniel Bell's statement that only in the last generation or so has the United States become a "national" society (cf. Bell, 1968: 19). One of the strik-

ing phenomena has been the immense increase in geographical mobility, not only for more or less permanent residence, but also, facilitated by ease, speed and relative cheapness of travel, for more temporary purposes, both recreational and occupational as well as others. Added to this is the new technology of communication, both person-to-person varieties, and the mass media, which are directed to nonspecific "audiences."

It was first noticed that these changes have brought about an immense increase in the mobility of the factors of production in the economic sense. The most notable is labor, although there is clearly still much "localism" in labor markets.[2] An even more dramatic change has occurred with respect to capital as a factor of production, especially through the ramified system of banking, credit arrangements, and securities markets, highly dependent as these are on the new communication system.

What is true of the factors of production in the economic sense can, however, be generalized to the factors of the other primary categories of "contribution" to societal functioning from the primary subsystems, namely, collective effectiveness, community solidarity, and the integrity of maintenance of value-commitments (cf. Parsons, 1969). All of them have come to be immensely more highly "mobilized," in the sense of assessibility to "mobilization" in the more active meaning. I may illustrate with reference to the case of solidarity, which is of special concern to the present paper. As I have argued elsewhere, the two most critical "factors of solidarity," corresponding to labor and capital as factors of production, are firm policy decisions of organized collectivities, private as well as governmental, and the commitments of units of the society to "valued association," which means to the socially organized collective frameworks within which the implementation of more general value-commitments can be carried out. Here mobility of policy decisions as a factor means an increase in the "extent of the market," within which what we have called "interest-demands" may be presumed to have a reasonable chance of "influencing—in our technical sense—the binding decisions which are necessary for effective implementation. In spite of the importance of the hierarchy of authority in any "politically organized" society, this broadened "extent" includes a wider range of alternative sources of bindingness as well as greater influence of "constituencies" on more centralized organs of decision.

In the field of what we call "valued association," similar considerations apply. Particularly important here is the increasing pluralization of modern society so that, not only with respect to geographical location, but also on several other bases, the unit, individual or collective, has a manifold of

---

[2] This is one of the several phenomena of what may perhaps be called "residual" ascriptiveness in modern societies, to which Leon Mayhew (1968) calls attention in his illuminating paper "Ascription in Modern Societies." In general I heartily subscribe to this analysis.

open alternatives among the associations to which he will make commitments. A particularly salient example is the double choice, first of type of occupation, second of employing organization. Another, of perhaps equal salience, is the hard-fought freedom of choice of marriage partner.

The more general upshot is that, not only with respect to economic production, but also with respect to all the other primary categories of contribution, there has been an immense broadening of the range from which factors may be drawn to bring about the valued outputs we speak of as contributions. Put in negative terms, the most obvious source of this increased mobility of factors lies in emancipation from ascriptive restrictions which have previously been operative, among which the territorial reference has always been prominent. More positively, however, we would like to link this with the outcome of processes of differentiation by which the factors, by which we mean human actors making decisions in roles, have shifted their focus of concern from the inexorably given conditions under which they had to operate, to concern for the "meaningfulness" of the goals which they sought and the functions they could *choose* to contribute to.

This has, in turn, led to an important shift in the structure of the very important relation which Shils and others have referred to as that between center and periphery. Centralization is a very controversial issue in modern discussions and of course centrality of geographical location is only one of the relevant concrete references, but always a vital one. Increased mobility in the senses referred to inherently creates some new forces making for what we may call *concentration* of opportunity and responsibility for valued contribution, though there are also sources of a tendency to decentralization. In any case, however, the weakening of ascriptive bases of centralization changes the character of whatever "centers" survive or appear. Thus every politically organized society must have a governmental "capital" in a specific location. In very many preindustrial societies, however, there were no clear productive centers in the economic sense. The question of centralization of the foci of solidarity is highly complex. With the general process of emancipation from the more massive historic ascriptions, there has been a tendency for macrosolidarities to oscillate between religious and governmental anchorage. There is perhaps a valid sense in which the Reformation was made almost inevitable by the fact that the center of Catholicism was unalterably anchored in the city of Rome, but that the main focus of Western society, in terms of governmental power, of economic productivity and the like had, by the sixteenth century, migrated north of the Alps. On the other hand, the new level of differentiated pluralism has made possible differentiation of territorial centralities by functions. Early "nationalism" tended to favor extreme concentration—not only for the government but for the whole cultural system. Thus, for example, no other location of academic appointment in France has been

closely competitive with those located in Paris. In the United States, however, both the Boston area and that of San Francisco Bay and part of the Middle West are at least competitive with, not only Washington, the seat of government, but also New York, the economic and the nonacademic cultural capital of the country.

This complicated matter of territorial concentration of functions is of course dynamically related to that which has ordinarily been called the context of "class." It has also, by and large, been the most recent primary focus of attention, especially as crystallized by the many versions and nuances of "Marxian" thought.

The thesis I should like to state as underlying the present analysis is that class in this sense represents a transitional phase in the development of the stratification systems which have become prominent in modern societies since the industrial revolution. The historically important pattern immediately preceding was that which divided a territorial population into two basic groups, the aristocracy and the "common people." We are, of course, aware of the many nuances involved, but this long remained the basic division.

The essential break in this arrangement had its roots in the fact that, since the Middle Ages, the urban sector of European society was characterized by a third group later called "bourgeois." This group has been widely held to have displaced the landed aristocracy in that, no longer land, but industrial capital became the primary controlling means of production, and the industrialization process generated a new subordinate class, the "workers" or proletariat.

Relative to the prevailing picture of early modern European society, this pattern involved two primary shifts. On the one hand, the newly dominant class had a position grounded in ownership of the newly important means of production; and, on the other, while it could be argued that the landed base of aristocratic predominance was rooted in the political power of government, of which aristocracies were an adjunct, government now came to be conceived to be dependent on the organization of the economy: it became the "executive committee of the bourgeoisie." Despite these shifts, however, two factors carried over. The first was the conception that "in the last analysis" the stratification systems must be conceived as a *two*-level affair, and the second that "membership" in each of the two classes was basically determined by status of birth, as in the case of aristocracy.

Both of these constant "givens" have now been brought into question. The "ascription" of superior status to ownership of property has largely broken down in favor of a highly diversified occupational structure which no longer displays a clear division between the "controllers" and the subordinate class. This occupational structure is characterized by a fine gradation of prestige statuses with respect to which authority-power relations

have come to be differentiated as one among several rationales of status-differentiation. Moreover, there is, especially perhaps through education, a far looser connection between adult position in the occupational world and status by birth than was assumed by the Marxian analysis. There has, however, remained a substantial component of ascribed status by family origin, though the "isolation" of the nuclear family has substantially reduced it, as have the other factors of mobilization just discussed.

Especially in view of the fact that modern societies generally—and the United States especially—are to a high degree "activistically" oriented in their values, this very general reduction in the ascriptive components of their social structure has opened up important new potentialities for inequality. These lie above all in two fields. First, modern society is characterized by an altogether new scale of organization, which is spreading not only in government but also through the private sector. Indeed, though with dubious correctness, "bureaucracy" is often said to be the dominant characteristic of modern society. However that may be, the prevalence of large-scale organization certainly makes for inequalities in authority and power. The second obvious potentiality is the greatly increased role of many kinds of competence, which invites the possibility of differentiating over a far wider range than, in general, was possible under simpler conditions. These factors have been institutionalized—for the individual, in the achievement complex, where achievement may involve either attaining a position of power or utilizing a special and superior competence, or both.

At the same time, the decline of ascription in certain respects weakens inherited bases of equality as well as of inequality—the decline of ethnic and religious homogeneity and of localism presenting good examples. Since the problem of equality is inherently central to the value systems of the whole of modern society, it is not surprising that a new level of intensity of concern with it has arisen in our time. Perhaps it is not too much to say that not since the later eighteenth century have defenders of various modes of social inequality been put so much on the defensive.

Equality and Social Class

It will be necessary, later on to spell out rather fully the contexts in which in modern society's egalitarian principles have been or are tending to become institutionalized. First, however, I should like to suggest that the most recent phase of the process has gone far enough so that there has been a shifting of burden of proof. The inequalities constituting a stratification system have previously tended to occupy the center of attention, with institutionalization of equalities regarded as manifestations of a need to curb excesses of inequality. Now the tendency is to emphasize the respects

in which societal units, but especially persons, are and should be treated as equals, and to place the burden of proof not only on the explanation, but above all the justification of components of inequality. The most general principle seems clear, namely, that grounds of justification must refer to functional needs of the various action systems which are objects of analysis.

Here, however, it is essential to remember that one of the salient features of modern societies is the pluralistic character of their structures, so that, however great the concentration of attention on a society as a whole, plural social system references must always be kept in mind.

In spite of this shift of emphasis, I shall here maintain my older view that the institutionalization of stratification, or more precisely of relations of inequality of status, constitutes an essential aspect in the solution of the problem of order in social systems through the legitimation of essential inequalities; but the same holds, *pari passu,* for the institutionalization of patterns of equality. Claims to equality of status, that is, must also be legitimized, and sometimes the problem of grounding such claims becomes complicated and subtle. What I am doing is to suggest the formulation of a dual, "dialectically" structured aspect of the "problem of order" rather than, as in the earlier papers, to treat equality as the limiting case where stratificatory differences disappear. Alternatively put, all societies institutionalize some balance between equality and inequality.

We have outlined above the secular trend to the weakening of many of the historic bases of ascriptive status such as religion, ethnicity, territorial location, and class in its older senses. In general, these changes have favored the rise to prominence of collectivities and roles (organized about functional specificity and universalistic standards of selection and performance) to a paramount position in the occupational system and in most modern authority structures. Such structures are related to the problem of equality through the principle of equality of opportunity. Even here, however, the kinship system retains an important residual status in favoring ascriptive continuities from generation to generation. It is difficult to see how these can be drastically reduced from the present level without virtually eliminating the family itself.

There is thus a sense in which the prototype of the collective structures within which the functionally specific and achieved types of inequality are least admissible is the family, which occupies an interestingly ambiguous position in modern societies. The range of obligatory solidarity and hence only very specifically justified inequality, as on the basis of age, has been enormously pared down by contrast with evolutionarily earlier kinship systems, in the residential nuclear family now constituting the main unit. In spite of the necessary difference of ascribed role by generation and sex, and, somewhat less essential, birth order and interval, internally the modern family is in some sense prototypically egalitarian. Since, however, its constituent membership roles cannot be neatly fitted into any of the

more instrumental specific-function structures of a modern society, the very survival of the family as a solidary unit serves as an agency of the perpetuation of some ascriptive discriminations which are in principle objectionable to a purely egalitarian ethic. This dilemma, of course, has been well known at least since Plato.

Put in pattern-variable terms, the problem arises from the facts that the family is both primarily diffuse rather than specific in function and that it is built on "quality," i.e., ascriptiveness, especially with respect to the status of children. A brief elaboration of these points may be helpful. The status of a child is less problematical in that neither his role nor his personality can, in the early years, have differentiated sufficiently to enable him to occupy other than primarily an ascribed status or to stand in functionally diffuse relations, by any standard, to his parents and siblings. The process of differentiation, with its other attendant features, is long and complex. The marriage relation is structurally quite different. It is, as Durkheim was one of the early observers to appreciate, in some respects the prototype of associational structure, as distinguished either from ascription or from hierarchical ranking. The institutionalization of the right of personal choice of marriage partner has gone very far indeed, as has the definition of husband and wife as basically equals and hence of their relationship as basically "consensual."

At the same time, for the partners, it is diffuse in the sense that, whatever other involvements the partners may have, e.g., in occupation, community affairs, etc., they are thrown back on each other in contexts both of daily living and of more ultimate personal security.[3] The fact that spouses are the almost universal primary beneficiaries of personal property arrangements emphasizes this point.

The fact that the typical marriage is expected to be complemented by parenthood and that therefore the ascriptive component comes to be heavily accented in the partners' relation to their children, in a sense skews the relationship away from the associational pattern. The recent tendency, however, has been to deemphasize the inherently hierarchical component of the generation difference within the family, and, in halting and tentative ways to try to "include" the children in the associational aspect, in ways which accentuate the associational relation of the parents to each other. From this point of view, the good family becomes in part a training ground in the arts of participation, not only granting children, according to the maturing of their capacities, rights to participate, but training them in the responsible use of these rights (cf. Weinstein and Platt, 1969). From one point of view, even though the recent increase in emphasis on independence training and participation weakens the hold of ascriptive features of identification with parental status, from another, it may increase the status-dif-

---

[3] Take, for instance, the marriage vow, "for better, for worse, for richer, for poorer, in sickness and in health . . ."

ferentiating influence of the family, in that the children of higher status parents derive special competitive advantages from their socialization, precisely in the form of capacities for more independent and more responsible action, so that their chances of maintaining or improving the parental level of status are actually improved, relative to children of less "advantaged" homes. This need not be a matter of family income level or access to the "best" schools and colleges though it is rather highly correlated with such factors (cf. Spady, 1967). Hence the seeming paradox arises, that the ascription of children by birth to the families established by the parental marriage, accentuates the child's competitive advantage in the institutions governed by the value of equality of opportunity, rather than compensating the status disadvantages.[4]

If the above is true of the substantially "democratized" family, the question naturally arises of whether similar things are not true of other solidary groupings, the constitutive basis of which is either only partially or not at all that of kinship. Ethnic groups are the prototype of the category partially constituted by kinship relations. They, of course, often coincide with religious and "national" groups. All of these, however, are internally stratified in the normal case, so that the problems of the scope and nature of mechanisms of mobility apply within them. Between such groups there is a problem concerning the extent to which such membership has implications of status in the system of stratification. This is often highly equivocal. The status of the Negro in the United States is a particularly massive example, but even here such phenomena as the "black bourgeoisie" make it clear that ethnic status is only one of the determinants of general "class" status, even though it may be the overwhelmingly important one for large numbers (cf. Parsons, 1965).

On the other hand, there are important classes of associational groups in the constitution of which kinship is a minimal factor, if it is present at all. Thus apart from the admittedly important question of the class and ethnic composition of residential neighborhoods, school classes and youth peer groups are nonascriptive relative to the family; their composition stands in structural contrast to the family statuses of their members, and even where the families are relative status-equals, the status of the member in the group is often different from that in the family. This is one general and important area of the residual ascriptions of modern society which are the subject of Mayhew's article (cf. Mayhew, 1968; Parsons, 1959).

Membership in such groups and the status attained within them inevitably constitute ascriptive bases which affect future or current status-oppor-

---

[4] This is a rather striking case of what Merton (1968) neatly calls the "Matthew Effect." Here, to symbolize cumulative tendencies to inequality, Merton uses the gospel aphorism "To him who hath shall be given, from him who hath not shall be taken away, even that which he hath."

tunities in other connections. Thus being in the "top ten percent" of the class in a high quality school or college substantially improves one individual's future opportunities compared to the case where another was near the bottom of an evaluative scale on either or both counts. Indeed the "better" the school or college, the more it may contribute to the Matthew effect, in that it may not only confer immediate "prestige" but also help train capacities and open opportunities which, if competently used, will improve the chance for achieving higher status than would otherwise be possible. Thus so long as the achievement complex and the related complexes of valuation of organizational effectiveness and authority and power persist, the "democratization" of the system through more rigorous institutionalization of equality of opportunity does not alone solve the problem of equality. What is true of families, schools, and peer groups is of course at least equally so of residential communities and occupational organizations.

Of the four primary historic foci of ascription that were briefly reviewed in the introductory section of this paper (religion, ethnicity, local and regional particularism, and social class), only the last, social class, was primarily focused about the problem of inequality internal to a society. Here it was suggested that the crucial background lay in the institution of hereditary aristocracy, but that in the more recent version heredity of status through kinship was specially combined with property relations in the emerging industrial economy. In recent, non-Marxian discussions of class, the specific reference to the ownership of the means of production has virtually disappeared; concern with the distribution of wealth and of power as well as with kinship, however, has remained.

In spite of its "oversimplification," the Marxian conception remains a very useful point of reference. It was not fully accurate, even in 1848, and has certainly become progressively less so for the principal modern societies. But what have been the principal changes? On the kinship side, the most important one has been the attenuation of lineages with their intergeneration solidarity, leading to an increased "isolation" of the nuclear family. The most important single shift has been from total or virtual "arrangement" of marriages to a situation of relatively high degree of individual freedom of marriage choice, not without ascriptive "preferences," but still allowing much more mixing across ascriptive lines than before. This in turn has been associated with the loosening of the ties of the family to the other three ascriptive contexts, namely, religious affiliation—indexed by the increase of "mixed" marriages—ethnicity, and local particularism. These more specific bases of class identification have tended to be replaced by more generalized "style of life" patterns related to income levels and access to consumers' goods.

On the "property" side, we can clearly no longer speak of a "capitalistic" propertied class which has replaced the earlier "feudal" landed class. The changes are principally of two types. One concerns the immense ex-

tent to which household income has come from occupational rather than property sources, extending upward in status terms from the proletarian wage worker to the very top of the occupational scale. This clearly leaves the problem of the relation of the income-receiver to the employing organization problematical, but it clearly cannot be simply dichotomized into the case of the classical "worker," who is simply paid by those who control the means of production, and the "owner," who, if he has a salary, essentially must be conceived to "pay himself." The second type of change is the relative dissociation of rights to property income from effective control of the means of production. Thus most of the recipients of corporate dividends have no more control of the enterprises in which they invest than do customers over those from which they buy.

The Marxian synthesis essentially asserted the *codetermination* of class status by economic *and* political factors—ownership of economic facilities giving *control,* in a political sense, of the firm as an organization. This in turn was conceived to be synthesized with the kinship system in its lineage aspect. The process of differentiation in modern society has, however, broken down this double synthesis, insofar as it existed at all, in classical nineteenth-century "capitalism." In consequence, not only has the mobility of economic and political resources been greatly enhanced, but the door has been opened to the involvement of factors other than the classical three of kinship solidarity, proprietorship, and political power in private organizations. One effect is to make it possible for other ascriptive factors to have a continued or even revived existence, in the enhanced independence of "minority" religious and ethnic solidarities, and also relative to the "microascriptions" of which Mayhew speaks. But the main macrosocial structure has moved much farther away from ascriptive foci, even that of class, than the Marxian analysis would have it.

At the same time, the "property" complex has become much more highly differentiated. Not only have the ownership component as claim to income and the political power component as right to control become differentiated from each other, but the variegated occupational system has developed a wide range of qualitatively different types. The most important new element is probably the injection, on a scale not even vaguely envisioned by Marx, of many kinds of trained competence as factors in effective occupational performance. This has established a set of links between the occupational system and that of education, especially higher education, which did not exist before. The growth of a vast range of white-collar occupations for which secondary education is prerequisite is one major consequence, but perhaps the most important is the emergence into a new prominence of the professions, dependent as these are on university level training.

Occupation rather than property having become the primary focus of household status, both through the prestige value of occupational positions

and functions themselves and through the income and style of life they ground, there is neither a simple dichotomy nor a single neat hierarchical continuum in the status system—and least of all is there such a continuum hinging on ownership as distinguished from employed status. There is, of course, an hierarchical dimension to the occupational system, about which we will have something more to say; but, especially in the upper ranges, it is only one of several dimensions of differentiation. It is particularly important that there is no clear-cut break between an upper and lower "class;" even the famous line between manual and nonmanual work has ceased to be of primary significance.[5]

In the light of these developments, we may suggest the usefulness of divorcing the concept of social class from its historic relation to both kinship and property as such; to define *class status,* for the unit of social structure, as position on the hierarchical dimension of the differentiation of the societal system; and to consider *social class* as an aggregate of such units, individual and/or collective, that in their own estimation and those of others in the society occupy positions of approximately equal status in this respect.

As we will argue later in the paper, class status and the "division of society into classes"—to use a phrase of Malthus'—represent a more or less successful resultant of mechanisms dealing with integrative problems of the society, notably those having to do with the balance between factors of equality and of inequality.

Certainly for the male individual as unit, the two primary foci of class status are occupation and kinship. The former is articulated with a variety of the other predominantly universalistic and functionally specific structures of the society, particularly the market system, with special reference to the very complex phenomena of the labor market and the structure of power and authority especially in specific-function organizations, and the educational system and other foci of the institutionalization of differences of kind and level of competence.

Kinship, on the other hand, is for both the individual member and the social system, diffuse in function; it is the most important residual basis of diffuse solidarity and personal security. It, then, is articulated with the other principal bases of diffuse solidarity, which include the massive historic ones of ethnicity and religion and the relations between household and more extended kinship groupings, as well as those of residential neighborhood and, extending from this, a complex variety of solidarities associated with territorial localism, extending up to the societal community

[5] It is well known that, in Communist countries, the higher nonmanual occupations, including those of industrial managers and scientists, are classified as belonging to the "intelligentsia," which is explicitly said to be part of the "working class." Of course theoretically in such societies there is no longer a "bourgeois" class.

itself. Class status, for the unit, must include the whole complex of membership in diffusely solidary collectivities.

Diffuse solidarities, in this sense, constitute the structure of modern "communities." It is important to our general argument to be clear that there is no one community in a sociologically relevant sense but that a modern society is a very complex composite of differentiated and articulating—sometimes conflicting—units of community. This is one of the two primary respects in which such societies are "pluralistic." The typical individual participates not in one, but in several of them. He is, of course, a family member; but there are two typical family memberships for each individual, not one. Both his ethnic and his religious identification may be in part independent of family membership—e.g., he may "intermarry" both ethnically and religiously. In even modestly high-status neighborhoods, he probably lives in one which is "mixed" from such points of view, as well as heterogeneous by occupational roles. Even at the level of the societal community as a whole there is major variation, e.g., as to the degrees to which people have transnational affiliations, on the basis of kinship, occupation or other grounds.

The other primary respect in which modern societies are pluralistic has to do with the functionally specific roles of which occupation is prototypical. Besides occupation itself, which is, like marriage, in the normal case a one-at-a-time involvement, this pluralism has above all to do with memberships in more or less formalized voluntary associations, which, for the participating individual, have immensely varying modes and levels of significance.

In order to throw more light on the nature of the integrative problems involved in the class hierarchy of a modern society, we must first turn to the aspects of their structure in which the egalitarian emphasis is strong and indeed newly prominent in the most recent phase of development. We have linked the emergence of this phase with the weakening of certain aspects of historic ascription of status. It should, however, be clear that equality versus inequality and ascription versus achievement should be treated as independently variable. We are suggesting here not their identity, but specific connections between them, namely, that the weakening of historic ascriptions "opens the door" to new modes and forms both of equality and of inequality. Hence a new situation comes into being for defining the relations between them.

Contexts of the Institutionalization of Equality

The case of Constitutional rights provides the most convenient point of reference for raising the question of the status of the relatively "uncon-

ditional" egalitarian component of the modern status system. The conception of equality of opportunity then forms, from the egalitarian side, the most important institutional link, not between equality and inequality generally, but between equality and that set of components of the latter which could be most fully integrated with the equality context, via achievement and functionally justified authority.

Especially since the work of T. H. Marshall (1965), the "rights" component of patterns of equality which he calls "civil" has come to be seen as part of a broader complex, which above all, following Marshall, may be said to include both "political" and "social" components. To these, should, I think, be added another which may in a rather vague and residual sense, be called "cultural." Each of the four categories is at the same time a focus of the institutionalization of components of equality of status and of the legitimation of components of stratification.

The rights that are institutionalized in the legal or civil context insure basic equalities with respect to freedom of the person, speech, assembly, association, and the like. At the same time, however, they institutionalize "equal freedoms" that permit those who enjoy them to engage in actions, the consequences of which are likely to produce differences of status. Thus the freedom of religion, as based in the first amendment to the United States Constitution, legitimizes the choice of a more prestigeful religious affiliation, given that denominations will in fact vary in terms of social prestige. Of course, the same applies to other aspects of the freedom of association. In this respect, however, probably the most important "legal" complex is that of the freedom of contract. The more commercial and financial aspects of contract have of course been highly important, but perhaps particularly important to stratification has been the inclusion here of the contract of employment. With the tendency of the occupational system to move its center of gravity from statuses of proprietorship—e.g., as peasant holder, craftsman or small business man—to that of functionally specific organizations, the immediate basis of the participation of the individual has tended to become increasingly contractual. The relation of freedom of contract to the pattern of equality of opportunity is clear.

The potentials of freedom of contract for facilitating inequality should not, however, be used to minimize the importance of the egalitarian trend of the "rights" complex. Recent legal trends in fields other than civil rights strongly emphasize this.

Similar dual involvements with the problems both of equality and of the legitimation of components of stratification should be seen in the second of Marshall's citizenship complexes, which he calls political. Historically, the central change came with an egalitarian thrust, namely, the enfranchisement of the mass of citizens through the democratic revolution. Rokkan (1960) in particular has shown how fundamental and universal,

within at least the "liberal" world, has been the institutionalization of equalities in this aspect of government. That parallel developments have occurred with respect to a vast welter of private associations does not need to be stressed.

This phenomenon of course raises the question of the other side of the coin. In one respect the development of the democratic franchise, governmental or private, constituted a response to a crisis in the legitimacy of "arbitrary" authority, i.e., that based on grounds other than the explicit consent if not mandate of the governed. It has, however, also given rise to a new basis of the legitimation of inequality, namely in the authority and power of incumbents of elective office relative to that of the larger numbers on whose electoral decisions this grant of power rests.

As noted, this new legitimation of inequality of power extends to the sphere of private associations. At the same time, it is not unrelated to the legitimation of authority in the more bureaucratic aspects of modern formal organization. The most obvious case is that of governmental executive organization where the authority of elective office legitimizes appointive powers. In modern governments this, of course, becomes a very extensive phenomenon indeed.

One special type of case is the business corporation which, historically at least, has been a quasi-democratic association in its top authority, based on the votes of shares of capital rather than numbers of persons participating. Historically, of course, this is in turn a derivative of the rights of proprietorship, which in its earlier phases was neither strictly political nor strictly economic in its functional significance. In the case of the corporation, its economic functions have taken precedence over the political and thereby largely escaped the egalitarian pressures of modern political organization.

To sum up the political aspect of the citizenship complex in Marshall's sense, the focus of equality has been the democratic franchise on the principle of one member, one vote. Most large democratic associations, however, are governed on a representative basis, with elected officers acting on behalf of their constituents. The representative principle is also often combined with that of the separation of powers, as in the cases of the American federal and state constitutions.

Recently there has been a new wave of advocacy of so-called participatory democracy which, in its more extreme form, would go so far as to erase the distinction between basic membership status and elective office— "every member his own officer." A common slogan has been the importance of people coming to "control the decisions which affect their lives." Again the sheer fact of social interdependence makes this an absurdity if carried to the extreme, because if A controls all the decisions which affect his life, he *ipso facto* must control many decisions which affect the lives

of others and thus deprive them of the order of control which he claims for himself. Nevertheless, the drive is clearly to extend participation well beyond the traditional limits of representative systems.

The largest scale American example has been the attempt to develop "maximum feasible participation" on the part of the "poor" concerning the administration of the programs associated with the "war on poverty" (cf. Moynihan, 1969a, 1969b). The principal targets in this case have been the welfare and secondarily educational "bureaucracies" which have had a primary responsibility to taxpayers as well as to clients and parents. In the more extreme cases there has been a direct bid of local groups to assume full control of the spending of such funds. Another major example, by no means confined to this country, has been of course the drive of student groups for more participation in academic decision-making, challenging not only the more bureaucratic component of university "administrations"—including their fiduciary boards—but also the professional prerogatives of faculties.

Again these movements are not altogether new. To take only the American case, "populist" movements were very prominent for a considerable time in our history and scored in such fields as the referendum, the recall and the popular election of judges.

It is indeed difficult to assess the limits of such movements; the history of populism would suggest that the limits for stable institutionalization are relatively narrow, though under popular pressure they may go quite far. It is, however, important to bear in mind that this participation movement concerns a complex balance among modes of what, in the analytical sense, is the political control of collective processes, and that there are at least three nonegalitarian modes which are being attacked, namely, the most obviously appropriate target, bureaucratic hierarchy, but also professional control of functions requiring special competence and, finally, the inequalities of power inherent in the institution of elective office, even though the procedures of election are thoroughly democratic. At one level the drive is to widen the scope of affairs organized in terms of the democratic association, but also beyond that, further to "democratize" the democratic association itself by reducing the powers of elected officers relative to those of the average member.

The third of Marshall's components of citizenship governed by egalitarian principles, he calls "social." It has often been said that this has proved necessary to give "substance" to the more "formal" legal and political equalities. It is of course notable that every "industrial" society has adopted more or less of the features of the so-called "welfare state." In terms of content it comes close to the jurisdiction of the American federal department of "Health, Education and Welfare."

From our point of view there is here, as in the other contexts, a striking duality of reference. The one aspect, focusing on income level, con-

cerns the state of economic welfare in which different sectors of the population find themselves. This includes access to health services and other conditions of welfare. The other aspect brings us back again to the opportunity complex, but with the implication that there will be inevitable differentiation among those who have equivalent opportunities at the start.

It is perhaps correct to say that, in American society at least, there has been a notable shift of concern over the last two generations, from worry about the inequities of the advantages enjoyed by the rich—today, in this context, it is much more inequality of power than of wealth which is the focus—to concern about the other end of the scale, namely the problem of poverty. It is also notable that the weight of evidence indicates that, in a generation, there has been relatively little change in the main pattern of income distribution.[6] Since the general level has been rising, the "poor" are not in any absolute sense "worse off," so that a major problem is raised as to why there has been such a wave of new concern.

As Rainwater (1969) in particular has made clear, the essential answer to the nondisappearance of the problem in the face of increasing general productivity lies in *relative deprivation,* a view which is of particular relevance in the present context. This is to say that those groups which, for whatever reason, have incomes sufficiently below the normal level of "average" families, are unable, in a variety of ways, to participate fully in normal activities and to utilize normal symbols of self-respect. The evidence indicates that the result tends to be a withdrawal, partly by self-isolation, partly by pressure of other groups, into a "subculture of poverty" which maintains a rather unstable partial integration in the larger society. There has been an increasingly vocal and impressive body of opinion arguing that by far the most effective single remedy for this situation is a massive redistribution of economic resources to the lowest sector of the income scale.

In this connection the emphasis is on the economic factor as such, but the development of the subculture of poverty seems to indicate that the main problem is societal integration and that we are here talking about one major condition of integrating a major sector of the population into the larger community. It seems reasonable, with respect to this integration, to distinguish two analytically separate components, although they overlap and interpenetrate empirically. One may be said to be that of the "style of life," which focuses on what are usually called "consumption" standards, which are not necessarily essential elements of the conditions of developing capacities to exploit opportunities. Much of the area of dress, housing, and furnishings, of food habits and the like belongs in this cate-

---

[6] S. M. Miller points out that the economic aspect of welfare would take three components into account, namely, income, assets and services. On income distributions, a convenient source is Herman Miller (1964).

gory. The other concerns the factors of capacity and motivation to take advantage of opportunities for some kind of social mobility.

Economic underpinning is exceedingly important to both, but its provision may probably be relied on to operate more nearly automatically in the former sphere than in the latter. Probably the most important case in point here is education. Whatever may be said about the inferior quality of slum schools, in any drastic sense the "poor" cannot simply be said to have been denied access to educational opportunity. There is of course much argument on various aspects of the problem, but both the findings of the "Coleman report" (1966) and of much recent research in class-linkages in the cognitive aspect of child development seem to indicate that a genuine component of capacity is prominently involved, and that this in turn is a function of the culture of poverty (cf. Bowles, 1963; Coleman *et al.,* 1966; Kagan, 1967). Equal access to education is clearly one of the most important components of the equality of opportunity complex, helping enormously to lift those who can take advantage of it out of economic dependency and to open doors to higher levels of occupational and other success. At the same time it is more than that, not only in the negative sense that the capacities of the deprived are seriously impaired, but also in the sense that levels of education become exceedingly important conditions of the more general participations which symbolize full citizenship. Here what is meant is participation in a sense which includes shares in collective decision-making, but which is more broadly the sense of belonging and "being accepted" in many situations of social interaction. Thus, much as highbrows tend to look down on the mass media and the cultural levels of what they purvey, genuine participation in many aspects of mass media culture is essential to a sense of belonging in the society—a participation which includes politics and more specifically "cultural" concerns.

In several connections I have stressed the importance to modern society of the so-called educational revolution (cf. Parsons and Platt, 1973). If this emphasis is well placed, it should follow that the equality–inequality "variable" should have a cultural dimension as well as legal, political, and economic dimensions. In a society where cultural advancement is a process of fundamental importance, it is out of the question that there should be a "flat" equality of cultural level in a large population. Indeed much has been made, often with strongly aristocratic overtones, of the differences between elite and "mass" culture (cf. Ortega y Gasset, 1932; White, 1961). However justified such distinctions may be, it does not follow that there is not an equality problem in this area and that it is not structurally similar to those in the political and economic spheres.

One aspect of the problem concerns the extent to which "elite" culture must be ascriptively integrated with diffuse patterns of stratification, as has conspicuously been the case in societies characterized by the strong

institutionalization of aristocracy. One major modern trend in this respect has been in the direction of increasing specificity of cultural bases of status, notable perhaps in the field of the intellectual disciplines and the professions. Cultural superiority as a component of the competence essential to an occupational role *is quite different* from the cultural "refinement" of the aristocrat.

If, as seems to be the case, modern society is strongly committed, on value grounds, to the minimization of institutionalized aristocracy, an acute question is raised about the nature and problem of what is sometimes called "general education" (cf. Parsons, 1966). Here there is a problem not only of equality of "levels" but of "commonality" in the sense of transcending specializations. On the side of equality, the modern commitment to mass education clearly implies that there must be a "floor" below which only the "mentally retarded" should be allowed to fall. This floor was first set at simple literacy, but has been steadily rising. Whatever the crudity of the demographic measures of educational level, it is a cardinal fact of the society of our generation that completion of secondary education has become normative for the *whole* of the age cohort. There is a "poverty" problem in the field of education as truly as in that of income, and it is the "drop-outs" who cannot or will not complete secondary education who are becoming the core of the "educational poor."

If cultural standards are to constitute, "across the board," a criterion of position on a scale of stratification, the question of what constitutes a "level" of cultural attainment becomes a critical one. In the lower reaches the problem is relatively simple; virtually no one extols the cultural virtues of illteracy or inability to understand simple arithmetic. The foundation clearly includes certain basic cognitive skills, and a fund of basic information. At more "advanced" levels problems clearly emerge having to do at least with differences of competence among the ramified branches of the cognitive universe, and then with ideological and religious differences.

The broad answer is that the factor of "communality" as I have called it is above all a function of the level of generality of cultural orientation, and hence of the capacity to "subsume" differing varieties in the cultural sphere under more general categories. The ecumenical trend in religion is perhaps the most conspicuous example in a socio-cultural field, where points of view previously treated as nearly totally alien to each other have come more or less to be "included" in a single meaningful cultural system. The application of this principle to the sciences is relatively clear. Specialization has, to be sure, proceeded apace, but so has the integration of the corpus of scientific knowledge; indeed this process has begun to bridge the gap between the "natural" and the "behavioral" sciences, perhaps even of science in relation to the humanities.

Another way of putting the point is to say that we have been living in an increasingly pluralistic culture, which is intimately linked to the plurali-

zation of the structure of modern society. In both cases, however, the differentiation which produces pluralization must be matched by corresponding integrative processes and patterns. In another idiom, the universalistic character of the more general cultural patterns has gained a certain ascendancy over the particularism of less generally significant "sectors" of the cultural universe. To me the only sensible way to define "general" education in a sense which permits progressive upgrading is in terms of participation in this process of universalistically defined generalization of the cultural traditions.

The System of Equality Dimensions

It has thus been possible to identify four principal contexts in which the equality–inequality problem arises, and to give at least reasonable indications why, in a highly differentiated and hence pluralistic modern society, they are to significant degrees independently variable. These are the "legal," political, economic, and social and cultural contexts. They all seem to open the door to opportunity for differential achievement which can be both legitimized and differentially rewarded in various ways. We have also reviewed some of the principal ways in which conditions have been or are being institutionalized, under which such differences are regarded as legitimate.

When the four are looked at as a system, however, an important element of asymmetry appears. This lies in the fact that, while economic, political, and cultural inequalities are legitimized under the general formula of equality of opportunity—and of course other conditions such as "fair competition" and the like—the same is not true in the same way for the legal category. The old constitutional formula about "inalienable" rights seems to be appropriate here. It is significant in particular that the principle of equality in the form of nondiscrimination has been institutionalized for two fundamental "boundary conditions" of human action, both in the formula common to the fifth and fourteenth amendments to the United States Constitution. The first of these concerns the ascriptive qualities of the organism as labeled by the terms "race" and "color." Presumptively other biological fundamentals are so closely related as to fall in the same broad category, namely age and sex. The second concerns the "ultimate" boundary at the cultural end of the cybernetic scale. Here the context is that of religion, and the constitutional word is "creed," but also the provisions about the "establishment" and the "free exercise" of religion in the first amendment are central (cf. Parsons, 1966: 9ff, Freund and Ulich, 1965).

Those considerations suggest, on theoretical grounds, that the "legal"

complex has, relative to the other three, pattern-maintenance functions. It has evolved in most modern societies to the point of institutionalizing the principle that there shall be a "base" in the status of citizenship, with respect to which all individual citizens stand as equals, and that these patterns of equality apply in at least three spheres, namely, the citizen's rights of participation *in* government, e.g., through the franchise, his rights *vis-a-vis* government, and, within a considerable range, his rights in contexts of private association. Here the situation is somewhat less obvious, but recent court decisions have made it quite clear that, especially *vis-a-vis* race, but also religion, the freedom to discriminate within private associational contexts is substantially restricted. It seems a fairly safe prediction that these restrictions will tend to increase rather than the reverse.

In my two previous general papers on stratification theory, I have strongly stressed the importance of values as legitimizing differences of ranking. If the present interpretation that in the legal complex we are dealing with a pattern-maintenance function is correct, I should like to suggest that this valuational emphasis applies not only, as is obvious, to the factors of differential ranking, but also to equality—that the evaluative backing of constitutional law in this case constitutes the *specification* of the general value system of the society to the level of the *normative structure of the societal community*. It amounts to saying that the modern societal community shall be "basically" a "company of equals" and hence, so far as empirically possible, legitimate inequalities shall be "won" from a base of equal opportunity and that the rewards which go to differential statuses and achievements shall be justified in terms of functional contribution to the development and welfare of the society (cf. Davis and Moore, 1945). It should be noted that this formula can legitimize some differential opportunity, through the kinship system, for the children of the more favored groups, if they can be held to sufficiently high obligations to contribute. What in effect such a qualification does is to extend the equality of opportunity pattern beyond the span of one generation; indeed it connects with the old aristocratic formula of *noblesse oblige*.[7]

In this connection it is particularly important to be clear about system-references. When I speak of the legal or civil component of the citizenship complex as having pattern-maintenance functions, I do *not* refer to the total society but to the *societal community* as the system within and on

---

[7] Earlier societies, notably in the Western orbit, however, positively institutionalized a pattern of *diffuse* inequality through the institution of aristocracy. This seems to link up with a conception of inherent "substance," i.e., quality in pattern-variable terms. In some respects the "class" division of the Christian church was similar, namely into the "religious" and the "lay" components. The process of "elimination" of this diffuse superiority–inferiority distinction has, significantly, typically taken the form of upgrading of the status of the "common" or "lay" component rather than the reverse. See Parsons, 1968. It is probably correct to regard the persisting stigmatization of groups on grounds of "race" and "poverty" or the combination of the two, as a residuum of this more general historic division.

behalf of which this component has pattern-maintenance functions. The societal community is here conceived as a primary, functionally differentiated *subsystem of a society* (cf. Parsons, 1969a: chap. 2). This is clearly to be distinguished from the pattern-maintenance subsystem of the society as a whole. The latter clearly centers in the system of institutionalized values at the general level and is in that sense especially closely related with the cultural system. The "value-premises" of the rights and obligations here regarded as both egalitarian and inalienable, should be conceived as residing in that more general value system, but the particular relevant "forms" they take, are specifications from these premises on the basis on which that aspect of value-commitments more generally have been analyzed (cf. Parsons, 1969b).

I have just argued that the equality component of the normative structure of modern society comes to focus in the legal or civil complex of citizenship with its presumption of basic equalities of rights—and correlatively of obligations. This complex is normatively grounded in the general societal value system. In a sense underlying the more specific contexts in which the equality–inequality problem arises, which have been reviewed on one level and will be discussed again presently, there are two particularly significant contexts of value-specification which go one step farther than the specification just discussed to the level of the societal community.

The first of these I shall call the *fiduciary* complex. It is grounded in the fact that one basis of inequality lies in the incapacity, for a very wide variety of reasons, of all members of a societal community to take effective responsibility for the protection and furtherance of their own rights and interests, hence there is a necessity for "entrusting" these interests to persons or groups on which such responsibility is focused.

This principle operates most obviously in those collectivities which have responsibility for the interests of dependent persons, an execellent example being the small child, whose interests are in the first instance entrusted to his parents, but also to various other agencies. In this sense there is a fiduciary component in virtually all differentiated responsibility for societal function. The connection with the legal system is, however, particularly prominent as in the case of the courts taking formal responsibility for the administration of such matters as wardships and guardianships, various kinds of trusts and the like. Indeed we shall note that the courts of law themselves are primarily fiduciary institutions in that small groups of persons are given responsibility for very widespread interests of others. There are, however, two particularly salient and more general cases, the "fiduciary board" as a governing body in organizations, and, in a more diffuse sense, the modern professions.

What I have called the fiduciary complex has an important though complex and often ambiguous relation to the legitimizing functions of

government. Indeed, there is an important sense in which the private corporation, in the modern world, has been said to constitute a "delegation" of governmental authority to private groups, as does the institution of private property itself, if we go farther back. Such a line of argument, however, depends on the view that government is the primary matrix from which a main process of differentiation occurs. It seems to me that the appropriate matrix is more the societal community than government and that in the modern phase of societal development government itself has been in process of differentiating from this more diffuse matrix, with the democratic franchise marking one main phase of that differentiation. Thus it seems sounder to regard property and the corporation on the one hand, and government on the other, as two different "branch" developments from the same evolutionary trunk. Both of them involve the institutionalization of authority and power, and hence the elements of inequality inherent in such institutionalization. Both, however, rest on a common basis of legitimation through common values, rather than the former of being legitimized by the latter. Not to understand this fact of differentiatedness may perhaps be called the "Rousseauistic fallacy."

The other component of the "fiduciary" complex which is particularly important to the modern world, and which should be looked at in the present context, is the complex of the professions. Among their basic characteristics is a level of special technical competence that must be acquired through formal training and that necessitates special mechanisms of social control in relation to the recipients of services because of the "competence gap" which makes it unlikely that the "layman" can properly evaluate the quality of such services or the credentials of those who offer them. Professional competence, in this sense, is grounded in the mastery of knowledge of one or a combination of the intellectual disciplines, though of course other factors than knowledge as such are also involved.

What I have called the "competence gap" necessitates a component of inequality in the professional complex, e.g., between physician and patient, lawyer and client, or teacher and student. At the same time, *within* the context of professional organization, in spite of differences in competence, there is a strong tendency to an egalitarian type of associationalism on the principle that a person either is or is not a member of the profession in question, or one of its subdivisions, such as a university faculty or department, and that all such members have a certain equality of status, including the democratic franchise in collective decision-making. This is the most important case where a system of occupational roles is organized on such a basis, which may be called collegial.

It is clear that, though the factor of competence makes for a critical element of inequality—with fiduciary responsibility—it also puts a premium on capacity independent of ascriptively particularistic considerations and hence enhances the general societal stress on equality of opportunity.

Indeed, this is particularly important because it operates in the higher levels of the modern occupational system. While classical bureaucratic organization is also in principle governed by equality of opportunity, it is at the same time bound up with an hierarchical pattern of operating organization, much more than in the case of the professions. On the other hand the operation of large modern organizations has become so complex and technical that neither "direct democracy" nor elective office, crucial as the role especially of the latter is, can cover a very large proportion of its functioning, though the latter can form "top" control.

The "educational revolution" has brought the professional complex to an increasingly prominent place in the structure of the society, a prominence by no means confined to the academic world as such nor to the traditional "practicing" professions, but above all permeating both industry and government on a large scale and substantially modifying their patterns of organization, including stratification. It has above all created a new basis of solidarity, cross-cutting the traditional divisions between such spheres as those of "government" and "business." Hence the professional complex, as I am calling it, has the potential not only of a powerful instrumental influence in societal functioning but also as a focus of integrative mechanisms. These can operate above all through a process of balancing the necesary differentiations based on competence and authority, with patterns of equality.

Professions, like many other structurally differentiated groups, also pose problems of control. Since on some level only their members are competent to judge the competence of their fellow members, there is a built-in possibility of monopolistic practices in several contexts such as the restriction of access to membership. In the United States the medical profession, especially through the American Medical Association, has perhaps gone farthest in this direction. This would seem to be one of the inherent hazards to the "public interest" in a modern type of social organization.

Another major point concerns the relations between the "rights" complex of egalitarianism and the "political" complex. In a general institutional context clearly the former takes precedence in that such rights as the democratic franchise must be legally grounded, as we often put it, at constitutional levels. From this point of view the system of courts, and their equivalents in other systems, does not consist only in a "third branch," e.g., of the federal government, but is the fiduciary guardian of the more general legal order within which government itself operates—the institution of judicial review of acts both of the executive and the legislative branches clearly asserts this. This is a special case of the fiduciary principle, which is not, in the usual sense, democratic. Furthermore it is notable that, in most modern societies, these functions are performed by members of an institutionalized professional group which is structurally

anchored in many nongovernmental ways in the society and has a long *cultural* tradition of its own which was not created by any act of government, nor of an electorate at any particular time.

The second field of specification referred to above is that of the generalized media of societal interchange, as I have called them. Earlier in the paper I have stressed the importance of the erosion of ascriptive structures and the consequent increase in the mobility of many kinds of resources and the related openness of opportunities. As first became clearly evident in the field of the economic market, the widespread openness of opportunities and extensiveness of markets, as well as high degrees of the division of labor, depended on the development of money as a medium of exchange, and beyond that, as an instrument of credit.

It has proved possible to extend the conception of a generalized medium of interchange beyond the case of money to include political power and what some of us have been calling influence and value-commitments (cf. Parsons, 1969a: chaps. 14–16).

The processes of interchange and the situations in which they occur open up greatly widened possibilities for units in the social system to pursue whatever goals and interests they may be committed to. The media themselves, however, cannot in the same sense be "managed" by unit-interests, but must in some sense become an object of fiduciary responsibility. This has become obvious in the case of money, where the monetary system is a fundamental responsibility of government and certain specialized organs of it. Similar things can be said of the constitutional aspects of the organization of poltical power, not only that of government, but also as institutionalized in private organizations. Such regulation seems to be necessary because it is the very process of the development of such media, and especially the mobilization of the factors of production and of collective effectiveness, which has opened up new possibilities of inequality and of "exploitation." Thus Marxian doctrine was not fortuitously associated with the maturing of the industrial revolution and its complex relations to the democratic revolution.

It is possible to say comparable things about the relation of value-commitments as a generalized medium to the institutionalization of the culturally interpenetrating pattern-maintenance systems of modern societies. Indeed one source of modern "anti-intellectualism" seems to be a sense of inferiority, and hence of being, if not "exploited"—certainly not in the strictly economic sense—"put upon" by the superiorities of those who have enjoyed superior access to cultural resources. Indeed, the educational revolution has shifted the locus of felt conflict away from the older foci, especially of economic inequality, but also of political power, in the direction of cultural inequality.

If what has just been said about the importance of money, power, and value-commitments is correct, what of the fourth, namely influence as that

especially institutionalized with reference to the societal community? My suggestion is that one principal function of influence as a medium, perhaps the most important, is as a mechanism for "handling" the tensions which continually arise in a dynamic society over the balances between the egalitarian and the elitist components of the normative structure of the society and the realistic implementations of this balance. In previous discussions of influence, it has been emphasized that one of the principal functions of the use of influence lay in the "justification" of actions which ego was trying to persuade alter ego to perform; here, justification has been specifically distinguished from legitimation (cf. Parsons, 1969a).

Here it becomes particularly significant that, in normative terms, the pattern-maintenance "base" of the modern societal community is essentially egalitarian. In this perspective, seen in the stratification context, a primary function of influence is to justify functionally necessary forms of *in*equality. At the "pure" social system level, we have argued, these can be reduced to three main types namely, (1) through control of monetary assets, access to generalized economic resources; (2) through political power, access to factors of collective effectiveness; and (3) through value-commitments, access to "cultural resources." The attempt, then is to *"persuade"* the otherwise given holders of such "resources" to make them available for societally justified functional use, *even though* this allocation stands in conflict with some previously established egalitarian "right." In this respect, for example, the equal rights of members of an electorate are "sacrificed" to the cause of effectiveness by the granting of power to elected representatives. Similarly, resources controlled through monetary mechanisms are differentially allocated among claimants. But the burden of proof is shifted to the side of justifying inequalities.

The Interpenetration of Subsystems

It is a very important feature of the theoretical scheme we have been using here that at each of the main boundaries of a given primary system or subsystem there is a "zone of interpenetration" between the system of reference and the adjacent system. This conception may be employed here by suggesting that certain crucially important equality patterns, all three of them cases of the more general principle of equality of opportunity, can be located in these zones of interpenetration between the societal community and the other primary functional subsystems of a society.

The first of these, at the boundary *vis-a-vis* the economy, is the "classical" economic conception of the purely competitive market. This has of course been conceived in contrast with monopoly and essentially means that all participants in the operation of such an ideal type of market

should have equal opportunities of access, either to the effective demand of consumers of the relevant product, or to the factors of production, or both. When, however, the reference is to pure *competition,* it is made clear that equality of *outcome* of the process is not to be expected. If, however, the competition is "fair," it is expected that differential success will be accounted for mainly by differential efficiency of the competing units, "ultimately" in "satisfying the wants" of consumers or of producing "utility." This then falls under our conception of contribution to the welfare of the societal system. The justification, in the above sense, of "free enterprise" competition thus rests in the assertion that a competitive element in economic production contributes to more efficiency than, for example, a centrally controlled socialist form of organization.[8]

This justification, however, is contingent on keeping monopolistic tendencies under control. Differential success in market operations inevitably produces, for the next stage, differential advantages in competition. If, as is the case for most economic analyses, the firm is taken as the unit entering into the competitive process, it is very unlikely that "pure" competitive equality will prevail realistically over a large share of the market system. If, on the other hand, the step is taken to the socialistic alternative, then the justification problem becomes a matter of the appropriateness of governmental machinery which, we would in general argue, cannot have the primacy of productive efficiency in the economic (but not technological) sense which a market-oriented firm can have.

Turning to the boundary *vis-a-vis* the polity, we conceive the democratic association to be a boundary structure here, which is part integrative, part political in function. The equality of membership rights, anchored especially in the "one member, one vote" principle, is primarily a constituent of the societal community, i.e., the integrative system. Other aspects of the equal rights complex are of course also involved, perhaps above all those associated with freedom of communication, so that the free play of influence can be protected.

Of course, the most conspicuous outcome of the democratic revolution has been the institutionalization of the democratic franchise in the citizenship complex. It should not be forgotten that major developments in this respect have been taking place very recently (viz, the recent U.S. Supreme Court decisions on legislative apportionment) and that the process is probably far from being complete even in democratically "advanced" societies. Second, however, is the exceedingly important development of the same basic set of principles in the organization of many types of private association.

---

[8] It may of course be contended that it is not efficiency of production so much as the opportunity of the individual producer to "do his own thing" (in contemporary phrasing) which justifies competition. On this whole complex problem area, see the famous essay of Frank H. Knight (1935).

In various discussions of the place of the polity in societal systems, we have argued that its principal value standard is *effectiveness* of collective goal-attainment. There is an obvious tension between the equality principle in the field of participation and the functional imperative of effectiveness (cf. Parsons, 1969: chaps. 13, 14). Effectiveness in turn is a function of concentration of authority and power, not necessarily maximal, but still—where memberships are large and collective functions are both complex and urgent—an appreciable concentration. The most generally evolved institutional solution for reduction—never complete elimination—of this tension is the institution of elective office. Here of course citizens— or members of other associations—exercise their equal rights in contributing to the choice of their elected representatives, but in so doing they establish a special form of *in*equality, namely, as between office holders and "ordinary" members. My suggestion is, in line with the above discussion, that the justification of this inequality must focus in the importance, to the collectivity of reference, of effectiveness in arriving at collective decisions—i.e., those *binding* on the collectivity—and implementing the decisions arrived at, above all through the mobilization of obligations to contribute to effective collective goal-attainment.

The incumbent of elective office, by virtue of his election, assumes a special share of responsibility, both for contributing to decision-making and for implementation. Especially on the implementation side, "he" is not often in a position to discharge this responsibility by his own action alone. This need for "help" is, in one context, the focus of the development of another major type of organization, namely the "bureaucratic." The ideal type, classically delineated by Weber, is one of an "apparatus" the participants in which are incumbents of full-time occupational roles, remunerated by money salaries, organized collectively in the interest of effective attainment of a goal or "goal-set" which is defined by *other* agencies, what Weber called the "non-bureaucratic top" of the bureaucratic organization. In modern political terms this latter tends to be focused in elective office—hence the bureaucracy is conceived as responsible to its elected chiefs, and the latter in turn to the electorate.

In terms of the theory of stratification, of course, bureaucracy is a paradigmatic case of inequality established on nonascriptive bases. Here the primary focus of inequality is authority and power, especially the famous concept of "line authority."

The primary value-basis of the justification of inequalities in the outcome of market competition we may say lies in their function as conditions of economic efficiency, which in turn may be interpreted to mean that the more successful units in market competition are presumptively more efficient and hence contribute differentially to the implementation of the societal interest in production or productivity, or both. Such a proposition, of course, is true only under carefully defined conditions, but eco-

nomic theory has gone rather far in clarifying the nature of these conditions. Similarly, the value-basis of the inequalities of power between ordinary association members and elective officials must, in strictly *political* terms, lie in the contribution of this concentration of power to collective effectiveness. Beyond this the involvement of bureaucratic "apparati" must have a similar justification. Here it is important that the same basic principles of justification apply in both the political and the economic spheres.

As a consequence of the introduction of inequalities to meet functional exigencies, in both cases it follows that certain "rights" meaningfully belonging to the "pure" egalitarian membership status in the societal community have had to be sacrificed. In the political case these would seem to center in rights which are currently often formulated as rights of "participation," or as quoted above, rights to "control the decisions which affect one's life." Our essential reference here is to the fact that the basic issue is that of striking the balance between units and collective rights and hence interests. Where the *functional* context is political, the imperative of collective effectiveness very often overrides interests in unit power and unit control, sometimes involving deciding against a unit interest in a direct conflict, but more often excluding the unit or class of units from participation in ways which avoid a confrontation of conflicting interests.

In the economic case what is sacrificed is not in the political sense power, but some kind or component of "proprietary" rights. In this connection we can call participation in the purely competitive market the case of the "fullest" proprietary rights, corresponding to associational membership participation without "delegation" of any decision-making power to elective officers, to say nothing of bureaucratic apparati—in short the ideal type of "direct democracy." In the economic case we might even say that the equivalent of elective office for the political sphere was the development of the joint-stock corporation, through which owners delegated certain of their proprietary rights to the corporation to administer on their behalf. This distinction between membership and proprietorship seems to be the basis of the justification of the "psuedo-democracy" of the corporation with its enfranchisement of monetary shares rather than members.

In both these functional contexts, the delegation of components of the rights complex is a condition of a process of differentiation by which, through "freeing" certain substructures from ascriptive involvement in the more general "matrix," and allowing or encouraging the development of specialized structures such as elective office, bureaucracy, and corporate proprietorship, far greater functional contributions to the societal system can be made in *these* subsystem terms than would be possible were the original ascriptions retained in force. At the same time, such differentiation heightens tension on the equality–inequality axis. The question arises

whether integrative mechanisms have developed or are likely to develop which can sufficiently mitigate this tension.

It is notable that the economic and the political are the two paradigmatic contexts of nontraditional or nonascriptive inequality problems in modern societies. It is important here that *both,* from the perspective of the society as a social system, are subsystems which mediate crucial relations between the society and its environment and, to be technical, its environments which stand lower than it does in the cybernetic hierarchy of the primary subsystems of action in general. In the larger theoretical framework this is formulable as a problem of adaptation. This is to say that, at certain stages of societal evolution, some types of inequality are part of the price paid for high adaptive capacity. Seen in this context it is perhaps not surprising that, under the pressure of the strains produced by processes of evolutionary change, the "sacrifices" of elementary equality which are at some level justified by economic efficiency and political effectiveness, are often held to be at best unnecessary, at worst, immoral, and that there is hence a movement for the restoration or the institution of "true" equality in one or both of these respects.

Indeed, it is striking that the "myth" of a primitive equality in these respects has been exceedingly persistent throughout the history of thought about society, certainly in the Western tradition. The processes of modification of this alleged egalitarian condition are pejoratively labeled as "exploitation" or "predation," underlining the presumption that all such departures are inherently illegitimate.

On the basis of our analytical paradigm, finally, we are obligated to include a third major context of interpenetration, namely between the societal community and the pattern-maintenance system. Here the relevant version of the equality principle seems to be equality of opportunity of access to participation in *cultural* "goods." This is a conception which needs considerable elucidation. One keynote is provided by the anthropological tradition that culture should be regarded as acquired by learning processes by contrast with biological heredity. This implies that it is capable of transmission through some sort of teaching process. Another major reference is to cultural content as modes or versions of human "orientation" organized as symbolic systems of meaning through "codes." This is the basis of an exceedingly important property, namely that the transmission of culture takes place without depriving the agent of the process of control of the "content;" the success of the teacher of a language is not measured by his *loss* of control of the language in favor of his pupil. On the contrary in this sense he relinquishes nothing. He does "spend" time and effort. Contrariwise, the seller of a commodity, if successful, transfers control of the commodity to the purchaser, relinquishing it himself.

It is of course possible, through imposing barriers to communication, to restrict access to cultural content, as by keeping items of information

"secret," and indeed the existence of such barriers is *one* basis of cultural inequality. More important, however, is the fact that the "mastery" of cultural content is a process of achievement, success in which requires not only situationally open opportunity, but also effort, ability and, in the most important cases, help. Hence the acquisition of culture in this sense is typically socially organized. An especially important aspect of it is the process which sociologists have come to call "socialization."

We have suggested that it seems justified to add a cultural component of the citizenship complex to Marshall's three. This in turn presumably has several layers and facets. There is a layer of truly common culture in modern societies, of which surely one of the fundamentals is language. Here it is significant both that differentiation by dialect has decreased and the difference between a standard language used by "educated" people and local dialects has decreased. It is also significant that societies with more than one language, like Canada or Belgium, undergo serious difficulties of integration on that account. On quite another level while "denominational" levels of religion have been considerably pluralized, there does seem to be something like what, for the U.S., Bellah calls the "civil religion," which is common to "all" (cf. Bellah, 1967).

In many connections we have taken the position that strategically the most important component of culture for the social systems is patterns of value which define the actor's own situation in crucial respects. Hence in the process of acquisition of culture by individuals, the internalization of value-patterns is a central aspect of socialization. It is because of this central significance of societal values that we have treated value-commitments as the generalized medium of interchange which is anchored in the pattern-maintenance subsystem of a society. The very emergence of such a medium, however, depends on the fact that the value-*system* of a society is highly complex, and not a unitary entity, which as such either is internalized by an individual or a class of them, or is not. There are variations both in "intensity" of commitment, and in selectivity of emphasis among the many different components and levels of a value-system.

In different types of society there may be many different bases of specialization in cultural matters, the base which emphasizes in religion having been particularly important. With the process of societal differentiation, however, such specialization becomes an increasingly important function and comes to be increasingly distinct from command of wealth or power. At the same time the cultural system itself comes to be more highly differentiated, especially with the emergence, from the matrix of religion, of the arts and the sciences. Finally institutionalization of values in the structure of the society comes to be more differentiated from their religious base. This process above all leads to the emergence of law as a "secular" cultural structure which is differentiated from direct religious prescriptions. In formal analytical terms, law constitutes, as we have said,

the focus of the normative structure of the societal community and articulates, through the mechanism we have called specification, with the moral value component of the cultural system.

Differentiation of cultural concerns from others of functional significance to a society leads to increasing importance of the nature of the capacities on the basis of which the differentiated function can be effectively performed. I suggest that the central role here must be played by *competence* as a capacity to implement the values of cognitive rationality. This is to say that the cultural specialist, as distinguished, let us say from the priest in less differentiated socio-cultural systems, must be superior to nonspecialists above all in his command of the *generalized* cultural structure of his domain and thereby its relevance to more particularized problems. This generalization, and the related systematization, in the first instance has to be cognitively oriented, which is another way of emphasizing the adaptive function with reference to culture (cf. Parsons and Platt, 1968, 1970; Parsons and Platt, 1973).

The cognitive is only one of four primary functional categories of a cultural system, the others being expressive-symbolic, moral-evaluational and "constitutive-symbolic." Undoubtedly cognitive primacy as a basis of expert capacity in the cultural sphere is accentuated in societies the values of which lean, as do those of the United States, in the direction of instrumental activism (cf. Parsons and White, 1961). It is also accentuated as a function of high levels of differentiation and hence pluralism of societal structure.

In view of the complexity of these issues, we can here only suggest the consequences of primacies of each of the other three categories. That of the component of constitutive symbolism is, I think, the well-known case of a society which gives structural primacy to its religious orientation. A particularly striking case was that of ancient Egypt, but the case closest to our Western experience is the European Middle Ages—in another cultural tradition the high tide of Hinduism in India also fits this pattern. In the last case the basic axis of stratification became the *ritual* purity of castes and subcastes.

Dominance of the moral-evaluative component of culture seems to be involved with the phenomenon of "legalism," i.e., the establishment of a system of normative rules which, though having strong religious grounding, are relatively autonomous as the main area of implementation of the religious mandate. The classic cases here are postprophetic Judaic and Islamic societies. There is something of this in the earlier phases of ascetic Protestantism, and a persistence of such features in the more "fundamentalist" branches in later phases.

The expressive-symbolic component raises particularly complex problems. It seems to be the most difficult of all to maximize as culturally dominant for a total society because of its particularistic and short-run

focus. Probably no society as a whole can be mainly a "work of art." Perhaps the closet approach is a type like that of classical China, which had primarily integrative emphases in its paramount values, but relatively slight activistic stress. Its orientation to stability and the particularistic character of its relational system then seem to have favored strong aesthetic emphases.

The more individualistic type of aesthetic concerns presents another type of problem. In the Western world the aesthetic and cognitive components have, since the time of ancient Greece, been closely linked, perhaps in a kind of "dialectic" relation with each other. There have of course been specially prominent aesthetic movements, such as that of the Renaissance, and of literature and art in the nineteenth century, but they have not gained cultural dominance in total societies.

However these complicated matters may be, we shall assume here that, in our type of society at least, cultural specialization tends to give a particularly prominent place, if not dominance, to the cognitive function. Thus our differentiated cultural system is organized more about *knowledge,* its transmission, acquisition, application, and advancement, than any other single focus (cf. Frye, 1970).

With of course many antecedents, this differentiated culture-dominated system has undergone an immensely accelerated development in what we call the educational revolution, with perhaps the greatest impact being exerted by the advent on the one hand of mass higher education, on the other of the "professional" levels of institutionally organized competence, including that in the advancement of knowledge itself, and the permeation of the whole higher occupation structure by professional components.

There is very much a problem, for modern societies, of the definition and institutionalization of a common base line for cultural level which all full members of the society can and should share. There seems to be evidence that, as suggested, this base line has been rapidly rising, as indicated above all by rising levels of educational attainment. It seems likely that the time will come when the "general education" component of higher education will be universalized and become, however redefined, both a prerogative and a requisite of full citizenship for everyone. There is also the problem of the institutionalization of access not only to the general level of education, but to opportunity for attaining levels both in specific fields and in unspecialized ways, which are well above the general (cf. Porter, 1968; Parsons, 1968a, 1968b; Ben-David, 1963-64).

However these two bases of equality are institutionally worked out, as in the economic and political cases, both the differentiation and the upgrading of the culturally primary subsystems of the society lead to increased differentiation in levels of competence and resulting achievement (cf. Parsons and Platt, 1970). Hence the greater the stress on cognitive achievement, through value-commitments and through access

to economic and organizational resources, the more it becomes necessary to *justify* the resulting inequalities, and to define the framework within which they, and their consequences, are felt to be justified—e.g., with respect to differential rewards.

As in the other two cases, the culturally "common man" must sacrifice here some of his egalitarian prerogative in recognizing the merits of cultural superiority. It is thus not surprising that there are new currents of what is sometimes called anti-intellectualism, and hence the idealization of a state of affairs where competence above the general level does not count—as well as derogation of the validity of claims to superior competence.

The line of justification of this category of inequalities clearly must rest first on assertions of the functional importance to the society of the institutionalization of the requisite aspects of culture, of its advancement, transmission, and application. The recognition of superiority then must be balanced by what I have referred to above as "fiduciary" responsibility. There must be institutionalized ways of assuring, with tolerable probability, that superior competence will be used in ways which are compatible with societal interests—as in the case of the medical assertion of concern for the "welfare of the patient."

If we are correct that the main center of gravity of the differentiation of that sector of the pattern-maintenance subsystem of modern society in which cultural interests have primacy is the system of higher education, it should not be surprising that the problem of the justification of inequality in matters of cultural competence should be particularly acute at the present time. Furthermore, among the classes of "laymen" in academic matters, students are particularly closely involved through their partial and somewhat equivocal membership in academic collectivities, in such ways that they are subject both to authority and to economic pressures in this relationship. This set of circumstances seems to be important in the background of the present wave of disturbances in the relations of students to universities and colleges.

The Integrative Process

We can now take up the problem of what are the integrative processes by which, on the one hand, these three different kinds of inequality can be, at least in part, reconciled with the egalitarian components of the institutional system; and by which, on the other hand, equality and inequality can be integrated with each other. We must not forget that presumably the major part in this integration is played by institutions which are not alterable on an *ad hoc* basis, but which have evolved over long periods.

They, of course, are also continually changing, only in part by conscious decision-making processes.

The more complex and pluralistic a society becomes, however, the more dependent its functioning comes to be on freedom of unit decision and on generalized mechanisms which facilitate and guide those decisions. The four generalized media of societal interchange *all* have, in their respective spheres, integrative functions. Thus it is almost obvious that without money as a medium of exchange the pluralism brought about by the economic division of labor could not be brought into a balance among the various participants in market relations, namely, consumers of myriad commodities and services, producers, employers, members of the labor force, et al. (cf. Parsons, 1969a: chaps. 14–16).

In the area where stratification is a particularly salient phenomenon, I shall, however, suggest that the complex of mechanisms which centers on influence as a generalized symbolic medium of interchange is crucial in that its functions are *doubly* integrative. We have defined influence elsewhere as the *generalized* capacity to persuade in the process of social interaction. On the one hand it involves, as such, no situational sanctions such as modes of coercion or inducement. On the other hand, as symbolically generalized, its use is *not* a mobilizing of "intrinsically persuasive" particular arguments; but, in parallel with money, is rather a capacity to persuade independently of intrinsic considerations—in the monetary case the relevant property is "value in exchange," not "value in use" (cf. Parsons, 1969: chap. 15).

We have long contended that the social system, within the general framework of action, is the primary focus of the integration of cultural with "motivational" factors. In the context of action, among the cultural modalities, the normative, the moral values, for obvious reasons takes precedence (vide the "problem of order"). Among the "motivational" components of action which are "subcultural"—i.e., pertain to personality and organic systems—we are assigning precedence to the category of *affect* because of its *inter*personal integrative significance (cf. Schneider, 1968) and at the same time its "access" to the more primordial motivational components, notably the erotic at the organic level.

In analytical terms, however, both moral values and affect are extrasocietal categories: each has to be "processed" before it comes to be fully "incorporated" in a social system. In the cultural case, moral values as part of the general "definition of the situation" must be conceived both to be institutionalized, as components of the structure of the social system, and *specified* to the level of norms. Both aspects are clearly involved in the conception of value-commitments as a generalized medium of the social system (cf. Parsons, 1969). Both also are conditions of the operation of influence as medium.

Affect we conceive to be a medium operating at the general level of

action, parallel to the "definition of the situation" in the primarily cultural reference (cf. chapter 10 in this volume). To be "transformed" into operative significance at the level of the social system, however, it also must be "institutionalized," or "socialized." This means two primary things. The first is what we call *identification* in the sense of motivational "acceptance"—at levels of "deep" motivational "commitment"—of membership in collective systems, most notably the society itself, which essentially is what we mean by solidarity, when seen from the point of view of function for the collective system, and secondly, internalization of some kind of priority system which structures the manifold of membership expectations for the individual—and somewhat differently for collective units.

Money and power are the obvious generalized foci for the assertion of unit-interest in the outcomes of social participation, and various units, especially persons, may have different levels of "investment" in the maximization of their money and power interests. Influence, as we see it, is a mechanism which *mediates* between these unit interests—with respect to which affective "involvement" is the most important subcultural and subsocial component—and collective interests—with respect to which solidarity presents the most important normative condition, which in turn "reflects" the underlying cultural commitments entering the social system via the institutionalization of values and the specification of these values to the level of norms.[9]

As a generalized medium, we hence conceive influence to operate in the first instance as a mechanism for integrating these two levels, *namely, that of collective solidarity in the implementation of values on the one hand and that of "motivating" units, especially individuals, to participate, including "genuine" acceptance of the obligations of membership, on the other.*

In the nature of the position of cultural components in the system of action, the reference to "justification" must call on more generalized considerations, must tend toward the pattern of universalism. In contrast, the reference to mobilization of "motivation" must invoke considerations special to the nature and situation of the unit of reference, hence more particularistic considerations. Seen in these terms, at the social system level, influence is a way of reconciling these two very fundamental constituents of social systems. As the history of law amply documents, justification must continually invoke "general principles." On the other hand, "appeal to interest" must invoke considerations more special to the particular characteristics and circumstances of units or classes of them. This

[9] The much discussed problem of the "protection of privacy" has a bearing here. From the perspective of one of an individual's fields of membership participation, e.g., in his family, his "right to privacy" is essentially the claim legitimately to prevent or curb "intrusion" stemming from the expectations generated by participation in *other* membership categories, e.g., in his occupational role.

process of mediation may be said to define the primary function of influence as a medium.

If the social systems with which we deal were structured as monolithic "confrontations" between units—especially individuals—and societies"—this formulation would be exhaustive. In fact, however, the most important systems are pluralistically differentiated. This fact introduces the relevance of two other functions of the influence mechanism, namely, contributing to the allocation of loyalties as among plural collective involvements by units, and to the level of responsibility to be assumed by each unit within the structure of each such collectivity.

It should, however, never be forgotten that the specification of societal values to the level of solidarity of the societal collectivity is a step in the direction of particularistic primacy from the more generally universalistic pattern of the value-system, but that at the same time the treatment of the individual societal member in the role of membership, e.g., citizenship for the societal community as a whole, involves a major "universalizing" of *his* orientations. From the point of view of the society, his identifications make him a relatively generalized resource for societal functions, which is capable of allocation among several such functions. At the same time the generalization of affect, socialized through identification, tends to make it motivationally meaningful for him to accept societal guidance in the allocation of his affective interests. At the other end, the specification of values to the societal community qualifies the purer universalism of the more general societal value system and creates a manifold within which a variety of such allocations can in our sense be justified.

It would seem to be the case, moreover, that the equality principle has its most important focus in the modern type of societal community at these two points. At the point of value-specification, the basic pattern of equality of membership status creates a presumption against the introduction of inequalities which are not positively functional for the system. At the point of effectively anchored interest, on the other hand, there is a presumption against the introduction of inequalities which either impose on the motivated unit the toleration of inequalities in the extra rewards of which he does not share or, contrariwise, imposes on units or classes of them, special status with respect to responsibilities, command of resources, rewards, etc., which are not shared by other members.

It thus follows that the *main* focus of the justification of inequalities should lie in the other two categories. These, it will be remembered, are, first, the differentiation of subcollectivities of the societal community in terms of their functional contributions to the societal community as a whole, and hence the development of differential prestige as a function of memberships in such subcollectivities. Thus obviously government can, for most modern societies, have special kinds of functional significance for the society as a whole. Second, within such functionally differentiated

subcollectivities, participating units will have to occupy statuses, individual or collective, which are differentiated on an axis of inequality, e.g., of command of resources, of authority and power, of cultural competence, or some combination.

The most general functions of influence then are first to "combine" and in that sense integrate the considerations of justification of allocations of societal units, the resources they command and the rewards and burdens they receive, among societal functions, and with this to reconcile these justifications with their interests, not only as conceived by the user of influence, but also by the units themselves. Since influence is conceived as a medium of persuasion, this implies the reaching of some kind of consensus between persuader and persuaded with respect to the integration of justification and interest.[10]

Within this more general framework, then, the functions of influence are secondly to bring about an allocation of subcollectivity organizations and their memberships on the one hand, of statuses and roles within them on the other, which can be said to be compatible with the "collective interest" or the demands of solidarity and at the same time with the interests of units. The same ideal standard of reaching consensus on such allocations applies here. In these areas in particular it will be necessary to justify important inequalities which, moreover, rest on *varying* combinations of bases, such as functional importance, competence, levels of authority, etc., and to reconcile these inequalities, both with the interests of the favored, and more difficult, of those who are disadvantaged by the allocative decisions.

If influence is to be treated as a generalized medium of interchange, it must be conceived to operate through a code. We thus conceive the insti-

---

[10] The term *justification* has been used several times in the last few paragraphs and with some frequency in other parts of this paper. It is meant here in a technical sense which is above all to be carefully distinguished from the related term legitimation. Both refer to the invoking of grounds of *normative* "authority" for a proposition or for a course of action, past or prospective. They differ in level of the generality of the grounds of normative acceptability. The most familiar example is that of law. In the American system the problem of legitimacy concerns the Constitutional level, in the broadest sense, of the legitimacy of the legal order, its general principles of "Rights" as reveiewed above and the powers of government and limitations on those powers. This sense of the concept legitimation is, I think, essentially the same as Weber's usage. Justification, on the other hand, concerns the lower level of generality where the main legitimating framework is assumed. In law it involves the justification of a decision by reference to a more particularized legal doctrine, e.g., decision that publication of a confidential medical record constituted an "invasion of privacy" and that the plaintiff is therefore entitled to damages. The decision in the case is here justified by the prohibition of unwarranted invasions of privacy.

A collective system in which influence operates as a medium must be legitimized as a system, including its normative order as a whole. More particular "allocative" decisions about rights and interests *within* the system, where actual or potential conflict is involved, must be justified. The necessity for the distinction arises out of the more general distinction between pattern-maintenance and integrative functions in social systems.

tution of property to be the code through which money as medium operates, and similarly authority to be the code of power. For the code which is central to influence as a medium it seems appropriate to choose a concept which has played a central role in stratification theory, namely *prestige*.

First let us suggest that, though of course it has a quantitative dimension, prestige should not be used only in an hierachical reference. In this respect it is similar to power—thus we speak of the possession of the franchise as having power. One vote per election is only a little power, but it quite definitely *is* power. Similarly I would suggest that *any* membership status in a solidarity collectivity carries prestige and hence influence, no matter how far from carrying special prerogatives not shared by other members. But of course some units, collective or individual, have higher prestige than others.

If membership status is a kind of minimal base-line for the concept of prestige, in line with our treatment of the problem of equality, then two qualifying considerations need to be introduced immediately. First, from the point of view of any given system reference, there may be those who are excluded from membership status, e.g., "aliens" relative to a national society, and they do not share in the prestige of "citizens." Similarly, the "poor" are said to be at least partly excluded (cf. Rainwater, 1969). Second, the structure of such a community is always more or less pluralistic so that different components of prestige will derive from memberships in different subcollectivities within the system—and of course also "intersecting" with it, as in the sense that some honorary societies have foreign members. Hence the prestige of a member unit, again individual or collective, is a function not of one membership status alone, but of some kind of integration of his or its plural membership statuses. In general, the higher the prestige of any of the collectivities of which he or it is a member, the more this membership contributes to his more general level of prestige. Conversely not belonging to given collectivities itself constitutes "membership" in "outgroups" whether the latter are lower in prestige or not.

The amount of influence a unit can command, and hence its level of prestige, is a function in particular of *two* sets of condtions, which need to be clearly distinguished from each other. The first, analogous to the money income of a unit of the economy, is influence deriving from interchange operations through connections of solidarity. Insofar as these operations involve implementations of values shared by others, they can establish what we have called "value-based claims to loyalty." Insofar as they involve assumption of collective responsibilities, especially in leadership capacities, they can also establish claims to reciprocal support; and insofar as they involve actual or prospective valued contributions to societal function, they can generate persuasiveness in assertion of claims to

the control of the necessary resources. Here the influence controlled by the unit is an *input* from others.

The other context is that in which such units can in fact "produce" influence in a sense parallel to that in which an authentically productive unit of the economy actually "makes" money, not only in that it enhances its own money income but that it adds to the amount of money circulating in the economic system. Capacity to make influence in this sense is a function of a second set of conditions, namely command of a set of "factors of solidarity" which are analogous to the factors of production in economic theory and of course of the effective use of the factors commanded. In addition to the specification of the general value-pattern to the relevant levels of valuation of solidarity (the equivalent of "land" as an economic factor), these are value-commitments to the relevant forms of association, capacity to invoke policy-decisions binding on the relevant collectivities, and actual control of the necessary generalized resources.

Taken together, these two sets of inputs to the influence system of an acting unit can be expected to produce higher levels for the unit of reference in the relevant prestige-scale in proportion as, first, the functions of the unit in question in the system, regarded as "contributions," are highly valued. These valuations of function, however, break down into two components which it is essential to distinguish. One of these, (a), is the function of the valuation of the collective unit of which the unit of reference is a "member." This may be a university of which a given scholar is a member as a faculty participant, or it may be an industry of which a given firm is a member. The other, (b), is the function of the valuation of the unit of reference itself. Thus a physicist may be valued more highly than a sociologist though they are members of the same faculty, and a "blue ribbon" firm more highly than a marginal one in the same industry.

Secondly, prestige is a function of the unit's capacity to participate in an extensive "influence-market" and thereby to extend and generalize its access both to influence-income and to factors of influence as these have just been outlined. The conception of extensiveness here is consciously modeled on Adam Smith's conception of the "extent of the market." In our case it refers to the scope or range of interpenetrating solidary collectivities with which a unit has contact, to which it hence enjoys "access" through its own and others' common membership. Thus, even within its differentiated sphere, a modern academic unit is part of a highly pluralistic social system. A professor in a particular discipline, e.g., sociology, in a modern university, has access not only to his colleagues in his own department, but to certain categories of students, to faculty colleagues in other disciplines, to colleagues in his own discipline in other institutions, to alumni, to "outside" groups who have an interest, as "lay" groups, in his contribution, etc. His capacity both to command an "income" of influence, and to generate it himself is clearly a function of the extensity of this

relational nexus. The familiar distinction between the "local" and the "cosmopolitan" is relevant here, because only cosmopolitans, with their more extensive "contacts," can reach certain of the higher levels of prestige.

The third basic factor of prestige is access to instrumentality significant resources, at a level cybernetically lower than the value-commitments themselves, but definitely including command of influence. This latter point is directly parallel to the sense in which the "market position" of a firm is a function of its access to *financial* resources as well as to non-monetary factors of production. Thus "funds" of influence may be available for operations analogous to investment in the economic sense.

Conclusion

A few crucial points can be made in conclusion which tie up the rather involved preceding analysis. The first is that, though difficult balances must be held within complex social systems between the imperatives of quality and those of stratification, both sets of imperatives operate in such a wide variety of different respects and contexts that there is no guarantee that they will cohere in a form which is functionally viable for the larger system unless there are mechanisms which are functionally specialized in the relevant modes of integration.

There is no simple alternative as between an egalitarian and a stratified society, or even a question of acceptable "degrees" of stratification in general. Four patterns for the "maximization" of one mode of balance may be noted. The first, which was more popular a generation and more ago than now, is based on the strict application of the model of the competitive economic market. The combination of the ideal of equality of opportunity with the justification of the inequalities generated in the competitive process seem to provide one basis of reconciling these two opposed imperatives, with the implication that the successful in the competition of the market "deserve" not only such rewards as high income, but also the larger share in control over the processes of the economy that the resulting concentration brings about.

Interpenetrating with this there are two political models. The one with egalitarian emphasis is that all integration on the equality–inequality axis should occur through the pattern of the democratic association, so that the only inequalities permitted should be the superiorities accorded to incumbents of elective office who are held strictly accountable to a fully democratic constituency. This is often held to be the sole basis of a principled legitimation of inequality which would in turn make possible the justification of more particular forms of inequality.

Largely antithetical with this is the model of the centralization of in-

equalities by the self-conceived bearers of a higher order of value-commitments; this in turn allegedly justifies the assumption of central control and all the other primary spheres of inequality—as exemplified in our time by the fascist and communist dictatorships. There is an important sense in which this pattern is the obverse of radical democratic associationalism in that both tend to bring matters to focus on the problem of *control* of collective decisions and resources and thereby to "politicize" the integrative process. Dictatorship in this sense is generally legitimized in terms of a pattern I have often called "value-absolutism." The stance is that "the values to which *we* are committed take precedence, at the value level, over any others operative in the relevant field, hence we have the legitimate right to take control and to suppress opposition." The content of the values may be economic, as in the communist case, nationalistic-political as in that of fascism, or religious, as in that of the early Calvinists; in our terms there is a basic similiarity of pattern.

As against all three of these "models" of integration, the kind of pluralistic society which has become dominant in the modern world is dependent for its integration on complicated cross-relations among these different bases of claims to equality and justification of inequality respectively. This has certain important consequences, of which three may be noted. First, bases of prestige, in the sense in which we have used that term, must be functionally diffuse, i.e., a resultant of plural components rather than any one. Thus in a professional case, competence alone is a limiting case unless it is combined with a reputation for "integrity" in the sense of concern for the interests affected by the use of such competence. The access to influence which results from a position of prestige—higher than average—is thus a function of *plural* factors in this sense.

Secondly, since we have taken the position that there is a presumption in favor of equality of status and hence inequalities need to be specifically justified, the problem of *accountability* has acquired a new salience. This very old concept has had its most prominent uses in the fields first of "moral" accountability symbolized above all in terms of accountability to a deity or to a "moral community" legitimated at the highest level. The democratic version of accountability to a constituency involves many familiar complications. That of competitive success in the economic sense attempts to eliminate the problem by suggesting that an automatic mechanism insures that the successful are also the "deserving."

We suggest that the problem of accountability cannot, in a pluralistic society, be "solved" by any one of these three ways or by any combination of them. Hence, third, we suggest that a fourth focus, which has been discussed at some length above, is necessary, namely, what we have called the *fiduciary* focus. Here the term "responsibility" seems to have a rather special resonance. In this, as in so many contexts, system-references are crucial. For my present purposes, therefore, fiduciary responsibility is

to be defined in terms of the social system of reference for most of this discussion, the society. In proportion as such a system is pluralistically differentiated, it becomes less meaningful to focus such responsibility in any one functional context—it is in this sense inherently "diffuse." Thus where government has come to be highly differentiated from the societal community, high governmental office has progressively less of a monopoly of fiduciary responsibility and, with it, prestige.

There is here an important kind of relativity. If we take the perspective of any one primary functional context, the fiduciary component must arise from its articulations with others. Thus the socially responsible business-man is one who has interests other than those in economic productivity in mind—similarly the socially responsible politician, interests other than those of effective government, to say nothing of his own power. In the academic world, assuming the primacy of cultural commitments, the socially responsible member of the profession is concerned with implementation of the relevant cultural commitments *plus* a concern for their impact on and conditioning by other factors in the society.

There was a sense in which, some centuries ago, a hereditary aristocracy could serve as the focus of fiduciary responsibility at the higher levels. This possibility has clearly been destroyed by the basic conflict of the modern egalitarian complex with the principle of heredity of status. In this structural reference it can perhaps be said that one of the greatest integrative needs of modern society is for a functional equivalent of aristocracy.

In discussing prestige and influence, we have stressed the aspect of "diffuseness." This, of course, is technically most directly evident in the range or scope of the "influence market" as a factor in prestige. Influence is both acquired in part by virtue of highly specific capacities and achievements and dependent for its genesis on such. But there seems also to be an important functional "need" for more or less visible symbolization of prestige. This is the context often discussed under the heading of style of life or sometimes standard of living. It is often referred to in various contexts in discussions of stratification but in my opinion has not had the careful analytical attention it deserves (cf. Laumann and House, 1970).

The family household has, of course, been the commonest point of reference for such discussions, but I think it should be made particularly clear that *any* unit of a societal system employs expressive symbolism in ways which are significant to its prestige or reputation. This is equally true of "negative" styles of life where, for example, certain of the younger generation use deliberately sloppy clothing as a symbol of protest.

To cite only a few examples of nonfamilial symbolization. A laundry of my acquaintance does not get its wash any cleaner by planting attractive flower beds along the side of the building, but the customers generally "like" it. A publisher generally does not make his physical product

as strictly utilitarian, from e.g., the point of view of readability, as possible, but employs book designers to make the product more "attractive." The general principles of "consumption style" hence should be worked out to include all societal units, not just family households.

A second main point needs to be made. The very ready tendency to derogate such symbolism often takes the form immortalized by Veblen in the phrase "conspicuous consumption," with the allegation that people lived in comfortable and tasteful houses, or wore attractive clothes, *in order,* for instrumental motives, to enhance their prestige. This was then held to be a dishonorable motive with no "intrinsic" connection with the "real" functions of the unit. The aspect of the problem which needs to be noted here is that it arises *wherever* generalized media of interchange are involved in human action. Thus it has often been alleged that participants in market systems, in particular businessmen, are motivated "only" by profit, politicians "only" by power, etc. Precisely insofar as influence has become differentiated out as a generalized symbolic medium, therefore, it has become tempting to allege that those who seek and use it are motivated "only" by prestige (cf. Packard, 1959). Of course it is in the nature of such a differentiated system that there is a structurally built-in interest in *both* enhancing command of the medium concerned *and* effectively performing the functions of reference. Thus ideally—though of course often not actually—the more efficient businessman gains higher profits and ideally the politician who prospectively and actually serves the public interest better gains more power. In the academic world ideally, and dare we suggest *sometimes* actually, the man who makes greater "contributions" through good research and teaching gains higher prestige. The nature and extent of the conflict between these two basic interests, i.e., in effective functional performance and in command of a generalized medium, is an *empirical* problem, not one solved by allegations that interest in the medium is "inherently" at the expense of achievement in the function.

Technical Note

For those readers who are concerned to follow the more technical and formal aspects of the theory of social systems as these have been presented in a rather long series of discussions, complete with diagrams, it may be worth while to attempt to fit the dichotomy equality-inequality formally into the more general scheme of paradigms. My starting point was the suggestion of Lipset that equality–inequality might be treated as a pattern variable. This is on the face of it a reasonable suggestion, but the pattern variable scheme, especially in the version presented a few years ago in

"Pattern Variables Revisited" has become a rather tightly integrated paradigm, and introduction simply of an additional pair would raise questions about the whole logical structure of the scheme. An alternative, of course, would be to identify, as another pair of terms, this dichotomy with one of those already in the scheme, but this clearly will not work. Here I present, schematically, a third possibility.

I should like to start with reference to Figure 1, the general "format" of a societal, or other action system, interchange paradigm, and then Figure 2, the six sets of four interchange categories between each pair of the four primary functional subsystems for the social system case.

With reference to the format presented in Figure 1, my suggestion is that the dilemma of equality vs. inequality can be used to characterize certain aspects of *both* of the *diagonal* interchange systems, namely *L–G* on the one hand and I–A on the other. Two important background references are relevant to the rationale of this choice. First, it will be noted that earlier in this paper (footnote 10) I have strongly emphasized the importance of the distinction between *legitimation* and *justification*. In Figure 2 it will be noted that these terms, quite independently of the composition of the present paper, appear, one in each of the two, namely legitimation in the formula "legitimation of authority," treated as a variant of value-commitments as a medium in L–G, and justification in the formula "grounds for justification of claims," treated as a variant of influence as a medium in I–A. The other influence component in the I–A interchange, "standards for allocation of resources" could of course readily be rephrased to include the term justification, as could "moral responsibility for collective interests" in the L–G interchange be rephrased to include the term legitimation. The inclusion of both terms in the analysis of the equality problem on the one hand, the distinction between them on the other, are certainly crucial to the general analysis.

The second background consideration concerns the relevance of these diagonals to Durkheim's famous distinction between mechanical and organic solidarity. The L–G axis concerns the relation between the system's pattern-maintenance base—especially its values—and its capacity for effective collective action in the analytically political sense, which comes very close to the "problem" of mechanical solidarity. The I–A axis, on the other hand, concerns the relation between the system's integrative norms and mechanisms and the problem of allocation of resources, including access to opportunity. The stress here is on pluralistic differentiation and the problem of maintaining solidarity among differentiated units and subsystems. The broad insight about the connection of the "diagonals" with Durkheim's scheme was attained in connection with the paper on "Durkheim's Contribution to the Theory of Integration of Social Systems" (Parsons, 1967b: chap. 1), and has served as a cardinal reference point ever since.

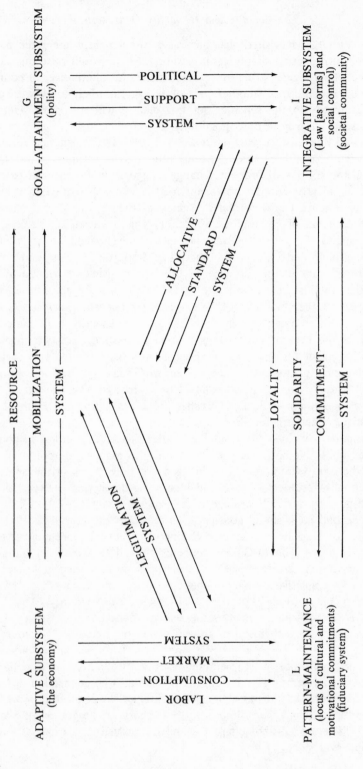

Figure 1. Format of the societal interchange system.

366

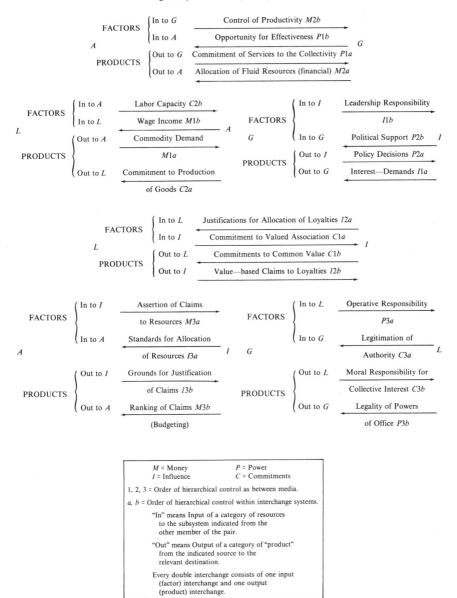

Figure 2. The categories of societal interchange.*

*See Parsons, 1969b, "On the Concept of Political Power," Technical Note; also 1973, *The American University*, Figure A-3.

Within this frame of reference, in the light of the considerations re-viewed in the present paper, it seems clear that the principal egalitarian components of modern society are anchored in the "internal" subsystems of the society, namely those of pattern maintenance and integration (or the societal community), respectively. On the other hand, the exigencies which legitimate and justify inequalities are predominantly functions of the relation of the system to its environments, notably in the political and economic, but otherwise adaptive contexts.

In the above discussion we have both strongly emphasized and distin-guished from each other two such contexts. The first of these constitutes the system of institutionalized basic rights, which is central to the pattern-maintenance system. For the United States their content is centered in the Bill of Rights, thus having constitutional status for the legal system. The essentially egalitarian character of this complex is clear, and has, as we have noted, become accentuated through the development of the law since the adoption of the Bill of Rights, especially through judicial interpreta-tion and further institutional amendments, but also through legislation and executive action.

The second context, also partly legitimized in the Bill of Rights itself, is the basic equality of membership status as the organizing principle of associational collectivities. The most fundamental is the "politically orga-nized" societal community as the constituency to which government is held to be formally accountable under the law. The symbolically focal institution is equality of the franchise on the one member–one vote prin-ciple; but a number of other egalitarian freedoms cluster around it, such as those of free speech, petition for the redress of grievances, and the like. Of course the basic principle of membership equality extends in general to a much wider range of associational collectivities.

Contrasting with these, we can distinguish two main contexts of positive sanctioning of inequalities. The first, diagonally opposite to the basic rights complex, is the goal-attainment subsystem, which it will be remembered we interpret analytically as the *polity*. The focus of this is the attainment and implementation of *binding* collective decisions in the interest of collective effectiveness. The criterion of bindingness involves the imposition on collectivity members of obligations which only in limit-ing cases can be fully equal; and both decision-making and implementa-tion require differential authority and power, as we have discussed above in connection with both the conceptions of elective office and of bureau-cratic administration. This, then, is the context in which Weber's famous conception of the *legitimation* of authority is central. Weber was thinking primarily of *differential* authority and power, which of course concerns the problem of inequality. It should, however, not be forgotten that mem-bership status as such entails binding obligations, some of which impose equal burdens on all members. Thus inequality is not "the essence" of

binding obligations, but is one fundamental condition of collective effectiveness and hence one principal focus of the problems of legitimation. In this connection we obviously have a triangular interchange relationship. What we are saying is that the enjoyment of political support by "leaders" or others who assume differential authority and power is not enough. Their legitimacy derives not, in the first instance, from their constituencies, but from the institutional framework, at the "constitutional" level, within which such differentials are provided for.

Diagonally opposite to the complex of membership status stands, what, in a highly differentiated reference, we call the *economy*. This, as a functional subsystem of a society, is in the first instance the structural locus of "production" through combinations of the factors of production. In its relation to the societal community, however, and hence to the membership complex, it is concerned with the problem of *allocation* of mobile resources. The *standards* which regulate the allocative processes, as distinguished from the concrete processes of allocation themselves, derive in the first instance from the nature of the societal community as an association of members. Here, as we put it, on the background of the egalitarian base of membership rights, unequal allocations require *justification* in the above technical sense of that term, a process which is in some respects at least similar to that of adjudication in its legal meaning. This is to say claims have to be evaluated and implicit or explicit "judgments" rendered.

A certain focus falls on the economic aspect of allocation, that is of fluid resources which are at the disposal of one unit or class of them relative to others. This aspect of the allocative problem, however, becomes bound up with two others in particular. One concerns the allocation of capacities to utilize resources, once available. The base line in this connection has been the distribution of the genetically given components of achievement capacity. On "top of" this, however, come the factors which enter into the development of capacities—or their extinction or diminution—all along the path of the life course. Here, of course, particularly important are "socializing influences starting with the family of orientation and the more "formal" aspects of education. Of course, fluid resource allocation constitutes one major factor in the development of capacities in these respects, hence operates again and again at different stages, e.g., through the allocation of societal resources to educational functions.

The second aspect of the allocative problem concerns what is often called the "opportunity complex." One factor here concerns the possession by units of fluid resources adequate to take advantage of available opportunities. The other, however, is less fluid, what may be called the "structure of opportunities." Thus the manifold of "places" in good institutions of higher education is not, at any given time, a simple function of the capacity of some agency to pay for them in the short run.

The upshot of this combination of capacities, resources, and oppor-

tunity structures, however, becomes the primary focus, in the structure of a modern society, of patterns of inequality in the distribution of valued achievements, whether of individuals or of collective units. The thesis is that such inequalities need to be *justified* in terms of their functional contributions to the social system.

The specific manifold of the distribution of authority and power in a complex society, including, but not confined to, the dimension of inequality in it with respect to both public and private power, requires, if it is not to be unduly disruptive of societal order, legitimation in terms of *generalized* mediation. I hence suggest that legitimation of such distribution constitutes one of the most important functions of value-commitments considered as a medium of interchange. In this context such commitments are *specified* (cf. Parsons, 1969b) to the functions of collective effectiveness—remembering the pluralistic structure of collectivities—and to various levels in the interpenetrating hierarchies of authority and power. Legitimation as a function entails denial of its positive version in cases which are judged to be incompatible with the integrity of the value-commitments in question. Value-commitments, however, at the same time have functions in other connections than the legitimation of authority, notably, that of commitment to participation in contexts of valued association and that of participation through "commitments to labor" in the instrumental functions of the society. The relationships just reviewed are schematically set forth in Figure 3.

When the relationships are set forth in this way the question is urgently posed of why I have stressed the two diagonal relationships; why not all six equally? There certainly are important relations, for example, between equality of membership status and inequalities of power and authority—a theme discussed above in connection with the institution of elective office in democratic systems. Similar things can be said about the other three interchange relations between primary subsystems.

My general rationale for selecting the diagonals, in addition to the considerations advanced above with respect to the distinction between negative and positive sanctions and between mechanical and organic solidarity, concerns a formal consideration which was prominent for a time

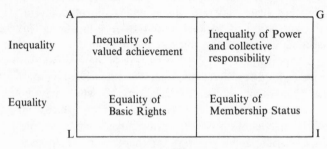

Figure 3.

in considering the general interchange paradigm, but which was not even included in the version which appeared in the Technical Note to the paper on Power (Parsons, 1969b, Figure 3) which is reproduced here as Figure 2. This is that the distinctions between the three pairs of interchange sets—namely, in the figures, horizontal, vertical, and diagonal respectively—had functional significance. Specifically, the horizontal interchanges had mainly adaptive significance, the vertical ones, goal-attaining, and the diagonals, integrative significance.

This is not the place to go fully into the rationale for this set as a whole. For the horizontal let me suggest only by illustration that the A–G interchange is the primary locus of the famous means–end relation. That fluid resources are means to goal-attainment goes without saying, but the relation is reciprocal, namely through the fact that political effectiveness (political in the analytical sense) is an essential means to efficient economic production. Hence the importance of the firm as political entity. In the vertical context, for households' attainment of an adequate standard of living is certainly a major goal, but so for the economy is the securing of adequate labor capacity as a factor of production.

It seems clear that, on the basis of the considerations reviewed in the present paper, the problem of equality and inequality is, as Lipset has often emphasized, of particularly clear integrative significance. This becomes evident in the first instance because, probably increasingly as ascriptive inequalities have lessened in significance, inequalities which are neither legitimized nor justified, in the technical senses in which we have used these terms, are likely to be especially disruptive of the social systems in which they actually or allegedly occur. The ubiquity with which aggrieved groups use such terms as "oppression" and "exploitation" surely strongly suggests this.

One of the virtues of working with a formal paradigm is that the existence of "empty cells" or other formal components to which no special significance is attributed, raises questions which keep nagging for answers. If the equality–inequality problem is to be especially related to the internal–external axis of the social system paradigm, the question naturally arises of whether another dilemma of comparable integrative significance should be related to the other, the instrumental–consummatory axis, again with special reference to its relation to the diagonal interchanges. Precisely in the course of working out the formal position of the equality–inequality problem as just presented, it gradually became clear that there was indeed another such dilemma which could be treated in a comparable way, namely the very old and much discussed one of freedom vs. constraint (for the latter, I deliberately select the term used by Durkheim).

That there has been a major dilemma in this area is probably obvious, as is the fact that it has taken rather definite theoretical shapes at least since Rousseau (cf. Weinstein and Platt, 1969). Starting then with the

assumption that these terms refer to genuine dilemmas of the human condition and that there is a certain coherence among their various meanings, it at least makes sense to try to fit them into a system paradigm. If, then, the instrumental–consummatory axis is chosen as a place to try the fit, the first question is, which of the two concepts in the paradigm fits which of the "horns" of the dilemma? It will be remembered that initially it was by no means obvious in common sense terms that equality has, as we have put it, its "anchorage" in the *internal* subsystems of the social system.

My suggestion here is that the key conception would be the relation of the freedom–constraint dilemma to the *temporal* axis of action systems, including the social system. If this is done, then it seems clear that the ongoing process of action is in one aspect always a matter of the foreclosing of previously open alternatives. To be sure a process of expenditure of funds may be balanced by an equal flow of income, but the *particular* funds commanded in the T_1 initial period, when they have been spent, are no longer available in T_2.

This seems to mean that, from the point of view of action, moving forward in time always means the sacrifice of some freedoms and the corresponding acceptance of some new constraints. This basic relation is of course balanced by what in some sense is a "feedback" phenomenon, namely that all along the temporal course of action processes, man-imposed constraints have to be "set up" (the ways in which this occurs are of course highly problematical) so that acting units or systems are never concretely as "free" as they "theoretically" might be, and, conversely, remaining freedoms have to be protected at later stages. To use a familiar illustration, much has rightly been made of the genetic plasticity of the human child—he presumably has the potential for example, of learning *any* language as his "native" tongue, but he cannot learn them all. Because he is socialized in a particular speech-community, his initial "freedom" is "constrained" by the linguistic institutions of that country. In principle the same things can be said of all other institutions, none of us is free to opt for *any* of the alternatives which have in some sense been intrinsically open to lines of human social, personal, or cultural development; we are always constrained by what is sometimes called the "history" of the particular action systems in which we are involved. This does not mean that they cannot change or be changed, but it does mean that processes of change must *start* from the state of affairs which exists at the time in that system, and in an abstract sense that is always "constraining."

Since we are here dealing with the analysis of social systems, we assume that concretely there is *never* either absolute freedom or absolute constraint, but that what we are presenting is a paradigm of components of both, in a sense in which *all* concrete states of affairs are combinatorial resultants. Under this assumption we therefore identify freedom with the instrumental side of the paradigm, constraint with the consummatory.

As in the case of equality–inequality, and in many other connections, it is likely to be necessary to carry analytical "breakdown" at least to the point of subdividing each of the main categories into two, on the basis of their relation to the other main axis of the system, the internal–external. For reasons of historical comprehensibility, it is probably better to begin with the constraint side. Here a striking fact is that the external–internal axis links very directly with Durkheim's last two of three meanings of the very crucial concept of constraint (French *contraint,* which fortunately presents no problem of translation). The first, constraint by the objective existence of situational "reality" need not concern us here. The second, however, was constraint by the imposition of sanctions through human decisions—the criminal law, and the exposure to legal penalties being for Durkheim clearly the paradigmatic case. This clearly fits in our general "political" context. It seems appropriate to designate it as "constraint by collective decisions and sanctions," assuming that the *authority* of the individual decider or imposer of sanctions is collective in origin.

Durkheim's third mode of constraint, our second, he called "constraint by moral authority." The moral authority of collectivities was thus felt to operate through the internalization of their normative orders in the personalities of their members. The sense in which such a member was not "free" to act in violation of these norms came to be that he accepted their legitimacy or justification and that violation would expose him to "internal" sanctions—if an individual is the actor of reference, guilt or shame. Durkheim conceived this type of constraint as definitely bound to solidary collectivities, so I have phrased it as "constraint by moral authority in a community."

The "freedom" side of the dichotomy again can be seen to involve two subtypes. One is the mode of freedom which is relatively independent of immediate normative controls in terms of the values of the social system. This connects with economic considerations and long-standing ideas about the "rational pursuit of self-interest"—the self of reference of course may be a business firm, rather than an individual. Hence an appropriate designation seems to be "freedom to pursue unit interest."

The other subtype concerns freedoms with respect to involvement in the normative obligations and commitments which are institutionalized in the system. In my paper on "The Concept of Value-Commitments" (Parsons, 1968b), I have stressed the importance of the combination of integrity of commitment to a value-pattern at high levels of generality, and freedom of the unit, individual or collective, to *allocate* his more specified commitments among functions, levels of specification and along the line collectivities and types of contribution. We may hence speak of "freedom of units to allocate commitments." This suggested ordering of the freedom–constraint dilemma is formalized in Figure 4.

Considerations very similar to those discussed in relation to the

	Freedom	Constraint	
A	Freedom to pursue unit interests	Constraint by collective decisions and sanctions	G
L	Freedom of units to allocate commitments	Constraint by moral authority in community	I

Figure 4.

equality–inequality dilemma serve to justify the emphasis on the diagonal relationships in Figure 4. I suggest that the L–G axis in this respect constitutes a kind of superordinate locus of "social control" in the relevant respects, in that, if the system is to be a *social* system, the unit freedom to allocate commitments at will must be constrained by concern for *collective* goals and interests. Furthermore, the "hard-nosed" suggestion is made, that if collective interests are to be sufficiently protected, it is not possible to rely *only* on moral authority, however fundamental that may be—and I personally think it is—but that *collectively binding* decisions, with the appropriate (including negative) sanctions are also functionally necessary.

These "hard" necessities of the L–G syndrome do not, however, exclude an equal importance being accorded to the other diagonal relation, namely between freedom to pursue unit interests on the one hand and constraint by moral authority on the other. In terms of the dual conceptions of the "division of labor," that of economic differentiation of function associated especially with the name of Adam Smith, and that of differentiation of the societal community (or pluralism) associated with that of Durkheim, this is on the one hand a sphere of especially increased "autonomy" on the part of units. *At the same time,* it is essential to recognize that such autonomy cannot be generalized in a social system without the complementary set of constraints which are "ideally" those of moral rather than coercively political authority.

Finally, when the two dilemma components are systematically related, in the above way, the question must arise of what the nature of the *resultant* patterns may be. The origin of such resultants is in the nature of the case clearly complex. It involves a "balancing" not only of equality and inequality and of freedom and constraint, but of both in relation to each other and in relation to the other exigencies of a social system.

I suggest that there is indeed a pattern of distinction among such resultants and that this pattern makes it possible to "locate" in terms of analytical "paradigming" certain syndromes which for a long time have appeared to be very important, but the exact theoretical status of which

	Freedom	Constraint
Inequality	Equality of opportunity for achievement	Equal Protection of the Laws
Equality	Fiduciary Responsibility (moral authority)	Institutionalized Individualism (class prestige)

A ... G (top corners), L ... I (bottom corners)

Figure 5. Resultant patterns of the balancing of legitimized and justified equalities and inequalities and freedoms and constraints.

has not hitherto been clear. An important principle of this last paradigm to be presented is that, presumably because of the importance of feedback considerations, each category involves a component of its "dialectical" opposite. Thus in the cell in which "justified or legitimized inequalities" have been located, a "secondary" principle of equality appears, and in the cells in which constraints constitute the keynote, special institutionalized freedoms appear. The same holds *mutatis mutandis* for the obverse relations. These resultants are presented in Figure 5.

Perhaps the least problematical is the A–Cell. In a modern society the justification of inequalities of achievement, and of course of the rewards which are in some sense inseparable from them as *social* phenomena, is dependent on equality of *opportunity* to attempt the kind of achievement in question. Here of course it is fundamental, first that the reference is to *unit* achievements and second that units are "free" to attempt such achievements, but not "forced" to do so. Finally, it is inherent in this syndrome that there should be a competitive aspect of the relational system.

The G–Cell combines inequality and constraint. In a society such as our own, where both equality and freedom are not only highly valued but in certain respects "insisted upon," this is empirically perhaps the most problematical case. Theoretically, however, the *legitimation* of the inequalities and the constraints in question demands that there should be "balancing" guarantees of equality and protections of freedom. My suggestion is that the great Constitutional principle of *equal protection of the laws* comes very close to formulating these conditions. It may be interpreted to mean that on the one hand binding collective action shall not infringe at the "basic rights" of units of the social system, and that units of the requisite categories are basically equal in these rights—notably, of course, individuals. On the other hand, such action shall not unnecessarily abridge freedoms—which are part of "basic rights"—either at the level of pursuit of interests, or that of allocation of commitments.

The I–Cell resultant seems to present a combinatorial synthesis of the two variables in that, on the one hand, it asserts the basic importance of

equality of membership status, but at the same time makes allowance for the inequalities which will result from achievement motives protected by equality of opportunity. On the other hand, this implies acceptance of the constraints by moral authority implied in membership in a community— which is pluralistically differentiated—which rests for its integration on the institutionalization of basically moral values. This is the syndrome which I, and a number of associates, have for some years been calling that of "institutionalized individualism," a concept of which the immediate intellectual ancestor was clearly Durkheim. It is indeed the spelling out of the conception of organic solidarity to a special conception of a balance, at the integrative core of social systems, between freedom and constraint on the one hand, equality and inequality on the other.

There seems to be a special set of implications of this balance for the theory of social stratification. First I would suggest that the more organic solidarity, the more the legitimacy of political inequalities is likely to be challenged, in the first instance in favor of equality of membership status. The repercussions of this may well strengthen claims to equality of opportunity, but may also activate claims to freedoms in the area of basic rights.

However these complex dynamic relations may work out in particular cases, this seems to be the focal center of social stratification, under modern conditions especially, but probably more broadly. In the body of the paper, I have used the concept of prestige as the primary institutional code of influence systems, corresponding to authority in the political context and property in the economic. Prestige is in the first instance an aspect of diffuse status, going beyond the specificity of particular capacities, achievements or powers or, for that matter, particular specified value-commitments. Inequality of prestige is in the first instance a function of the relation of cases to the institutionalized standards of justification, inter-related as these are with standards of legitimation. Institutionalized stratification then is a scale of relative prestige among units in the structure of the social system on reference. Such a scale is of course possible only if there are institutional mechanisms which render qualitatively diverse components comparable. This is, in general, precisely what the generalized media of interchange, as used by actors of course, in fact do. In this sense all of them perform integrative functions, but influence is the integrative medium in a double sense, in that it develops a higher order integration of the integrations already accomplished by the other three. Only when this has worked out according to the standard we have called "consensus" (Parsons, 1969c), can we speak of an acceptable *generalized* prestige status of a societal unit. Because of the trend of modern societies toward a high level of the institutionalization of freedoms, such a prestige scale must, so far as the location of particular units or classes of them is concerned, be highly fluid.

The L–Cell in Figure 5, finally, provides a theoretically meaningful location for another major concern of the body of this paper, namely the *fiduciary* complex. Here, in a sense parallel to that in which equality of membership status is balanced in the resultant syndrome by inequalities of prestige among units, so equality of basic rights is balanced by inequalities of responsibility, though all members bear some fiduciary responsibility. The inequality component has been illustrated by the professional case. By virtue of his special competence, which in the nature of the case cannot be equally shared by "laymen" relative to his profession, notably of course his clients, but also others, the professional bears a special responsibility for the legitimate and justified use of that competence. In particular, we have made *integrity* a criterion, on a par with competence itself, of institutionalized professional status. This means integrity of commitment to the relevant values which are in principle shared by professional and laity in the case of the sphere of competence. In the academic world, for example, a crucial value is what we call cognitive rationality, which, however, must be fitted into a broader and more general value system. The academic professional has a special responsibility, by virtue of his competence both for the implementation of this specified value, and for its "fit" in the broader value system from which it constitutes a specification.

These interpretations of the suggested content of Figure 5 perhaps show why, in a social system, accountability *only* to the wishes of a democratic constituency, *or* to the discipline of the market, *or* to formally enforceable law, cannot suffice for the institutionalization of responsibility in the functioning of social systems generally. There must also be a sphere in which the responsibility is not to any identifiable specific social agency or category of them but to the actor's own "conscience" in the sense of his commitment to the values he accepts and to their implementation. His action will of course be evaluated by others, hence the immense importance of value-consensus for the stability of a social system.

I have suggested that the stability of fiduciary responsibility is to be to a very high degree a function of the actor's capacity to command moral authority, the more so the more stratified in the relevant respects such assumptions of responsibility become.

References

BELL, DANIEL (ed.)
    1968   Towards the Year 2000: Work in Progress. Boston: Houghton Mifflin. P. 19.

BELLAH, R. N.
    1967   "Civil religion in America." Daedalus (Winter): 1–21.

BEN-DAVID, J.
1963–64 "Professions in the class system of present day societies: a trend report and bibliography." Current Sociology 12:247–330.

BOWLES, F.
1963 Access to Higher Education. New York: Columbia University Press.

COLEMAN, J., et al.
1966 Equality of Educational Opportunity. Washington, D.C.: U.S. Office of Education.

DAVIS, K., and W. E. MOORE
1945 "Some principles of stratificaton." American Sociological Review 10, No. 2:242–249.

FREUND, F., and ULICH
1965 Religion in the Public School. Cambridge, Mass.: Harvard University Press.

FRYE, NORTHROP
1970 "The critical path: an essay on the social context of literary criticism." Daedalus (Spring).

JENCKS, C., and D. RIESMAN
1968 The Academic Revolution. Garden City, New York: Doubleday.

KAGAN, J. (ed.)
1967 Creativity and Learning. Boston: Houghton Mifflin.

KNIGHT, F. H.
1935 "The ethics of competition," in Ethics of Competition. New York: Harper.

LAUMANN, EDWARD O., and JAMES S. HOUSE
1970 "Living room styles and social attributes: the patterning of material artifacts in a modern urban community." Sociology and Social Research 54 (April).

LIPSET, SEYMOUR M.
1960 Political Man. Garden City, N.Y.: Doubleday.
1963 The First New Nation. New York: Basic Books.
1966 "Value patterns, class and the democratic polity." Pp. 161–171, in R. Bendix and S. Lipset (eds.), Class, Status and Power. New York: The Free Press.

MARSHALL, T. H.
1965 Class, Citizenship and Social Development. Garden City, New York: Anchor Books.

MAYHEW, LEON
1968 "Ascription in modern societies." Sociological Inquiry (Spring): 105–120.

MERTON, ROBERT
1968   "The Matthew Effect in science." Science 159, No. 3810 (January):
      56–63.

MILLER, HERMAN
1964   Rich Man, Poor Man. New York: Signet Books.

MOYNIHAN, DANIEL P.
1969a   On Understanding Poverty. New York: Basic Books.
1969b   Maximum Feasible Misunderstanding. New York: The Free Press.

ORTEGA Y GASSETT, J.
1932   The Revolt of the Masses. New York: Norton.

PACKARD, V.
1959   The Status Seekers. New York: David McKay.

PARSONS, TALCOTT
1954   Essays in Sociological Theory. New York: The Free Press.
1959   "The school class as a social system." Harvard Educational Review
      29, No. 4 (Fall): 297–318.
1965   "Full citizenship for the Negro American? a sociological problem."
      Daedalus (Fall): 1009–1054.
1966a   Societies: Evolutionary and Comparative Perspectives. Englewood
      Cliffs, N.J.: Prentice-Hall.
1966b   "Youth behavior and values." in E. Landy and A. Kroll (eds.),
      Needs and Influencing Forces, Cambridge, Mass.: Harvard Gradu-
      ate School of Education.
1967a   "Pattern variables revisited." in Sociological Theory and Modern
      Society. New York: The Free Press.
1967b   "Durkheim's contribution to the theory of integration of social
      systems." Sociological Theory and Modern Society. New York:
      The Free Press.
1968a   "Professions." in David Sills (ed.), The International Encyclopedia
      of the Social Sciences. New York: Macmillan Company and The
      Free Press. 12:536–547.
1968b   "The academic system: a sociologist's view." The Public Interest
      13 (Fall): 173–197.
1968c   "The problem of polarization on the axis of color." in John H.
      Franklin (ed.), Color and Race. Boston, Mass.: Houghton Mifflin.
1969a   Politics and Social Structure. New York: The Free Press.
1969b   "On the concept of influence"; "On the concept of political power";
      "On the concept of value commitments." in Politics and Social
      Structure. New York: The Free Press.
1970   "Some problems of general theory in sociology." in J. McKinney
      and E. Tiryakian (eds.), Theoretical Sociology: Perspectives and
      Developments. New York: Appleton-Century, Crofts.

PARSONS, TALCOTT, R. FREED BALES, and EDWARD SHILS
1953   Working Papers in the Theory of Action. New York: The Free
      Press.

PARSONS, T., and G. M. PLATT

1968 "Considerations on the American academic system." Minerva VI, No. 4 (Summer): 497–523.

1970 "Decision-making in the academic system: influence and power exchange." in Sheldon Messinger and Carlos Kruytbosch (eds.), The State of the University: Authority and Change. Beverly Hills, California: Sage Publications.

1972 "Higher education, changing socialization, and contemporary student dissent." in Matilda Riley, *et al.* (eds.), Aging and Society. New York: Russell Sage Foundation.

1973 The American University. Cambridge, Mass.: Harvard University Press.

PARSONS, T., and W. WHITE

1961 "The link between character and society." in Lipset and L. Lowenthal (eds.), Culture and Social Character. New York: The Free Press.

PORTER, J.

1968 "The future of upward mobility." American Sociological Review 33, No. 1: 5–19.

RAINWATER, LEE

1969 "The problem of lower-class culture and poverty war strategy." in Moynihan (ed.), On Understanding Poverty. New York: Basic Books.

ROKKAN, STEIN

1960 "Citizen participation in political life." International Social Science Journal 12.

SCHNEIDER, D.

1968 American Kinship: A Cultural Approach. Englewood Cliffs, New Jersey: Prentice-Hall.

SPADY, W.

1967 "Educational mobility and access: growth and paradoxes." American Journal of Sociology 73, No. 3 (November): 273–286.

WEBER, MAX

1946 "Politics as a vocation." in H. Gerth and C. Wright Mills (eds.), Essays in Sociology. New York: Oxford University Press.

WEINSTEIN, F., and G. M. PLATT

1969 The Wish to Be Free. Berkeley: University of California Press.

WHITE, WINSTON

1961 Beyond Conformity. New York: The Free Press.

WILLEY, R. J.

1969 "Taking the post office out of politics." The Public Interest 15: 57–71.

13. Some Theoretical Considerations on the Nature and Trends of Change of Ethnicity

IT SEEMS TO BE GENERALLY agreed that what we call ethnicity is a primary focus of group identity, that is, the organization of plural persons into distinctive groups and, second, of solidarity and the loyalties of individual members to such groups. It is, however, an extraordinarily elusive concept and very difficult to define in any precise way.[1] Perhaps the best way to introduce the problem is in terms of a sketch of some of the principal historic and contemporary contexts in which the conception has figured prominently. Following this we will undertake a more careful consideration of the definitional question.

Clearly one primary reference point is to the ideal-type conception of the population of a "nation-state," meaning a politically organized society which has historically enjoyed a legitimate claim to independent existence.[2] The ideal type calls for a coincidence of what in a broad sense we may call common culture and territory of residence. For the typical individual both his residence within the territory and his sharing of the common culture have been conceived as given by his birth, that is, he has acquired the ethnic identification of his parents. Ethnicity, then, has very generally been interpreted as having a biological base sometimes explicitly stated in terms of racial distinctiveness.[3] If we take, however, the popula-

---

From *Ethnicity: Theory and Experience*, edited by Nathan Glazer and Daniel P. Moynihan (Cambridge, Mass.: Harvard University Press, 1975), pp. 53–83. Article copyright © 1975 by Talcott Parsons.

[1] See, for example, H. S. Morris, "Ethnic Groups," in D. L. Sills, ed., *International Encyclopedia of the Social Sciences* (New York, Macmillan and the Free Press, 1968), V, 167–172.

[2] Cf. Hans Kohn, *The Idea of Nationalism: A Study in Its Origins and Background* (New York, Macmillan, 1944).

[3] Carleton Coon, with Edward E. Hunt, Jr., *The Living Races of Man* (New York, Knopf, 1965).

tions of a variety of the classical nation-states, it is to a very varying degree that they can be called racially distinct. But some kind of relative homogeneity has generally been presumed.

On the more specifically cultural side again religious uniformity has historically played an important part, though in the Western world since the Reformation for most nations it has become increasingly problematical.[4] A particularly prominent aspect of cultural identity, then, has been language. Even though what is essentially the same language, as in the case of English, may be spoken in more than one nation, linguistic uniformity has served as one of the primary criteria. Language, in turn, has been closely associated with a relatively diffuse conception of a common cultural tradition. This, of course, has been both oral tradition and in the more evolved societies a tradition embodied in documents of written language; in the broadest sense, a "literature." It is, however, exceedingly difficult to specify such a common cultural tradition more precisely. At a certain common sense level, however, we think we know fairly definitely what is meant by referring to French culture or English culture or Italian culture.

Certainly the development of what we call national states was one of the primary processes involved in the establishment of modern societies, though the European system cannot be said ever to have even come very close to universalizing the ideal type of what in the above imprecise sense would be called an ethnically homogeneous population. The premier classical examples of England and France are perhaps the best approximations, but neither of them has ever been completely pure. Thus the politically organized England has not been confined to "Anglo-Saxon" populations, but has included Celtic components in Wales, Scotland, and, of course, Ireland. In the case of France there has been shading off into the German cultural world toward the east, as, for example, in Alsace and Lorraine, and toward the Italian world in the south. At the other extreme, there have been major historical political units, such as the Austro-Hungarian empire, which have never even approached being an ethnically homogeneous entity, but were put together out of a considerable variety of different ethnic groups for the most part, however, territorially concentrated as in the case of German-speaking Austria, Czech-speaking Bohemia and Moravia, and Hungarian-speaking Hungary.

The various components which have figured historically in the ethnic complex have by no means been uniformly involved over time. A notable case has been that of religion. There were, to be sure, many centuries of integrity of Western, that is, Roman Catholicism in Europe, with only

[4] Wilbur K. Jordan, *The Development of Religious Toleration in England,* 4 vols. (Cambridge, Harvard University Press, 1932–1940). Also, James Hastings, ed., with the assistance of John A. Selbie, *Encyclopedia of Religion and Ethics* (New York, Scribner's Sons, 1908–1915).

very small enclaves of Diaspora Jews who were not Catholics. Since the Reformation, however, that has changed, and though for a time the famous formula of the Peace of Westphalia, *euis regio euis religio,* held, it has gradually been attenuated and most of the populations of European nation-states have become religiously pluralistic with Protestants, Catholics, and Jews represented in varying proportions. The establishment of the American republic constituted a major step in this process through the institutionalization of the separation of Church and State. In the nineteenth and part of the twentieth centuries there were important attempts to identify ethnicity and nationality with race. The most sensational and disturbing was the attempt of German Nazism to purify the "Aryan" composition of the German people, and to include so far as possible all ethnic Germans in the Reich.[5] By contrast the Jews were also alleged to constitute a distinctive race and cultural characteristics of both groups were held to be derivable from their racial natures. This particular set of views, however, has lost ground most conspicuously.

American society, on the one hand by virtue of its political constitution, on the other hand by virtue of the history of immigration, pioneered in the establishment of a multi-ethnic society. If there is a single formula for ethnic identity in the American population, probably the conception of "national origin" is the most accurate designation for most groups. Certain kinds of exceptions have to be made where color is a major factor, but in the case of the so-called blacks there is the common geographical origin from Subsaharan Africa. The Jews constitute another distinctive case because of the religio-ethnic character of the historic Jewish community.[6] Broadly speaking, ethnic pluralism on something like the American model has been coming to be increasingly characteristic of modern societies.

A notable recent development has taken place in Europe with the establishment of the Common Market and, as one of its primary features, the removal of many previous restrictions on the geographical mobility of labor. Hence, a process of in-migration of "foreign" elements into the most important European industrial societies has occurred on a big scale, creating situations which in some respects are parallel to that of the United States in an earlier period occasioned by mass immigration from diverse European sources.

Finally, with the emergence of the so-called Third World, new nation-states have been created with populations ethnically diverse in one or another sense.

[5] Stephen H. Roberts, *The House That Hitler Built* (New York and London, Harper and Brothers, 1938).

[6] Oscar Handlin and Mary Handlin, *A Century of Jewish Immigration to the USA* (New York, American Jewish Committee, 1949).

A General Characterization of the Ethnic Group

In spite of the difficulty of being specific about criterial features and components, what social scientists have called ethnic groups do belong to a relatively distinctive sociological type. This is a group the members of which have, with respect to both their own sentiment and those of non-members, a distinctive identity which is rooted in some kind of a distinctive sense of its history. It is, moreover, a diffusely defined group, sociologically quite different from collectivities with specific functions. For the members it characterizes what the individual *is* rather than what he *does*. Thus we say, whether resident in Ireland or not, he may be ethnically Irish; whether resident in Israel or not, ethnically Jewish; and so on. This is to say it is a primary collective aspect concerning the identity of whole persons, not of any particular aspect of them. Common culture is probably the most important general core, but it is a culture which has some feature of temporal continuity often reaching into an indefinite past. An ethnic group is, of course, always a group consisting of members of all ages and both sexes and ethnicity is always shared by forebears at some level. It is thus a *transgenerational* type of group.

Ethnic groups are traditionally mutually exclusive. This would be rigorously and uniformly the case, however, only insofar as they are consistently endogamous. There are many cases, however, of the marriage of members of different ethnic groups. The question therefore of the ethnic adherence of a married couple can become indefinite and the same is of course true for their children and for their further descendents. Indeed in such cases there may be a certain optional rather than ascriptive character to ethnic identity.

Functionally diffuse time-extended solidary groupings are indeed not exclusively recruited by birth, and this has become conspicuously true of the population of the modern state in the existence of appreciable numbers who have become members or citizens by, to use the American phrase, "naturalization." This points to the fact that national communities share with ethnic groups the involvement of a component of voluntary adherence. This has been classically formulated in social and political theory under the conception of the social contract: a conception which has recently been revived by the philosopher John Rawls in his influential book *A Theory of Justice*.[7] Politically organized societies do have on occasion specific points of origin such as for the United States the combination of independence from Great Britain and the setting up by the recently independent group of a distinctive autonomous constitution of

[7] John Rawls, *A Theory of Justice* (Cambridge, Belknap Press of Harvard University Press, 1971).

its own.[8] This kind of thing is the nearest to a general social contract establishing a national community which is empirically possible. But as an analytical concept, the establishment of solidarity by voluntary adherence is an extremely important social phenomenon.

Every social system of the very important type we call a society is in one of its primary aspects what may be called a societal community. At one time this was identified ideally at least with what is called ethnicity—a societal community was almost by definition an ethnic entity. It is exceedingly important to be aware that this is no longer the case even as an ideal type for a number of the important national societies, most conspicuously of course for that of the United States. At the same time it is extremely important that any societal community, so far as it has the central property of solidarity, essentially in Durkheim's sense, is of the same *generic* sociological character as is the ethnic group. This is to say that it is a diffusely defined collectivity which has the property of solidarity and is a major point of reference for defining the identity of its members.[9] To be identified as an American is not to have one's ethnic status identified, but it very definitely is a primary aspect of the "identity" of any given individual so designated.

The generic sociological type to which references here are made has the two primary aspects: first, that of a common distinctive cultural tradition applying to a "population" of members; and second, something of the equivalent of a social contract, that is, a component of membership status which is in some essential respect voluntary. This is to say it is the creation of the members independent of rigid and complete determination by past tradition. The modern community is characterized by a balance between these two vital components, that of tradition and that of "contract."

The Collectivity with "Diffuse Enduring Solidarity"

We have reached the point of cardinal importance that in the contemporary world what we have been calling societal communities or "nations" are to a decreasing degree ethnically homogeneous entities. A significant aspect, however, of the importance of the ethnic group as a social phenomenon lies in the fact that it is one primary example of a large genus of types of social collective organization which might be called the diffusely

[8] Seymour M. Lipset, *The First New Nation* (New York, Basic Books, 1963).

[9] Talcott Parsons, *Societies: Evolutionary and Comparative Perspectives* (Englewood Cliffs, N.J., Prentice-Hall, 1966), chap. 2, pp. 5–29; and T. Parsons, *The System of Modern Societies* (Englewood Cliffs, N.J., Prentice-Hall, 1971), chap. 2, pp. 4–28. Both chapters reprinted in Talcott Parsons, *Politics and Social Structure* (New York, The Free Press, 1969), as chaps. 1 and 2.

solidary collectivity.[10] I should like to devote this section to a brief outline of this generic organizational type before returning to some further considerations specifically about ethnicity.

The best single empirical point of reference seems to be what may be called the societal community. This is one primary aspect of the structure and functioning of the extremely important type of social system we call a society. It is that aspect or subsystem which has primarily integrative functions for the society as a whole.[11] The societal community presumes a relatively definable population of membership, which at this level we ordinarily call citizens for the modern case, and presumes as well that the collective organization of reference is politically organized on a territorial basis, that is, it maintains normative order and certain political decision-making processes covering the human events which occur within a defined territorial area.[12] Finally, as a third primary criterion, at some level it is characterized by a common cultural tradition, the nature of which will be further discussed presently.

One of the primary characteristics of a societal community is that it has the property which David Schneider, with special reference to American kinship, has called "diffuse enduring solidarity." We should, however, understand that solidarity in this sense is not a matter of presence or absence, but varies in degree and in type in important ways. Solidarity in this sense should be considered to be a property of the system. The corresponding property of individual members which may be called dispositional or motivational seems best called loyalty. Clearly the solidarity of the collective system is among other things a function of the level and distribution of loyalty of its members but not synonymous with it. Following the cultural structure which Schneider has elucidated for the case of kinship, we may stress two culturally symbolic elements of our generic type of collectivity which correspond to the roles of "blood" and "law" as symbolic definitions of a kinship unit.[13] The equivalent of blood is the transgenerational tradition to which reference has been made above. As I have pointed out, it is exceedingly difficult to specify exact criterial components of its content. It is essential then to consider it first as definitely cultural. Second, it is to be considered as broadly shared in com-

---

[10] See David M. Schneider, *American Kinship: A Cultural Account* (Englewood Cliffs, N.J., Prentice-Hall, 1968); and David M. Schneider, "Kinship, Religion and Nationality," in V. Turner, ed., *Forms of Symbolic Action, Proceedings of the 1969 Spring Meeting of the American Ethnological Society* (Seattle, University of Washington Press, 1969).

[11] Talcott Parsons, "Durkheim's Contribution to the Theory of Integration of Social Systems," chap. 1 in *Sociolgical Theory and Modern Society* (New York, The Free Press, 1967), pp. 3–34.

[12] Cf. T. H. Marshall, *Class, Citizenship and Social Development* (Garden City, N.Y., Doubleday & Co., 1964).

[13] Schneider, *American Kinship.*

mon by the whole population of a societal community. This transgenerational tradition could be broken down down into three primary elements. The first is a common language which has been inherited by the current members of the community from its past and those aspects of the cultural tradition which are most closely associated with language. Language is not, however, an infallible criterion as such cases as the multilingual societal community of Switzerland remind us. A second primary reference may be referred to as the "cultural history" of the community. This concerns a series of events and symbolic outputs of the past which have contemporary significance because those who experienced or produced them were "our" forebears. This sense of a shared history applies to those who themselves or whose immediate forebears have joined the community long after certain other crucial events took place. Thus the American achievement of independence and the establisment of the Constitution involved a population of nearly two centuries ago who were actual ancestors of what is (probably) only a minority of the contemporary population of the American community. Nevertheless, those whose forebears were immigrants much more recently still consider this to be part of "their" history.

Third, the extension of the temporal continuity of tradition is operative not only retrospectively with reference to the past, but also prospectively with reference to the future. A major aspect of solidarity in the present sense is the sharing of a common fate by virtue of common membership in the particular societal community. So long as the community itself persists, this continuity will be a central feature of it. A major aspect of the diffuseness of the solidarity system lies in the fact that it is impossible to isolate the symbolic meaningfulness of temporally specific events and prospects from the temporally extended continuum. Just as in the kinship context an individual is ascriptively the child of his parents, so in a societal community the citizen is ascriptively one of the heirs of his forebears in the societal community and will be one of the "progenitors" of the future community so that many of the consequences of the actions of contemporaries cannot be escaped by future members in new generations.

The types of social structure just under discussion belong to a general type the nature and significance of which has recently been substantially clarified in my own mind.[14] This type I have called the "fiduciary association." The adjective fiduciary derives mainly from the element of transgenerational "tradition" that has just been discussed. At any given time the current membership exercises, and is expected to do so, a fiduciary responsibility for the maintenance or development of such a tradition in its place in the larger society, including those inside its boundaries who cannot be expected to assume the highest levels of such responsibility. It becomes a "moral community" in Durkheim's sense.

[14] See Talcott Parsons and Gerald M. Platt, *The American University* (Cambridge, Harvard University Press, 1973), esp. chaps. 2 and 3.

I hold that, in a highly differentiated society, there are four principal subtypes of fiduciary association, the kinship association, the societal or similar community, the religious association and the educational-cultural association. In the modern type of family, the unit is established by a contract in the above sense, that is, a marriage, but if the couple has children they as parents assume a fiduciary responsibility for their welfare and proper "bringing up." Parties to the marriage also assume such responsibilities for each other and the proper mode of married life, obligations which of course obtain even for childless couples. In the communal type special fiduciary responsibilities devolve upon holders of associational office [15] and those members of the community of association who exercise more than the average levels of influence, both for the welfare of less powerful and influential groups and for the integrity of the tradition. In the case of the religious association it is above all what we call the clergy and other specially committed groups on which such responsibility focuses. Finally in referring to the educational–cultural subtype I have had in mind above all the university or other institution of higher education, but various other types of culturally oriented institutions such as museums or musical organizations can also be included. In the university case a particularly conspicuous focus of fiduciary responsibility is members of faculties, both vis-à-vis students who do not yet command the same level of competence and experience, and vis-à-vis the integrity of the tradition itself, in this case with a special concern for the "advancement of knowledge." I have tended to interpret these fiduciary responsibilities of faculties as the set of obligations which underlie and legitimate the elements of special privilege which are often referred to as "academic freedom." [16]

I think of the ethnic group as belonging by and large to this same category of fiduciary association, especially by virtue of the element of continuing tradition which has been emphasized above. It does not seem, however, to belong unequivocally to any one of the above four subtypes. My inclination is to treat it as a kind of "fusion" of the community and kinship types. This would mean that the two have not yet come to be clearly differentiated from each other where ethnicity is involved.[17] Such differentiation has clearly been going on in recent times.

[15] It seems to me that there is a major sense in which the fulfillment of fiduciary responsibilities in the present sense on the part of both elective officials, notably the President, and those holding appointive office, notably those on his staff, constitutes the most important focus of concern in the recent and current activities of the House of Representatives Judiciary Committee, and the office of the Special Prosecutor.

[16] On this last point again see Parsons and Platt, *The American University*, esp. chap. 3. I am greatly indebted to David M. Schneider, especially in the course of a collaborative seminar at the University of Chicago, Fall Quarter 1973, for clarification of the nature of what I am here calling fiduciary associations.

[17] As we shall see below, in recent developments the voluntary "contract" element is by no means absent from the current picture of ethnicity.

Some Primary Features of the Current Situation of Ethnic Groups

In order to drive home the relevance of the above theoretical sketch it may be worthwhile in the remainder of this chapter to speak fairly briefly of three empirical topics. The first concerns certain developments in the relatively advanced modern societies with special reference to ethnic relations in the United States without special concern for the status of the blacks. Second, in light of the fact that a tenth anniversary of the *Daedalus* study entitled *The Negro American* is approaching, it might be worthwhile to undertake a brief stock-taking review of where some of the problems of that study stand in the light of developments since it was made.[18] Finally, third, it seems worthwhile to say something about developments in the so-called "new nations."

I have already strongly emphasized that in spite of its origin as what has sometimes been called a WASP community, the American societal community is no longer in the older sense of its own history and of the classical pattern of the national state an ethnic community. This is not to say that ethnic groups have ceased to have significance. In certain respects quite the contrary is true. The most salient point, however, is that it is an ethnically pluralistic community where even the previous vague and informal stratification of ethnic subgroups has ceased to have its previous importance.[19]

At the same time the complete assimilation leading to the disappearance of ethnic identities and solidarities, which was much discussed in the earlier part of the present century and greatly feared by some groups, has also not in any simple sense taken place. Indeed, full assimilation, in the sense that ethnic identification has virtually disappeared and become absorbed within the single category of "American," is very little the case. For example, Schneider reports as one of the conspicuous findings of the recent study of families in the Chicago area, on which his theoretical book *American Kinship* is based, that "Almost every family identifies with some ethnic unit—they were Italians, Jews, Bohemians, Polish, Czechs, and so on."[20] Those who identified themselves as Anglo-Saxon on Schneider's

[18] Talcott Parsons and Kenneth Clark, eds., *The Negro American* (Boston, Houghton Mifflin, 1966); first published as *Daedalus* 94.4 (Fall 1965) and 95.1 (Winter 1966).

[19] For the situation of the 1920s, see André Siegfried, *America Comes of Age: A French Analysis*, trans. H. H. Hemming and D. Hemming (New York, Harcourt and Co., 1927). The present volume will provide a general review of the current situation.

[20] Schneider, *American Kinship*. This quotation and the ones that follow are taken from an informal memorandum written by Professor David Schneider, De-

and other evidence often also use regional categorization and sometimes that in terms of a type of community as in the case of being "ordinary Midwestern farmers" or various types of Southerners.

Schneider goes on to make some exceedingly interesting observations about this situation, saying "It was true that when they [that is, the interviewers on his project] collected the genealogies of those who most vehemently and affirmatively claimed they were Italian, they discovered a succession going backwards of Irish and Polish mothers and grandmothers. That is, upwardly mobile Italians marry 'blond' Irish and Polish Catholics. This is a well-known phenomenon. Yet, despite this intermarriage, the affirmation of Italian identity was quite clear, affirmative, and positive from even the Irish and Polish mothers and grandmothers. They had 'become' Italian and proved it, for instance, by cooking according to the Italian stye. eating according to distinct Italian traditions (elbows on tables, eat, eat)."

This seems to be a notable confirmation of the general point we made earlier in the chapter about the optional and voluntary component of ethnic identification, at least in the United States. It seems to be especially the family household which tends to adopt such an identification and in the process to pass over the actual ethnic origins of various of its members and members of recognized extended kin groupings.

How, however, is this possible? Schneider goes on to make two extremely interesting observations. The first of these is that, however strongly affirmative these ethnic identifications are, the ethnic status is conspicuously devoid of "social content." Again, as Schneider puts it, "It does not require the learning of a totally new social role for the Irish girl to marry the Italian; they are both Catholic at least and she picks up some Italian, learns some cooking styles, and, lo, the symbolic identification is set." He goes on to say, "The marks of identity are in a very important sense 'empty symbols.' Symbols empty of elaborate social distinctions, and thus they are able to function freely and smoothly in this multi-ethnic social system while maintaining a distinct cultural-symbolic identity as markers." Perhaps it is legitimate to interpret this as saying that the symbolization of ethnic identification is primarily focused on style of life distinctiveness within the larger framework of much more nearly uniform American social structure. This social structure is differentiated by class, by region, and by type of community, for example, metropolitan contrasted with small town, but not very greatly on an ethnic basis. Schneider recounts another example of a family of Greek origin who were visited by the parents of one member of the married couple who, after

partment of Anthropology, University of Chicago (1972) and quoted with his permission. He and I have also had long discussions and correspondence over these topics, culminating in a joint seminar on cultural symbolism held at the University of Chicago in the Fall Quarter of 1972.

a brief sojourn in the United States, had returned to Greece. The younger couple, as Schneider says, "were vehemently, indeed belligerently Greek, and explained all sorts of special Greek traits and customs to us." The old couple from Greece, on the other hand, "complained bitterly that these young people claimed they were Greek and made all kinds of noises about being true Greek, but they were nothing but common Americans underneath all that empty talk."

Schneider's second pertinent observation is particularly interesting at the role level. He reports that he and his staff were repeatedly told in respondents' explanations of what underlay their ethnic identity that if the identity was Irish, it could be understood only if one understood "the Irish mother." The interesting point, however, is that the assertion about the crucial role of the mother was repeated for group after group. You could not understand Jewish family life unless you understood the Jewish mother, similarly with Polish, and so on. Whatever the situation with respect to cultural relativity in these respects and, hence, differences in definition of mother roles in the various ethnic groups, there seems to be a striking uniformity with respect to focusing on the mother as the symbolic guardian of the ethnic identity.

These observations clearly indicate that the development of what we have called ethnic pluralism in American society has involved major changes in the character of the ethnic groups themselves compared to what they were, for example, as embodied in the life of the first-generation immigrants in question. As Schneider puts it, there is a certain sense in which they have been "desocialized" and transformed into primarily cultural-symbolic groups. This does not preclude solidarity at certain levels such, for example, as preferences for residential contiguity or, if not that, selective relatedness. Thus, people who identify as Italian in Schneider's sense may well feel more comfortable in associating in a variety of respects with others who also identify themselves as Italian, whether or not they reside in predominantly Italian neighborhoods. Similarly, members of such groups may crystallize their solidarities, for example, about political interests, but here it should be kept clearly in mind that there is an element of voluntary selectivity. Especially for the case of the non-Italian mothers and grandmothers to whom Schneider refers, there is option with respect to what identity to emphasize for particular purposes. Very important here is the relation between ethnicity and religion. Again, as Schneider notes, Irish, Italians, and Poles in the current American ethnic sense are all predominantly Catholic. On questions involving the relation of Catholicism to other denominational religious groups, obviously Protestants and Jews, a certain cross-ethnic solidarity is possible. It should not be forgotten that this applies to the Jews, since from the usual point of view, American Jews are far from being ethnically homogeneous, although they hold special allegiances to the wider international Jewish com-

munity. On such matters as support for Israel they would be likely to be rather highly solidary in spite of their own internal divisions and differences. Furthermore, there are many distinct Protestant denominations.

The phenomena we have called "desocialization" of ethnic groupings do not stand alone. A good many observers have contended that in recent years, even apart from specifically disadvantaged groups, there has tended to be something like an intensification of ethnic solidarity and a certain tone of militancy in the defense or promotion of what are conceived to be ethnic interests.[21] If such a tendency exists in the United States, two further points need to be made about it. First, it is at least in part of a piece with patterns of the intensification of feelings of both ethnic solidarity and "rights" that have been involved in a number of recent movements in other countries, some of which approach the boundary line of political separatism. Our neighbor, Canada, provides a conspicuous example, though the intensity of the French Canadian movement seemed to have subsided somewhat in the most recent period. Another case of which somewhat similar things may be said has been the conflict between the French-speaking Walloons and the Flemish-speaking population of Belgium, which at certain points has been very acute indeed in recent years. Even though it is less in the international news than it was for some time, recently we had the very striking announcement that the French-speaking sector of the University of Louvain has not only become separated in local operations from the Flemish-speaking sector but has decided actually to move its location to another community. Finally, we are all exceedingly conscious of the situation in Northern Ireland which has seemed so very difficult to cope with.

The second extremely important point is that the accentuation of group solidarity and militancy in insistence on rights has not been confined to ethnic groups. Though trade union movements in general have not been particularly militant in recent times, an interesting problem is created by certain cases among which urban civil service groups seem quite conspicuous. The time when the right to strike was effectively denied to almost all classes of government employees at whatever levels seems far behind indeed. Such disturbances have, of course, often been connected with ethnic issues, thus in the case of the New York City Teachers Union of a few years ago, the fact that such a large proportion of unionized teachers in the city were Jewish certainly played a part in the situation, producing what many would consider the somewhat bizarre phenomenon of a wave of black anti-Semitism.[22]

We think it important to emphasize that the phenomena under dis-

---

[21] Cf. Nathan Glazer and Daniel P. Moynihan, *Beyond the Melting Pot* (Cambridge, Harvard University Press and MIT Press, 1963).

[22] Daniel Bell, *The Coming of Post-Industrial Society: A Venture in Social Forecasting* (New York, Basic Books, 1973).

cussion are not related to the political position of members of the groups in question in any simple way. They are probably particularly conspicuous both on the Right and on the Left, but even this identification need not be infallible. Many movements such as that backing Governor Wallace of Alabama in recent presidential elections have a baffling combination of what by ordinary standards would be called radicalism and conservatism. There are many features in common between such movements: the discontent of urban government employees and some of the more militant movements of the Left, particularly in the academic world. The blacks have occupied a very special position on which a special comment will be made.

Finally, in enumerating the above types of groups, those organized about some kind of religious solidarity should not be forgotten. Such phenomena are most conspicuous in the case of Protestant Fundamentalist groups, but the militant right-wing Jewish group led by Rabbi Kahane should not be left out of the picture. Many of the Protestant Fundamentalists who are militant in this sense are in part motivated by a WASP identification and of course the Jewish group just referred to is both ethnic and religious in identification.

A particularly important phenomenon in this whole connection may be considered to be the obverse of the desocialization of ethnic solidarity and identification which I have discussed. Under conditions of rapid social change and certain tendencies to anomic social disorganization and alienation, intensification of "groupism" and the high emotional loading of the status of group membership and identity is one major type of reaction. Like many other such phenomena it may involve a complex combination of potential and, to a certain degree, actual disruptive consequences for social solidarity and, at the same time, a kind of constructive mode of reintegration of population elements into structures which are less anomic and alienative than their members might otherwise be exposed to. In attempting to analyze and appraise the forces involved in such phenomena, it is very important not to identify what is found too closely with actual historic antecedent conditions, if by that would be meant for the ethnic case the restoration of a pattern of life and of values and sentiments which is identical with that which the first waves of immigrants brought with them. One would expect some kind of a compromise formation between tendencies to such restorationism and the recognition of many of the facts of current life in modern society which are incompatible with the old patterns.

There does seem to be a common feature which is conspicuous in the ethnic field and also more broadly of social processes which bears a certain analogy to the phenomenon of regression in the psychological sense and which, in terms of motivational dynamics, is undoubtedly associated with regression, but by no means identical to it. I have found it useful

to refer to this common factor as "de-differentiation." Its nature and significance should be seen against the background of the very powerful incidence, in recent developments of social structure, of universalistic standards of mobility and of the development of relatively enhanced freedoms, which, however, can easily turn over in anomic directions. Perhaps the most important focus, however, is the pluralization of modern social structure by virtue of which the typical individual plays multiple roles, no one of which can adequately characterize his identification as a "social" personality. The de-differentiating tendency is to select particular criteria and use these as identifying symbols for what the persons who constitute the group actually *are*. This, for example, has been particularly conspicuous in the racial context. But Daniel Bell adroitly points out, what are we to think of the identity expressed by a reference to a "black woman sociologist"? In some connections the salient feature of her identity would be her racial position, in others it would be her sex, and in still others it would be her occupational role. For certain subcategories of each these do go together, but from the point of view of the larger social structure they are very far from being identical or, in general, ascribed to each other. There are white sociologists and there are male sociologists as well as black and female, and there are many blacks and many females who are not sociologists, to say nothing of there being many females who are white and not black. These are very elementary considerations, but it is extremely important that their relevance should not be overlooked.

One further general consideration should be commented upon in the present context. Among various others, Daniel Bell in particular has recently emphasized the problems of the shift in many quarters from emphasis on equality of opportunty to equality of result. This is particularly conspicuously manifested in public policy with respect to so-called "affirmative action" in relation to minority groups. In one prominent context, for example, either academic admissions or appointments to teaching positions, there is strong pressure to assert some kind of quota-defined right of "representation," that is, essentially the same proportion of members of a minority group in a given status such as students or teachers in a given institution of higher education as there are in some probably vaguely defined larger community. The shift is from treating admission or appointment as a selective process guided by criteria of universalistically defined qualifications individual-by-individual to a collective group right. Therefore, it gives an enhanced legitimacy to particularistic criteria.

This tendency seems to us quite definitely to fit in the general category of processes of de-differentiation. Differentiation of role and opportunity among the members of a given group on the basis of universalistically defined qualifications of promise or achievement tends to be played down in favor of some criterion of identity, such as membership in a minority or other such group based on race, sex, or ethnicity, for example. It can

also be extended to religious groups, community of residence, and other such criteria.

There is an important bearing here on the problem of equality. Equality is by no means a simple entity which is either present or absent or which varies only in degree along a linear continuum. It is a matter of qualitatively different components. As Bell notes, one of these components which is very generally called equality of opportunity is tending to be sacrificed to certain others such as group membership status, as ascertained independently of the universalistic criteria to which we have just referred, so that it comes to be that opportunities should be equal by *groups,* not for individuals.[23]

Recent Developments in the Situation of American Blacks

Nearly a decade ago I as well as several other contributors to this book was a participant in a major study of what was then called "The Negro American." [24] It seems pertinent to the theme of this chapter to consider briefly the status of my own contribution to that enterprise and perhaps introduce a few considerations which were not taken account of at that time.

First, attention may be called to two interesting and I think significant shifts in symbolism as applied to this particular "minority" group in American society. The first has been introduced on the initiative of members of the group itself but has spread much more widely, namely, the adoption of the term "black" in the place of "Negro." The latter term was used not only in the title, *The Negro American,* but pretty consistently throughout the discussion and papers of the project. In going back to my own contribution, I have been struck by the consistency with which I used the term "Negro" and did not use "black." [25] The new term stands in a very frank and explicit contrast, of course, to white, and is a good Anglo-Saxon word in contrast to Negro which has a Latin origin.

The second symbolic change is the introduction of the reference to African origin so that, by sharp contrast with the situation a decade ago, we now have frequent references to "Afro-Americans." This has the interesting effect of introducing a new parallelism between the status of

[23] Daniel Bell, "Meritocracy and Equality," *The Public Interest,* no. 29 (Fall 1972), 29–68.

[24] *Daedalus* 94.4 (Fall 1965); *Daedalus* 95.1 (Winter 1966); and Parsons and Clark, *The Negro American.*

[25] Talcott Parsons, "Full Citizenship for the Negro American? A Sociological Problem," in Parsons and Clark, *The Negro American,* pp. 709–754.

the black group and other ethnic groups in terms of what we have referred to above as "national origin." [26] Thus symmetry is established between the definition of black Americans as an ethnic group and other white Americans. If this interpretation is correct, it is connected with an interesting change of perspective. I recall the frequency with which it has been contended, especially in the discussions at the time of the *Daedalus* study, that the "problem" of the status of the black or Negro American was inherently and fundamentally different from that of white ethnic groups and that any attempt to treat it comparatively with the others under the same general analytical scheme was inherently illegitimate. In my own contribution, I begged to differ with this very prevalent view, and might consider this symbolic change to be a certain straw in the wind of vindication of my own view.

The replacement of the term "Negro" by "black," however, seems in a certain sense to have the opposite significance in that it very explicitly accentuates the *racial* focus of the identity of members of the group as somewhat distinguishable from the greater relative importance of the cultural component in the case of the principal white ethnic groups.

A further interesting change since the older stereotypes of the status of blacks came to be established has been the change of status of one set of groups who are of different racial origin from the predominantly European majority. These are, in the first instance, those whose forebears migrated from East Asia, most prominently the Chinese and Japanese. It will be remembered that when they first arrived in substantial numbers, the indigenous American white population showed quite violent antagonism to them with such dramatic episodes as the Chinese Exclusion Act and much later the World War II internment of Japanese-Americans.[27] If I remember correctly, it was in particular Daniel P. Moynihan who in the 1964 *Daedalus* conferences strongly emphasized that being of Chinese or Japanese origin was no longer considered to be a stigma for the most part

[26] At a *Daedalus* conference subsequent to the Negro American enterprise, which was held in Copenhagen in 1965, I distinctly remember the question in a discussion of the apparent anomaly that Negro Americans did not refer to themselves nor were they frequently referred to in terms of any equivalent of the concept of national origin. I suggested the possibility that this gap would be filled and that the most likely way of doing so was a reference to Africa as the area of origin. Somewhat to my surprise, this suggestion was not taken seriously by the overwhelming majority of other participants in the conference. I think the feeling was that Africa was an area inhabited predominantly by "primitive" peoples and that black Americans would not wish to be identified with it in this respect. It was not very many years, however, before the identification in fact became common. Not least is the movement which swept the institutions of higher education for the establishment of what have usually been called "Afro-American programs of study." The papers issuing from this conference were published in *Daedalus* 96, no. 2 (Spring 1967), and in John Hope Franklin, ed., *Color and Race* (Boston, Houghton Mifflin, 1968).

[27] See Alexander H. Leighton, *The Governing of Men: General Principles and Recommendations Based on Experience at a Japanese Relocation Camp* (Princeton, N.J., Princeton University Press, 1945).

in this country.[28] There seems to be a certain congruence between this development and the process by which Afro-Americans, if we may use this term, became accepting of an accentuation of the salience of a category of race as the primary identification symbol.[29] There is probably also a certain connection between this and the recent emergence of concern with the American Indians as another minority ethnic group, after a long period of relative neglect by nearly everyone except anthropologists. Thus we may speak of a racial, as well as in more general terms an ethnic, pluralism of the American population consisting of black people, yellow people, red people, and white people.

It also seems clear that these symbolic changes with reference to American ethnic designations where a criterion of race can be relevant have been affected in an important way by events outside the United States. With respect to East Asia, in the case of the Japanese we can speak of a course of American attitudes changing from a kind of indifference mixed with romanticism to a phase of acute hostility culminating in the Second World War and back to a phase of pronounced favorable attitudes strongly reinforced by the great recent economic and social achievements of the Japanese nation. The Chinese case is somewhat different, but the consolidation of revolutionary China in the recent period has made it much less plausible to think of the Chinese in the old terms of a certain kind of social incompetence, as "the sick man of East Asia," comparable with Turkey in the period of the First World War. The consolidation of the revolutionary regime, of course, provoked acute hostility in this country which has only recently given way to a new orientation which seems to be association with a widespread attitude of respect.

Third, the great development in Subsaharan Africa, of course, has been the achievement of independence by a number of formerly colonial societies. Here also a certain contrast between these predominantly black new nations and the racism of the white minority-dominated Union of South Africa and Southern Rhodesia has tended to give the black African

---

[28] D. P. Moynihan in "Transcript of the American Academy Conference on the Negro American, May 14–15, 1965," *Daedalus* 95.1 (Winter 1966), 343.

[29] Cf. Talcott Parsons, "The Problem of Polarization on the Axis of Color," in John Hope Franklin, *Color and Race*. This article was written after the *Daedalus* conference in Copenhagen, referred to in note 27 above, and was not included in the issue of the journal which resulted. It is concerned with a rather general analysis of the phenomenon of polarization, with examples from the fields of religion and class as well as race. It is also world-wide in reference and not confined to the United States and is hence particularly pertinent to the concerns of the present volume. One of the principal polemical targets is the paper "Color, Racism and Christianity" by Roger Bastide in *Color and Race*. (The article by Edward Shils in the same volume should also be compared.) As in the present paper I argue there that, while for the short run the American pattern by which a person is *either* black *or* white with no intermediate status category may impede inclusion of blacks, or integration of blacks and whites, for the longer run a case can be made that the American pattern is more favorable. That this is the case is a major argument of the present section of this article.

nations something of a good press. Similarly, the case of the American Indian has probably been helped by social changes in Latin America in those countries in which a very large proportion of the population consists of persons of Indian origin who have recently become politically active on new levels.

Finally, with respect to the distinction between race and cultural tradition, it is pertinent to point out that the designations of racial groups by color are themselves cultural symbols.[30] When the four colors just mentioned, black, yellow, red, and white, are used in this connection it is clearly in major part a *cultural* phenomenon. This is true in a sense parallel to that in which the symbol, blood, as used by Schneider in the context of kinship analysis, is a cultural symbol and not simply the name for a physiological entity.[31] In this connection it is worth noting that the "blood relationship" par excellence is that of a mother and her own child. Physiologically speaking, however, they do *not* share the same bloodstream; the child's bloodstream develops independently and what passes to it from the maternal organism through the placenta includes a great many other elements, but definitely not blood. "Blood relationship" here is a symbol, not a description, of a physiological relationship.

Precisely in this kind of context the symbol black has certain particularly interesting features. As is true of African populations, a certain proportion of members of the American ethnic group who are now called and call themselves blacks have skin color which is a close approximation to the physical color of black. Unlike Africans, however, the black Americans who approximate this skin color in fact are clearly a minority of the whole group. The predominant reason for this is the history of what used to be called "miscegenation," that is, racial mixing as between black and white people with the offspring as in this sense a hybrid group. In America, however, sociologically the definition of a Negro is not, and has not been historically, in terms of skin color, but in terms of parentage. Any person, one of whose parents was socially classified as Negro or black, has been by *social* ascription Negro or black. Even in South Africa there is a distinctive group called "colored" as distinguished from either white or black. These are descendants of mixed unions of one kind or another; there is no such category on the American scene.[32]

The designation of Negroes or black as an ethnic group through a

---

[30] Thus Shils (in Franklin, *Color and Race*) is at least partially wrong in designating color as an almost purely "primordial" criterion with the implication that it has virtually *no* other significance than biological characterization.

[31] Schneider, *American Kinship*.

[32] One aspect of the meaning of the symbol black came out in classroom discussions held under the impact of the assassination of Martin Luther King, Jr. I had remarked on the emergence of this symbol and asked for suggestions of explanation. A black woman, a member of the class, made the following interesting point: it concerned, she said, the internal stratification of the black community and the correlation between lightness of color and high status. She then said that one of the reasons for identification of all as blacks was to counteract this tendency to stratifica-

symbol designating color is a tag which has made it possible or easier to attribute biologically hereditary characteristics to the group. I think particularly of the allegations, which have been especially prominent in Southern racist ideology, to the effect that blacks are either like children or like animals.[33] Quite apart from the more general question of whether there is a hereditary component in the differences of races which bears on capacity for performance according to the standards of current society, this ideology flies in the face of the massive fact of the heterogeneity of origin, precisely in terms of inherited genes, of the members of the black community. One is reminded in this case of Schneider's comment on the Irish and Polish mothers and grandmothers of ethnic Italians.[34] The black community in a certain sense has chosen to forget or in a symbolic sense to "deny" the relevance of the white component in its ancestry. One might speak of this as "getting back" for the obverse denial of the relevance of parenthood where a white person, notably a father, was a biological parent of a "black" child.

It has, of course, long been known to sociologists and others that even with indelible visibility of skin color, for a certain fraction of members of the black community, there are options of choice of ethnic identity through the phenomenon known as "passing." Cases, for example, have been known where an individual passed as white in an employment situation, but with reference to residential associations functioned as a member of the black community.[35]

It has been almost a sociological commonplace, and was strongly emphasized in my own *Daedalus* paper, that a primary feature of the status ascribed to the blacks has been the stigma of somehow inherent inferiority.[36] That there should be a group thus stigmatized seems in turn to be to an important degree a function of a society in which the achievement complex, with its inherent competitive aspects, has been so prominent. This also goes a considerable distance toward making it understandable that racial prejudice has centered rather more in the lower ranges of the stratification of the white community than in the upper. No matter how relatively "unsuccessful" such people may seem to be and think of themselves as, this view provides a floor below which they cannot fall, that is, to maintain this fiction of black inferiority it can be seen that it has been exceedingly important to maintain the salience of a *single* identifying characteristic of the group which is both visible and indelible, namely,

---

tion and be sure that the least advantaged members of the group were fully included. In a sense this is a case of making a virtue of necessity.

[33] Thomas Pettigrew, *A Profile of the Negro American* (Princeton, N.J.: D. Van Nostrand, 1964).

[34] D. Schneider, informal memo. See note 22.

[35] The obverse is also known to occur, namely, the "passing" of whites as black. This has been true by marriage, but also otherwise.

[36] Parsons, "Full Citizenships for the Negro American?"

color.[37] This has not, however, prevented a certain amount of differentiation among other things because the color characteristic is, as we have just noted, empirically not uniform.

Inferiority of status, however, has been to a substantial degree a self-fulfilling prophecy. The allegation that blacks as such were incapable of the higher orders of achievement has been a major factor in preventing them from having the opportunity for such achievement. In American society, actual development of what is usually called upward social mobility, which is linked with personal achievement, therefore becomes particularly important in breaking the symbolic rigidity of the old stereotypes. It is, therefore, a matter of profound interest that, in spite of a good deal of unevenness, the last decade or so since the Civil Rights Movement gathered force has seen a pretty massive process of upward mobility among blacks. Among specialists there is considerable skepticism of the statements made by Wattenberg and Scammon in their recent article in *Commentary* that it can now be said that slightly over half of the black population (52 percent) should be classified as middle class.[38] For example, a very knowledgeable and judicious student of the problem, Thomas F. Pettigrew, has estimated (by personal communication) that the proportion is closer to 35 percent. However this may be, there seems to be no question but that a strong current of upward mobility has been under way, including a shift in the distribution of income, of occupational status, of educational levels, and a variety of such criteria resulting in an increasingly large cohort of the more successful blacks.

It seems that this change either already has or soon will reach the point of making a very fundamental difference to the symbolic impact of the success of a select number of outstanding blacks like Justice Thurgood Marshall, the late Whitney Young, or Senator Brooke. There will be the impact of the familiarity of very substantial numbers whose social characteristics, apart from their color or status as blacks, are very similar to those of the majority of non-black middle-class Americans. It may thus turn out in the longer run that acceptance of the more radical symbol of identity, black, will have favored rather than hindered the process of inclusion in the American societal community on a basis of something like parity with other ethnic groups, the inclusion of which has preceded that of the blacks in time.[39]

In spite of such indications, however, the situation should not be

---

[37] See Edward Shils, "Color, the Universal Intellectual Community, and the Afro-Asian Intellectual," in *Daedalus* 96.2 (Spring 1967), 279–295; this article also appears in Franklin, *Color and Race.*

[38] Ben J. Wattenberg and Richard M. Scammon, "Black Progress and Liberal Rhetoric," *Commentary* (April 1973). Also, "Letters, An Exchange on Black Progress: Ben J. Wattenberg and Richard M. Scammon and Critics," *Commentary,* 56.2 (August 1973), 4–22.

[39] Cf. Talcott Parsons, "The Problem of Polarization on the Axis of Color," and Roger Bastide, "Color, Racism and Christianity," in Franklin, *Color and Race.*

oversimplified. The symbolic change around which this discussion has been organized has also underlain and in part been caused by a tendency to militant separatism on the part of a substantial proportion of the politically activistic blacks, finding its extreme manifestations in such phenomena as the Black Panthers and the Black Muslims; escalating polarization of the separation has occurred at many points and been highly visible. It is clear, however, that this polarization trend does not stand by itself, but that the inclusion-pluralization trend is also present to an important degree. Again, following Schneider, we would like to reemphasize that insofar as these latter tendencies become more prominent, there will tend to be a considerable process of desocialization of black ethnicity which is parallel to that which has occurred with other American ethnic groups.

Insofar as this does take place, it will have the interesting implication that the status of the ghetto blacks becomes increasingly anomalous. There has been an understandable tendency to assume that the ghetto pattern of existence was the "natural" mode of living for urban blacks. With, however, a substantial decrease in the proportion of those identified as blacks found in the ghetto pattern of life, it will become increasingly difficult to maintain this attitude. It may be said that during the critical period of the Civil Rights change, non-ghetto blacks have tended to be more or less ignored and pushed out of the center of national awareness. In a comparable sense the non-black poor have had a similar fate, though it has always been well known to experts that though a very large proportion of blacks relatively speaking have been counted among the poor, in fact they have been a minority of the poor, the substantial majority of whom have been white.[40] Perhaps with these developments the problem of poverty as one cutting entirely across ethnic lines will undergo a certain reinstatement which should eliminate a good deal of confusion.[41]

A Word on Ethnicity and the New Nations

A disproportionate amount of the space of this chapter may have been devoted to American and other Western-type modern societies. I have, however, a firm conviction that the kind of theoretical analysis which has been used here can legitimately be tested by its relevance to quite different empirical conditions. I should therefore like to illustrate this by rounding out the discussion with a few points about the so-called

---

[40] Cf. Daniel P. Moynihan, ed., *On Understanding Poverty*, Perspectives on Poverty Series (New York, Basic Books, 1968); and Herman P. Miller, *Rich Man, Poor Man* (New York, The New American Company, 1964).

[41] This is not to say that I am unaware of the salience of many "backlash" phenomena such as the appeal of anti-busing slogans in the current situation. It seems, however, unlikely that these will prevail in the longer run.

new-nation world. I think the same fundamental problems of the relation between the diffuse transgenerational solidarities of ethnic and other groups and their place in the structure of the total society are to be found in different form with the same components occurring in different combinations in other types of society.[42]

We may emphasize in this area three aspects of the problem field. The first has to do with the fact that it is rare that a new nation is composed of a population that in any simple sense approaches ethnic homogeneity. The commonest formula used to describe the lack of such homogeneity is "tribal" diversity. Second, for the most part the definition of national boundaries which has resulted from independence from the colonial powers has failed to coincide with territorial-ethnic boundaries and has tended to include diverse tribal groups and to cut many important such groups in two or more pieces by placing them on different sides of a political boundary.

Tribal diversity, to continue, is in turn associated with a good deal of diversity with reference to a number of the factors I have discussed which tend to be used to define ethnic identity. A prominent case is language and it is notorious that a large proportion of these societies have very complicated language problems. The linguistic diversity of the "common people" is apt to be so great that the most convenient medium of communication for the leading strata involved in government and other such affairs has continued on a large scale to be the language of the former colonial power. Central Africa is thus very broadly divided into areas where the "elite" are English-speaking on the one hand, French-speaking on the other. Naturally, this dependence on the language of a previously hated colonial power creates substantial ambivalence.

This is compounded by the fact that the culture of the elites has been, in respects other than language, strongly influenced by the colonizing nation, and as one important manifestation, many of the generation which have taken political and other responsibility in the new nation have been educated in the "metropolitan" country, to use the French term. It should thus not be forgotten that the two great emancipating heroes of Indian independence, Gandhi and Nehru, were both British-educated. India has been a focus of intense conflict over language problems with an attempt to institutionalize the general usage of indigenous languages which, however, has run into very severe difficulties. English remains the lingua franca of the substantial majority of the upper groups.[43]

---

[42] Cf. Reinhard Bendix, *Nation-Building and Citizenship* (New York, Wiley and Sons, 1964).

[43] That these problems do not operate only at political and governmental levels is illustrated by an interesting phenomenon. Dr. Bennetta Jules-Rosette in her recently submitted doctoral dissertation analyzed a new religious movement called the Apostles, which, from a Protestant missionary background, has spread in Zaire, the former Belgian Congo, and certain neighboring countries, notably Kenya. The

To stress the third problem, it is clear that the problem of ethnic diversity and the threats it poses to some kind of "national unity" is a ubiquitous problem in almost all the new nations. Though certain personnel who have, as it were, inherited their status from previous colonial regimes have retained some kind of residence and functions in many of these societies. In Africa and India, for example, the racial factor is not a primary one in this diversity. It is simply a consequence of the particularistic localism of so much of the indigenous society.

The obverse problem derives from the historically arbitrary division of ethnic groups as between two or in some cases even more politically organized societies. This clearly is a phenomenon which has also been exceedingly prominent in European history. In a national solidarity sense are the French-speaking components of Switzerland or Belgium members of the French nation or not? Or are the German-speaking Swiss members of the "German nation"? It is clear from the historic record that the answers to these questions are seldom simple. Even where geographical location is very distant indeed, the same problem has arisen with respect to what significantly is called the "Francophone" group in Canada. Some of the separatist-oriented French Canadians, egged on by de Gaulle, have made a great deal of the definition of their ethnic identity as French and thus in some symbolic sense as inherently part of the same French ethnic community as metropolitan France, and hence to be separated from "Anglophone" Canada.

Political realities, however, are such that it is no more likely in the new nations than it has been in European history that neat correspondences between traditional ethnicity and political allegiance can be worked out for the system as a whole.

There are, therefore, powerful incentives toward commitment to ethnically pluralistic national societal communities in a sense which involves at least some resemblances to the problem of the evolution of a

---

boundary with which Dr. Jules-Rosette was most concerned was between the former Belgian Congo and a neighboring former British colony which cut across ethnic lines. She observed and described, however, an exceedingly interesting linguistic phenomenon. In certain of the rituals of the Apostles there is alternate "preaching" and "singing" introduced by various members of the group participating. The interesting point is that the ritual is conducted in several different languages. Some of the participants chose to speak or sing in French; others used not one, but several, different indigenous tribal languages, most of which are, however, sufficiently closely related as to be with some approximation mutually understandable. The religious movement, as such, is clearly a cross-tribal phenomenon which is forming links of solidarity independent of tribal affiliations. It is, however, as it were, paying its respects to tribal identities by institutionalizing the use of plural tribal languages in the same ritual performance. It seems legitimate to interpret this as a case of maintaining a delicate balance between the creation of new solidarities and respectful recognition of tribal diversity. See Bennetta Jules-Rosette, "Ritual Contexts and Social Action: A Study of the Apostolic Church of John Marangue." Unpublished doctoral thesis. Harvard University, Cambridge, Mass., June 1973.

type of community like the recently emerged America. It is almost commonplace that an important factor underlying the intensity of "nationalistic" sentiments in many new nations is a function of the tensions occasioned by this diversity and the fact that the new nation is incompatible with many of the traditional conceptions of sub-ethnic independence. I suppose it could be said that the recent civil war in Nigeria, which was structured mainly on this kind of basis, is a classic example from the field of the new nations, but, of course, there are many others.[44]

It is an important fact bearing on the possibilities of development in pluralistic directions that, important as race and color have been in many instances, this symbolic focus of ethnic identity is very widely cross-cut with others, thus producing, even from the beginning, the kind of structural pluralism which in the long run strongly inhibits polarization.

Conclusion

It is quite clear that in this chapter it was possible to deal with only a small part of the problems and topics which are relevant to the theme of ethnicity on a world-wide basis. I hope, however, that it has been helpful to try to show not only how deep-rooted are the forces which make for stress on an ethnic type of solidarity, but also some of the relations of ethnicity to different but related modes of establishing solidary groupings. Finally, I hope that the differences between the various relevant groups in the United States, notably white and black, and the differences and similarities between American developments and those going on in other parts of the world will prove illuminating. It is hoped that this chapter can serve as a modest contribution to the development of a more general theory of the nature, variety, and functions of groups in which diffuse enduring, that is, transgenerational, solidarity is a salient characteristic. If so, comparative sociology in this area would be greatly facilitated and the resort to the mere assertion of uniqueness less necessary or tempting.

[44] Robin Luckham, *The Nigerian Military: A Sociological Analysis of Authority and Revolt* (Cambridge, England, Cambridge University Press, 1971).

Index

Index